The Grateful Dead FAQ

Series Editor: Robert Rodriguez

The Grateful Dead FAQ

All That's Left to Know About the Greatest Jam Band in History

Tony Sclafani

Backbeat
Books

An Imprint of Hal Leonard Corporation

Published in 2013 by Backbeat Books
An Imprint of Hal Leonard Corporation
7777 West Bluemound Road
Milwaukee, WI 53213

Trade Book Division Editorial Offices
33 Plymouth St., Montclair, NJ 07042

The FAQ series was conceived by Robert Rodriguez and developed with Stuart Shea.

Book design by Snow Creative Services

Printed in the United States of America

Library of Congress Cataloging-in-Publication Data is available upon request.

ISBN 978-1-61713-086-1

www.backbeatbooks.com

To Sharon, for answering the musical question
"How does the song go?"

Contents

Foreword

I first became aware of the Grateful Dead in 1966. I was about eleven years old. I grew up in San Francisco in the heyday of the Haight-Ashbury renaissance. I loved the Dead, but I also loved Quicksilver Messenger Service, Jefferson Airplane, the Sons of Champlin, Moby Grape—all those bands. The Dead were definitely a huge influence on my friends and me, but there weren't even any Deadheads back then. Nobody followed the band on tour. All that came much later.

In spring of 1998, when I got the call to try out for the Other Ones, the Grateful Dead had become not much more to me than a warm, fuzzy touchstone of my youth and early musical influences. I was (and still am) pretty fond of *Live/Dead* and the album many lovingly refer to as *Skullfuck*, as well as *Europe '72, Workingman's Dead, American Beauty*, and *Wake of the Flood*. Those records were all in my collection, and I listened to them over the years and loved them, but I hadn't played that music myself in a very long time.

The truth is, I was surprised when I ended up getting the gig. I previously hadn't had much success at auditions. I'd get nervous, try too hard, and freeze up. When I went to the Other Ones audition, I assumed I wasn't going to get the gig and just thought, "Wow, how awesome . . . I get to play with the guys I grew up watching and listening to as a kid." I had a really fun time, and I think that's why they liked me. It was pretty amazing.

Getting to tour with "the boys" was fun, rewarding, surreal, and incredibly confusing all at the same time. They ended up taking both Steve Kimock and me as twin lead guitar players. The thing was, in classic Grateful Dead fashion, we never worked out any details about who would do what, or when. Plenty of times, Steve and I would just look at each other when it came time to play the lead guitar parts and say, "I don't know—you wanna go or should I?"

It was humbling to become part of the music that had been so much of an influence on my early history. I think the biggest gift I got from playing with the Other Ones (and with Bob Weir and RatDog) was rediscovering a very real sense of musical freedom and rediscovering my passion for music for the sake of the music, not for commercial success. Coming back into the "family" was an opportunity to reconnect with what drew me to music in the first place.

I think there's sort of an idealized vision of who the Grateful Dead are and what they represent from the fan perspective, but to me they're just humans like any others. I know them now as friends—people I've actively collaborated with. But I'm also very aware that they were responsible for the development of an entire approach to music—what's become known as the "jam band." I believe that the Dead originated the whole idea of doing things differently and giving rock 'n' roll as much room to improvise and express itself as jazz had traditionally gotten. Of course, a lot of jam bands don't seem very musically influenced by the Dead, yet conceptually, their roots are there. I think the Dead will always be seen as a huge source of inspiration and innovation in the history of rock 'n' roll music.

There are now huge numbers of people worldwide who fit the term "Deadhead." Part of that group is, of course, the "hippie" community, but many modern Deadheads are now stockbrokers, insurance salesmen, and the like. It's like the bumper sticker says: "Weir Everywhere." Sociologically, this entire segment of the population are bound together by their common love of the music of the Grateful Dead and the particular sort of social ethics and sense of community that has been created as an extension of that love. I can't think of too many bands that have had such a far-reaching impact. Maybe the Beatles.

Mark Karan
2013

Mark Karan has played guitar and sung for artists ranging from Dave Mason to Delaney Bramlett to Huey Lewis. In 1998, he was picked (along with Steve Kimock) to play lead guitar in the Other Ones, a group made up of all the former members of the Grateful Dead, along with Bruce Hornsby on piano and Dave Ellis on saxophone. He has also been the lead guitarist of Bob Weir's RatDog since 1998 and has performed with Mickey Hart's Planet Drum and Phil Lesh and Friends. A cancer survivor, he released his first solo album, *Walk Through the Fire*, in 2009.

Acknowledgments

E ven though this book bears the name of one author, a lot of people influenced the writing of it. I'd like to extend special thanks to the following people:

Sharon Balan, for being a collaborator, editor, proofreader, sounding board, and so much more.

Toni Brown, David Gans, Mark Karan, Carol Latvala, Dennis McNally, and David Lemieux, who took the time to explain a lot of details.

Arion Berger, my former editor at the *Washington Post Express*; Denise Hazlick, editor at NBC.com; and Peter Lindblad, the former editor of *Goldmine*, for assigning Dead-related articles that led to the writing of this book.

Stuart Dahne, Rich McManus, and Eric Schwartz, for the scans of tickets and picture sleeves.

Josh Baron, for tons of *Relix* covers.

Traci Balter Tyo, for creating a Facebook post that led to a chapter.

Jean Pfefferkorn at the Howard County Public Library, for background information and explaining how those strange, old microfilm machines work.

Rob Bleetstein, Annemarie Hunt Dauer, Kathi Abernethy Dunsmore, Dean Grabski, Emily Vitullo Martin, Cathy Garland Meyers, Sue Smith, and John Sybert, for the quotes and stories.

Gary Gebler of Trax on Wax Records, for vinyl discoveries.

Barbara Kellner of the Columbia Archives, for old news clippings, info, and support.

Steve Sclafani and Dave Lax of the Baseball Factory, for help with scans.

David Vitagliano, for being the first to encourage me to pursue writing and for bringing up "Dark Star" during tenth grade journalism class.

Thanks also to Cary Baker, Warren Belasco, Mike Duffy, Todd Everett, Russ Grabski, Karl Groeger, Skip Groff, Richie Latvala, Carrie Lombardi, John Lynskey, Ellie MacKnight, Bernadette Malavarca, Rosie McGee, Nicholas Meriwether, Chris Mosher, Allon Porter, Robert Rodriguez, Audrey Fix Schaefer, Susan Sliwicki, Michael Valentine Smith, Jon Stebbins, Liz Stewart, Jason Thrasher, Alan Trist, and Bob Weir. And thanks to Backbeat Books and the Hal Leonard Group for allowing me to indulge professionally in the type of thinking and topics that earned me disapproval from guidance counselors and other figures of "authoritah."

Introduction

Box of Rain

I first connected with the music of the Grateful Dead in the pouring rain, during a frighteningly loud thunderstorm. When I was at work.

It was a dark, dreary Monday night—June 20, 1983—and I was a teenager working a summer job as a parking lot attendant at Merriweather Post Pavilion in Columbia, Maryland. The Grateful Dead were playing a two-night stand, and no one seemed happy about having to direct traffic with sheets of rain crashing down. The storm grew worse and chaos started to reign—pun intended—so a bunch of us ran from the parking lot into the concert park, where we took cover under an awning and attempted to dry off. (Confession: we snuck in past the distracted security guards. Hope I don't get retroactively fired for this.)

I was a fan of punk rock and new wave at the time; I had little patience for bands with beards, paunches, and touches of grey in their hair. And besides, I was a wannabe teen rock critic, and critics couldn't be Deadheads, after all—could they? Wouldn't be prudent.

And then the band launched into a grungy version of "Little Red Rooster," the slide guitar–fueled Willie Dixon/Howlin' Wolf blues tune I knew from *The Rolling Stones Now!* "What are they doing playing this tune?" I asked my work buddies. No one knew. Or cared. But they did have a lot to say about the drugs, the male Deadheads who seemed to be locked in 1968, and, of course, the scantily clad, rain-drenched female fans.

A few days later, I headed to the library expecting to find a book about the Dead's music. I found none. As the years rolled by, books did eventually appear, many of which gave detailed, first-hand accounts of the band's affairs. I came to know and love such tomes, some of which were written by authors with whom I've become friendly, including Dennis McNally and David Gans. With *The Grateful Dead FAQ*, I made a conscious attempt not to reiterate the same ideas found in these books. Instead, what I've tried to do is explore areas I seemed best qualified to analyze, using my knowledge and experience as a music writer and overall pop music fanatic. Whenever possible, I've tried to bring in information from the world of pop and rock to show how the Dead functioned in it, influenced it, and drew from it.

(For example, while researching double live albums for a completely non-Dead-related article, I discovered that the Dead pioneered the "double live" concept, which came to rule throughout the 1970s. Who knew?) I've also tried to expand on subjects that were only touched on in books or blogs, such as what roles some of the lesser-known band members played, and what a final, 1990s-era album by the Dead would have been like.

Getting into the Dead isn't like discovering most other artists, whose studio albums constitute their main legacy. The Dead built their legend being a live band—some would say *the* live band. Consequently, their studio recordings haven't always been given the analysis they deserve. I've tried to rectify that here and take a close look at their studio albums, placing each one in the context of its time. Even though the band's albums were considered second-rate, in retrospect, it's evident that they contain more classic songs and hidden gems than many people might realize. They also show a bold experimental spirit that went largely unrecognized at the time. To enjoy the down-home charm of *Workingman's Dead* or the panoply of influences on *Grateful Dead from the Mars Hotel*, you don't need to be "on the bus" (Grateful Dead slang for people who jump aboard as fans). Nor do you need to be a Deadhead to appreciate the first-rate songs that formed the foundation on which the Dead built their legendary jams. I've also tried to separate myth from fact. As with Elvis, the Grateful Dead's iconic aspects often overshadow their artistic achievements. But in the end, artistic achievement, not myth, was really what the Grateful Dead were about.

In their three decades of existence, the Grateful Dead went from being thought of as a group of counterculture weirdoes to being hailed as rock 'n' roll heroes. Vice President Al Gore and his ex-wife, Tipper, confessed to being Deadheads, as did conservative agitator Ann Coulter. As for the music, the Dead are "a large part of why the jam band scene exists now," Bruce Hornsby told me when I interviewed him in 2010 for an MSNBC.com article about Jerry Garcia. Garcia's championing of roots music now seems prescient, as scores of other artists in the Americana and alt-country genres now use some of his same influences to make new music.

How did all of this happen? Why did the band become more iconic when a lot of their contemporaries either fell by the wayside or became laughingstocks, doing things such as attempting to build (metaphorical) cities out of rock 'n' roll? This book will attempt to answer those questions. Considering that the Dead never really had the goal of being a "commercial" band, their influence and continuing pervasiveness in the culture is nothing short of astounding.

On the other hand, the deeper I dug into the Deadosphere, the more I learned that all that was Dead wasn't necessarily great. So, I've addressed what I came to see as the band's missteps as well. In all, I've done my best to present a road map into the magical but sometimes confusing world of this unique band.

A few notes, before we begin in earnest.

Throughout this book, I'll be using the word "Dead" as an abbreviation of the group's full moniker, not to connote the incarnation of the band that came together after Garcia's death that was called The Dead (unless I'm speaking specifically about that band).

Donna Godchaux is referred to by her current, married name, Donna Godchaux-MacKay. I've done this not only for accuracy's sake, but also because referencing her as simply "Godchaux" is confusing, as there was another Godchaux, her late husband, Keith, in the band.

When writing about songs that the Dead covered, I've used the titles the band put on their albums, which were sometimes slightly different from the titles the original artists gave their songs. So, even though Martha and the Vandellas recorded a song called "Dancing in the Street," for example, it's referred to here as "Dancin' in the Streets," because that's how the Dead titled it on the single and on the *Terrapin Station* album.

All of the chart information for album and single releases was sourced from Billboard reference books, which are listed in the bibliography.

All of the information about songs the Dead played live was gleaned from Deadbase.com, which Dead experts David Gans and David Lemieux (both of whom were interviewed for this book) said was the most reliable source.

I also wrote up a chapter I decided not to include because I ultimately didn't feel it fit the book. It's a recommendation of other recording acts that I think will appeal to Dead fans. I've instead made it available on my website at www.tonysclafani.com.

If anyone reading this is new to the band, I hope this book will spark your interest in the Dead the same way seeing the band play live that first time sparked mine.

Oh, and about that Merriweather show from 1983? It sounded great all over again when I heard it unexpectedly one day within the confines of my warm, dry home. It popped up on Grateful Dead Radio (www.gdradio.net), a 24/7 online station that streams concerts recorded by fans and is a testament to the Dead's longevity. The Dead's version of "Little Red Rooster" was as fab as I remembered it to be, even when it wasn't playing as a backdrop to waterlogged concertgoers and thunderbolts lighting up the night sky.

Tony Sclafani
Winter 2013

I Am Who I Am

A Primer on the Grateful Dead's Twelve Official Members

Founded in 1965, the Grateful Dead consisted of five founding members at its outset: lead guitarist Jerry Garcia, rhythm guitarist Bob Weir, harmonica and organ player Ron "Pigpen" McKernan, bassist Phil Lesh, and drummer Bill Kreutzmann. All but Kreutzmann sang. With the exception of Pigpen, who died in 1973, all of the band's original members stayed with the group until their dissolution in 1995 following the death of Garcia. Over the years, seven other members were added to the band at various points, making a total of twelve official Grateful Dead members. Keyboardist Bruce Hornsby, who played regularly with the group starting in 1988, was not considered an official member.

Jerry Garcia

(Jerome John Garcia; born August 1, 1942; died August 9, 1995) San Francisco native Jerry Garcia was largely the creative force behind the Grateful Dead's music. With lyricist Robert Hunter, he wrote the music to such signature songs as "Dark Star," "Uncle John's Band," and "Touch of Grey." As a guitarist, he pioneered the idea of improvisation in rock 'n' roll, and his fretboard work on stage served as a template for countless other guitarists. Garcia, who was named after composer Jerome Kern by his jazz musician father, was a natural musician, taking up banjo, then guitar as a teenager. He worked for a while teaching guitar at a music store where future Dead drummer Bill Kreutzmann also worked. One of Garcia's students was future Dead guitarist Bob Weir. As years passed, Garcia also became a cultural icon, and although he did not actively seek celebrity, he became one of the symbols of the 1960s counterculture. He also earned the distinction of getting a flavor of Ben & Jerry's ice cream, Cherry Garcia, named after him. As a musician, he kept active during the Dead's downtime, forming his own group, the Jerry Garcia Band, and performing with such diverse players as bluegrass mandolinist David Grisman and the late keyboardist Merl Saunders. Garcia died of a heart attack at a residential drug treatment center at age fifty-three.

Around the time this 1987 publicity shot was taken, Jerry Garcia had become a celebrity in the mainstream media, having survived a coma and making a triumphant return with a hit Grateful Dead album and single.   *Author's collection*

Bob Weir

(Robert Hall Weir; born October 16, 1947) Bob Weir, who was also born in San Francisco, was still in high school when he met Garcia and Pigpen, with whom he formed Mother McCree's Uptown Jug Champions, a jug band that predated the Dead. Weir struggled in school because of undiagnosed dyslexia; as such, he attended several high schools, including Fountain Valley School in Colorado, where he met future Dead lyricist John Perry Barlow. The youngest member of the original Dead, Weir played a supporting role in the band during their beginnings. But by the early 1970s, the singer-guitarist had become a driving force in the band, co-writing and singing lead on some of their most popular songs, such as "Truckin'," "Sugar Magnolia," and "The Music Never Stopped," all minor hits. Whereas Garcia sang most of the ballads and mid-tempo songs, Weir was the band's resident rocker, especially in concert, where he sang the Chuck Berry covers the band performed during their encores. During his time in the Dead, Weir cut two solo albums and cut albums with his bands Kingfish and Bobby and the Midnites. He then formed the band RatDog, with which he continued playing for fifteen years after the Dead ended. In 2008, Weir joined with Phil Lesh to form the jam band Furthur, which mostly revives old Dead tunes.

Phil Lesh

(Phillip Chapman Lesh; born March 15, 1940) Berkeley-born Phil Lesh may have been the Dead's bass player, but his influence on the group went far beyond that role. As a trained trumpet player and fan of jazz and avant garde modern composition, he brought these elements into the band, where they helped shape the group's early albums and live improvisations. He also sang lead vocals on a couple of key early cuts he co-wrote, notably "New Potato Caboose" from the band's second album, *Anthem of the Sun.* Never a prolific songwriter, Lesh nonetheless wrote a handful of songs that became fan favorites in the 1970s. Lesh's aggressive style of bass playing included not only bass leads but also chords. He was the first member of the group to earn a "fan section" of the concert audience, which was named "The Phil Zone." After the Dead disbanded, Lesh continued to tour with a rotating cast of musicians in a group called Phil Lesh and Friends. From there, he joined up with several other former Dead members to perform as the Other Ones, and he later joined forces with Weir in the group Furthur. A bout with hepatitis C caused his liver to malfunction; he received a transplant in 1998 and has since become an advocate for organ donation.

Robert Hunter

(Robert Christie Burns; born July 23, 1941) Garcia's longtime collaborator Robert Hunter was a lyricist for the Grateful Dead, not a performer with the group, but was listed as an official band member on the albums *American Beauty, Blues for Allah,* and *Shakedown Street* and is pictured on the cover of *Workingman's Dead* (on the far left). When the Dead were inducted into the Rock and Roll Hall of Fame, the San Luis Obispo, California, native was inducted along with them. Hunter and Garcia's friendship predates the Dead; the pair met at a theatrical production in 1960 and played coffeehouses together as the folk duo Bob & Jerry. Hunter co-wrote the majority of Grateful Dead originals, and his use of classic American imagery and metaphor gave the Dead their distinctive voice. He also had a knack for coming up with phrases that passed into the common

Special Allen Woody Tribute Issue

Hittin' the note ™

The Road Lesh Travels

ISSUE 29 • U.S. $6.00
$6.00 U.S. $8.00 CAN

29>

0 74470 97699 8

Also: Taj Mahal, Frogwings, 1970 Byron Pop Flashback and much more!

After the demise of the Grateful Dead, bassist Phil Lesh kept musically active, playing in a number of groups, including Phil Lesh and Friends, who made the cover of *Hittin' the Note* magazine in 2001.   *Courtesy of* Hittin' the Note *magazine*

language, the most famous of which was the line "What a long, strange trip it's been," from "Truckin'." He also collaborated as a lyricist with Bob Weir, Phil Lesh, and Pigpen and cut nearly a dozen albums on his own during the Dead's era. Hunter is also a published poet, and his 1993 poem "An American Adventure" gives an account of the Dead's history.

Bill Kreutzmann

(William Kreutzmann; born May 7, 1946) Bill Kreutzmann of Palo Alto played drums for the Grateful Dead for the band's entire three-decade run, and it was his combination of steadiness and willingness to move outside the bounds of conventional drumming that allowed the band to expand their music as much as they did. Kreutzmann first met Jerry Garcia when the drummer was working at Dana Morgan's Music Source and Garcia came in looking for a banjo. After the breakup of Mother McCree's Uptown Jug Champions (Garcia, Weir, and Pigpen's jug band), Garcia and Pigpen recruited Kreutzmann for an electric band originally called the Zodiacs, then with Weir onboard called the Warlocks, the Emergency Crew, and finally the Grateful Dead. Along with Mickey Hart, Kreutzmann played the percussion solos, known as "Drums," at Dead concerts. In 2009, Kreutzmann formed the band 7 Walkers, which played a hybrid of rock and swamp music he called "swampadelic." The group released an album in 2010, for which Hunter wrote some lyrics.

Mickey Hart

(Michael Steven Hartman; born September 11, 1943) New York native Mickey Hart joined the Grateful Dead in September 1967 after meeting Bill Kreutzmann and being asked to sit in with the group on a set. After jamming on versions of "Alligator" and "Caution (Do Not Stop on Tracks)," the band members realized the unique power they'd have live with two drummers, so they made the very unconventional move of adding a second drummer. Hart's background in drums ran deep: his father, Lenny Hart, was a champion rudimental drummer. The elder Hart also came to manage the band and was arrested for embezzling money from them, resulting in Hart taking a leave of absence from the Grateful Dead from February 1971 to October 1974. In 1980, Hart won critical acclaim for the score he put together with the Diga Rhythm Band for the film *Apocalypse Now*. He's also written four books, most notably 1990's *Drumming at the Edge of Magic: A Journey into the Spirit of Percussion* and 1991's *Planet Drum: A Celebration of Percussion and Rhythm*. In 2011, a collection of world music recordings he compiled for Smithsonian Folkways Recordings, the nonprofit record label of the Smithsonian Institution, was released under the title *The Mickey Hart Collection*.

Ron "Pigpen" McKernan

(Ronald Charles McKernan; born September 8, 1945; died March 8, 1973) Pigpen and Jerry Garcia were the first members of the Grateful Dead to meet. A native of San Bruno, California, and the son of a blues and rhythm and blues disc jockey, Pigpen grew up steeped in African American music and brought his love of both of the above genres to the band, which he sometimes fronted. Pigpen played organ and harmonica with the Dead and sang lead vocals on such R&B cover songs as "Turn On Your Love Light" and "In the Midnight Hour." Depending on whom you believe, Pigpen earned his nickname either from a friend because of the way he lived or from a girlfriend who believed his personal grooming habits to be similar to those of the unkempt character in the *Peanuts* comic strip. Pigpen was also notable for the biker clothes he wore. By his mid-twenties, years of alcohol abuse had caused him health problems, and he died at the age of twenty-seven of a gastrointestinal hemorrhage. He was the first member of the Grateful Dead to pass away.

Keith Godchaux

(Keith Richard Godchaux; born July 19, 1948; died July 23, 1980) Seattle's Keith Godchaux first met Jerry Garcia at a Grateful Dead concert he attended in 1971 along with his wife, Donna Jean Godchaux-MacKay. Godchaux had been performing with Dave Mason's band at the time and wanted to join the Dead, but he was reportedly too shy to ask. He became a member after some lobbying on the part of Donna, who joined the band a few months later herself. Godchaux mostly played acoustic piano with the group, although he was also known to sometimes play the popular electronic keyboard of the day, the Fender Rhodes. During his tenure with the group, he only wrote and sang one song, "Let Me Sing Your Blues Away." Along with his wife, Godchaux added new life to the Dead, who were in a period of transition with Pigpen's failing health (they joined while Pigpen was still playing in the band). Deadheads widely believe that the "Keith and Donna Years" constituted the best era of the band, concert-wise. Eventually, Godchaux grew weary of the Dead's music, and the band also reportedly became disenchanted with his approach to keyboards. He and Donna left the band in February 1979, forming the Heart of Gold Band together. A year and a half later, he died in an automobile accident near where he and Donna were living with their son, Zion.

Donna Jean Godchaux-MacKay

(Donna Jean Thatcher; born August 22, 1947) The Dead's only female member was asked to sing with the group as soon as her husband, keyboardist Keith Godchaux, joined, but Donna Godchaux-MacKay deferred and made her onstage debut on December 31, 1971. Godchaux-MacKay was born in Florence, Alabama, and grew up listening to Southern soul and gospel. Those influences are clear in the way she sang with the Dead, most notably in her lead vocals section on "The Music Never Stopped" and on her own "Sunrise" and "From the Heart of Me." Her inclusion as a full-fledged member of the Dead is arguably one of the reasons the group attracted a substantial female fan base during a period in rock when most guitar solo–oriented rock bands didn't. Before her stint with the Dead, which lasted from March 1972 to February

1979, Godchaux-MacKay sang with a vocal group called Southern Comfort and appeared as a backing vocalist on records by Percy Sledge, Boz Scaggs, Aretha Franklin, Neil Diamond, and others. After she left the Dead, she suffered the loss of husband Keith in a car accident and stepped away from the music business for more than a decade after becoming a Christian. She remarried, to bassist/pastor David MacKay, and now fronts the Donna Jean Godchaux Band with Jeff Mattson, formerly of Phil Lesh and Friends and the Dark Star Orchestra.

Tom Constanten

(Thomas Charles Hills; born March 19, 1944) A friend of Phil Lesh's from college, Long Branch, New Jersey–born Constanten was an avant garde classical composer and keyboardist who joined the Dead during the recording of its second album, *Anthem of the Sun*. He brought his avant garde sense to that record, plus the following one, *Aoxomoxoa*, to which he added a plethora of keyboard textures. On stage, Constanten played organ and can be heard on the album *Live/Dead*. His tenure in the band was short lived, from November 1968 to January 1970, but he made his influence felt during that experimental period in the band's history. Constanten went on to compose modern classical pieces and teach piano. He also performed with Garcia collaborator Merl Saunders in Saunders's Rainforest Band and with Dave Nelson of New Riders of the Purple Sage in the Dead Ringers. He recounted the events of his musical life, including his stint with the Dead, in his 1992 autobiography *Between Rock and Hard Places: A Musical Autobiodyssey*.

Brent Mydland

(Brent Richard Mydland; born October 21, 1952; died July 26, 1990) Brent Mydland joined the Dead in April 1979, after the defection of Keith Godchaux and Donna Godchaux-MacKay. The German-born keyboardist came into the Dead's circle through his association with Bob Weir, with whom he toured in 1978 as part of the Bob Weir Band. Mydland got his professional start with the duo Batdorf & Rodney, then joined the country rock group Silver, which scored a #16 hit with the song "Wham Bam" (also called "Wham Bam Shang-A-Lang"). As a player, Mydland added distinctive ethnic musical touches to some of the band's concert staples. As a composer, he contributed a handful of songs, all featuring his bluesy, soulful vocal style and some featuring lyrics by Weir collaborator John Perry Barlow, who went on record saying that his lyrics were intended to help the depressive keyboardist find some hope in his life. But Mydland descended further and further into substance abuse and was found dead just after the Dead wrapped up a run of shows in late July 1990. Mydland died the same way comedian John Belushi had eight years earlier—by an overdose of cocaine and morphine, commonly known as a speedball.

Vince Welnick

(Leo Vincent Welnick; born February 21, 1951; died June 2, 2006) Vince Welnick was the Dead's final keyboard player, performing with the group from September 1990 until July 1995. The Phoenix, Arizona, native began his musical career in the 1970s when he moved to San Francisco and joined the band that became the theatrical/satirical rock act the Tubes. He went on to play with Todd Rundgren, who had produced the Tubes, before joining the Grateful Dead. Welnick brought "depth of feeling, musical finesse and a nice sense of weirdness" to the band, according to *MOJO* writer Ken Hunt. Welnick also wrote the song "Samba in the Rain" with Robert Hunter, which became a live fan favorite. During his stint with the Dead, Welnick was diagnosed with cancer and emphysema, but he recovered enough to later perform with RatDog. The illness threw him into a depression he couldn't overcome, though, and he ended up taking his own life at his home, making him the fourth Dead keyboard player to die an early death.

Prelude

A Brief History of the Grateful Dead

The history of rock music is filled with cult artists like Big Star and Laura Nyro and popular acts like the Rolling Stones and Led Zeppelin. But there never was any band that spent two decades playing to a cult audience and then suddenly exploded into the mainstream, becoming a cultural phenomenon in the process.

Until the Grateful Dead.

Quoting one of the band's most popular songs, "Truckin'," and saying that the Dead's odyssey was a "long strange trip" reeks of cliché. But it also rings true. The Grateful Dead weren't your average rock band. The group's career, which lasted from 1965 until leading light Jerry Garcia died on August 9, 1995, really was unique in the history of rock. Even though the basic points of the band's career path have been written about before, some facts bear repeating here, if only to save readers the trouble of having to use Google or head off to the library when they come across information that needs some context in order to be fully understood.

The origins of the Grateful Dead can be traced back to early 1961, when Garcia moved to the town of Palo Alto, having been discharged from the United States Army after less than a year of service. The town, which is located around thirty-three miles south of San Francisco, is where Garcia met future Dead lyricist Robert Hunter when Garcia was working the lights for a local theater company. Hunter and he began performing as the folk duo Bob and Jerry with Garcia on acoustic guitar and Hunter on upright bass. It was a short-lived act, and Garcia, who was also adept at banjo, went on to play in a variety of folk and bluegrass groups, including the Sleepy Hollow Hog Stompers, the Badwater Valley Boys, the Wildwood Boys, and Jerry and Sara, a duo he formed with his first wife, Sara Ruppenthal.

One of Garcia's Palo Alto hangouts was a bookstore called Kepler's, and it was there that Garcia got to know a bunch of local musicians, including blues-loving teenager Ron "Pigpen" McKernan, who would become the Dead's first keyboardist as well as their front man when the group performed blues covers. Garcia also began teaching guitar and banjo at Dana Morgan's Music Shop in downtown Palo Alto, which is where he met future Dead drummer Bill Kreutzmann, who was teaching drums at the shop.

The acoustic roots of the Grateful Dead can be heard on the *Mother McCree's Uptown Jug Champions* CD, issued in 1999. The disc is now out of print and commands high prices on eBay.   *Author's collection*

Meanwhile, over at the University of California, Berkeley, trumpet-player-turned-modern-composer Phil Lesh had become disenchanted with the lack of support in the school's music department and left the program. The future Dead bassist gravitated toward Kepler's, where he met Garcia. On New Year's Eve 1963, future Dead rhythm guitarist Bob Weir and a friend wandered by Dana Morgan's and heard Garcia playing banjo inside while waiting for his students, apparently oblivious to the fact the day was a holiday. Weir, who was then a teenager from the wealthy suburb of Atherton, had met Garcia before, but it was here that they discussed putting together a band.

That group became Mother McCree's Uptown Jug Champions, a jug band that included Garcia, Weir, and Pigpen. Two factors influenced the group's switch to an electric format around the beginning of 1965: Pigpen's yen to play the blues and the influence of the Beatles on the pop music scene. Recruiting Kreutzmann on drums and music shop owner Dana Morgan's son, Dana

Morgan, Jr., on bass, they began to play amplified instruments and changed their name to the Warlocks. Garcia was unhappy with Morgan's bass playing, however, and when he spotted Lesh during a set break at a gig at Magoo's Pizza Parlor, he asked the more experienced musician to take on bass guitar duties, even though Lesh had no experience playing bass.

Birth of the Dead

The fearsome fivesome got their chops together in 1965 playing long sets at a bar south of San Francisco called the In Room in Belmont. They eventually gravitated toward San Francisco itself when they got an engagement at a strip club called Pierre's. Toward the end of the year, the group felt confident enough to audition for the local label Autumn Records, best known for its hits by the Beau Brummels ("Just a Little," "Laugh Laugh"). The group recorded half a dozen songs for the label under a new moniker, the Emergency Crew, because Lesh had come across a record by another group called the Warlocks. The band didn't get signed to Autumn but did use the occasion of having to change their name to find a better one. They settled on the Grateful Dead after Garcia came across the phrase in a dictionary.

Around this time the band had gotten to know writer Ken Kesey and his group of LSD enthusiasts known as the Merry Pranksters. The band played for the first time under their new name at one of the Pranksters' LSD parties, which were called Acid Tests, on December 4. Their first gig was on December 10 at the Fillmore Auditorium; it was a benefit for a mime troupe that was promoted by Bill Graham, who would go on to own the Fillmore and several other rock venues and to develop a close association with the Dead while becoming one of the top promoters in the rock and roll business.

But all that was in the future. In late 1965, the Dead were just looking to get a record out. The band ended up auditioning for another label, Scorpio Records, which put out a Dead single composed of the songs "Stealin'" and "Don't Ease Me In." The Dead weren't happy with the recording and few copies were pressed. The Dead eventually became the house band at the Acid Tests and by 1966 were one of a number of groups that made up the burgeoning San Francisco scene, which also included Jefferson Airplane, Quicksilver Messenger Service, and Big Brother and the Holding Company featuring Janis Joplin. All of these groups played the Fillmore, which was renamed the Fillmore West when Graham bought another venue in New York and named that one the Fillmore East.

By this point, Garcia, Weir, and Pigpen were living in a communal house at 710 Haight Street in Haight-Ashbury, a neighborhood that had become a hub for a new breed of discontented teenagers and twentysomethings who came to be known as hippies. Sensing a "scene," record companies came around, and the Dead decided to sign with Warner Bros. because the company offered the group the most control over their music. The band's self-titled first album was released on Saint Patrick's Day 1967, and although it only got to #73 on the Billboard album chart, it became a celebrated example of the then-new genre of psychedelic rock, even though the group's music on their first album was mostly drawn from folk and blues sources. More than any other San Francisco band, the Dead came to be seen as a symbol of the countercultural revolution. This came about partially because of the musicians' penchant for eschewing commercialism in favor of jamming in concert and partially because of the image the group projected, especially when it came to Garcia's hippie style and ideas and Pigpen's biker chic.

High Time

The Dead's profile was raised considerably when the band's management shrewdly had them play at the Monterey International Pop Festival on June 28, 1967. The three-day event was attended by more than fifty thousand people and kicked off the Summer of Love while also launching the careers of Jimi Hendrix and Janis Joplin. In September 1967, the group added a second drummer, Mickey Hart, and became one of the first bands to try a two-drummer set-up.

The band started performing more and making more complicated music in the studio. To that end, they added yet another member: Tom Constanten, a classically trained musician who had been Lesh's college friend. Constanten first performed with the group on November 23, 1968, and played on the albums *Anthem of the Sun*, *Aoxomoxoa*, and *Live/Dead* (he can also be heard on several live albums released after the Dead split up).

The group performed at the Woodstock Music and Art Fair on August 16, 1969, playing a short set that was marred by technical difficulties caused by both rain and confusion about how to set up the group's equipment. The Dead didn't perform at the Altamont Speedway Free Festival on December 6, 1969, where a concertgoer was killed by one of the Hells Angels who had been hired as security guards. The group flew in by helicopter but left before playing, after hearing that a Hells Angel had knocked out Jefferson Airplane guitarist Marty Balin with a punch.

By 1970, the winds of change were blowing in popular music, and the Dead altered their sound to reflect a new back-to-basics trend in rock. In the Dead's case, that meant returning to some of the band's roots in acoustic music, and their next two albums, *Workingman's Dead* and *American Beauty*, reflected this change. These albums also contained some of the band's most popular songs, such as "Friend of the Devil," "Uncle John's Band," Truckin'," and "Sugar Magnolia," the last three of which became moderate hits on the Billboard pop singles chart (as well as staples of the then-new FM radio format).

By January 1970, Constanten had parted ways with the band, his departure coming after a much-publicized January 31 drug bust in New Orleans (immortalized in the song "Truckin'," which was recognized in 1997 by the Library of Congress as being a national treasure). Hart took leave of the group after a

When the Grateful Dead were just starting out, few people would have thought that their history would one day warrant an archive or that their artifacts would one day make up an exhibition. But that's just what happened when the Grateful Dead Archive at the University of California, Santa Cruz, opened in April 2012 and concurrently showcased the exhibition *A Box of Rain: Archiving the Grateful Dead Phenomenon*, which featured a poster by David Singer. *© David Singer and the Grateful Dead Archive Used with permission*

February 18, 1971, show after discovering that his father, Lenny Hart, who was managing the group, had absconded with the band's record company advance money. He would return to the fold on October 20, 1974, at a concert filmed for *The Grateful Dead Movie*.

In October 1971, the Dead added another classically trained keyboardist, Keith Godchaux, to the fold. Godchaux was brought into the band to help

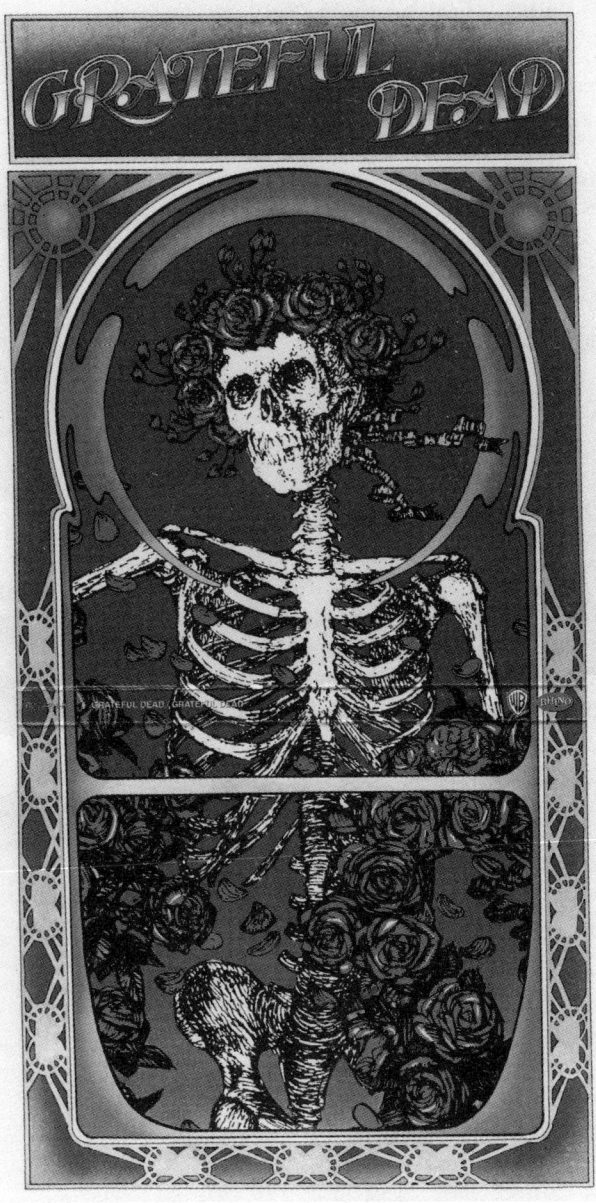

The skeleton image that has long been associated with the Grateful Dead made its debut on the band's self-titled 1971 album, which is often referred to as *Skull and Roses*. It was designed by psychedelic poster designers Alton Kelly and Stanley Mouse and was based on an image by British book illustrator Edmund Joseph Sullivan.   *Author's collection*

assist Pigpen, who had become an alcoholic and was suffering from health problems, including hepatitis. On March 25, 1972, Godchaux's wife, singer Donna Jean Godchaux-MacKay, officially joined up with the Grateful Dead and became their first and only female member. She had extensive experience as a singer, as she'd been part of a female vocal group in her teens and worked as a session singer in Muscle Shoals, Alabama, where she performed on such records as Elvis Presley's "Suspicious Minds."

The Dead performed a series of concerts in Western Europe in the spring of 1972, and these shows formed the basis of one of the band's most celebrated albums, the triple live set *Europe '72*. They were also among the last shows the ailing Pigpen would play with the group. He died of a gastrointestinal hemorrhage on March 8, 1973.

Also in 1973, the Dead left its longtime record company, Warner Bros., and founded a label to release their own albums, Grateful Dead Records, as well as another label, Round Records, to release solo albums and other projects with which the band was involved. Both would last until 1976 when the Dead signed with Arista Records.

Dawn of the Deadheads

By the early 1970s, the Dead were well established as a mainstream rock band, but with one crucial difference. Where most rock groups seemed to be on an upward trajectory, always reaching for bigger audiences and more record sales, the Dead became a cult group, content to play to the fans who came to see the band regularly and sometimes even followed them from town to town. Their followers started to be called Deadheads (after originally being called "Dead Freaks"), and they became something unique to rock: a subculture built around a single band (whereas subcultures such as mods or greasers revolved around genres of music).

Deadheads came to be known for their hippie fashions, nomadic lifestyles, and penchant for either recording Dead shows or swapping tapes with other fans. Detractors took to calling Deadheads "throwbacks" or leftover hippies from the 1960s, and they often became the target of overzealous law enforcement types who assumed that every Deadhead was carrying some sort of drug.

Beyond the sociology of Deadheads (which has been studied elsewhere), their continued support of the Dead put them in a unique position in rock starting around 1973, just after *Europe '72* came out. The group's records were selling, but not in massive quantities. Most made the Top 20, but the Dead never did place a #1 album during their career. On the other hand, they found they could sustain themselves through regular touring. Unlike most groups, the Dead didn't record albums and then go on the road to "promote the product." The road became their home-away-from-home, and studio records such as *Wake of the Flood* from 1973 and *From the Mars Hotel* from 1974 were recorded when enough new songs were worked out at live dates.

Because of this schedule, burnout was inevitable, and in 1975, the band decided to take a year off from touring, only playing four gigs the whole year. Instead, they worked on a new album, *Blues for Allah*, which became their first album made up of material that hadn't been road-tested. That album nearly cracked the Top 10, becoming the band's most successful album to date. Its success may have spurred the band to take a more experimental tack for their next two albums.

Or maybe it was the changing times that made the Dead begin to morph from a jam band (even though that term hadn't been coined yet) into a sleeker, more modern-sounding unit on the 1977 effort *Terrapin Station*, which only just grazed the Top 30 but eventually ended up going platinum. The album featured as its second side a long, multi-part suite of music that was composed, not improvised, which brought the group closer to progressive rock. Also in 1977, the group released *The Grateful Dead Movie*, which was directed by Garcia and mostly made up of concert footage shot in October 1974.

That was more palatable to fans than what the Dead did with their next record, *Shakedown Street*, a dance-oriented affair produced by Little Feat's Lowell George. Arriving in the fall of 1978, it was recorded during the year Americans fully embraced the rhythmic '70s style of music and kept the Bee Gees (and related acts) near the top of the singles charts for nearly the whole year. These sounds seemed to rub off on the Dead, and *Shakedown Street*, which didn't even crack the Top 40 on Billboard's album chart, became derided as the "disco Dead" record. Just before *Shakedown Street* came out, the Dead made a high profile trip to Egypt, becoming the first rock band to perform at the pyramids. The sojourn was undertaken at the behest of Phil Lesh, who wanted the band to perform in a "place of power" that had been part of the ancient world.

Meanwhile, tensions were building within the band, resulting in both Keith Godchaux and Donna Godchaux-MacKay leaving the fold. Their final show was February 17, 1979 (Keith later died in a car accident on July 23, 1980). A replacement was found in Brent Mydland, who was best known as the keyboardist with the country rock act Silver, which had scored a #16 hit with the song "Wham Bam" in 1976. With Mydland in the fold, the group recorded a comeback album of sorts: *Go to Heaven*, a rootsy effort that got to #23 and yielded a minor hit, "Alabama Getaway." Garcia then began to develop serious problems with drugs. The group did not release another studio album until 1987.

Into the '80s

By the mid-1980s, few bands came across as removed from the mainstream of music as the Grateful Dead. MTV, the cable channel for music videos that had been established in 1981, had helped to create a new crop of videogenic young rock and pop stars who emphasized looks more than talent and promoted their newest records instead of acquiring musical chops. The Dead, meanwhile, hadn't even released an album since 1980 and were more than ever playing to their cult of Deadheads, who were now probably a few years older than the average rock fan.

In the age of Bon Jovi, Madonna, and other glossy pop stars, the last thing anyone would have expected was for the grey-haired members of a twenty-year-old band such as the Dead to explode into the mainstream. But that's exactly what the Grateful Dead did when they placed their first Top 10 single ever, "Touch of Grey," which became a hit in 1987, twenty years after they released their first record. The accompanying album, *In the Dark*, became the Dead's biggest album ever, getting to #6.

Several factors contributed to the Dead's sudden surge in popularity. In 1985, they celebrated their twentieth anniversary with a lot of accompanying media fanfare. During this period, several other acts from the 1960s were also enjoying revivals of some kind because of a phenomenon known as "the twenty-year nostalgia cycle," in which the culture of a particular generation gets revived when that generation becomes old enough to get nostalgic and flex its economic muscles, and a new generation simultaneously picks up on it. MTV also ran a promotion called "Day of the Dead," which featured the band's music and fans at regular intervals for one full day.

Also, in 1986, Garcia had the first and most serious of several health scares during his lifetime. An undiagnosed diabetic, he'd unexpectedly collapsed on July 10 of that year and lapsed into a coma, only coming out of it after four days. He had to re-learn to play the guitar, and the whole chain of events caused people who weren't even Dead fans to consider the possibility that a rock icon they may have ignored previously could have been gone forever. When it was released, "Touch of Grey," with its chorus of "I will get by / I will survive," sounded like an anthem for Garcia as well as the whole aging Baby Boomer generation.

The Dead soldiered on, releasing another album, *Built to Last*, in late 1989. Less than a year later, the title would come to seem sadly ironic when Mydland died of a drug overdose. He was replaced by former Tubes keyboardist Vince

According to the late Owsley Stanley via his website, the skull and lightning bolt image used for the cover of the *Steal Your Face* album was designed by Stanley Mouse and graphic artist Bob Thomas in 1969. Their design became far more popular than did the album with which it's associated.   *Author's collection*

Welnick, while Bruce Hornsby, an '80s rocker and Deadhead who was fronting his own band, sat in on second keyboards during this transitional period.

The post–"Touch of Grey" era saw the Dead in a weird phase of their career. They were more popular than ever, now regularly filling stadiums. But in the wake of their hit, the group had acquired a new breed of younger, rowdier fans who regularly caused problems with the law (not to mention veteran Deadheads) at concerts. The expansion of the Dead's touring apparatus also meant more responsibility for the band, including Garcia, who was battling heroin addiction by the early 1990s. In a 1991 interview, Garcia spoke to a *Rolling Stone* reporter about the band's "huge overhead" and how they felt responsible for keeping the touring juggernaut going because they didn't "want to take people's livelihoods away."

By 1995, Garcia was in seriously poor health, and his physical tribulations were so great that they're exhausting even to read about in the various accounts that have surfaced since. One week after the Grateful Dead played its last show on July 9, 1995, the fifty-two-year-old Garcia checked himself into the Betty Ford Clinic in Rancho Mirage, California. By his fifty-third birthday, on August 1, he'd checked out before completing the program. He then checked into the Serenity Knolls drug rehabilitation facility, which is where he died on August 9, with the cause listed as a massive heart attack.

Garcia's death effectively ended the Grateful Dead, although all of the band's members performed with each other in one configuration or another afterward. Garcia's passing also showed how much of a mainstream figure he'd become, with both *Rolling Stone* and *People* putting him on their covers.

Even with Garcia's passing, though, the music never stopped, as the Dead once sang. In 1993, the band inaugurated a CD series, *Dick's Picks*, which featured tapes recorded through the soundboards at concerts throughout their career. These tapes were derived from the band's "Vault," a storehouse of recordings dating back to the Dead's inception and running through their last concert as a working band. The Vault, which was bought by the Rhino Entertainment Company in 2007, continues to be a source of archival material, which the company releases on a regular basis.

The Grateful Dead were said to have played 2,317 concerts in front of a total of 25 million people during the thirty years the group toured.

3

Friends of the Devil

Who's Who in Deadland

ohn "Marmaduke" Dawson, David Lemieux, and Merl Saunders are a few of the names people come across when reading about the Grateful Dead or perusing the credits on the band's CDs. But how do these people relate to the band? Like most rock groups, the Dead established a roll call of associates over the years. Some, like Dawson and Saunders, worked with the band in a musical capacity. Others might not have played music, but they played a role in the band's history in one way or another. The following is an overview of the Dead's colleagues, friends, and associates who all played a significant role in the band's story.

Rebecca G. Adams

A tenured professor of sociology at the University of North Carolina at Greensboro, Adams was the pre-eminent pioneer of bringing the Grateful Dead into the academic world, teaching courses about the band and their following. Her most celebrated course in this area may have been her first, "Applied Social Theory and Qualitative Research Methodology," which was known colloquially as "Deadhead 101" and took twenty-one students on tour with the band in the summer of 1989. Adams is a longtime fan of the band who first caught them live in 1970. She's also written about the Dead in academic journals, exploring such subjects as "Stigma and the Inappropriately Stereotyped: The Deadhead Professional." Adams also served as co-editor for the 2000 book *Deadhead Social Science*, a collection of papers that looks at various aspects of Deadhead subculture.

John Perry Barlow

A friend of Bob Weir's since their teenage days together at the private Fountain Valley School in Colorado, Barlow is primarily known to Dead fans as the lyricist of Weir's tunes, although he also wrote songs with keyboardist Brent Mydland. Barlow is something of a modern-day Renaissance man, and his pursuits include projects as varied as running a cattle ranch, co-founding the Electronic Frontier Foundation, and serving as a campaign coordinator for Dick Cheney in the 1970s. He was also a pioneering advocate of the World Wide Web and these days is active in fighting for digital freedom or "cyber rights." His work in this area has led to him becoming a fellow at both the Institute of Politics at Harvard University and Harvard Law School.

Candace Brightman

The appropriately named Brightman served as the lighting designer for the Dead from the early 1970s until the band's dissolution. Brightman first became known for her lighting work at the Fillmore East, and Garcia purportedly took note of what she was doing when he caught the Mahavishnu Orchestra there. He invited her along on the Dead's 1971 European tour, and she eventually became known for her subtle coloring effects that cleverly seemed to reflect or even anticipate the mood of the band's songs.

Toni Brown

A musician, publicist, and music journalist, Brown is perhaps best known to Deadheads for her role as editor and publisher of *Relix* magazine from 1981 through 2001. Brown helped the magazine morph from a Dead fanzine into a national music publication. Today, *Relix* is the longest-running music magazine in the United States, save *Rolling Stone*. These days, Brown fronts her own musical ensemble, the Dead-influenced Toni Brown Band. She's released three CDs of original music and has been part of the jam band touring circuit since the mid-1990s. A dedicated Deadhead since 1969, she released a book documenting the band, *Relix: The Book; The Grateful Dead Experience*, in 2009. Brown is not to be confused with the Toni Brown who led the Bay Area band Joy of Cooking.

Bill "Kidd" Candelario

Candelario got his start with the Dead as a roadie who looked after the band's keyboard and bass gear. Around 1972, he took over regularly recording the band's shows, a concept devised by the band's then soundman Owsley Stanley, who wanted to move into other areas. Candelario's tapes were stored by the Dead in the storage space they called "the Vault," and they eventually emerged when the group began releasing their *Dick's Pick's* archival series (see the Dick Latvala entry).

Betty Cantor

Along with Bob Matthews, Betty Cantor (now Betty Cantor-Jackson) was part of the "Bob & Betty" team who engineered or produced such classic Dead albums as *Aoxomoxoa, Live/Dead, Workingman's Dead, Europe '72*, and the self-titled 1971 album also called *Skull and Roses*. She also co-engineered *Go to Heaven* along with producer Gary Lyons and co-produced *Reckoning* and *Dead Set* with Garcia and Dan Healy. Cantor worked with the band from the late 1960s through the 1980s, often manning the recording console for live concerts. The soundboard recordings she made became popular with fans, who affectionately dubbed them "Betty Boards." Cantor was one of the pioneering women in the field of sound engineering and continues to work at her craft today, shaping sound for several outfits, including the Dark Star Orchestra.

John Cutler

Cutler worked as a live audio engineer before co-producing with Garcia the band's final two studio efforts, *In the Dark* and *Built to Last*, as well as the live album *Dylan and the Dead*. Along with Phil Lesh, Cutler went on to co-produce a passel of live releases, including *Without a Net*, *Hundred Year Hall*, *Dozin' at the Knick*, *Fallout from the Phil Zone*, and *Live at the Fillmore East 2-11-69*. He now works in computer hardware and is not to be confused with Sam Cutler, the Rolling Stones tour manager who came to work for the Dead after the ill-fated Altamont Speedway Free Festival.

John "Marmaduke" Dawson

Guitarist and songwriter Dawson became friends with Garcia when they both lived in Palo Alto, California, in the early 1960s. In 1969, the pair formed New Riders of the Purple Sage along with Lesh, Hart, and several other musicians. Around this time, Dawson also contributed to a trio of Dead studio albums, starting with *Aoxomoxoa*. But his most enduring contribution to the band's legacy is his composing of the main hook for "Friend of the Devil," which he and Robert Hunter co-wrote (Garcia added the song's bridge later on). Dawson continued to lead various incarnations of New Riders until the mid-1990s. He died of stomach cancer in 2009.

David Gans

For nearly three decades, Gans has made it his mission to make sure the music of the Grateful Dead never leaves the airwaves for long. Since 1985, he's served as host of *The Grateful Dead Hour*, a syndicated program where he specializes in playing rare live cuts and interviewing Dead-related musicians. He also co-hosts another program, "Tales from the Golden Road," which can be heard on the SiriusXM Grateful Dead Channel. Gans is also the author of several books on the Dead. An active musician, he has gigged and released CDs since the late 1990s. These days, he is working on another Dead book, which he says will be "an opinionated listening guide" to the band's music.

David Gans is one of the foremost authorities on the Dead's oeuvre, and he unearths obscure live recordings for his weekly radio show, *The Grateful Dead Hour*. He also co-produced the box set *So Many Roads (1965–1995)*, which featured his essay "Everybody Is Playing in the Heart of Gold Band."   *Courtesy of David Gans*

Carolyn Adams Garcia (Mountain Girl)

A former Merry Prankster, Adams Garcia was Jerry Garcia's main love interest during the Dead's most creative years and also lived with the band in their legendary house at 710 Ashbury Street. The pair had two daughters together, married in 1981, and divorced in 1994. In 1997, she made an unexpected appearance on Court TV as part of a trial in which she defended herself against another ex-wife of Jerry Garcia, Deborah Koons, in a battle to receive part of her late ex-husband's estate (she won). She was later a founding member of the Hulogosi book publishing company, which put out Tom Constanten's auto-biography. She now sits on the boards of the Dead's charitable non-profit Rex Foundation and the Furthur Foundation, which "assists progressive groups working on environmental and social issues in the Bay Area and around the world."

Lowell George

The co-founder and main artistic voice of the country-funk band Little Feat, George was tapped by the Dead to produce their funkiest record ever, 1978's *Shakedown Street*. George can be heard singing on a version of "Good Lovin'" included as a bonus cut on the 2004 CD reissue of that album. He died of heart failure on June 29, 1979, less than a year after the album's release.

Bill Graham

One of a handful of rock legends who wasn't a performer, Graham was a concert promoter who eventually ended up running the legendary Fillmore West and Winterland in San Francisco, as well as New York City's Fillmore East, all of which hosted the Dead, among other big league rock acts. Graham was also a larger-than-life personality, with a charismatic edge that made him more famous than some of the acts he helped promote. Born in Germany and orphaned after the Holocaust, Graham was raised in a foster home in New York and moved to San Francisco to be closer to one of his two surviving sisters. It was there that he moved into promoting bands after an initial foray into theatrical production. Graham was killed on October 25, 1991, in a helicopter crash. He was 60.

Wavy Gravy

A peace activist and entertainer known for his hippie-clown persona, the former Hugh Nanton Romney came into the Dead's orbit when he was part of the Merry Pranksters, riding along on the Pranksters' cross-country bus trip and attending the Acid Test parties. He also ran the Hog Farm, which somehow ended up morphing into the entertainment company that ran the light shows at the Los Angeles Shrine Exposition Hall for the Grateful Dead and others. Like Garcia, Wavy Gravy also had a Ben & Jerry's ice cream flavor named after him. However, while Garcia's namesake product, Cherry Garcia, became the company's top-selling flavor, Wavy Gravy ice cream fell out of favor with the public and was discontinued in 2007.

David Grisman

Acoustic music virtuoso Grisman met Garcia at a bluegrass concert in the 1960s, and they stayed friends until the end of Garcia's life; their close relationship was even chronicled in a documentary, *Grateful Dawg* ("Dawg" is a nickname Garcia gave to Grisman). In 1973, Grisman and Garcia formed the bluegrass group Old & in the Way along with several other musicians, including Vassar Clements, John Kahn, and Peter Rowan. Grisman and Garcia also performed live together after the dissolution of that group, and the pair went on to record several duo albums together, some of which appeared after Garcia's death. Grisman still tours and releases albums on the Acoustic Disc label he founded in 1990.

Dan Healy

Sound engineer Healy met Garcia through John Cipollina of Quicksilver Messenger Service; he began working for the Dead doing equipment repair and upkeep and went on to design the band's early sound system. Healy also helped the Dead raise their profile early on when he recorded the band at a studio in which he worked, Commercial Recorders, and then played the tapes on his own radio show on KMPX-FM, one of the burgeoning underground FM stations. After leaving the fold for a while, Healy returned to help devise the Wall of Sound, an enormous public address system the band used live in 1974 that had stacks of speakers for each instrument set up behind each musician. He then became the band's senior engineer and mixer. Healy is credited as co-producer on the *Shakedown Street* album. Healy also produced the first two *From the Vault* live CDs and mixed the third. The Dead and Healy parted company just before Garcia's death, but he continues to work in audio and has served as a panelist at university conferences about the group.

Bruce Hornsby

Hornsby was an unofficial member of the Dead from September 1990 to March 1992. The group had hired Vince Welnick to officially replace the recently deceased Brent Mydland, and Hornsby sat in on piano to provide additional keyboards. He got his start playing Dead music live with a college band he and his brother Bobby formed, Bobby Hi-Test and the Octane Kids. Hornsby became a nationally known pop star in 1986 when his band the Range had a chart-topping hit with the politically charged song "The Way It Is." The Dead then asked Hornsby and his band to open some shows in 1987. Since then, Hornsby has worked as a session musician and guest musician, collaborated with Ricky Scaggs, wrote songs for a Broadway musical, and continued to work with Grateful Dead–related bands such as RatDog, The (post-Grateful) Dead, and the Other Ones.

Blair Jackson

A longtime chronicler of the Dead and Garcia in particular, Jackson, with his wife, Regan McMahon, published the fanzine *The Golden Road* from 1984 through 1993. In addition to writing countless articles, Jackson wrote the biography *Garcia: An American Life*, which was published in 1999. His other books include *Grateful Dead: The Music Never Stopped* and *Goin' Down the Road: A Traveling Companion*. Jackson serves as editor of *Mix*, a professional audio trade magazine.

Donald "Rex" Jackson

A Grateful Dead roadie who later became the band's road manager, Jackson died in 1976 in an automobile accident. The band's charitable non-profit organization, the Rex Foundation, was named in his memory.

John Kahn

Kahn was Garcia's bassist of choice for the guitarist's outside projects, playing in all of the various lineups of the Jerry Garcia Band as well as the Garcia and Merl Saunders groups Legion of Mary and Reconstruction. Kahn is also credited as associate producer on *Shakedown Street*, an album for which he also contributed horn arrangements. He died of a drug overdose in May 1996.

Matthew Kelly

Kelly is a harmonica and guitar player who was a close friend of Weir's and performed alongside him in several musical projects. In 1973, Kelly co-founded the Bay Area band Kingfish, which Weir later joined around the time the Grateful Dead took a hiatus from touring in 1975. He had previously performed with bluesman T-Bone Walker. Kelly's most familiar performance for Dead fans, however, is his blues harp wailing on "I Need a Miracle." He's also credited with playing harmonica on *Wake of the Flood*, although he's either buried in the mix or his play was mixed out, because it's hard to tell exactly what he contributed. In the early 1980s, Kelly joined Weir in his side project Bobby and the Midnites. Kelly and Weir stayed connected over the years, and Kelly makes a significant contribution as a guest artist on RatDog's first studio album, *Evening Moods*.

Ken Kesey

Most people know Kesey as the author of the 1962 novel *One Flew Over the Cuckoo's Nest*, a sympathetic look at the mentally ill that was made into an Academy Award–winning movie starring Jack Nicholson in 1975. But in the world of the Dead, Kesey's main role was as ringleader of the Merry Pranksters, a group of non-conformist psychedelic drug enthusiasts who threw the Acid Test house parties at which the Dead played. Kesey became a counterculture icon after the publication of Tom Wolfe's book *The Electric Kool-Aid Acid Test*, which chronicled part of the Pranksters' 1964 cross-country bus trip. Kesey died in 2001 after years of health troubles.

Les Kippel

A pioneer of taping shows, Kippel co-founded the First Free Underground Grateful Dead Tape Exchange, which begat the tradition of tape swapping among Deadheads, which helped grow the band's reputation as a premiere live act. Along with fellow taper Jerry Moore, Kippel founded *Dead Relix* in 1974 as a publication for tapers, and it grew into the national music magazine *Relix* over the ensuing years.

Dick Latvala

A lifelong music fan and an avid Dead taper (and trader) in the early days, Latvala became the Dead's official archivist in 1985 after working several jobs in the Dead's office. When the band decided to release the two-track stereo concert recordings they had made to scrutinize their work, Latvala was tapped to choose which of the fifteen hundred or so tapes he'd organized would make the best CD sets. The culmination of his work resulted in the *Dick's Picks* series, which started in 1993. Latvala, who was also active in the Dead's online community, died in 1999 at age fifty-six following a heart attack.

Eileen Law

Law was hired by the Dead in 1972 to run their fan club and went on to become the office chief of Grateful Dead Productions. For years, she was the liaison between the band and their fans, helping to answer fan mail and maintaining the group's mailing list. Law also served as the band's original archivist and is credited as archival researcher for many of the Rhino Records CD reissues of the band's original albums. Weir's song "Cassidy" was named after the daughter Law had with Rex Jackson, the Grateful Dead roadie and road manager.

David Lemieux

After Dick Latvala's passing, Lemieux stepped into the role of the band's archivist. The Canadian native has a deep background in academia, having majored in history at Carleton University in Ottawa and film studies at Concordia University. He also received his master's degree in film archiving at the University of East Anglia in Norwich, United Kingdom. Lemieux continued to release *Dick's Picks* sets until 2005, when the series ended, and also oversaw another series of live recordings, *Road Trips*. In 2011, he began curating a live CD series bearing his own name, *Dave's Picks*. Lemieux has also co-produced Rhino Records' reissue editions of the Dead's studio releases.

Branford Marsalis

The virtuoso jazz saxophonist and band leader opened shows for the Dead in the early 1990s and sat in with the band on a handful of occasions. The most notable instance of this was on March 29, 1990, at the Nassau Coliseum, where Marsalis performed with the group through the entire second set. One song from this date, "Eyes of the World," was placed on *Without a Net*, the live CD released later the same year. In the summer of 2012, he also appeared as a special guest of Bob Weir's at both the All Good Music Festival and Gathering of the Vibes.

Bob Matthews

Matthews was a high school buddy of Weir's as well as a banjo student of Garcia's before very briefly becoming a member of Mother McCree's Uptown Jug Champions, then hopping aboard the Dead's train and working as a live sound engineer for the band. When that didn't work out, he moved into studio work, first receiving credit as assistant engineer on *Anthem of the Sun*. After that, he worked with Betty Cantor and the pair became known by the handle "Bob and Betty," which appeared on the albums they engineered or co-produced, *Aoxomoxoa*, *Live/Dead*, *Workingman's Dead*, *Europe '72*, and the self-titled 1971 album also called *Skull and Roses*. Matthews returned as an engineer for *Shakedown Street* and an additional engineer for *Go to Heaven*. Matthews also played bass guitar in an early formation of New Riders of the Purple Sage. Most recently, he's worked with the Dark Star Orchestra and Donna Jean Godchaux-MacKay's Heart of Gold Band.

Nicholas Meriwether

A Deadhead and academic, Meriwether heads up the Grateful Dead Archive at the University of California, Santa Cruz, which houses the massive collection of memorabilia that the band and their associated acts accumulated over the years. Meriwether holds a Bachelor of Arts degree from Princeton University (where he discovered the band in the 1980s), as well as a master's in Library Science with a specialization in archives from the University of South Carolina. He's also written about the Dead and edited several books on the band, including *All Graceful Instruments: The Contexts of the Grateful Dead Phenomenon*, which was published in 2007.

Dennis McNally

McNally has been part of the Dead scene since Garcia invited him to become the band's official biographer in 1980, after Garcia learned that McNally had authored a biography about novelist and poet Jack Kerouac, *Desolate Angel: Jack Kerouac, The Beat Generation, and America*. McNally then moved on to become the band's publicist in 1984, a job he continued with until 2004. During that time period, he helped raise the band's profile in the press, most notably by staging a promotional campaign around the band's twentieth anniversary in 1985. The job caused him to put the Dead biography on the back burner, but he began writing it in earnest shortly after Garcia's passing in 1995. The book, which came out in 2002, is titled *A Long Strange Trip: The History of the Grateful Dead* and is the most definitive insider's account of the band's legacy published yet.

Dennis McNally worked as the Grateful Dead's historian, publicist, and biographer. When the Grateful Dead disbanded, he went on to become an independent publicist and worked with RatDog, Little Feat, and Steve Kimock, among others.
Photo by Susana Millman

Keith Olsen

A Grammy Award–winning producer who became sought after for his work on the big-selling 1975 *Fleetwood Mac* album, Olsen became involved with the Dead and then produced Weir's 1978 album *Heaven Help the Fool*. The project he produced for the Dead was *Terrapin Station*, their most orchestral and progressive rock–oriented record. Olsen went on to produce such acts as REO Speedwagon, Pat Benatar, Heart, Starship, and Kim Carnes. Olsen is not to be confused with

Elton John drummer Nigel Olsson, who appeared on the US pop chart with a pair of hit songs in 1979.

Steve Parish

A native of the rough-and-tumble New York streets and Riker's Island, Parish became a bad boy "name roadie" during his three decades on the road with the Dead. He eventually graduated to being Garcia's personal roadie as well as manager of the Jerry Garcia Band. In 2003, he published a personal account of his time with Garcia, *Home Before Daylight: My Life on the Road with the Grateful Dead*, a book that details in painful nuance Garcia's descent into harder drugs during the early 1980s.

Merl Saunders

Hammond B-3 wizard Saunders was one of Garcia's closest musical compatriots outside of the members of the Grateful Dead. After playing on the 1971 *Skull and Roses* album, the pair began a collaboration in the 1970s that included the Saunders/Garcia Band (which produced three albums) and the Legion of Mary. The prolific Saunders, who also played on several of Garcia's solo albums, was sidelined in 2002 when he suffered a stroke. He passed away in 2008 from complications due to the stroke.

Eric Schwartz

Since 1992, Schwartz has hosted and produced the *Lone Star Dead Radio* program that can be heard on KNON 89.3 FM, whose signal is also accessible online. The program, which was started in 1983 by "Grateful" Dave Moynihan, showcases the music of the Dead and their various offshoot bands for two hours every Friday night. Schwartz is also a record collector, and his program's website (lonestardeadradio.com) features images of his massive collection of memorabilia, which includes super-rare import 45s, privately pressed records, and old-school photos of Dead members.

Rock Scully

Scully managed the Dead from their Warlocks days in 1965 to a few years before they exploded with the hit "Touch of Grey" in 1987. He oversaw the band's transformation from a Bay Area act to a major label rock band that played such high profile festivals as the Woodstock Music and Art Fair. His time with the band is chronicled in a book he co-wrote with *Rolling Stone* founding editor David Dalton, *Living with the Dead*.

McGannahan Skjellyfetti

McGannahan Skjellyfetti is not a real person, but a pseudonym devised to connote collectively composed numbers on the original vinyl and CD copies of the band's first album and *Live/Dead*. The Rolling Stones had devised a similar idea by crediting early group compositions like "Empty Heart" to the imaginary Nanker Phelge. But where the Stones' moniker was derived partially from a real-life acquaintance—their roommate James Phelge—the Dead took their name from a novel, Kenneth Patchen's *Memoirs of a Shy Pornographer*. Songs credited to McGannahan Skjellyfetti include "The Golden Road (to Unlimited Devotion)," "Cold Rain and Snow," and "New, New Minglewood Blues" from the first album and "Feedback" from *Live/Dead*. The Rhino Records CD reissues of these albums used the band members' names in the songwriting credits.

Ihor Slabicky

Slabicky is the author of *The Compleat Grateful Dead Discography*, a website that scrutinizes the various album pressings and editions in detail. If you're looking to determine whether your copy of *Anthem of the Sun* with the white background on its cover is the remixed version or the original, Slabicky's site will tell you that and more. It can be found by Googling his name or visiting tcgdd.freeyellow. com/tcgdd.txt.

Owsley "Bear" Stanley

Owsley, as he was known to the public, was the chemist who supplied the LSD to Ken Kesey and the Merry Pranksters for their fabled "Acid Tests," a series of Bay Area parties where LSD was used liberally. The Dead were the house band at these parties, and Owsley soon signed on to work as the group's audio engineer. He also designed the "Steal Your Face" lightning bolt skull logo, came up with the idea of regularly recording the band (as a way to monitor his own mixes), and with Dan Healy helped devise the massive Wall of Sound system. Owsley produced and compiled the 1973 live album that bore his nickname, *History of the Grateful Dead, Volume One (Bear's Choice)*. Owsley eventually relocated to Australia, where he worked as an artist. He died in an automobile crash in March 2011.

4

Sing Me Back Home

Ten Artists Who Influenced the Grateful Dead

ike every other artist or group in the history of recorded music, the Grateful Dead came about their sound through others' influence. The difference with the Dead is that they grew up listening to a wildly divergent array of sounds, taking in everything from modern American classical music to traditional folk songs to the country and rhythm and blues hits of the day.

All of these influences came to the fore at different points in the Dead's career, but some of them also emerged at the same time, giving the band's music a crazy quilt quality. At times, such as on the group's second album, *Anthem of the Sun*, that quilt got a bit too crazy, shoving conflicting styles up against one another. But most of the time, the Dead's influences worked their way into the music seamlessly, and the group used the ideas of the musicians that came before them to build a new type of sound. These are ten of the artists whose sound infused the Dead's.

Chuck Berry

When the late Adam Yauch of the Beastie Boys was asked, in the early days of his fame, why America had made his group's debut album the first #1 rap album, he answered that Chuck Berry had invented rock 'n' roll, yet America considered Elvis Presley the king of the genre. He was addressing racial issues, but he made an excellent point about Berry and summed up Berry's place in the world of both early rock 'n' roll and its unruly younger brother, 1960s rock. Berry's influence cannot be overstated. If there needs to be a Founding Father of Rock 'N' Roll, then the Chess Records recording artist is it.

Berry emerged in the 1950s with a string of hits including "Maybelline," "Sweet Little Sixteen," "Roll Over Beethoven," and "Rock and Roll Music." These songs defined the guitar style of the genre. His lyrics often hid their keen social observations behind a wry sense of humor. The dense rhyme schemes in his songs even pointed the way towards rap ("Little Queenie," an often-covered B-side that became a minor hit, even includes a couple of rapped lines). Although Berry's sound is buried somewhere in every band that ever picked up an electric guitar, his influence on the Grateful Dead is explicit, as the Dead often covered his songs (the top three being "Promised Land," which got played 427 times; "Around and Around," which was performed 418 times; and "Johnny B. Goode," which the band broke out for 284 concerts). Bob Weir sang these songs, and his own songs, such as "Money Money," often bore similarities to them. Berry's influence kept the Dead grounded in rock 'n' roll as they sometimes threatened to fly off into the realm of unstructured improv.

Bobby "Blue" Bland

There are a lot of blues artists who could be counted as influences of the Grateful Dead, specifically on their resident blues fanatic, the late Ron "Pigpen" McKernan. Some of these artists include Muddy Waters, John Lee Hooker, and Howlin' Wolf. But the late Bobby "Blue" Bland has to count as the biggest influence, because in the early days, the Dead used to play the hell out of his 1961 rhythm and blues hit "Turn On Your Love Light," which also climbed to #28 on the pop charts. Bland isn't as well known anymore as other blues players who thrived during the same era, but, in his time, he was not only a musical force to be reckoned with—being a first-rate singer—but also a pop chart phenom of sorts. Despite never having a smash hit, he managed to rack up some thirty-seven entries on the Billboard Top 100 chart.

What Bland did was bring a more modern, soulful edge to traditional blues. And that's exactly what Pigpen used as a jumping-off point to develop his vocal style, which wasn't a traditional blues style, but a modern approximation of one. Bland also blended elements of gospel and rhythm and blues into his sound, and although the Grateful Dead aren't exactly known for their gospel stylings, Pigpen's shout-outs to the crowd during the band's long versions of "Love Light" do have their roots in gospel. Bland pretty much ceased being an influence on the Dead when Pigpen ceased being a member, but back in their salad days, the Dead did play the blues, and Bland was a touchstone for their forays into that genre.

John Coltrane

A ferociously inventive saxophonist, Coltrane, who lived from 1926 to 1967, performed solos that radically altered the way jazz players approached their music. In the late 1950s and early 1960s, he released a series of albums that helped define the bebop and hard bop subgenres of jazz, which took improvisation into a realm beyond anything anyone had heard in pretty much any genre. This, in turn, influenced the rock guitarists who came later, specifically, the musicians of the late 1960s who brought improvisation to the forefront of their own music. One of these was Duane Allman, who took rock to a new level by expanding the form in much the way Coltrane did with jazz. The other was Jerry Garcia, who listed John Coltrane as a major influence and covered "Russian Lullaby,"

Bob Dylan's influence is obvious on the pre-Dead track "Can't Come Down" (recorded under the name the Emergency Crew) and more subtly felt in the Dead's early 1970s work. In 1987, Dylan and the Dead would perform together, and some of the results would be released on the *Dylan and the Dead* album, the inner sleeve of which is shown here.
Courtesy of Sharon Balan

an Irving Berlin song done by Coltrane on his *Soultrane* album in 1958. Garcia once said in an interview that he'd been influenced by Coltrane, from whom he learned the idea of making musical statements that "sound like paragraphs," rather than copping the saxophonist's licks.

Yet, for all the jazz influence inherent in Garcia's six-string work, it was Phil Lesh who counted himself as a true Coltrane disciple, which explains his unconventional approach to playing bass guitar. In his autobiography, *Searching for the Sound*, Lesh writes, "Coltrane just blew me away. His sound was so radical—not smooth and breezy, but solid and edgy, as if it were carved out of bronze—and his ideas! Chords stacked upon chords, phrases looped over the tiniest fraction of the beat, all with the most soulful inflections and passionate intensity." When the Dead began to make long-form jams a regular part of their live shows, it was Coltrane's influence that allowed the whole thing to work the way it did. Had Garcia not met Lesh and ended up playing with a bass player who hadn't been steeped in Trane, as the late musician is affectionately known, the Dead as an improvisational powerhouse might never have come to be. Finally, in the years before his death from liver cancer in 1967, Coltrane augmented his quartet with a second drummer and began extending his live songs so that they could last for more than half an hour. Lewis Porter's biography, *John Coltrane: His Life and Music*, speculates that Coltrane may have been using hallucinogenic drugs around this time. Any of that sound familiar?

Bob Dylan

As with Chuck Berry, it's hard to overestimate the influence of Bob Dylan on both popular music and the Grateful Dead. Most folks know the basic story of this Minnesota-born rock legend: He started his professional career as a folk singer in the early '60s playing in Greenwich Village, and he wrote a handful of songs that became anthems in their time, like "Blowin' in the Wind" and "The Times They Are a-Changin'." He then infuriated his original audience when he moved into playing rock 'n' roll with a wild abandon previously unheard among most major label artists. As a lyricist, he brought new modes of expression to the genre, drawing on everything from French poet Arthur Rimbaud to old, weird traditional folk ballads to his own absurdist view of modern life. Then there was his voice. It's one of the most expressive in rock, but it's also one of the least disciplined.

When Dylan's breakthrough hit, "Like a Rolling Stone," was released in 1965, the (deliberate) lack of professionalism in his vocals and frankness of his lyrics opened the door for rock music to encompass a more "real" tone. The Grateful Dead built on what Dylan pioneered. Lyricist Robert Hunter took his cue from Dylan's lyrics and fashioned Dead songs that drew from older songs ("Dupree's Diamond Blues," "Stagger Lee"). The band themselves copped Dylan's passion-over-professionalism approach to musicianship and learned to value energy and spontaneity. And the idea of either Jerry Garcia or Bob Weir fronting a band seems unthinkable without Dylan there to get the public used to singers who weren't necessarily "vocalists."

Merle Haggard

At this stage in pop music history, the Bakersfield, California-born Haggard is a revered country legend, beloved by Toby Keith, name-checked in a song by Shooter Jennings, and even given a Grammy Lifetime Achievement Award. But back in the 1960s, Haggard's influence on country music was a bit like the Grateful Dead's influence on rock music. He changed the form into something bigger and badder and upset "the establishment" while doing so. Haggard emerged in the mid-1960s, but hit his stride a few years later with a string of country hits that helped define the "outlaw" movement of the genre. Two of these, "Mama Tried" and "Sing Me Back Home," were covered by the Dead, and it's telling that Weir sang one and Garcia the other, meaning that Haggard's songs weren't getting through to just one member of the band.

It's easy to see why both Weir and Garcia could relate to Haggard's music. Like the Dead's, Haggard's sound was unpolished (though compared to the Dead's, it's pretty polished; compared to the orchestrated "countrypolitan" hits of the time, it's pretty rough). Haggard spent some time in reform school while Weir was expelled from several private schools. Unlike Weir, Haggard didn't straighten up and join a band but wound up doing a stint in prison. Haggard's country hits included covers ("(My Friends Are Gonna Be) Strangers"), self-penned political anthems ("Okie from Muskogee," "If We Make It Through December"), and countless love songs, but like the Dead, he didn't have much impact on the pop charts. He only made the singles chart seven times and only once cracked the Top 40 ("December" hit #28 in 1973). As such, Haggard's outsider status in the pop world probably endeared him to the Dead, whose singles weren't exactly embraced by Top 40 radio either.

Charles Ives

Charles Ives was an American classical music composer who lived from 1874 to 1954 but was not really appreciated in his lifetime. These days, though, his symphonies are played by ensembles as renowned as the London Symphony Orchestra, the New York Philharmonic, and the Kronos Quartet. Frank Zappa also counted Ives as an influence, name-checking him on the inside cover of the first Mothers of Invention album and naming a song after him. So why on earth is Ives being mentioned as an influence on the Grateful Dead? Two words: Phil Lesh. Lesh counted Ives as an influence, zeroing in on the composer's experimental side, in which he melded European art songs with traditional American music, among other things. Ives's ideas pushed classical music beyond its normal boundaries, and without his concepts, it's hard to imagine the Dead embracing freeform, experimental onstage jams such as "Space" or studio weirdness such as "What's Become of the Baby" and the title track of *Blues for Allah*.

The best place to read about the connection between Ives and the Grateful Dead is in the 2010 tome *The Grateful Dead in Concert: Essays on Live Improvisation*, put together by California State University's Jim Tuedio, a professor of philosophy and director of the university's honors program. One of the book's essays is a piece by Shaun O'Donnell called "American Chaos: Charles Ives and the Grateful Dead," and it makes the case for Ives's being "a real, tangible direct influence on the band." Although this might not go over well with those who prefer the band for the pop stylings of "Sugar Magnolia" or the *American Beauty* album, Deadheads who smile each time they hear the band take off on some odd tangent on a concert recording will probably find O'Donnell's essay fascinating—much the way Lesh and company found Ives's music.

Motown Records

It seems a bit desultory to throw Motown Records out as a Dead influence as opposed to singling out its many brilliant individual artists, all of whom had their own styles and ideas. But the members of the Grateful Dead were influenced by so many artists that were on this innovative independent American label that it's not fair to leave any of them out, either. First and foremost is the girl group

Martha and the Vandellas, who churned out more than a dozen mid-1960s hits that influenced acts ranging from the Who (who covered "Heat Wave"), to the Jam (ditto), to Laura Nyro, who made an oldies tribute album featuring three of the group's songs. The Dead took Martha and the Vandellas #2 hit "Dancing in the Street" and made it a staple of their live repertoire, performing it some 123 times. They also covered it on their *Terrapin Station* album. The song's tone—celebratory, but with a gritted-teeth tension underlying its lyrics—infused such Dead songs as "U.S. Blues" and "The Music Never Stopped."

All told, the Dead did around a dozen Motown covers, either as a band or in solo mode. These covers included songs by Marvin Gaye, the Marvelettes, Smokey Robinson and the Miracles, and Stevie Wonder, among others. Motown recordings could sometimes bury subversive ideas in their commercial hooks ("Dancing in the Street" is said to be a very subtle commentary on the race riots of the 1960s), and the Dead drew from their playbook when they finally penned their own major hit, "Touch of Grey," which neatly manages to make its disturbing verses seem palatable with a triumphant chorus.

The New Lost City Ramblers

When people speak of old-time folk music, they talk a lot about Pete Seeger, the political activist and singer-songwriter who reshaped the form into something more immediate. They don't, however, talk much about Seeger's half-brother Mike Seeger and his trio the New Lost City Ramblers, who helped kick off a revival of traditional music in the late 1950s that influenced Bob Dylan, Jerry Garcia, and Robert Hunter. The New Lost City Ramblers were both a revival band and musical archivists: they took songs they heard on dusty old records and brought them back to life using banjo, fiddles, autoharp, mandolin, and hammer dulcimer. What Garcia and Hunter took from the Ramblers was that respect for tradition—the idea that older songs had worth beyond novelty value. When the Dead "went acoustic" in 1970 with *Workingman's Dead* and *American Beauty*, they sounded different from other bands who attempted an unplugged sound around the same time (such as the Eagles and Crosby, Stills and Nash). That's because instead of relying on acoustic pop hits for inspiration, the Dead looked to older influences, many of which the Ramblers helped unearth.

This is why a song like "Dire Wolf" sounds convincingly traditional and why "Cumberland Blues" was mistaken for a cover by one concertgoer (immortalized in several books) who didn't realize it was an original and marveled at how whomever had written the song would probably be pretty freaked out knowing the Dead were "reviving" it. While the Ramblers had to comb through stacks of old 78s to find their material, all anyone has to do now is pop their name into YouTube to hear them perform "Man of Constant Sorrow," the exact kind of song that led to the Dead's more old-timey efforts.

The Rolling Stones

The Rolling Stones brought a rougher, harder-edged element to the rock scene, paving the way for Bob Dylan and the Grateful Dead to do the same years later. Unlike those acts, though, the Stones eventually became celebrities, due to both their massive number of chart hits and the massive, headline-inducing drug intake of some of the group's members. These days, the Stones are like Madonna in that everyone from every generation seems to like something the band did. But back in the old days, the Stones were a very real threat to the rock establishment, with their explicit lyrics infuriating radio programmers and Jagger's onstage moves thrilling those under age twenty-five and perplexing everyone else. As with Bob Dylan, it was the Stones' lack of professional sheen that rubbed off on the Dead. According to the Rolling Stones' manager, Andrew Loog Oldham, in his autobiography, *Stoned*, they were the first group not to wear suits when they appeared on television. The Stones were also the first major pop group to put their guitars first and foremost in the mix of their records, emphasizing their raw sound over their vocals, which were also pretty raw, come to think of it.

All of these elements worked their way into the Dead's sound, especially in their earliest incarnation as the Warlocks/Emergency Crew, where they come off sounding pretty Stonesy, as can be heard on the *Birth of the Dead* double CD collection. Around this time, the band covered one of the earliest Stones originals, "Empty Heart," and later on took to performing its hits "The Last Time," "(I Can't Get No) Satisfaction," and "It's All Over Now." They also covered songs the Stones covered, notably "Little Red Rooster." As with Chuck Berry and Bob Dylan, it's hard to find an artist anywhere who hasn't been affected by the Rolling Stones. But the Stones practically rolled out the red carpet for the public to accept more earthy bands like the Grateful Dead in the 1960s, so the Stones have to be counted as a major influence on the group.

Harry Smith

Smith wasn't an artist per se. Rather, his type of artistry could be compared to that of a great disc jockey, in that he knew what songs would connect with an audience. Smith put together a multi-album package called *The Anthology of American Folk Music*, which collected songs by a slew of forgotten artists who had made great 78 records in the 1920s and 1930s. As released in 1952, the *Anthology* came out in three volumes, each comprising two albums, perhaps unwittingly setting the stage for the way the Grateful Dead would put out live albums (kidding). What these records actually did was kick off the folk music boom that took hold around ten years later. As with the New Lost City Ramblers, this music influenced not only Garcia and Hunter but also Dylan, Joan Baez, Phil Ochs, and scads of others.

These days, it's easy enough to find a song like the Carter Family's "John Hardy Was a Desperate Little Man," for example. But back in 1952, when televisions weren't common, much less the Internet, the work of an archivist like Smith was the only way the general public was going to hear songs like this. The *Anthology* has been easy enough to come by since it was reissued on CD in the late 1990s. It figures heavily in Greil Marcus's book about Bob Dylan from 1997, *The Old, Weird America,* originally titled *Invisible Republic: Bob Dylan's Basement Tapes.* And although the Dead never covered any of the songs on *Anthology,* their influence is clearly evident. Just check out Furry Lewis's "Kassie Jones," about a train engineer.

5

A Band Beyond Description

A Dozen Elements That Shaped the Dead's Music

he sound any band makes is made up of more than just the notes the musicians play and sing. There are also musical influences, sociological factors, and personnel combinations at play. In chapter 4, we looked at ten artists who influenced the Grateful Dead. Here, in roughly chronological order we'll examine some of those mysterious "other factors" that made Dead music Dead music.

The City of San Francisco

Despite the influence of mass media in the post–World War II era, local music scenes still managed to thrive independently of what was being played on radio. This was definitely the case in San Francisco, where a musical culture developed in the mid-1960s that was singularly different from anywhere else. It wasn't just that bands such as the Grateful Dead, Quicksilver Messenger Service, Jefferson Airplane, and Big Brother and the Holding Company turned up the volume a bit louder and kicked out the jams a bit longer. It was that they were able to attract an audience that accepted all that and didn't walk out or demand Top 40 covers.

This wasn't always the case. Even in cities as ostensibly open minded as New York and Los Angeles, the Velvet Underground and the Mothers of Invention had a hard time getting regular gigs (the Velvets' summer 1970 residency at Max's Kansas City was considered a homecoming, as they rarely played there, and Frank Zappa lamented the Mothers' lack of L.A. shows in a track on the *Uncle Meat* album called "If We'd All Been Living in California . . ."). Why would San Francisco, of all cities, have been the place the Grateful Dead was able to nurture their sound?

"For a musician, San Francisco provides the ideal climate in which to create," writes Jeff Tamarkin in his book *Got a Revolution! The Turbulent Flight of Jefferson Airplane*, and "Seiji Ozawa, a former conductor of the San Francisco Symphony, once said, 'There is a very free feeling in this city. People who live here have very free minds, which is very important for me to make music.'" Tamarkin also notes that the city was once described as being "resistant to authority and control" and "served as a final refuge for those whose ideas and lifestyles are too unacceptable, or just too bizarre, to survive in the mainstream." In other words, it was a perfect locale for a band that preferred taking musical trips instead of going on a pop star trip.

Garcia's Car Accident

When Jerry Garcia was nineteen years old, he was involved in a serious car accident in which one of his friends was killed. Like a lot of people who experience brushes with death, he was changed by it. In Garcia's case, he went from being a self-described screw-up to seriously focusing on his music. Had Garcia not been in that car at that particular time, would he have continued living his life with little focus? It's hard to say. But what's easy to see is that behind his hippie image, Garcia was one of the more driven musicians, at least early on.

It's likely the car accident fired that ambition, and that ambition is what led Garcia to work at his craft as a guitar and banjo player a bit harder and eventually seek out musicians with whom he could play professionally. Garcia is quoted in Blair Jackson's biography, *Garcia: An American Life*, as saying that the crash is where he felt his life really began. It's telling that Garcia didn't cite the beginning of the Dead or the founding of their acoustic predecessor, Mother McCree's Uptown Jug Champions, as the start of his life. It's likely he realized that without the accident, he might not have discovered the drive to start either group. "This accident put some focus, some intensity and desire, into our life," explained Garcia, speaking about himself and the other surviving passengers to interviewer Alice Kahn in the *San Jose Mercury News West Magazine* in 1984. "It's like somebody important was gone from our little scene, someone who had real talent and who might have been great—it was necessary now to fill in, to take up the slack," he said.

The Pre-Beatles 1960s

In America's urban areas in the late 1950s and early 1960s, a counterculture was developing before anyone thought to call it that. It was primarily made up of young people who had grown dissatisfied with the conformity that marked the time of Dwight D. Eisenhower's presidency, which spanned the years from 1953 to 1961. That era can be glimpsed in any number of TV programs from this time or by listening to the big hits of the day, which veered away from the rough-and-tumble early rock 'n' roll sound and began to edge more toward conventional pop. Even though John F. Kennedy officially became president in January 1961, the 1960s as we know them didn't quite start until the Beatles landed in America in February 1964.

Before then, teens or twentysomethings who were looking to live lives different from the unadventurous ones in the popular black-and-white TV shows of the time took to listening to folk music and reading the work of the alternative writers who became known as the Beat Poets. It was during this time that the ideas that would come to shape the music of the Dead and bands like them were forged. This period has been called "the pre-Beatles 1960s" but could also be termed "the pre-counterculture era."

It was around this time that Garcia had grown bored with rock 'n' roll and began to explore traditional folk and bluegrass music. He found kindred spirits in Robert Hunter, another folk aficionado who also wrote poetry, and Ron "Pigpen" McKernan, who studied old blues records in much the way Garcia studied traditional music. Like Bob Dylan, the Dead took from the pre-counterculture era several important elements that would find a home in the band's own work, such as a healthy disregard for the conventional norms of society, a skepticism about commercially oriented music, and an identification with outlaw and bohemian culture.

LSD

No serious discussion about the music of the Grateful Dead can leave out the band's experimentation with the drug lysergic acid diethylamide, commonly known as LSD. The drug wasn't yet illegal in 1965 when Garcia first took it with some friends and when Ken Kesey and the Merry Pranksters held their Acid Tests. At the time, LSD was being used for government and psychiatric purposes and wasn't widely known by the general public. But when word got out that long-haired types like the Dead were using it to "trip," the government stepped in really fast, and by October 6, 1966, it was made illegal in California.

LSD is part of what helped the band make the leap from the garage band affectations that are heard in their early work to the mind-blowing psychedelia of albums such as *Anthem of the Sun* and *Live/Dead*. Where the Beatles' amphetamine use during their early days gave their music a hyper edge, the Dead's use of psychedelics influenced their early music to be wide open spaces and new frontiers. In a 1979 interview with *Feature* magazine, Garcia admitted that his "most palpable experiences have all been psychedelics" and went on to explain in detail how powerful some of his experiences with LSD had been.

Virtually all the members of the band used LSD on at least a semi-regular basis during the band's early days. The group's signature jam tune, "Dark Star," is, musically speaking, something of a musical adaptation of the psychedelic experience, with its ever-shifting, improvisational melody lines and drum parts. LSD also gave the Dead an identity as a psychedelic group to the uninitiated kids who bought the group's first album. The first time that the masses would see Jerry Garcia's name, after all, was on that LP's back cover, where he's listed as "Jerry 'Captain Trips' Garcia."

Adding a Second Drummer

The Grateful Dead were not the first band in history to sport two drummers after bringing Mickey Hart into the fold in 1967. One of the Dead's influences,

John Coltrane, had tried out double drumming two years before (around the time he was rumored to have used LSD, for what that's worth). In the rock world, the Los Angeles psychedelic band Clear Light originally formed in 1966 with two drummers. But the Dead were the first major rock act to use such an approach and as such sent the message that rhythm was an element of the band they wanted to emphasize.

This had a marked effect on the band's music. More drumming or additional percussion meant that the Dead were a band you could groove to: there was a thrust to their sound that was lacking in the sound of many of their contemporaries, whose drums were often mixed into the background, even in live situations. It also put the Dead, perhaps unwittingly, in the vanguard of contemporary music as the 1970s wore on. The album *Shakedown Street* might have been derided as "disco Dead" by some, but the Dead already had that genre beat by several years when it came to incorporating polyrhythms and putting the groove in your face. One reason most of the Dead's post-1970 music has dated so well is that it anticipated popular music's emphasis on rhythm, which would come to dominate the music of the 1980s and beyond.

Robert Hunter's Adages

Lots of lyricists come up with brilliant phrases. But few devise as many quotable lines in songs as well as Robert Hunter did. One of Hunter's gifts was that he could come up with his own adages and slip them into unexpected places in songs. For example, in the middle of what appeared to be a conventional love song, Hunter would throw in a line that seemed to speak of a larger, universal truth.

The best example of a Hunter adage is probably "Once in a while you get shown the light in the strangest of places if you look at it right," from "Scarlet Begonias." His most popular line is "What a long, strange trip it's been," from "Truckin'," which went on to become a phrase used everywhere from headlines to everyday language. "If you plant ice you're gonna harvest wind," from "Franklin's Tower," is yet another. Phrases such as this make listeners stop to consider what a given song is really saying, or to think about what such a line means outside the context of the song. Hunter's uncanny ability to coin quotable phrases gave the Dead's music an intellectual heft it might otherwise have lacked.

Sharing the Singing

In his 1977 book *The Beatles Forever*, the late Nicholas Schaffner pointed out that one reason people related to the Beatles so well was that they came across as more of a band than most other acts did. A lot of this had to do with the fact that the Beatles had two main singers in John Lennon and Paul McCartney, plus they let members George Harrison and Ringo Starr take the mic on occasion, so each member got his say, so to speak. By the early 1970s, the Dead were doing

Vol.5 No.1
Mar.-Apr.
$1.50

Hot Tuna

McGuinn,
Clark &
Crosby

Papa John
Creach

and more!

Grateful Dead
lyricist:

Robert
Hunter

When Robert Hunter started writing lyrics full-time for the Grateful Dead, the band's music fully took shape. The poet and songwriter never had much success as a solo act, but many songs he co-wrote with Garcia are among the best known in rock.

Courtesy of Relix Media Group

much the same thing, letting virtually all their members take a lead vocals spot (with the exception of the drummers). In concert, Garcia and Bob Weir usually alternated on lead vocals, with other members stepping into the vocalist slot once in a while. On the group's most beloved album, *American Beauty*, the first four songs are sung by four different group members. On the debut album, three different vocalists take the lead on the first three songs.

This set-up gave the Dead's music a scope that other bands didn't have. Each of the lead singers had his own style, and that meant the band could move from whispery ballads into screaming rock 'n' roll with more finesse than groups who relied on a lone voice to carry them could. Sporting two main singers also allowed fans to feel that they'd gotten to know the band more closely because there were two voices with which they could identify instead of one. As with Beatles fans, some Deadheads favored one singer more than the other, and this sometimes made for spirited debate among fans about which version of the band they liked better—just the type of engagement that could never have occurred had the Dead relied on one singer.

Finally, having two main singers was also a built-in way for the Dead to maintain quality control. If one lead singer was having an off night, the other one could always be counted on to take up the slack. This is a major reason old Dead shows remain eminently listenable: *someone* is usually on fire in the vocals department. And it doesn't get much better than those magical occasions when both Garcia and Weir are at the top of their respective games.

Not Having a Front Man

There's a story that in the heyday of the Go-Go's, lead singer Belinda Carlisle didn't like it when rhythm guitarist Jane Wiedlin took lead vocals on parts of the band's songs because it left Carlisle standing in the center of the stage with nothing to do. Now imagine if the Grateful Dead had formed with a dedicated lead vocalist who didn't play any instruments but just wanted to stand front and center and sing the songs. He or she might have tired really quickly when Garcia decided to take off on one of his six-string flights of fancy, and the idea of the Dead as an improvisational unit might never have gotten off the ground. (While Pigpen did function in this capacity in the early days, he was also the band's organist and could hop behind his Hammond when the band moved into long instrumental passages.)

It was the Dead's set-up that enabled them to grow into the instrumental powerhouse they became by the time of 1969's *Live/Dead*. Without having to answer to a prancing front man like Mick Jagger or Robert Plant, the band could sing for one verse, then jam for ten if they felt like it. The Allman Brothers had a similar arrangement, and it's probably not a coincidence that their music evolved along similar lines. This flexibility allowed the band to do whatever they chose and is one of the reasons the Dead's music is defiantly different from and less commercially focused than the acts they came of age with—the ones who had a front person for whom they felt they had to play a backing band role.

Segues

Transitions from one song to another were part of the Grateful Dead's live performances almost from the beginning. Some of them, like blending "China Cat

Sunflower" into "I Know You Rider," became so commonplace that they almost made two songs seem like one song with two parts. The Grateful Dead were the first major rock group to make song segues a regular part of their repertoire. Before the Dead, bands performed medleys of their songs, but these consisted of fragments of whole tunes strung together to create a bigger musical piece. The Dead took whole musical pieces and tied them together.

Segues themselves could sometimes result in original music, because the band had to spontaneously come up with ideas to tie a pair of songs together. Tapers of the Dead's music took notice of this quirky habit and accordingly began to denote segues with a symbol of an arrow (>) on their reel-to-reel tape covers or cassette j-cards. When the *Dick's Picks* concert recordings series made its debut in 1993, it also used the arrow symbol to signify when one song segued into another.

Lesh Not Locking In

In most rhythm-based genres of music, the bass guitar "locks in" with the drummer to create a punchy, powerful rhythm section. Not with the Grateful Dead. One of the elements that made the Dead's music irresistible to believers and nerve-racking to detractors was the disregard bassist Phil Lesh had for this convention. Before Lesh ever picked up a bass guitar, he had already studied classical violin as well as trumpet and avant garde composition. This informed his approach to bass, which was different from virtually any other bassist's in the rock era save the Who's John Entwistle, a player who also defied convention.

Often in jams, Lesh would play his own bass leads while Garcia was performing his own guitar runs. This left rhythm guitarist Weir and whoever was playing keyboards to hold down the rhythm section with the drums. A good example of this can be heard on *Dick's Picks Volume Thirty* during the jam section of "Not Fade Away." Lesh's approach to playing against the rhythm section instead of with it ran completely counter to the way bands such as the Rolling Stones or Creedence Clearwater Revival "anchored" their music with tight rhythm sections. If anything took the Dead's music away from conventional rock, it was Lesh's loosey-goosey bass lines and his refusal to play basic root notes, opting instead to play harmony lines using thirds or fifths. He also threw in occasional bass chords and thunderously low notes using a six-string bass.

Deadheads

When you have a large, roving pack of fans that follow you around from city to city and keep audio records of what you play on any given night, you can't really get away with playing the same songs all the time. While the Dead would never have been the kind of glad-handling band that used touring as a way to promote their latest product to the masses, their rabid followers made sure the band never fell into any sort of complacency that mimicked that kind of conventional

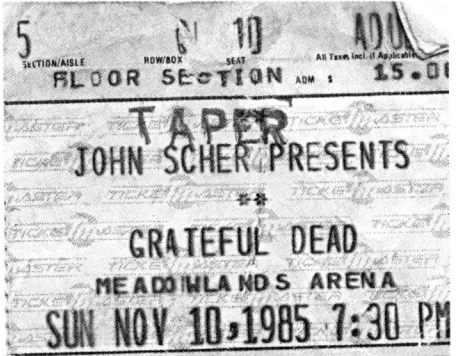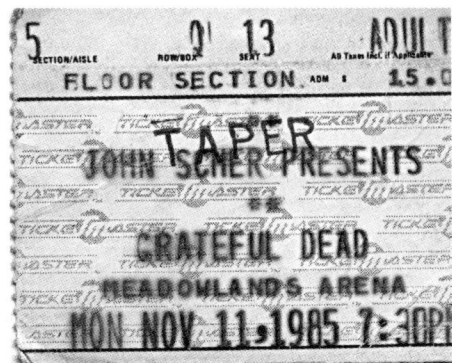

The Grateful Dead were the first major rock act to allow fans to record their concerts, even going so far as to issue tapers' passes such as these, for the band's November 10 and 11, 1985, shows at New Jersey's Meadowlands Arena (now known as the Izod Center).   *Courtesy of Stuart Dahne*

music industry set-up. The band may have challenged audiences with music, but the audience challenged the band right back by being such close listeners.

Deadheads, in other words, had an influence on the band by pushing them to try out new ideas on stage on a much more regular basis than was common in rock music. The group kept a reported 100 to 115 songs in rotation at any given time. Although there were songs that the band played regularly, such as "Me and My Uncle" and "Sugar Magnolia," the set lists overflowed with surprises. These included as-yet-unrecorded new songs, new arrangements of old songs, and songs no one seemed to quite expect, such as older tunes the band hadn't performed for more than a decade. One noteworthy example of this is when they broke out "Box of Rain" on March 20, 1986, after not having played it since July 28, 1973.

Occasionally, guest musicians would perform with the Dead, including jazz saxophonist Branford Marsalis, who played with the band in March 1990. The band didn't so much pander to the expectations of an audience as it kept in mind the symbiotic relationship between audience and performer. And that had an impact on how the Dead went about making music, at least when it came to live shows.

The Tapers

The Grateful Dead's music inspired a dedicated group of fans in the early 1970s to start recording shows and swapping the tapes they made. They were known as "tapers," a network of fans built up through *Dead Relix* magazine (later renamed *Relix*). As the 1980s dawned, and as the tapers became more and more a part of the Dead's scene, the band took the opposite approach of most artists, who called in heavy-handed security thugs to confiscate equipment. On October 27, 1984, the group became the first major band to officially sanction the live taping of concerts by setting aside a "Tapers' Section" behind the mixing board.

One member of the Dead's crew who couldn't help notice the tapers was the soundman, Dan Healy, who occasionally let them plug directly into his mixing board to capture a clean "board recording," which took the sound directly from the band's microphones into the tapers' recorders (as opposed to an audience recording, where tapers captured the sound of both the band and audience). After a while, Healy became interested in hearing what the tapers' recordings sounded like. Sometimes he didn't like what he heard.

Before you could flip a cassette, Healy had made some changes because he felt there was room for improvement in the band's live sound, according to a taper named Bob Menke, who is quoted in a Blair Jackson article titled "Deadheads: A Strange Tale of Love, Devotion and Surrender," which ran in the April 4, 1980, issue of *Bay Area Music* (*BAM*) magazine. "We gave Healy copies of some tapes we'd made in early '78," Menke is quoted as saying. "He heard some weakness in his mixing through our tapes and in early '78 he re-arranged the stage and developed a new mix." So, tapers had a direct influence on the way the band sounded after 1978, as Healy enhanced the group's sound because of them.

6

That's When It All Began

The San Francisco Scene of the '60s

lmost no recording act develops in a vacuum. There is usually a community in which artists develop. This was definitely the case with the Grateful Dead, who emerged from San Francisco's underground rock scene in the 1960s, a fertile musical space that encouraged artistic freedom. For the most part, the artists who came from San Francisco during this time period valued adventurousness over commerciality, had a preference for rock grittiness over pop polish, and included more women than were usually found in rock bands at that time.

All of these elements would come to influence the Dead. The following are some of the artists who came of age in or around the Dead's home base. Some played on the same bills with the Dead or jammed with the band on occasion. Others were pop and folk acts that came before the Dead, but paved the way for San Francisco in the 1960s to become a hub for rock acts.

Big Brother and the Holding Company

Before Janis Joplin was a rock legend, she was the main singer of this heavy rock ensemble, which she joined in mid-1966, around a year after they first came together. Big Brother and the Holding Company was something of a kindred spirit of the Dead's, playing many of the same venues and appearing with the Dead at the Monterey International Pop Festival in 1967. The rush of attention Joplin received at that festival helped intensify the spotlight the media had already shone on the city. With Joplin, Big Brother scored a #12 single with "Piece of My Heart" in the late summer of 1968 and released two albums, a self-titled debut and the mega-hit *Cheap Thrills*.

The Beau Brummels

Earthy folk rock without the professionalism of the Turtles or the piousness of the Byrds, and predating them both on the singles charts, the Beau Brummels formed in 1964 and scored two big hits in 1965 with "Laugh, Laugh" and "Just a

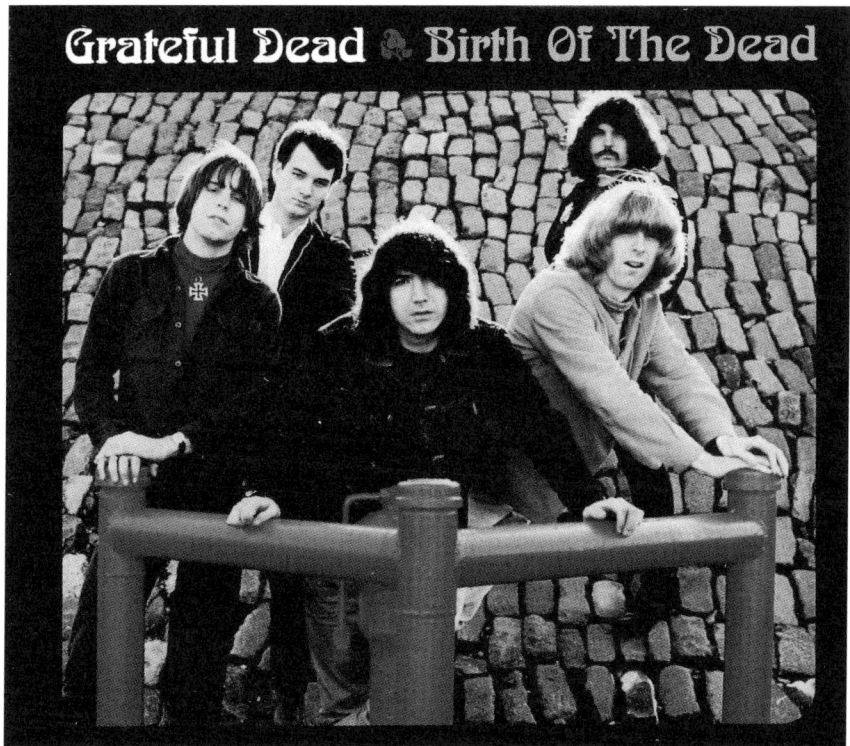

They're a garage band: on *Birth of the Dead*, the 1965 edition of the Grateful Dead (temporarily called the Emergency Crew) sounds at times like one of the obscure mid-1960s garage rock outfits featured on the *Nuggets* or *Pebbles* compilation series. The band would find their voice soon enough.   *Author's collection*

Little." They also had a few smaller hits that predicted the acoustic-rock sound R.E.M. brought into vogue in the early '80s. The band is credited with introducing a prototype for the San Francisco sound and recorded for Autumn Records, which almost signed the Dead in 1966. Although the Beau Brummels never got to capitalize on that, they have received posthumous critical acclaim for a pair of classic albums released in 1967 and 1968, *Triangle* and *Bradley's Barn*.

Blackburn and Snow

This obscure male-female folk duo began playing in coffeehouses in Palo Alto early in the 1960s and might have bumped into Jerry Garcia and his first wife, Sara Ruppenthal, had that pair stayed together as Jerry and Sara a bit longer. As it ended up, this pair, whose full names were Jeff Blackburn and Sherry Snow, only stayed together long enough to put out two singles, although twenty songs were unearthed when a CD of their recorded legacy was put out in 1999.

The originality of this duo's music shows how much the region was a breeding ground for talent before it became a rock mecca. Snow later joined another local outfit, Dan Hicks and his Hot Licks.

Blue Cheer

Known at the time as the loudest rock band around, the members of Blue Cheer began playing with one another in 1967 after three of them moved to San Francisco to be part of its rock culture. They didn't really share the hippie aesthetic of Jefferson Airplane or the Dead, though, and Blue Cheer's success helped take San Francisco from being a genuinely interesting musical town to being the media's idea of a "trendy" town, like Seattle was in the 1990s. Blue Cheer did, however, help invent heavy metal with their Top 20 remake of Eddie Cochran's "Summertime Blues."

The Charlatans

The Charlatans came together in the summer of 1964 and brought with them many of the same musical influences that made their way into the Dead's sound: rock, jug band, country, and blues. They were hamstrung by bad luck, though, getting their first album shelved and only having two non-charting singles issued during their heyday in 1966. The excitement had worn off by the time the Charlatans eventually released their self-titled debut album, which was co-produced by Dead soundman Dan Healy. The band's original first album finally came out in 1996 on CD as *The Amazing Charlatans*.

The Chocolate Watch Band

This quintet (originally a septet) originally hailed from nearby San Jose, but they helped define the region's psychedelic music sound with their outlandish name, which defied the more conventional monikers of the time, and their 1967 debut album, which contained fuzz-drenched rockers such as "Dark Side of the Mushroom" and "Expo 2000." The band created three albums, the first of which contained "Let's Talk About Girls," immortalized on the landmark compilation album *Nuggets: Original Artyfacts from the First Psychedelic Era, 1965–1968*.

The Count Five

Also hailing from San Jose, this grungy garage band also helped focus attention on the region with their surprise hit single, "Psychotic Reaction," which hit #5 in the fall of 1966. A true one-hit wonder act, The Count Five never charted again and split up after just one album.

Country Joe and the Fish

The work of "Country" Joe McDonald helps connect the world of San Francisco's folk music of the early 1960s with the rock that came later. As early as 1965, McDonald released an early version of his anti-war anthem, then called "The I-Feel-Like-I'm-Fixin'-To-Die Rag," as part of a seven-inch extended play record, *Rag Baby: Songs of Opposition*. The song later formed the basis for the title of his second album, which along with his first, *Electric Music for the Mind and Body*, helped define the San Francisco psychedelic sound. McDonald became something of a counterculture icon after his performance of the song at Woodstock.

The Flamin' Groovies

The Flamin' Groovies were a pop band that was mainly popular with critics. Founded in 1965, the band didn't record until 1969 and didn't become influential until after the punk era dawned. It was then that songs such as "Shake Some Action," from 1976, came to be seen as important to the power pop genre, which helped beget new wave. The band's no-frills approach to rock also provided a link between San Francisco's hippie scene of 1967 and its punk scene, which exploded ten years later when bands such as the Avengers, the Nuns, and the Dead Kennedys sought to shake up the establishment in much the same way the psychedelic bands had.

Frumious Bandersnatch

Taking their name from the Lewis Carroll poem "Jabberwocky," this group only could have come out of the psychedelic era, and their heavy sound was indicative of the San Francisco scene in 1967, the year they formed. The group only released one three-song EP in their day (although more recordings came out later) and is most notable for some of the members' later joining the Steve Miller Band and Santana.

The Golliwogs

The Golliwogs first released records in an early rock style as Tommy Fogerty and the Blue Velvets and by 1970 were one of America's biggest bands, Creedence Clearwater Revival. In between, they were a band who were in search of a sound when they released four singles on Scorpio Records. Scorpio was a subsidiary of Fantasy Records and released the first-ever record to bear the name of the Grateful Dead, the single "Stealin'" backed with "Don't Ease Me In." The Golliwogs didn't hail from San Francisco but El Cerrito, located about sixteen miles east. Still, they played some of the same venues as the early Dead, including Longshoreman's Hall.

The Great Society

Now known as the training ground for future Jefferson Airplane singer Grace Slick, the Great Society were one of the earliest proponents of acid rock, making their debut in late 1965. After releasing only one single, an early version of "Somebody to Love" titled "Someone to Love," Slick defected to the Airplane. The Great Society never released a proper studio album while they were together, but after they split up, two albums were released in 1968 to capitalize on the Airplane's success. Both albums are evidence of how the Great Society helped open the door for heavier forms of rock in San Francisco.

It's a Beautiful Day

The eccentrically named band didn't form until 1967 and were kept from playing locally by their manager. They didn't even release an album until 1969, but the self-titled debut they came up with is an eclectic blend of rock, jazz, folk, and classical, featuring the FM staple "White Bird," a song illustrative of the gentler side of San Francisco rock. The band was also notable for featuring Linda LaFlamme, a multi-instrumentalist whose presence helped underscore the importance of women in the San Francisco rock scene.

Jefferson Airplane

The Airplane started in the summer of 1965 and along with the Dead were one of San Francisco's most famous exports. The difference between the two bands was that the Airplane were the far more commercial, racking up two massive 1960s hits with "White Rabbit" and "Somebody to Love." The group's debut 1966 album, *Jefferson Airplane Takes Off* (with singer Signe Toly Anderson), might have been a rather safe dry run for what came later when Grace Slick hopped aboard. But it's one of the earliest fully realized rock albums that puts across the basics of what came to be known as the San Francisco sound.

The Kingston Trio

The Kingston Trio, a clean-cut, commercially oriented folk group, were not part of the city's rock scene. But when most of the rockers were still learning to pick their guitars (or banjos), the Kingston Trio were helping to launch the folk music boom of the early '60s and were doing that from their home base in San Francisco, even cutting a live album at the city's hungry i nightclub. Along with the Smothers Brothers (also based in San Francisco for a while), the Kingston Trio deserve credit for setting the stage for the city's folk rock scene in the mid-1960s, if not the rock scene that exploded a few years later.

The Loading Zone

One of the more commercially oriented but least successful psychedelic groups to emerge from the Dead's backyard (actually from Oakland originally), the Loading Zone got their start playing the Trips Festival at the Longshoreman's Hall in January 1966, a three-day Acid Test that made the Dead local celebrities of sorts. The Loading Zone then released a truly weird self-titled debut album in 1968, which blended avant-jazz horns, rock beats, and operatic soul vocals from Linda Tillery. A self-released second album, *One for All*, is so obscure it's become a holy grail among collectors of psychedelic records.

Steve Miller

Miller might be from Wisconsin, but when he formed the Steve Miller Band (originally the Miller Band) in 1967, he moved to San Francisco to do it. His debut album, *Children of the Future*, was psychedelic rock filtered through the lens of British producer Glyn Johns, and it set the stage for his many successes to come (such as *Fly Like an Eagle*, *Book of Dreams*). Decades later, in 1992, Miller would tour with the Dead and jam with them on stage. It might have seemed like a weird combo unless you knew Miller had once traveled all the way to Deadland in order to build his own musical house.

Moby Grape

Started in 1966 by former Jefferson Airplane drummer Skip Spence and that band's then manager Matthew Katz, Moby Grape released one of the definitive psychedelic rock albums borne out of the San Francisco scene in 1967. Moby Grape's self-titled debut album, though a Top 30 hit, suffered from an ill-conceived promotional campaign by Columbia Records, who released almost all the songs as singles, sparking a backlash or at least lots of confusion. The band never quite recovered after that, and Spence descended into mental illness. He released a cult favorite, *Oar*, in 1969, after which he slipped into obscurity before passing away in 1999.

The Mojo Men/Mojo

Formed in 1965, when folk rock bands were sprouting like weeds, the Mojo Men started out doing more rocking fare, with their first single, "Dance with Me," placing at #61 late that year. Their biggest hit, though, came in 1967 when their cover of the Stephen Stills–penned Buffalo Springfield song "Sit Down, I Think I Love You" rose to #36, making it one of the many San Francisco–based hits of the time. By that time, the group had a female member in singer/drummer Jan Errico (also known as Jan Ashton), so the Mojo Men changed their name to the sexless Mojo and released an album in 1968. Several compilations of the band's early work have been issued since.

Quicksilver Messenger Service

A guitar-oriented ensemble if there ever was one, Quicksilver Messenger Service helped build the foundation of the San Francisco rock scene when they started playing in 1965 (but didn't release an album until three years later). The group became known for the guitar playing of the late John Cipollina and eventually featured the late songwriter Chet Powers, who wrote the Youngbloods' mega-hit, "Get Together," under the pseudonym Dino Valente and Quicksilver's biggest hit, "Fresh Air," under the moniker Jesse Oris Farrow. Got that? Quicksilver's first two albums are considered quintessential examples of psychedelic rock, even though they came a bit late in the game.

Santana

Santana didn't form until 1967, after San Francisco had been established as a breeding ground for creative musicians. Nonetheless, Carlos Santana, the band's founder and creative force, helped fuel the feeling that the city was in the midst of a musical Renaissance when he unleashed his heady new style of guitar-heavy Latin rock. From then on it was Woodstock, hit albums and singles, Grammy Awards, and legend status.

The Savage Resurrection

This obscure act started in 1967 when psychedelic music was trending, and released their lone album the next year. The barely-produced, raw-sounding, guitar-driven self-titled record turned out to be the band's only one and is indicative of how the Dead's stomping grounds were now spawning bands with sounds that were miles away from the folk- and blues-derived music that helped drive the scene in the beginning.

Sly and the Family Stone

Rhythm and blues music was never quite the same after Sly and the Family Stone broke through in 1968 with their first big single, "Dance to the Music," a wildly influential piece of progressive soul. The band had been around in some form since 1966, though, and it made perfect sense in the context of San Francisco rock that an R&B band from the area not only would mix and match musical genres, but also would sport a lineup with musicians of various races and genders. Before all that, band leader Sylvester Stewart (aka Sly Stone) had also produced the Beau Brummels, the Mojo Men, and the Great Society, and as such was one of the architects of the city's rock sound.

The Strawberry Window

An obscure psychedelic band probably better known to today's aficionados of the genre than they were in their time, the group, which started in 1966, played pounding, guitar-heavy rock that sounds intense even now. Unfortunately, it didn't net them much interest from record companies. Some live and studio recordings from 1967 were belatedly released on CD in 2009, offering a fascinating look at a band on the periphery of the Dead's world.

The Vejtables

Hailing from a city west of San Francisco, Millbrae, the Vejtables serve the same purpose as the Beau Brummels when it comes to the story of the Dead. The rough-hewn brand of folk rock the Vejtables started playing in 1964 paved the way for the San Francisco sound that was to come. The group never released an album, but did score two minor hit singles in 1965: the rocking "I Still Love You" (#83) and a cover of the Tom Paxton favorite "The Last Thing on My Mind" (#117). Singer Jan Errico (also known as Jan Ashton) also played drums and later drummed and sang for the Mojo Men, exemplifying how women were especially integral to the rock scene in San Francisco.

We Five

We Five were a short-lived San Francisco–based folk rock phenom in mid-1965, taking a cover version of Ian and Sylvia's "You Were on My Mind" to #3 and Dino Valente's "Get Together" (under its original title, "Let's Get Together") to #31. They were fronted by Beverly Bivens and originally formed by Michael Stewart, the brother of John Stewart (the Kingston Trio, "Daydream Believer"), who later went on to produce two Billy Joel albums, including *Piano Man*. As with the Beau Brummels, We Five's success focused attention on their hometown.

William Penn and His Pals

Another group that played in the Dead's backyard with little widespread recognition, William Penn and His Pals only released one non-charting single, "Swami"/"Blow My Mind" (as William Penn V) in 1966, but the group recorded enough material to fill a rather short CD that came out in 2003. Mickey Hart is said to play drums on an alternate version of "Blow My Mind" contained on the CD.

More Music: Looking High, Looking Low

A good number of the aforementioned acts didn't have nearly as high a profile as the Grateful Dead, so it's not always easy to seek out their music. But it can be done; you just have to poke around.

The best resource for hearing the San Francisco sound of the '60s is the four-CD box set *Love Is the Song We Sing: San Francisco Nuggets 1965–1970*, which Rhino Records issued in 2007 to commemorate the fortieth anniversary of the Summer of Love. The set was the fourth in a series of box sets called *Nuggets*, which followed the tradition of the landmark 1972 compilation *Nuggets: Original Artyfacts from the First Psychedelic Era, 1965–1968*, by showcasing obscure material by unheralded bands.

There are popular acts here, such as the Steve Miller Band, Sly and the Family Stone, and Santana, but their tracks rub elbows with songs by some of the lesser-known acts mentioned in this chapter. Liner notes by compiler Alec Palao along with Ben Fong-Torres and Gene Sculatti put it all in context.

Also in 2007, the British label Ace Records came out with a one-disc collection, *You Got Yours! East Bay Garage (1965-67)*, that brought together two dozen tracks by largely unknown local acts of the time. The compilation was also researched by Alex Palao, and his liner notes describe the musical happenings in the blue collar backyard of the Dead's stomping grounds, the East Bay. The collection brings together a handful of obscure singles and a slew of unreleased tracks by bands that include the Baytovens, the Blue Lite Conspiracy, and the Harbinger Complex, the latter of whom has long been a favorite of garage music aficionados.

You can dig even deeper into the history of obscure 1960s San Francisco bands by checking out a five-volume series of downloadable sets called *California Love-In*. These sets cover music from local scenes other than San Francisco, offering some interesting perspectives on what was happening in other localities during the fervent musical period in which the Dead came of age. Some of the San Francisco acts featured include super obscure bands such as Initial Shock, Spring Fever, and the Travel Agency. Of special interest to Dead fans should be a 1966 version of "Morning Dew," a song the Dead covered on their first album, which is done by San Francisco's Bethlehem Exit in a jangly fast-paced style and was released under the title "Walk Me Out." These collections are downloadable from the Yahoo group U-Spaces and are sometimes available on various music blogs that specialize in psychedelic sounds.

7

The Music Never Stopped

Why Does the Grateful Dead Still Interest People?

The scene is the Rams Head Live! concert hall in Baltimore, Maryland. The date is August 10, 2005, nearly ten years to the day after the Grateful Dead's leading light Jerry Garcia died, but the room is packed in anticipation of a concert by a group led by former Dead member Bob Weir. Weir's group, RatDog, have attracted not only a capacity crowd, but also an audience that looks for the most part as though they're in their twenties and thirties.

Nearly three years later on August 1, 2008, the ritzy Meyerhoff Symphony Hall in the same city is swarmed with people who want to hear the world premiere of composer Lee Johnson's symphonic suite of Grateful Dead songs, *Dead Symphony No. 6.* This unusual orchestral work recasts tunes such as "St. Stephen" and "Mountains of the Moon" into big, symphonic pieces. The concert, held on what would have been Garcia's sixty-sixth birthday, also brings out two Dead-related celebrities who sit in the audience. When Carolyn "Mountain Girl" Adams (Garcia's ex-wife) and John Perry Barlow (Weir's lyricist and buddy) are introduced at the concert's outset, both get greeted with thunderous cheers that probably frightened the Meyerhoff's season box-seat ticket holders.

Scroll ahead four years, and in nearby Columbia, Maryland, Weir and former Dead bassist Phil Lesh stop into town with their band, Furthur, which mostly plays the music of the Grateful Dead. The two aging musicians play for nearly three hours to a crowd of all ages that probably would have stayed the whole night had they not been finally ushered out by the concert's security staff.

As Bob Dylan once sang, something is happening here. It's easy enough to know what it is: the Dead's music still has an audience nearly two decades after the band called it quits in the wake of Garcia's death. But why is it happening? Why do people still fill the concert halls, buy the reissued CDs of old albums, and cause the runs of concert series like *Dick's Picks* to go on for thirty-six volumes? Why are the Dead still referenced in popular culture?

The easy answer is to say, "People loved the band's music." While there's no doubt lots of truth in that, it can't possibly be the whole answer. Other artists from the 1960s and '70s actually had more people who loved their music, if you

⟨ 2856432	JOSEPH MEYERHOFF SYMPHONY HALL

Tie-dye mixed with tuxedos when legions of Deadheads filled Baltimore's Meyerhoff Symphony Hall for the premiere of Dead Symphony no. 6. The concert, which was officially billed as "A Tribute to the Grateful Dead," was sold out, proving that interest in the band remains high, even when there are no guitars in sight.   *Author's collection*

judge by record sales. But those artists aren't really part of the culture now. It would be hard to imagine Gary Lewis and the Playboys, for instance, filling up concert pavilions with twentysomethings year after year—yet that group had more hits than the Dead had, plus a chart topping song, "This Diamond Ring." The Dead never even had a Top 10 single until 1987.

No, the Dead had something else about them that went beyond the music. Call it a mystique or an image. Call it something that the band accidentally came by or deliberately fostered. Whatever you call it, it still exists, and it's the reason the Dead are still an influential force in music, not a half-forgotten oldies act whose name befuddles the contestants on TV's *Jeopardy*.

Mysteries Dark and Vast

To get to the center of this riddle, we need to look beyond the music and get into some sociology by peering back at the 1960s, the era in which the Dead formed. While a good argument can be made that the Dead were more a '70s band than a '60s one, as that's when the Dead were at their best in concert and on vinyl, most people associate their presentation with the 1960s. And they're right to do so. In no other era could such a band have been launched. In the 1950s, the group's scruffy appearance and free-for-all meshing of musical styles would have kept them from getting signed by a major label, thereby relegating them to bush league status. In the 1970s and 1980s, well, the same thing probably would have happened.

Had the Dead formed around the time indie acts such as the Replacements and Hüsker Dü started in the early '80s, the Dead would have made for one hell of an indie label act. But they also might not have survived their early period without the backing of a big record company, as it took them several years to find their footing musically, and none of their first four albums made the Top

40. Also, without a major label backing them at some point, it's doubtful that their cultural influence would have become as big as it did.

In the 1960s, bands as weird as the Dead, Frank Zappa's Mothers of Invention, and the Velvet Underground all not only could get major label deals, but also put out multiple albums on those labels without getting dumped at the first sign of failure, which is what happens a lot today. Although the Dead was considered cool in music circles, the music they were making when they were signed was somewhat out of step with the public. The garage sound of their early records was too rough for radio, and the way the Dead extended songs wasn't yet in vogue, even among musicians. Meanwhile, their association with the burgeoning drug culture wouldn't be accepted for a while by the masses, either.

How different was the culture into which the Dead dropped their first album? Consider this: the group signed with Warner Bros. in October 1966, and the final episode of *The Donna Reed Show* was broadcast on March 19, 1966. Even though we know now that hippies were ultimately embraced by the public, there was a chance the whole long hair thing could have ended up a fad. Still, the Dead ended up on a major label.

Zappa (along with co-author Peter Occhiogrosso) spoke of the open-mindedness of record companies in the 1960s in *The Real Frank Zappa Book*, which was published in 1988:

> One of the good things that happened in the sixties was that at least some music of an unusual or experimental nature got recorded and released. So, who were those wise, incredibly creative executives that made this Golden Era possible? Hip young guys with Perrier breath? No—they were old cigar-chomping guys who listened to the tapes and said, "I dunno. Who knows what the fuck it is? G'head—put it out there! Who knows? I dunno."

"We were better off with that attitude than we are now," Zappa continues. "The 'bright young men' are far more conservative—and more dangerous—than the old guys ever were . . . There is something to be said for an executive who is willing to take a chance on an idea, even if he doesn't like it or understand it. The new guys don't have that spirit."

When the Dead were signed, they were not only obviously "weird," looking like a classic "menace to the public," but they also weren't even quite ready to be recorded, what with their rickety early sound and lack of original songs. Then there was the fact that most of the band members were either average looking or below-average looking. It didn't matter much then; it matters a hell of a lot now. Since cable TV took over the homes of America, appearance matters far more in virtually all facets of media, from news anchors to talk show hosts to the pretty-boy bands and scientifically engineered women that get priority on the music channels.

While not everybody knows the ins and outs of the music industry, a good number of people get a sense that we now live in a more corporate-controlled environment, one in which a record company would show the young Dead the door or exploit them for one album and then unceremoniously drop them. People look back to a time when it wasn't this way. Their longing for a less corporate-controlled, more individual-driven era is a reason we have nostalgia for the Dead in their heyday (it's also the reason for another burgeoning sub-culture, the people who make up the Occupy Wall Street, or OWS, movement).

People perceive the Dead as having stood for individuality, for bucking the system. To most people, that means the Dead lived out the classic 1960s ideal of "doing your own thing." The first generation of kids who bought into the Dead's new ideas were called the "counterculture" for a reason. They created their own culture to counter the mainstream one that they felt was going wrong for reasons too numerous to list here.

If the Dead's fans were idealistic, they were only following the lead of the band themselves. The Dead's former manager, Rock Scully, said as much in a 1996 article in *Relix* magazine: "It was a time of huge idealism," Scully said. "I went out to the Haight to live there, and Rock was like the Minister of Culture . . . I see it as a utopian venture, and in a way, the folly which nobody really saw at the time was you can't build a revolution or a society on pop music. It helped change people's minds, but I mean, we really thought, or I really thought, that a new culture was coming. We were not so materialistic, and everything was gonna be like it was in the Haight."

The Dead may have been signed by a major label, but they weren't *of* the mainstream culture. They used the label's resources as a springboard for what they wanted to do as opposed to having themselves "molded" into a record company's idea of what they should be. Again, such molding is what record companies did in the eras before and after the Dead were signed, and the Dead had the luck to come up in a period where they got to make the kind of albums they wanted and no one pulled the plug on what they were doing when they didn't "increase the revenue stream" right away. The Dead seemed to be the antithesis of corporate culture, even though in later years they became a sort of mini-corporation themselves. And it was partially people's disgust with the burgeoning corporate culture that drew them to the Dead then and continues to draw them to the band now.

The Corporate Curse

Droning on about the troubles of living in a corporate-dominated society can seem both cliché and overwrought—unless someone presents evidence that the business world has, in fact, dramatically altered the way we live. Douglas Rushkoff does exactly this in his anti-corporation tome *Life Inc.*, which details the many ways that big business gradually came to dominate everyday life during the twentieth century. Anyone seeking a deeper understanding about why subcultures like the Deadhead community or OWS have evolved will find insight into that in his book.

Progressive Review editor and author Sam Smith makes an argument similar to Rushkoff's in an essay he wrote for that online journal called "The Corporate Curse: How Business Culture Dragged America Down with It." In it, he outlines how American business has become both dysfunctional and ineffectual and how this has been caused by the rise of the new "management class" that has come

Back in the late '70s, if you didn't want to buy tie-dyed shirts on Shakedown Street (the nickname for the vendors' section of concert parking lots), you could always buy an "official authorized" T-shirt for $6 by mail order. Back then, decals set you back $1 and card sets $3.   *Courtesy of Relix Media Group*

with the massive increase in graduates with Master of Business Administration degrees. Smith noted that in the 1950s, the country's universities turned out fewer than 5,000 MBAs a year. In 2005, they graduated 142,000. This, he says, has affected virtually every industry, including the music industry:

> We have created an economy based not on actually doing anything, but on facilitating, supervising, planning, managing, analyzing, tax advising, marketing, consulting or defending in court what might be done if we had time to do it. The few remaining truly productive companies become immediate targets for another entropic activity, the leveraged buyout.

It's instructive to note that a lot of the very people attending the aforementioned concerts either work for businesses that engage in such "entropic activity" or grew up with the influence of corporations as an inescapable backdrop to their own lives. It's little wonder that a subset of people find themselves drawn to music made by musicians who are some of the last remnants of the counterculture.

Smith goes on to explain how the business class's obsession with the bottom line affects the music we hear today:

> The corporate virus even affects the arts, that supposed haven from our lesser selves. Watch *American Idol,* for example, and count the number of times corporate interests intrude on the proceedings—from the participants taking part in a loudly cheered automobile ad to a handful of listener questions that serve no purpose other than to promote a phone company. You think you're above *American Idol?* Think again. More votes were cast in a recent American Idol poll than Bill Clinton got the first time he ran for president. Even if we hate such manifestations of corporatized culture, we can't hide from their effect.

Smith goes on to ask, "Why don't I like more songs? Why does the audience become so hysterical about so little? Whatever happened to melody? Why do looks and attitude swamp talent?"

They don't in the world of the Grateful Dead, where many who can't abide the larger culture have sought refuge year after year since the band began.

Deadheads of the World Unite

By the dawn of the Reagan era, the hippie counterculture of the 1960s and early 1970s had receded into the past like a dream, or like a nightmare if you hated hippies. But a funny thing happened on the way to the future: A subculture of Dead fans known as Deadheads didn't fade into history. In fact, their numbers grew with each succeeding year. They followed the band around from city to city, swapped concert tapes, and often kept detailed records of what the band played at each gig. They were the people who tuned away from Top 40 music, who weren't slaves to the newest fashions, and who didn't watch all the trendy shows—if they even owned a TV. Odds are that today's equivalent of these folks aren't watching *American Idol.*

Critics scoffed at Deadheads for being relics of a bygone era, but they didn't consider the demographics of the group. By the 1980s, the average Deadhead wasn't necessarily an "aging hippie," but could be anyone from almost any age group. On virtually every college campus and in some high schools, a small collection of the tie-dyed faithful could always be spotted among the preppy masses. You'd see them playing Frisbee on the quad or strumming guitars outside the dormitories.

Some of the new generations of Deadheads sought the scene out not only because of the music, but also because it looked to them like the only current embodiment of 1960s culture. Critics dismissed this as nostalgia but failed to ask why a cult of nostalgia had developed for the Dead. Why not for Gary Lewis, for example? Others dismissed Deadheads as people only in it for the drugs, but if that were the case, why didn't they just stay home and get high? Why go through all the trouble of following a band around?

The very fact that a "Deadhead culture" had evolved into becoming a permanent part of the social landscape was enough to give the Grateful Dead a mystique that almost no other band had. Throw in the fact that the Dead hadn't sold nearly as many records as other 1960s bands that didn't have such fanatical followings had, and you had a bona fide phenomenon on your hands. If only Gary Lewis had attracted such a cult, he'd probably be a hot touring ticket today, too.

When the Dead scored a Top 10 hit with "Touch of Grey" in 1987 and finally did get played on MTV, the band's audience exploded. The concert halls where the band played were never exactly empty, but by late 1987, the parking lots overflowed with kids wanting in on this odd cultural phenomenon.

The new fans, called "Touch Heads," seemed to glom onto the Dead's scene more for the drugs and (presumed) sex than for the music. But when that brief period of Deadmania subsided, a lot of new fans stuck with the band, because they had discovered the back catalog and the magic of seeing the band live.

They'd also discovered an alternate culture, whether they knew it or not. It was a culture where fans who had graduated into the working world took weeks off to go "on tour" with the Dead, a culture in which "regulars" knew each other and didn't sell bootlegs for profit but swapped tapes for free.

The sad irony of all this is that while the Dead avoided making their music more corporate, their expanded audience did cause their organization to become a corporate monster. This, in turn, put stress on Garcia, whose health had been deteriorating since a diabetic coma he'd survived in 1986. Garcia's agreeing to go out on the band's final tour in 1995 likely hastened his early death that summer. So, the Dead became the victims of a corporate culture that was their own doing. Then again, had the band not become so big, they wouldn't have been nearly as influential and wouldn't have helped generate a whole alternative rock culture in the jam band scene.

As time went on, bands began to form that were put together by people in and around this scene. Phish was one. Blues Traveler was another. There were dozens more. Before you knew it, the "jam band scene" was being written about in the mainstream press, and kids weaned on MTV discovered that there was an alternative to mainstream music culture.

All of this came just in time. A few years after a bunch of jam band acts came together to tour under the banner of the H.O.R.D.E. Festival (which stood for Horizons of Rock Developing Everywhere), Garcia died. But the cult he'd spawned had grown to the point where it was now part of mainstream culture, at least temporarily. For a brief period, H.O.R.D.E. bands such as the Spin Doctors, Blues Traveler, and the Dave Matthews Band were all over pop radio. Add to that the music of H.O.R.D.E. veterans Joan Osborne, Natalie Merchant, and Fastball, and you have another generation—or two—who came of age listening to music inspired in some way by the Grateful Dead.

That these people still crowd concert halls shouldn't be a surprise, considering the influence the Dead had on 1990s music. And that these same people seek an alternative to a corporate-dominated society shouldn't be shocking either, considering how different the country is today from what it was forty or so years ago.

Revolution and the Dead

And yet there had to have been something about the music the Dead played that helped spark the Deadhead phenomenon to begin with. A lot of this had to do with the way the group went about playing their music. The music the group played live was partially improvisational in nature. Garcia in particular had a knack for developing melodies on the fly during the band's signature jam tune, "Dark Star," but all the band members could jam when the occasion presented itself.

The concerts the band played weren't the same night after night, which is often the case with other bands, even ones from the same era (I remember seeing the reunited Monkees play in two cities once, and not only was their set the same, their supposed ad-libs were nearly identical). Sometimes fans would see the Dead and enjoy an evening full of their favorite songs. Other times the band would play sets of tunes almost no one seemed to like. Some nights they were on fire, playing better than anyone imagined. Other nights they were uninspired. But no matter what they played or how they played it, everyone knew they were at least getting something real.

The Dead made each concert a singular artistic experience, not a preconceived "presentation." Whether people knew it or not, the Dead's stage show was the embodiment of a wildly anti-corporate attitude. What could be less corporate, after all, than making your "product" totally unpredictable?

But the Dead's do-your-own-thing aesthetic is what made the Dead the Dead. The group's philosophy came to serve as a template for a way Deadheads could lead their own lives. This especially appealed to the group's followers who had no interest in conforming to the narrow ways of living prescribed by parents, teachers, guidance counselors, religious leaders, and other folks who'd never think to eat an avocado sandwich, much less prepare one in advance for a concert.

People who came in contact with the band in their later years (or after they split up) easily sensed that something different was afoot with the way the Dead approached their music. People either hopped onboard the Dead's train or ran

New York–based Brookvale Records' decision to release the first two *Dick's Picks* volumes on vinyl seemed like a quirky idea when it was first announced. But sales proved so strong (with the second volume selling out) that the company decided in November 2012 to put out the entire series in the good old LP format.

Courtesy of brookvalerecords.com

screaming in the other direction. Those who "got it" usually stayed onboard, as the Dead were never exactly a trendy band that people would discover as tweens and then leave behind due to embarrassment. So, something of a snowball effect developed, which had the group picking up new fans year after year.

Thus, we now have the phenomenon of sold-out concerts nearly two decades after the Dead have ceased to function as a band.

In his landmark book about the music of the Fab Four, *Revolution in the Head: The Beatles and the Sixties,* the late British writer Ian MacDonald lamented the growing sameness in popular music, which he says is and was largely due to producers' increasing use of computerized drum machines and sequencers, which removed the "human element" from the sound. MacDonald wrote that he believed such devices made modern pop songs "regularized and formularized, their harmonic movements banal and predictable, their vocal lines devoid of independent melody and constructed from pre-fabricated melody/lyric clichés bolted together as if by mechanics on an assembly line."

It's not difficult to see this as a metaphor for what's happened in modern life. With the rise of both corporations and technology, life itself has become more and more "regularized and formularized" as well as "banal and predictable." Such changes in society—along with the fear-mongering of the invasive media culture—have caused Americans to become alienated from one another, a dispiriting situation described in Robert D. Putnam's landmark 2000 book, *Bowling Alone: The Collapse and Revival of American Community*. In this book, the Harvard professor examines how civil engagement in America has declined, with fewer and fewer people involved in community and social groups. This situation presents an answer to why people continue to find refuge in the Deadhead subculture, with its promise of community and acceptance of individuality.

Considering all of this, maybe the question that needs to be asked about the Dead's continuing popularity isn't "Why does the Dead still interest people?" but "Why aren't even more people tuning in, turning on, dropping into the scene?"

8

False Alarm

Why Naysayers Were Wrong About the Dead Not Being a Studio Band

T here is nothing like a Grateful Dead concert" was a legend from an old bumper sticker as well as a saying among Deadheads. If you were a newcomer on the scene and spoke to any Dead freaks, you'd hear about the network of tape trading that went on, and how this concert from New York or that show from Chicago was their favorite.

What you didn't quite hear was how good the Dead's studio albums were. Back in the day, the band's records got a bum rap. With one or two exceptions, the records were thought to be poor approximations of what the band *really* sounded like, the stories went, but to truly experience the band you had to see them live. This wasn't completely true. The Dead made more than their fair share of great studio albums over the years, and that fact is coming to light more and more as the band recedes into history and as decades of hindsight allow people to get a better perspective on the Dead's music.

The Grateful Dead's reputation as a substandard studio band took hold because of three factors: rock critics, the band members themselves, and the fans. With all these negative elements with which to contend, it's amazing the band did as well as it did with the studio albums it released, placing ten albums in the Top 40 during its lifespan. Here is a breakdown of why each of these factors claimed that the Dead-on-LP experience wasn't so hot and why they are wrong.

Call Your Soul a Critic?

First, the critics. There were a lot of rock critics who didn't take to what they disparagingly called the Dead's "three-hour jams." Fair enough; not everyone likes long-form music. But this attitude spilled over onto the LPs. Because of what the band did on stage, critics heard the albums with jaded ears, assuming that the Dead were unfocused or indulgent. The main culprit of damaging the Dead's reputation as a studio act was the original *Rolling Stone Record Guide*, put out in 1979 and then updated in 1983. It's hard to overestimate the influence these books had on would-be fans of the band. In fact, it's hard to overestimate the effect the books had on fans of any artist. When I interviewed Laura Nyro biographer Michele Kort for an article about why Nyro's influence wasn't fully appreciated over the years, Kort didn't hesitate to answer: "*Rolling Stone*. That's what a bible *Rolling Stone* is."

These books were all most rock fans had back in the pre-Internet era and back before the rock audience became mature enough to sustain its own mini-book industry. So, what *Rolling Stone* said went. This could sometimes have a positive effect on artists, such as the Beach Boys, whose *Pet Sounds* earned its reputation largely from these books. But it could also have negative consequences, such as when the wrong critics were assigned to bands. This is what happened with the Dead in the first two editions of the *Rolling Stone Record Guide*.

In the first, reviewer John Milward acknowledges that the Dead are capable of "sparkling jams," but goes on to say that "they are just as likely to wander aimlessly." Additionally, he notes that "only a bunch of hippies could survive this long without a first-class singer," totally disregarding Garcia's uniquely subtle approach to vocalizing.

What mostly damaged the band's reputation as album artists, though, were the ratings the albums earned. The *Record Guide*'s rating system awarded "stars" to each LP in accordance with its supposed entertainment value. None of the Dead's records received more than a three-star rating in the original 1979 *Record Guide*. Even the bona fide classics *Workingman's Dead* and *American Beauty* only warranted three stars each. Also, the Dead's hits collection, *Skeletons from the Closet*, only rated three stars in the 1979 book, which is really odd. Usually, when bands that critics dislike put out "best of" albums, the critics at least acknowledge that such albums distilled what was best about those artists and give the album a high rating. This didn't happen with the Dead, though.

Cue the imaginary footage of fans and non-fans passing by the Grateful Dead bins as they searched record stores back in the days of denim and long hair. And believe it or not, it actually gets worse from there.

For the 1983 *Record Guide*, the Dead entry was written by the book's co-editor, Dave Marsh. Marsh scrunched the entry down to just a few paragraphs and lowered the album ratings so much that ten of the nineteen albums reviewed got one-star ratings. *Wake of the Flood*? One star. *Blues for Allah*? One star. *Terrapin Station*? One star. And the classic *American Beauty*? Well, that at least got two stars. Writes Marsh,

> The Grateful Dead epitomize hippie rock & roll and if you're a hippie yourself, you might want to invert the judgments expressed in the ratings system above. But unless you are, this is one assuredly major oeuvre that's virtually worthless except for documentary purposes.

Marsh goes on to say that Garcia has a "pedestrian set of chops" as a player and that what's most impressive about the group is the "devotion of its fans to a mythology created in Haight-Ashbury and now sustained in junior high schools across America."

Marsh actually had that wrong. Anyone in junior high back then knew that kids were most devoted to whichever bright and shiny new pop star MTV was showing at the time, not to the Grateful Dead. I admire Marsh as a critic, and his writing has been a big influence on my own, especially his book *The Heart of Rock and Soul*. But Marsh favors working-class rock and R&B and doesn't seem to have much interest in jam music, and therefore wasn't the best reviewer to tackle the Dead's catalog, as he was clearly hostile to their music.

Decades later, the idea of jam bands would find favor with critics who began to see the burgeoning genre as a viable alternative to the ever-growing commercialization of mainstream pop. But back in 1983, Marsh was emblematic of a breed of critics who didn't quite get what the Grateful Dead did and trashed the band, casting a pall on their recorded work. Around the time the jam band scene got started, a completely new, retitled edition of the book was put out called *The Rolling Stone Album Guide*. It was fairer to the band's recorded work, but the damage had already been done, with several generations of rock fans buying into the myth of the Dead making poor studio albums.

The Interviewer Plays the Band

The second reason the Dead's albums were never accorded much respect was the band members themselves, most of whom never seemed happy with what they'd done in the studio. For Garcia, this feeling took hold early on, apparently: in Rock Scully and David Dalton's book *Living with the Dead: Twenty Years on the Bus with Garcia and the Grateful Dead*, Garcia is quoted as repeatedly saying, "God, we make shitty records."

In an interview with James Henke in a 1991 issue of *Rolling Stone*, Garcia elaborated on this feeling. Henke starts his questioning by regurgitating the party line and asking Garcia, "Why do you think the Dead have had such problems making good studio albums?" Leaving aside the issue of why an interviewer would ask such a leading question, let's consider Garcia's answer. He says, "Well, I think we have made a few good ones. *From the Mars Hotel* was an excellent studio album. But since about 1970, the aesthetics of making a good studio album is that you don't hear any mistakes. And when we make a record that doesn't have any mistakes on it, it sounds fucking boring."

Garcia continues, "Also, I think we have a problem emoting as vocalists in the studio. And there's a developmental problem, too. A lot of our songs don't really stand up and walk until we've been playing them for a couple of years. And if we write them and try to record them right away, we wind up with stiff versions of what the song finally turns into."

It's telling of Garcia's mindset that he didn't attempt to reframe the interviewer's question and say something like, "What are you talking about saying we don't make good studio albums? Even if we made five great albums, that's a pretty good track record." But Garcia played into the interviewer's hand. Looked at from a broader view, the idea of "making mistakes" on records was never quite the norm in pop (classic pop records with mistakes are beloved in spite of said mistakes, not because of them), and most artists—even commercial pop ones, not just the Dead—allow their songs to evolve in concert.

Then there's Phil Lesh, who also played into interviewer Tucker Carlson's frame when the conservative talk show host interviewed Lesh on his *Unfiltered* PBS television show on May 8, 2005. Carlson asks why the band couldn't capture their sound in the studio. Lesh answers, "We—you know, I don't think any of us ever believed it could be done. Because there's just so much . . . there was just so much range to it. Not necessarily only dynamic range or—but there's just so much emotional range to it and we just—we found ourselves in the studio always trying to tone it down, which really isn't what we do. We're not about turning it down. We're about opening it up."

"I never bought your albums when I was little," Carlson goes on to say. "I just got tapes for free."

A better answer from Lesh might have been that no band captures their live sound in the studio. That's what live albums are for. Rather, most artists develop a distinct studio sound that works when we consider records as records per se. But whatever Lesh had answered, his response wouldn't have convinced a lot of people that the group knew what they were doing each time the red Record light got turned on in a recording studio. That leads us to the third and probably the most important reason the Dead were never thought of as a premiere LP act: the band's original legion of fans who coveted tapes like Beatles fans coveted rare 45s.

How Does a Pop Record Go?

To understand why Deadheads saw the band's music as working best in a live medium rather than a recorded one, we need to break down what a "record" is and why that medium has become central to the twentieth- and twenty-first-century listening experience, as opposed to the live medium.

A record is different from a song. A record is not just words and notes; it's a recorded moment, preserved with whatever technology is available at the time. Rock 'n' roll was the first genre of music that was more about records than about live performance. As much as rock 'n' roll is said to be all about spontaneity, as a sound it's largely been a studio creation. The early 45s Elvis Presley made for Sun Records, for example, are sonically defined by the tape-delay echo that producer Sam Phillips used. The most celebrated albums by the Beatles and Pink Floyd, *Sgt. Pepper's Lonely Hearts Club Band* and *Dark Side of the Moon*, are as much triumphs of effects and technology as they are models of great songwriting. All those effects helped define the record.

Even when the rockers of yore didn't rely heavily on technology, they had a "sound" depending on what studio they were in and which producer they were using. Artists or bands would make records, go out on tour, and hope they

The Dead added keyboardist Brent Mydland (far right) in 1979, right around the time they were being written off as a studio band. The group surprised everyone when they made a comeback in the late '80s, cutting the most successful studio album of their career, *In the Dark.*   *Author's collection*

could re-create that sound decently. Or they hoped fans wouldn't mind if they couldn't.

The Grateful Dead did not subscribe to this process. They rarely attempted to make their live sound match the sound of their records. Instead, the Dead behaved more like a jazz act than a rock or pop band, as they made spontaneity, not sonic re-creation, the hallmark of their music. This doesn't mean the band didn't have a "studio sound." The Dead had a signature sound on record, which they defined around 1970 and expanded on throughout the rest of their career. But that sound did not define the band outside the studio.

Instead, the Dead saw their stage show as a separate thing, a venue that allowed them to improvise, try out new songs, stretch out songs for more than half an hour, or even make atonal noise. The Dead didn't make like other groups and go on tour to "promote the product." Instead, they played pretty much whatever they felt like no matter what record they had out at the time.

The band's fans knew to expect this. From the beginning, the Dead had attracted a breed of fans that enjoyed their improvisations, whether those moments took the form of Pigpen's vocal excursions on blues tunes, Garcia's unpredictable guitar lines, or Lesh's bass runs.

While all this was happening, a gigantic taping community was taking shape. Fans would record shows, make copies of their tapes, and then trade with other fans. While concerts of other bands would occasionally get bootlegged and wind up on albums, the Dead's network of tape traders was unique in that it seemed to suggest that almost everything the band did was worth hearing, not just specific concerts. Because of all this, most Deadheads learned to assess the band as an improvisational act who were at their best "in the moment." This is similar to the way jazz fans appreciate jazz players, and totally unrelated to the way most pop or rock fans relate to their favorite artists, whose ultimate moments are thought to be captured on records.

The downside of this is that the Dead's records got the short shrift from fans, as records in and of themselves are made up of captured, contrived moments, not live improv. Dead fans came to hear the studio versions of their favorite band's songs in the exact opposite way rock and pop fans hear the records of their favorite bands. Dead fans heard the studio songs as performances that happened to take place in a studio and usually didn't compare to the ever-evolving live versions. Fans of virtually every other act heard their favorite act's studio creations as "records."

Let's use the Beatles as an example, because they're a group that most everyone knows. When the Beatles committed "Drive My Car" to tape for the *Rubber Soul* album in late 1965, they used some very specific arrangement ideas: a piano, a cowbell, and falsetto backing vocals are three of the standout ones. When fans hear Paul McCartney perform the song live, they expect at least one of those elements to be in place. They're not listening for the song itself so much as they're listening for *the record*. And they're not comparing McCartney's latest version of the song to the one he played at some other concert because, odds are, the version at the other concert was probably pretty similar because it also aped the record.

The opposite thing happens when a seasoned Deadhead plays the band's records. Instead of hearing, for example, the delicate acoustic guitars of "Friend of the Devil" as the ultimate way that song should be performed, they're comparing it to many, many live versions that can be heard—and wondering where the band will take it next. As the Dead played the song more and more, they slowed it down and gave it a loping reggae beat. After hearing enough versions of this song, the studio rendition does, in fact, begin to sound "stiff" as Garcia said. Maybe "embalmed" would be a better word, because the live versions are just so . . . alive.

Hence a situation evolved where older fans would rave about their favorite concert tapes to newer fans and in doing so made the band's studio work seem irrelevant or like an afterthought. When judging the band's songs by this criteria, it's easy to think of them that way. But if you forget this and you judge the Dead's records as records per se, and/or against the recorded works of other bands, they sound pretty damned good.

To appreciate the Grateful Dead's records, you have to concentrate on elements the band couldn't bring to the table in a live setting but could play up in the studio. There are the "stacked" harmonies, where band members would overdub their voices several times to create a deep, rich sound you can only get in the studio. There's the subtle way Garcia's guitar is highlighted with just the right amount of equalization and reverb. There are also the little oddball touches that add to the atmosphere—you're not going to get that spacey whooshing sound in "Unbroken Chain" on any concert recording.

Then there are things you don't even think about. Things like the concept of the fade-out, which was almost unheard of in the pre-rock days. Fade-outs aren't always just an easy way to end a song that doesn't resolve. They can also be used as an effective tool to lull the listener into an emotional state where the song seems "bigger" because it fades into the (imaginary) sunset rather than coming to a halt. This can be particularly effective when a song with a long, slow fade closes a good album, and it's rarely been used as effectively as the Dead used it on "Ship of Fools," which ends the *Grateful Dead from the Mars Hotel* album. There's something distinctively melancholy about the way Garcia and company slowly march off into the distance as the song's volume gets lower and lower, and it's the type of moment you can only get on a record. This is just one example of how Dead records have elements that are undervalued.

There is also one more reason the Dead's records aren't appreciated by fans. It's because the Dead were, in fact, making substandard albums during the time period when a lot of people discovered them. That was in the late 1970s, when the band signed with Arista Records and got paired with producers who didn't quite get the music. So there was a falloff in quality from the band's output during the 1970s, which had previously been almost uniformly excellent. The Dead's experiment with outside producers at Arista lasted just three albums, but it was enough to taint the band's studio reputation retroactively.

Blues for Everyone

Rather than sift through the many great moments on Dead records, which is done elsewhere in this book, the fact that the Dead made great albums can be proven by employing a hypothetical.

Let's say you were a visitor from another planet and the authorities in charge decided for whatever reason to acquaint you with pop music, so they put you in a room with a handful of CDs, MP3s, and old records by artists from the 1940s until today. You know nothing about Chuck Berry, Frank Sinatra, or Lady Gaga, but in playing their recordings, you get a sense of why their music connected with these humanoids at some point in history. You have no idea of who the Grateful Dead are, but they've given you an old LP called *Blues for Allah*. You put it on the contraption they have called a "turntable." As it plays, you get a sense that the record contains four really great songs in "Help on the Way," "Franklin's Tower," "The Music Never Stopped," and "Crazy Fingers," plus a few good ones, and some interesting experimental material. There are no other performances of any of the songs by which to judge the material, so you dig the mellow grooves the band put out, and instead of wishing for different versions of songs from different cities, you come to appreciate how the band can be both danceable and subtle at the same time. Who else did that?

All told, having four standout songs is not a bad batting average, considering what most albums have to offer. Even that *Dark Side of the Moon* CD the security humanoid from NASA keeps telling you is the greatest thing ever has about that many great songs and is equally waterlogged with strange effects. So, taken outside the context of concerts and tape trading, it seems, *Blues for Allah* is pretty great. And it's not even the Dead's best album.

All told, the Dead made more than their fair share of classic albums. It's just that the critics and the context in which the fans listened kept everyone from appreciating them. Hopefully, this essay will inspire a few listeners to break out *Mars Hotel*, fire up a pair of headphones and dig the way Donna's voice lights up the layered harmonies of the band's male cast. Just the type of thing you can only experience on one of the Dead's studio records.

9

Trouble Behind, Trouble Ahead

Five Reasons People Hate the Dead

'll be grateful when they're dead."

Somewhere along the way, most every Deadhead has heard that clichéd but admittedly funny saying. Hard as it is to believe, some people just don't take to the Grateful Dead. OK, so that isn't really so hard to believe at all. Like a lot of idiosyncratic, individualistic artists, the Grateful Dead's weirdness and refusal to bow to most mainstream conventions put a lot of people off. There's nothing wrong with that, really. Any artist in any genre that comes off different from the norm is bound to attract some haters. But why? Here are five reasons the Dead have engendered the enmity of some.

Guitar Solos

If you want people to listen to your music, Frank Zappa once noted, you need to have vocals in there somewhere. In all styles of popular music that sell big, vocals reign supreme. The Grateful Dead sang, of course, but they were among the first rock bands to expand their music to encompass long instrumental passages. While that might seem de rigueur to jazz and jam band fans, it was anything but run-of-the-mill when the Dead started pioneering this approach in the latter half of the 1960s. Before then, when rock groups played live, they would mostly play their hits the way they sounded on their records. Some bands, such as the Beatles, even shortened their songs in live settings, perhaps to better engage the short attention spans of their teen audiences.

The Grateful Dead acted as if this way of performing was already buried in the deep past when they started to garner an audience. They didn't temper their edgy rock approach with "eager to please" audience pandering the way many of the British rockers who had paved the way for the Dead's bluesy approach did. No, the Dead jammed. And jammed a lot. They jammed to the point that when they put out their first official live album in 1969, there were only seven songs on the four sides. It would have been unthinkable for any band to do this even two years earlier, but it worked for the Dead. And, apparently, it also worked for the band's audience.

But it didn't quite work for the Dead's detractors. Unfortunately for the Dead, many of those detractors worked for companies that bought ink by the barrel. Critics groaned about "three-hour solos" (a standard phrase you'll find while perusing back issues of magazines like *Creem*), often viewing the Dead's style of playing as indulgent rather than adventurous. This gave a lot of people the impression that the Dead's music was made up of little but formless instrumentals.

OK, so sometimes it was. But that's not all it was. And even when the going did get way out there—like on the improvisational "Dark Star"—the playing was exploratory and not the mere "noodling" that some critics claimed it was. Solos didn't go on for three hours (although maybe some concerts did). The fear-mongering about endless solos caused a lot of listeners to be surprised when they finally caught an earful of Dead studio albums such as *American Beauty* or *Go to Heaven*, in which instrumental passages were kept to a minimum. Even the live set *Steal Your Face* doesn't put many solos in the listener's face.

Critical drubbings aside, Garcia's guitar playing was rarely boring or indulgent and gave the band the energy it fed off of for years. It's easy to see that in hindsight, but some were blinded to it by those who lacked foresight. Still, no matter how inspiring Garcia was, there will always be the type of music fan who hears a live show and asks, "Aren't they going to sing?" Instrumental music doesn't do much for a lot of music fans, and that's why Garcia will always be guitarist non grata to a segment of the popular music audience.

Deadheads

If you were on a college campus at any time from around 1975 through 1995, odds were you'd spot a Deadhead before too long. Deadheads usually sported longer hair, wore a lot of tie-dye or concert T-shirts and generally dressed as if they were completely oblivious to whatever the style of the moment was. During the day, they'd hang on the quad, where they'd toss Frisbees or kick around Hacky Sacks. Or they'd sit in small circles and strum guitars. When party nights rolled around, they'd usually avoid the beer bashes and often indulge in other substances while holed up in someone's dorm room or apartment.

This might have represented something of the norm in the 1970s. But by the early 1980s, the music kids liked had gone from rock to pop, fashions edged toward the preppy look, and long hair was something your uncle had. Deadheads, with their penchant for old music, denim, and shaggy hair, became the kids who didn't quite fit in with the ones who embraced mainstream culture. Blair Jackson observed as much in a 1980 article for *Bay Area Music* (*BAM*) magazine, where he noted that younger Deadheads back then were defensive about charges that they were "trapped in an anachronistic fantasy world that is hopelessly out of step." Starting around the Reagan era, the Deadheads sometimes became an object of derision or at least bewilderment for some. This usually didn't happen so much on a personal level but on a conceptual one. At

Jerry Garcia jamming with Dickey Betts of the Allman Brothers Band circa 1972 might be Guitar Nirvana to jam band aficionados. But to some critics, the Dead guitarist's six-string excursions were self-indulgent and took concerts into the realm of tedium.   *Courtesy of BigHouse Archives*

any college you'd find Deadheads sitting among straight-laced-looking kids at cafeteria tables, but ask some of those kids what a "Deadhead" was, and you'd usually get descriptions like "dirty," "smelly," or "drugged out."

When Deadheads decamped to a town where the band was playing, it was a much different experience for the townspeople from when Journey or Bob Seger fans paid a visit. With the latter acts, they'd pop into town for the concert, then leave. Deadheads arrived in packs and often made themselves at home hours before a show, then set out at whatever time worked for them. While they weren't known to wreak havoc or cause violence, they nonetheless seemed to scare the moms and dads who felt as though they'd been time warped back to 1967, seeing roving bands of longhairs trolling about (see chapter 32 for a detailed account of how one town reacted after hosting Deadheads for three summers in the mid-1980s).

By the 1990s, the Dead had become accepted (or at least tolerated) by much of mainstream society. As Deadheads moved from campuses and into workplaces, people began to realize that the woman who was doing their taxes or the guy who wrote their computer code was one of *those* people and was really not so scary—or unhygienic—after all. But there were some holdouts.

The most notorious of these was conservative columnist George Will, who went out of his way to bash Deadhead culture around the time of Garcia's death by pointing out some Deadhead parents who had abandoned their three-year-old kid as indicative of the whole scene. Will's column, which was titled "About That Sixties Idealism," drummed up about the amount of fuss that media-contrived "controversies" usually do. But when the dust had settled, most people came to realize that most Deadhead parents didn't, in fact, abandon their kids. As for conservatives, well, Ann Coulter eventually outed herself as a Deadhead, the news of which probably sent more minds reeling than the discovery of those lost "Houseboat Tapes" from the summer of 1971 that make up the thirty-fifth *Dick's Picks* set.

Drugs

Anyone who has ever seen the unintentionally funny 1937 anti-drug film *Reefer Madness* knows that illegal drugs have long been a bogeyman in American culture. Every few decades, it seems, someone mounts some sort of anti-drug effort. There was Nancy Reagan's "Just Say No" campaign in the 1980s and the enactment of mandatory sentencing laws in the years that followed. No matter that legal substances can be even more dangerous than illegal ones, especially alcohol—drugs represent some sort of amorphous evil to a segment of the American population, notwithstanding the fact that a good number of these

"Deadhead" by DC's Teen Idles attacked the Dead's infamous subculture, although there was some humor implicit in the lyrics. The song was from the Teen Idles' 1981 EP *Minor Disturbance*, the label of which is shown here.   *Courtesy of Chris Mosher*

people apparently have no qualms about giving questionable drugs such as Ritalin to their own children.

But the drug LSD wasn't equated with negativity on a large scale when the members of the Dead began using it. When the Grateful Dead met Ken Kesey in 1965 and performed at his drug-fueled Acid Tests, the band saw LSD as a gateway to mind expansion, not necessarily hedonism. LSD advocates were trying to reach for the unknown and devise a new type of society based more around spirituality and self-awareness than around materialism and conventionality.

It didn't quite work out that way. Drugs, including LSD, did in fact harm a lot of people. On the other hand, the *Reefer Madness* crew was wrong as well: not everyone who used drugs wound up on skid row or in an early grave. The hysteria such zealots engendered caused a lot of thinking people not to take their messages seriously at all. This was a shame, because a rational, cooler-headed approach to the growing drug culture in the United States by authorities might have prompted young people to more seriously consider which drugs they should ingest and how much.

Throughout most of the Dead's career, the grievances directed toward the Dead and Deadheads were rooted in such anti-drug hysteria. Sure, you'd find troubled druggies at Dead concerts. But there were also thousands upon thousands more concertgoers who made it to and from the concerts safely and went to work or to school the next day—some of whom used drugs recreationally. Beer drinkers also get out of hand at sporting events, but panic doesn't ensue as to whether to shut stadiums down. Beyond all that, there were Deadheads and casual fans who went to the concerts and didn't use drugs at all.

Implicit in all of this was the idea that you had to be drugged out to enjoy the Dead's music. Anyone who has ever bumped into a Deadhead unexpectedly and heard him or her rattle off exact dates and places where specific songs were played knows that such listeners couldn't be too drugged out to remember all these obscure facts and figures. So, drugs and the "Dead experience" aren't entirely intertwined.

And then came the 1980s. In the wake of the band's hit "Touch of Grey," legions of fair-weather fans descended on the parking lots at Dead concerts with what appeared to be the sole intention of partying and getting rowdy. Yes, fans liked to do all that in the early days, but it had been on a much smaller scale and thus was less troublesome to authorities. By the early 1990s, drug dealing outside concert venues became so commonplace that even the most liberal and tolerant Deadheads became disgusted. Arrests followed, unsurprisingly, and at least a handful of concert halls made good on threats not to have the Dead return.

By the summer of 1990, keyboardist Brent Mydland was dead from drug-related causes. Garcia died five years after that. Both of these deaths were proof, if any was needed, that while some drugs might have led to the expansion of minds, others caused the destruction of bodies. So, drug use did, in fact, have a negative impact on the band in several respects, and the negativity directed toward the Dead because of drugs was, in part, warranted.

All that said, the Dead's reputation as a "druggie band" only spoke to one part of what they were about. But it was a pretty obvious part. Because of that, the Grateful Dead's name will always first and foremost evoke the "drugs" part of the phrase "sex, drugs, and rock 'n' roll."

"Touch of Grey"

For a Top 10 hit, "Touch of Grey" sure had its share of detractors when it rose up the charts in the summer of 1987. On one side, you had the serious-minded alternative music crowd, which was peeved that a group of old fogies were invading the space they felt should have been rightfully occupied by newer acts like Hüsker Dü, X, and the Replacements. On the other hand, you had Deadheads who were mortified that the band had ostensibly "sold out." Few things were more discomfiting than seeing your mom or your little brother bopping around to the very same band they'd spent years telling you to turn down on your bedroom stereo. By the end of the summer, the song's chorus of "I will get by" was heard blasting from radios and TV sets so frequently that most everyone was sick of it.

The haters on both sides missed the point, though. First, from today's perspective, members of the Dead weren't quite the relics of ye olde days that the alternative crowd imagined them to be. The group had only been around for just more than two decades, which is really not much considering that down the road both the Rolling Stones and the Beach Boys would be celebrated for their fifty-year anniversaries. In the years following "Touch of Grey," both Eric Clapton and Carlos Santana would have massive hits, but by this time, a new appreciation for classic rockers had set in, and there was a lot less resentment among youth-minded critics.

As for the Deadheads who disliked the tune, that had more to do with the fact that the band's popularity began to snowball after it made its first official MTV video. It came as something of a surprise that the channel broke from its usual diet of hair metal and dance music and put the video into heavy rotation. This resulted in legions of younger, rowdier fans unexpectedly showing up at concerts and altering the dynamics of the scene for the worse.

The song itself, however, was not a contrived effort to create a hit single and became a hit more because the Dead happened to release the right record with the right video at the right time. "Touch of Grey" had been in the group's repertoire for half a decade, after all, and although its studio incarnation came across as glossy and airplay-ready, so did other relatively recent singles like "Dancin' in the Streets" and "Don't Ease Me In," and neither of those had a fraction of the success of "Touch." Also, the band didn't seek out a music industry songwriter like Diane Warren to pen them a hit (as Starship and Aerosmith did) or contract a "song doctor" like Desmond Child to help commercialize their songs (as did Bon Jovi, KISS, and Aerosmith again).

The Teen Idles' sleeve for the 1981 EP *Minor Disturbance*, which contained "Deadhead," reflected the punk rock artwork of the time, which was far removed from any images that graced the sleeves of Grateful Dead albums.   *Courtesy of Chris Mosher*

The fact that "Touch of Grey's" success was a fluke became clearer when none of the Dead's follow up singles charted at all. That's actually unfortunate, because a few more hits, even minor ones, might have meant an infusion of cash that could have kept the Dead's road schedule lighter and allowed the band time to address the health issues of two members who would be dead in less than ten years' time.

The Influence of Punk Rock

Punk rock gave a much-needed shot in the arm to the moribund rock scene of the late 1970s. Not only that, but it set the stage for artists to emerge who rivaled the classic rockers of the 1960s in terms of greatness and influence. The

Ramones, the Clash, and Talking Heads come to mind, but there are scads more that followed in the wake of the initial punk rock explosion of 1976–77.

But the underlying theme of much of punk was that the generation that had come before needed to be put out to pasture, the old ways needed to be smashed apart to make room for new ideas, hippies were embarrassing relics, etc. If you opened the magazines, you saw Sex Pistol Johnny Rotten in his "I Hate Pink Floyd" T-shirt. The B-side of the Clash's first single was a rocker called "1977" that sported the lyrics "No Elvis, Beatles, or the Rolling Stones in 1977." All of a sudden, the music of an entire generation (or two) was deemed irrelevant and outdated. It's instructive to note that many of these ideas fermented before the Dead's youngest member at the time, Bob Weir, had even turned thirty.

Rock critics, never ones to miss a trend, hopped aboard the punk band-wagon. And for good reason: a lot of the music was truly great, and a lot of what wasn't great was at least exciting. But in doing that, many of them made like the punk rockers and felt the need to trash almost everything that had come before to justify why the new music was relevant and the old wasn't. Punk bands played short songs. The Grateful Dead didn't. Ergo, pop music began to be judged by the standard of how "economical" it was. The Dead weren't usually concerned with being "economical," although in the studio they could turn out a set of tightly-written tunes with the best of them when they were in the mood. So, critics used Garcia's alleged "three-hour solos" as a negative comparison point when judging the supposed worth of music. Because punk songs harkened back to the music of the pre-hippie era, jam-oriented bands and progressive rock began to seem like a bad detour rock had taken before it, you know, righted itself with punk.

The critics and punks did have a point. You'd be hard pressed to find songs that moved at a slower pace than "Row Jimmy" or "Stella Blue." The Dead definitely took their sweet time playing these songs, too, sometimes stretching them out on stage until they were longer than entire sides of Ramones records. But what critics missed was the fact that the Dead had already tried their collective hands at punk music, of a sort, and developed their own music out of punk.

Had anyone bothered to go back to the Dead's first album, they'd have found that the band's speeded-up tempos, trebly guitar attack, rinky-dink organ, and low-fi sound bore an uncanny resemblance to the new music they were currently touting. The Dead didn't exactly start out as proto-punks in the mold of the Kingsmen or early Love, but neither did the Dead set out to be well-scrubbed pop idols. Before that first album, the band's sound was even rougher. When the recording sessions that preceded the debut album were released in 2001 as *Birth of the Dead*, the band's early sound was revealed to be uncannily close to that of the '60s garage punk band the Music Machine.

Beyond their early, unpolished sound, the Dead had a do-it-yourself aesthetic and a disregard for polite conventions that were precursors to the punk era. What other band would seriously lobby record executives to call an album *Skullfuck*, as the Dead did with their self-titled 1971 effort (the *Skull and Roses* album)? But few people outside the band's cult studied them closely. So, kids who grew up in the shadow of punk rock—and its commercially minded little brother new wave—came of age thinking the Dead was the antithesis of punk rock, not an unlikely precursor to it, in however small a manner.

The aversion of punk rockers toward all things Dead-related even got immortalized on record. In 1981, the Washington, DC–based proto-hardcore punk band the Teen Idles came out with an anti-Dead song called "Deadhead" on their sole release, the EP *Minor Disturbance*. The group included Ian MacKaye, who later became an important figure in the DC punk scene, founding the seminal indie label Dischord as well as the bands Minor Threat and Fugazi. Like a lot of hardcore punk songs, "Deadhead" was pretty funny in its intent to be as nasty as possible. Lines like "Troubles behind, troubles ahead / The only good Deadhead is one that's dead" were clearly intended to be taken with a healthy dose of irony. But comedy aside, the song underscored the disdain directed toward Deadheads by much of the punk scene. In much the way *South Park*'s Cartman likes to point the finger at hippies for all he considers wrong with society, punks sometimes liked to point to Deadheads as an example of all that was wrong with music.

The ethos of 1977 didn't last forever. In a few years, the Clash would release albums that no one would call "economical," Talking Heads would embrace the kind of percussion-oriented world music Mickey Hart had long championed, and bands such as XTC would pay tribute to the very psychedelic era they supposedly wanted to make disappear.

10

Cryptical Envelopment

The Dead's Studio Recordings, 1967–69

T he three studio albums that the Grateful Dead recorded in the 1960s don't sound much like the band that Deadheads came to know later on from concert tapes or albums released in the early 1970s. Often on these early efforts, they seem like a whole 'nother band. Part of the reason for that is the primitive recording technology that was available at the time. But a bigger part was that the Dead's style hadn't been fully established. Still, there are enough buried treasures on these albums that make all of them worth hearing and one of them essential listening.

The Grateful Dead

What's most striking about the Grateful Dead's maiden effort isn't what they chose to do, but what they chose not to do. First, the Dead avoided diving headfirst into psychedelic rock, the new genre of freeform, outré music that had become popular in the months before they began recording the album in January 1967. Even though the album's trippy cover montage seems to indicate that its contents would be beyond weird, the Dead eschew overtly psychedelic songs along the lines of the Electric Prunes' "I Had Too Much to Dream (Last Night)," the Byrds' "Eight Miles High," or the Beatles' "Tomorrow Never Knows," all from 1966. Also missing are the Dead's covers of songs the Rolling Stones were performing at the time. The Dead might have done nice 'n' nasty versions of "Walking the Dog," "Pain in My Heart," and "I'm a King Bee" (all of which can be heard on the *Rare Cuts and Obscurities 1966* album), but committing them to vinyl would have marked the Dead as copyists like San Jose's Count Five, who put two Who covers on their first (and only) album. The Dead also avoided covering the same songs everyone else did, such as "Tobacco Road," which had recently been put out by Jefferson Airplane, Nashville Teens, and Blues Magoos, and "Hey Joe," done by the Leaves, Love, the Byrds, and eventually Jimi Hendrix, among others.

The Dead also were careful not to fill their debut album with original songs that were derivative of the work of other artists. The album only had two self-penned cuts out of its nine songs, but that wasn't for lack of writing chops. The

Dead had several originals they could have used, such as "Can't Come Down" or "Mindbender (Confusion's Prince)." But those sound a bit too much like Bob Dylan and the Strawberry Alarm Clock, respectively, nice as they are (both can be heard on the 2001 collection *Birth of the Dead*).

Finally, the Dead didn't allow the rough edges of their sound to get sanded down by either a producer or the record company they'd signed with, Warner Bros. To that end, the Dead chose Dave Hassinger, who had engineered the Rolling Stones' *Out of Our Heads* and *Aftermath* albums. In a March 1967 interview, Jerry Garcia said, "I think our album is honest. It sounds just like us at a job. It even has mistakes on it and stuff like that. But it also has a certain amount of excitement."

So what exactly did the Dead do on their self-titled debut? They brought together a bunch of different strains of American roots music with the songs they chose to cover and made sure their originals fit in with those songs. The Dead also played most of these tunes at breakneck tempos and ornamented some of them with Pigpen's very '60s organ sounds, which makes the album very unlike the Dead people would come to know later on. The first album also introduced audiences to the Dead's voices for the first time, all of which sounded unschooled and rough in one way or another. But the band's limitations in this area also worked to their advantage because they kept the Dead from ever sounding too phony or too highfalutin'.

The album kicks off with the group-written party number "The Golden Road (to Unlimited Devotion)," which appears to be a lot more trippy than it is because of its title (which does not appear in the lyrics). With lyrics such as "See that girl, barefootin' along / Whistlin' and singin', she's a carryin' on," the song follows in the great tradition of rhythm and blues dance numbers, like Robert Parker's #7 hit "Barefootin'," which it resembles rhythmically and probably references lyrically. By emulating African American musicians—as opposed to copying English bands who were copying African American artists—the Dead gave their music an authenticity that less roots-conscious bands didn't have. Released as a single, with another album cut, "Cream Puff War," on the flip side, it didn't chart.

Speaking of authenticity, Pigpen's vocal on Sonny Boy Williamson's blues classic "Good Morning Little School Girl" is surprisingly authoritative considering he was twenty-one at the time. This song was the one number the Dead covered that had been done by another rock band, in this case the Yardbirds. But the Dead's take on the song stays truer to its menacing spirit than the Yardbirds' jangly Beatles-esque rewrite of it. Another reason for that is Bill Kreutzmann's powerful drumming, which was something of a secret weapon on these early releases.

The Dead as we would come to know them emerge for the first time on Bob Weir's vocal number, "Beat It on Down the Line," a hitting-the-road tune written by San Francisco bluesman Jesse Fuller. The Dead's performance of this song—which they would come to play more than three hundred times—gels a lot better on the original mono mix of the album, which has never come out on CD, but was issued on 180-gram vinyl for Record Store Day in 2011.

The band's version of "Morning Dew," which would also become an onstage standard, also provides a connection to the later Dead, as it doesn't sound that different from how they usually played it. The song is a Cold War–era anti-nuclear lament by Canadian folksinger Bonnie Dobson, but Garcia probably learned it from Fred Neil and Vince Martin's 1964 album *Tear Down the Walls*, as the pair changed the opening line from "Take me for a walk in the morning dew" to "Walk me out in the morning dew," which is how Garcia sings it. (That album also features a version of another Dead favorite, "I Know You Rider.")

The other original, "Cream Puff War," would fit in on any collection of mid-1960s garage rock with its frantic tempo and wheezy organ—so, for that matter, could the equally rushed cover of the Mississippi Sheiks' country blues kiss-off song "Sitting on Top of the World," which wasn't nearly as giddy in its original version. The Dead's penchant for taking the jug band standard "Viola Lee Blues" and turning it into a long jam had already evolved on stage, as the ten-minute live version from the summer of 1966 on *Birth of the Dead* indicates. The song had been done more traditionally as "Viola Lee" by Jim Kweskin & the Jug Band on the 1966 album *See Reverse Side for Title*, but the Dead bring a tour de force quality to the instrumental section, which serves as a portent of things to come.

The traditional bluegrass favorite "Cold Rain and Snow" (also known as "Rain and Snow") is interesting in that Garcia kicks it off with the verse he usually sang as the second verse ("Well, she's comin' down the stairs / combing back her yellow hair") and relegates the more provocative opening verse to the second verse ("Well I married me a wife / She's been trouble all my life"). Maybe the lyrics hit a little too close to home for Garcia, who was divorcing his first wife around this time. The song, which the Dead played some 241 times, must have had some personal resonance for Garcia. He also sang it on New Year's Eve 1981, the night he wed his longtime on-again-off-again paramour Mountain Girl, which the pair reportedly did for tax-related reasons. That night, Garcia left the first verse intact.

The Grateful Dead was released on March 17, 1967. It entered the Billboard album chart on May 6 and rose as high as #73.

The expanded CD reissue from 2003 adds five studio outtakes. The most interesting is the poppy band-written "Alice D. Millionaire," apparently penned as a tribute to Owsley Stanley, whom a newspaper had called an "LSD million-aire." It's sung by Phil Lesh, who wouldn't sing a full lead vocal on a Dead album until 1974. Garcia takes the lead on a version of the jug band blues "Overseas Stomp (The Lindy)" (also done by Kweskin), while Pigpen sings his own late-night blues "Tastebud," which arguably would have been a stronger addition to the album than were several songs that made the cut. An alternate heavily edited take of "Viola Lee Blues" is also included, as is an instrumental version of the Reverend Gary Davis's "Death Don't Have No Mercy."

The reissue also includes a live version of "Viola Lee Blues" recorded September 3, 1967, at the Dance Hall in Rio Nido, California. Finally, the reissue features "full-length" versions of "Good Morning Little School Girl," "Sitting on Top of the World," "Cream Puff War," "Morning Dew," and "New, New Minglewood Blues" that each run about thirty seconds longer than they did on the original vinyl version of the album.

Anthem of the Sun

Most artists release a difficult album at some point—an album that requires some work on the part of fans to figure out. The Dead did this with their second album, *Anthem of the Sun*. With this record, the Dead dived head first into psychedelic music, writing a bunch of strange songs, recording them in a strange way, and even mixing them in a completely weird way. The album is also unique in that it mixes and matches live and studio performances into a long, strange continuous trip of an album. If you're looking for a Dead album to listen to with headphones, start here.

To fully understand why *Anthem of the Sun* came to sound the way it did, two factors need to be taken into consideration. The first is where the band members' heads were at. By the time of their second record, the Dead were no longer looking to recreate their stage act in the studio, having already done that with the first album. For their second go-round in a recording studio, they were looking to flex their artistic muscles and translate some of the experiences they'd had with LSD onto vinyl. The band had already expanded their sound on stage by adding percussionist and drummer Mickey Hart. In the studio, the Dead would add yet another member in additional keyboardist Tom Constanten, a classically trained musician who was a college friend of Lesh's.

The other factor that made *Anthem* so different is the time period in which it was recorded. Even though psychedelic music is said to have peaked in popularity in 1967, with the Beatles, Bob Dylan, and the Beach Boys returning to a rootsier sound by early 1968, most other artists didn't get the message. Quite the opposite: there were probably more psychedelic albums released in 1968 than in 1967, because trends take a while to disseminate. Beyond the tons of San Francisco bands that had emerged as psychedelic acts (Country Joe and the Fish, Jefferson Airplane, Quicksilver Messenger Service), there also were British ones (Nirvana, Pink Floyd, Tomorrow). And in 1968, an explosion of such acts from around the country released records, including Ultimate Spinach, Creation of Sunlight, the Daughters of Albion, Haymarket Square, and the Troll. Psychedelic ideas also began to crop up in songs from artists as disparate as the Association, the Buckinghams, and the Temptations.

As the Dead were in the thick of the San Francisco psychedelic scene, *Anthem* can be seen as their one genuine contribution to the genre. Depending on your point of view, it's either a sonic adventure or a mess. Producer Hassinger considered it the latter, and left the sessions before even half the project was

The addition of second drummer Mickey Hart to the fold broadened the musical scope of the Grateful Dead. Hart's fascination with the traditions of percussion stemming from different cultures would prompt him to cut a series of solo albums that helped invent the world music genre.
Author's collection

finished. Listeners were probably confused when they went to play the album: on the original vinyl there are no bands separating each track, and it's all edited as one long suite with only a break between the two sides. In this way, *Anthem* foreshadowed the Dead's habit of segueing songs in concert.

Where the first album began with some spirited organ and guitar fanfare, *Anthem* creeps up on the listener by starting with a slinky Garcia song snippet called "Cryptical Envelopment," which is one of four sections of a seven-and-a-half minute suite called "That's It for the Other One." When the band took to playing this live in later years, they dropped this section, but on record it works as a way to ease listeners into the song, which moves into a jam section edited in from live tapes called "Quadlibet for Tender Feet." After that comes the familiar Weir-sung "Spanish Lady" section, which was originally titled "The Faster We Go the Rounder We Get," but became known as simply "The Other One" when the band played just this section live. The song then returns to Garcia's first section before it dissolves into live tapes of the band jamming on its main riff. It all closes with some dissonant space-ageish piano tinkling by new kid Constanten that seems specially designed for headphones. Constanten was also indirectly responsible for the now-classic album cover, a fire-wheel motif interpolating the band members' faces that was painted by his friend Bill Walker.

Blink and you'll miss the transition into Phil Lesh and friend Bobby Peterson's "New Potato Caboose," an acoustic shuffle than evolves into a jam with the band seemingly split into halves on each side of the stereo spectrum. That leads into Weir's first solo original composition for the Dead, the rollicking "Born Cross-Eyed," which sounds much more powerful in its mono single mix included as a hidden track on the 2003 CD reissue. The single, released three months before the album, was paired with the non-LP studio version of "Dark Star," which can be found as a bonus track on the CD reissue of *Live/Dead*. It didn't make the singles chart.

The last two songs, which made up side two of the original album, are co-written and sung by Pigpen. "Alligator" features the first Robert Hunter lyrics on a Dead album, while the jam tune "Caution (Do Not Stop on Tracks)," which had been in the band's sets since late 1965, was said by Weir to be based on "Mystic Eyes," Them's chugging rocker known for its long instrumental introduction. The mix of the live version on *Anthem* is mainly made up of Pigpen rapping over a lot of percussion. Of these two songs, "Alligator" works better because Hunter's lyrics are intriguing and the jamming toward the end catches fire, especially Garcia's extrapolation of Donovan's "There Is a Mountain," which the Allman Brothers took and made into their live showcase "Mountain Jam."

Anthem loses its plot on its last two songs because the band's concept doesn't serve the Pigpen-led songs: his long blues jams sound unfocused when given the cut-and-paste editing treatment. Montages work better when they juxtapose diverse ideas (such as in the Beach Boys' "Good Vibrations" or the band's own songs on side one), not when they're interrupting the flow of otherwise interesting jams. Would the Dead have been better off making side two a live side featuring Pigpen? Probably. It would have been more artistically satisfying and also would have kept the band's recording budget from spiraling out of control. But the album wouldn't have been nearly as psychedelic without all the weirdness thrown in.

Psychedelic music started to fade away as a trend around 1969. But it left its traces in pop music for years to come. Its long jams were absorbed by hard rock; its multi-tiered song structures were taken up by progressive rock; its kitchen-sink arrangements found a home in new wave and indie rock; its repetitive drones were co-opted by house and trance; and its mix-and-match editing was a precursor to sampling. So, while *Anthem* might be the Dead's most dated album in one way, in another way it's the band's most forward-looking album.

Anthem of the Sun was released on July 18, 1968. It entered the Billboard album chart on August 31 and rose to #87.

The 2003 CD adds the aforementioned "Born Cross-Eyed" single mix, plus superior live versions of "Alligator" and "Caution" recorded at the Shrine Center in Los Angeles on August 23, 1968. From this same show, there is also a four-minute blast of freeform jamming and weirdness titled "Feedback," as on the *Live/Dead* album. The original vinyl credits all songs collectively to the group, while the 2003 CD reissue breaks down individual authorship, which is what was referenced here.

Aoxomoxoa

Despite the acid-tinged look of its cover and the palindrome of its title, 1969's *Aoxomoxoa* represents a step away from the psychedelia of the Dead's previous album and a move toward the more roots-oriented approach the band would soon fully embrace. It also marks a gigantic leap forward in songwriting: all of the album's eight songs are originals from the team of Garcia and Hunter, and most of them are not only well-crafted and tuneful, but emotionally engaging as well. (The original album's sleeve credits Lesh for composition, but the CD credits only list him as co-composer for "St. Stephen.") There's almost nothing on *Aoxomoxoa* that anyone could have expected from the group judging by their previous albums. The "dean of American rock critics," Robert Christgau, gave the album an A rating at the time, calling it "fantastic," save its one experimental cut (more on that later).

As with any growth, artistic or otherwise, there were some growing pains. For the Dead, those involved briefly firing Pigpen and Weir, who Garcia and Lesh felt weren't keeping up musically with the rest of the band. Because of that, Pigpen isn't on *Aoxomoxoa*, and Weir's presence is barely felt, all of which is quite a switch from the previous album, where they dominated the proceedings. While Garcia and Hunter's coup couldn't have been good for band morale, it did help the pair hone their vision of what the Dead should sound like and update the group's sound. The ideas they first brought to *Aoxomoxoa* would shape the band for most of their career. And what was the duo's vision for the future of the Dead? Going back to the past! With this album, Hunter and Garcia took tentative steps back toward the traditional music they'd played in bluegrass and folk ensembles, and blazed a path that would lead to the group's next two breakthrough efforts.

It helped that being old-timey had suddenly come into vogue thanks to the Band and Creedence Clearwater Revival, two "new" bands that actually had been around a while before they hit it big. Both revived early rock 'n' roll or pre-rock sounds and themes in their music. The Dead didn't completely jump aboard this bandwagon with *Aoxomoxoa*; after all, the album boasted both a title and a cover by the psychedelic poster artist Rick Griffin. Plus, it had all sorts of strange keyboard sounds played by Constanten. But Hunter and Garcia's songwriting was rooted in motifs from the music of the past, and their collaboration resulted in music far different from anything the band had put on their first two albums. The group, which were now producing themselves, sometimes let the arrangements get too ornate for their own good, but for the most part the production serves the songs.

Aoxomoxoa starts on a high note, with the anthemic fan favorite "St. Stephen," which grabs the listener from all sides as it cleverly reimagines the religious figure as annoying and confused rather than saintly, all the while driving the point home with a killer riff. The song also introduces a Hunter specialty, the quotable pull-out line that stands apart from the song to tell a larger truth (in this case, "One man gathers what another man spills"). This version of "St. Stephen" doesn't emphasize the riff as much as the ones the band recorded but didn't release, or the ones they played live. But it's an exuberant performance of a first-rate song, and Constanten's bell-like sounds on the bridge are enhancements, not distractions.

"Dupree's Diamond Blues" might even be better. Here, Hunter takes the basic folk story of Betty and Dupree (most recently heard in a 1960 hit by Chuck Willis) and makes it more powerful by rewriting it as a first-person tale of lust and bad judgment. Garcia's banjo plucking on the chorus and Constanten's pumping organ make the song sound as if it's being phoned in from a fairground somewhere in America's collective past. Hunter's first verse is unrelated to the

"Dupree's Diamond Blues," with "Cosmic Charlie" on the B-side, was the Grateful Dead's third Warner Bros. single; like the first two, it didn't make the pop charts, despite its perky melody and intriguing story. With their next single, "Uncle John's Band," the Dead would finally connect with listeners, radio program directors, and the Billboard singles chart.

Courtesy of Eric Schwartz

song's story, but works because it hangs a philosophical shadow over the rest of the verses, making them symbolically more meaningful than if they were to unfold as straight narrative. Released as a single with "Cosmic Charlie" on the flip, it became the band's third consecutive 45 not to chart, which was probably not a surprise to anyone, as the Dead were not by any means attempting to be a "singles band" at this juncture.

Both "Rosemary" and "Mountains of the Moon" are intimate acoustic recordings that almost sound like warm-ups for the band's next two albums, except for psychedelic touches like the phase-shifted vocals in the first and the harpsichord ticklings on the second. In "Doin' That Rag," Garcia's slippery melody is brought to life by Hunter's country and gospel imagery. Proof of the duo's sophisticated songwriting can be found at the song's end: it has a coda that not only is essential to the song's structure, but is also the catchiest part of the song. Had the band been paired with a pop producer, they probably would have been asked to rewrite the tune using the coda ("Is it all fall down / Is it all go under") as the main chorus hook.

The original vinyl's side two started with "China Cat Sunflower," which the group made a stage favorite, playing it well over five hundred times. The studio version also has a lot to offer, though, like Lesh's very pop-oriented high-pitched backing vocals and Garcia's spindly leads. Unfortunately, the next track, "What's Become of the Baby," doesn't really work in the context of the album: it's made up of eight minutes of eerie, near–a cappella vocal weirdness. This track might have worked on an album filled with similarly spooky music, such as Nico's macabre 1974 masterpiece *The End . . .* , but it never fit in among the bubbly psychedelia and proto-roots rock of *Aoxomoxoa*.

A bootleg containing outtakes from *Aoxomoxoa* features an early version of the song with Garcia's acoustic guitar louder in the mix, which makes it sound like a haunting folk ballad, similar to what British songstresses such as Bridget St. John or Vashti Bunyan were doing at the time. That might have fit the album. Also on the bootleg is an early version of the jam tune "The Eleven," which came to follow "St. Stephen" in concert and would have fit in better with *Aoxomoxoa*. The album closes with a cult favorite that wasn't played live too much but works great in the studio, the lazy shuffle "Cosmic Charlie."

Despite its one ill-fitting track, *Aoxomoxoa* is the first of several classic Dead albums. It would have been unfair to compare the fledgling Dead's earlier efforts to what big league acts such as the Beatles or Stones were doing at the time, but with *Aoxomoxoa*, the Dead had entered the big leagues, and *Aoxomoxoa* stands up favorably against the albums those bands put out in 1969. It also has a connection to grunge music by association because it features a four-year-old Courtney Love on the back cover, sitting up front toward the right in the "family" photo (which was probably inspired by the Band's "Next of Kin" photo in the gatefold of their *Music from Big Pink* album). According to Dead scholar David Gans, Love is pictured because her father, Hank Harrison, was a road manager for the Dead at the time.

Aoxomoxoa was released on June 20, 1969. It entered the Billboard album chart on August 21 and rose to #73.

The 2003 CD adds four extra cuts, three of which are live studio jams recorded on August 13, 1968, at Pacific Recording Studio in San Mateo, California. These include "Clementine Jam," "Nobody's Spoonful Jam," and "The Eleven Jam." The CD closes with a live version of "Cosmic Charlie" from January 25, 1969, at the Avalon Ballroom in San Francisco.

A Note About Remixes

Both *Anthem of the Sun* and *Aoxomoxoa* were remixed in 1971 because Warner Bros. wanted to put out more editions of the albums, but no one could locate the master tapes. *Aoxomoxoa* was given an extensive overhaul, and its remix became the standard on vinyl editions and, later, CDs (the difference between the mixes on that album's two versions are discussed at length in chapter 13).

In the case of *Anthem*, the original mix has become the standard; the remix was only used for albums in the 1970s and some early CDs. It was hardly the sonic overhaul that *Aoxomoxoa* was, and maybe that's one reason the band decided to use the original mix when CDs became the norm. The remixed version is *not*, by the way, on the 2010 box set of 180-gram vinyl albums, *The Warner Bros. Studio Albums*.

Because the remixed *Anthem* was only in print around a decade, and because it doesn't sound all that different from the original, it's become hard to track down. One thing that doesn't necessarily connote a remix is the "white cover" edition of the album, in which the purple background on the front cover was reconstituted as white. Some of these may contain remixes; others don't.

The way to visually spot a remix is by looking at the runoff grooves of the vinyl. Pressings marked with "RE-1" after the serial numbers are the remixes. The other way is to play the album. Side one of the remix starts with a hard organ note instead of a fade in and ends with a loud chord at the end of "Born Cross-Eyed" instead of a fade-out on the words "by and by." Those are about the only changes in the album's mix, other than some altered stereo placement of vocals and edits.

High Time

The Dead's Studio Recordings, 1970–75

The Grateful Dead released their four best studio albums in the early 1970s and one that was nearly as good in 1975. Like the Velvet Underground, the Dead got their innovations out of the way early on, freeing them to concentrate more on songwriting than on experimentation as their career progressed. And what songs they had. Lots of tunes on these five albums became concert staples; some went on to become rock anthems. All the albums from this period were self-produced (with only occasional help from members of the Dead's sound crew), and three were on a new label the band themselves founded—all of which gave the Dead an ample amount of artistic freedom that served them well.

Workingman's Dead

Workingman's Dead was the first Grateful Dead album to have a chance of attracting a mass audience outside of the cult following the band had already developed. The music is likable on first listen, the lyrics are easily understood, and the instrumentation is simple and to the point. The album also plugged into the trend of acoustic rock and country rock that was in its heyday during the early 1970s.

At the time *Workingman's Dead* came out in mid-1970, the psychedelic wave the Grateful Dead had rode in on had crested. Some of the British rock musicians who had defined themselves by psychedelia defected to progressive rock (Pink Floyd, Soft Machine) or moved into hard rock (Steve Marriott, Deep Purple). American musicians, conversely, took to scaling back their ambitions. This was probably because of the influence of the Band and Creedence Clearwater Revival, both of whom had released records in 1968 that showed rock could have a simpler sound without sounding simplistic. On the country rock front, the Byrds and Poco had already released pioneering albums by 1970, and the Eagles would make the genre big business when their first album came out two years later. In the commercial realm, Crosby, Stills and Nash and James Taylor were all the rage. Heck, even the moms and dads of the day were going acoustic and trading in their Herb Alpert records for David Gates's new soft rock ensemble, Bread (or was it the teenage sisters who bought all those records?).

Workingman's Dead sported a cover that made the Dead look like they had been transported into the Old West. It accurately reflected the fact that musically, the album was a 180-degree turn away from the electrified and very improvisational *Live/Dead*, which had been released only seven months earlier. As such, the Dead were perceived by some to be climbing onto the acoustic bandwagon. This wasn't really true. The Dead's previous studio album, *Aoxomoxoa*, had already pointed the way toward a more song-oriented, less electric approach. And while the Dead were no doubt influenced by the music of the day (as all artists are), their move into country rock was really a return home for Jerry Garcia, Bob Weir, and Pigpen, all of whom played in the acoustic jug band Mother McCree's Uptown Jug Champions. The musical roots of Garcia and Robert Hunter (the latter now listed as a full-fledged band member) went even deeper. They both played, apart and together, in various traditional music groups in the early 1960s, including Bob and Jerry, Jerry and Sara, the Black Mountain Boys, the Sleepy Hollow Hog Stompers, and the Wildwood Boys.

A song like "Cumberland Blues" might have seemed to come from left field with its bluegrass feel and first-person lyrics about working-class woe. But it wasn't all that different from a song such as "Standing in Need of a Prayer," a number Garcia and Hunter performed with the Wildwood Boys in 1963. Little wonder that the Dead could pull this kind of material off without it sounding forced or phony—in fact, Garcia sounded more comfortable than ever on acoustic numbers such as the regretful lost love ballad "High Time," or the mournful, bluesy deathbed hymn "Black Peter," the latter of which made it onto three hundred Dead set lists.

Beyond the unplugged numbers, *Workingman's Dead* also saw the band perfecting the light, harmonious rock numbers that they'd started writing on *Aoxomoxoa* and that would eventually become a hallmark of the band's style. The Dead produced that album themselves, but dressed up the songs with unconventional instrumentation. But on *Workingman's*, they kept the frills to a minimum, partially because they wanted a change of style and partially because they wanted to avoid having to pay the type of massive studio fees they'd racked up on their last two studio efforts. Another element that *Workingman's* had in common with *Aoxomoxoa* is that its lyrics were entirely written by Robert Hunter. His songwriting, with its philosophical underpinnings and references to historical America, would come to define the band as much as Garcia's music did.

"Casey Jones" might have been inspired by the story of a conductor who caused a train wreck way back in 1900, but Garcia and Hunter recast it as a chugging rocker that's a sort of allegory about hippie excess. Its opening lyric, "Driving that train / high on cocaine," became one of the most famous in all of rock and left the song open to all sorts of interpretations that the composers probably didn't intend. "New Speedway Boogie" was apparently written as a response by Hunter to the murder at the Altamont Free Festival that the Dead had backed out of playing. But the cooking shuffle Garcia puts it to overshadows the lyrics, so you don't need to know the backstory to enjoy the tune.

The opening number, "Uncle John's Band," was the Dead's most accessible number to date and remains one of the best songs in the Garcia-Hunter catalog. With its "stacked" three-part harmonies (a technique of overdubbing multiple voices that the band learned from Crosby, Stills and Nash), the song was ear-grabbing enough to become the Dead's first FM staple. It also fared reasonably well on AM radio, climbing to #69 in the late summer of 1970 and staying on the chart for seven weeks. The song itself is a deceptively simple number that works as a story-song about a mythical group and as a metaphor for the band and its followers. "Uncle John's Band" was the musical equivalent of the American flag hat that Garcia sported on the band's first album cover: a signal that the Dead saw itself as a part of American tradition, not a repudiation or rejection of tradition (which is how some perceived hippies at the time).

As on the previous album, Bob Weir and Pigpen play minor roles. Pigpen sings a song solely written by Hunter (the only such occurrence on a Dead studio album), "Easy Wind." It's a percussive blues that eventually opens up to become the only long jam featured on the album. Weir sings a verse of "Cumberland Blues," and an early version of "Dire Wolf" included as a live bonus track.

If *Workingman's Dead* has any shortcoming, it's that at thirty-five minutes, the album was a bit too short in its original vinyl incarnation. A Garcia-Hunter song left off the disc, "Mason's Children," was said to have turned out too pop-oriented for Garcia's tastes, but would have made a nice inclusion. It's an odd-but-entrancing number that juxtaposes a lilting melody against rather morbid lyrics about a burial of a beloved friend that goes wrong. The recording found its way onto the 2000 box set *The Golden Road (1965–1973)* but is not included in its studio version on the CD reissue of this album. Also not included is the single edit of "Uncle John's Band" that is dissected in chapter 31, "Searching for the Sounds: Fifteen Obscure Dead Collectibles."

Workingman's Dead was released on June 14, 1970. It entered the Billboard album chart on July 11 and rose to #27.

The expanded CD reissue from 2001 adds an alternate mix of "New Speedway Boogie," an old radio ad (which is a hidden track), plus six live recordings from six different venues. "Dire Wolf" was recorded on June 26, 1969, at Santa Rosa Veterans Memorial Hall in California; "Black Peter" was taped on January 10, 1970, at Golden Hall Community Concourse in San Diego; "Easy Wind" was recorded on January 16, 1970, at Springer's Ballroom in Portland, Oregon; "Cumberland Blues" was recorded on January 17, 1970, at the Oregon State University gym; and "Mason's Children" was taped on January 24, 1970, at the Civic Auditorium in Honolulu. "Uncle John's Band" is listed as being recorded on December 23, 1970, at Winterland in San Francisco, but Archive. org reveals that it's really an October 4 recording from the same venue.

American Beauty

Producer Joe Boyd once went on record as saying that he felt that the late folk singer Nick Drake's second album *Bryter Layter* was so perfectly rendered that it was the only album he'd worked on that he wouldn't go back and alter in some way. For the Grateful Dead, *American Beauty* is that type of album: a note-perfect encapsulation of everything great about the group. The ten-song collection, which was released at the end of 1970, is one of those rare classic rock albums that lives up to its reputation, and then some.

Unlike works by the Beatles, Pink Floyd, and Bob Dylan that critics and fans choose as the "best album of all time" in magazine polls, *American Beauty* contains no weak tracks, no questionable musical experiments, and no dated "you-had-to-be-there" lyrics. Taken as a whole, the album still sounds remarkably up-to-date, and that's because its bare-bones arrangements rely heavily on acoustic guitar, an instrument that never really goes out of style. The album was written and recorded during a period when Lesh's father was dying and Garcia's mother had unexpectedly died after an auto accident, and the resulting strain of melancholy that runs through most of the songs keeps them grounded in a reality to which everyone can relate.

Another reason the album works so well is that it still sounds so good. This was the Dead's third attempt at a self-produced effort (the fourth if you count the half of *Anthem of the Sun* they did themselves), and they finally learned how to give each individual instrument enough room to really ring out. More than forty years later, the acoustic guitar Phil Lesh strums on the opening of his "Box of Rain" sounds as though he's playing it to you in the same room. The song, co-written with Hunter as a tribute to Lesh's dying father, is also structurally innovative, containing four verses before hitting the chorus, which doubles as a coda and feels positively cathartic by the time it finally rolls around.

The band's singing had gotten better, too. The three-part harmonies that sounded somewhat shaky on "Uncle John's Band" come across far more professionally this time around. The lover's ode "Attics of My Life" would work fine with one voice, but by employing a cloud of harmonies throughout, the Dead are able to achieve a vocal blend that sounds as heavenly as the best doo-wop (e.g., Nolan Strong and the Diablos' 1954 classic "The Wind"). Even Pigpen, who usually shouted his blues songs, was able to find a new sensitivity in his vocals on this album. His singing on his defeated-by-love ballad "Operator" is heartbreaking in its pathos. Not only does it underscore the song's fragile lyrics, but it serves as an unintended commentary on Pigpen's own declining health at the time. Two years later, folk singer Jim Croce would score a big hit with a song that had the same title and the same lyrical premise.

American Beauty also has two of the Dead's best-loved songs in "Sugar Magnolia" (a Weir-Hunter composition) and "Truckin'," also co-written by that pair along with Garcia and Lesh. The first song is pure Dead nirvana, with its

If a trivia question ever comes up that asks what the Grateful Dead's most successful single was before "Touch of Grey," the answer is "Truckin'." The 45, which had a different mix than the album version, made its debut on the Billboard Top 100 and stayed on the chart for eight weeks, rising as high as #64—a chart placing that sells short the song's enduring popularity.   *Author's collection*

fetching melody perfectly complimenting Hunter's description of a woman who comes off as the ultimate female Deadhead. Hunter also does something in this song that songwriters rarely do: he breaks the "fourth wall" (the imaginary barrier between audience and performer) and addresses the audience in real time with the line "waits backstage while I sing to you." It's one of his many best lyrical moments. Released as a single in its live version from *Europe '72*, it peaked at #91 in February 1973.

"Truckin'" became an anthem for the Dead and for good reason. It's a road song by a rock band that isn't filled with clichés. Its most celebrated line, "What a long, strange trip it's been," became so much a part of the vernacular that many years later it was unwittingly criticized as a cliché by a writer, to whom Hunter had to explain that he was the one who'd invented that phrase to begin with (Hunter's letter to the writer is reprinted on David Dodd's *Annotated Grateful*

Dead Lyrics website). Beyond its many clever lyrical turns of phrase, "Truckin'" is something of a musical wonder, with its complicated, multi-part structure seeming far simpler than it actually is. Released as a single with a different mix and some different instrumentation, it rose to #64 in late 1971.

"Ripple" is a folk lullaby with a melody so enchanting that it was also realized by British composer Andrew Lloyd Webber, who used it for the song "Any Dream Will Do" in his musical *Joseph and the Amazing Technicolor Dreamcoat*. Webber's song allegedly pre-dates the Dead's, but it's doubtful Garcia could have heard the melody, as Webber's tune had only been performed at two small school productions in 1969 and 1970 (a soundtrack was recorded in 1969 but not released until October 1970, according to Ken Bloom's *Broadway: Its History, People, and Places*).

Best of all might be "Friend of the Devil," an outlaw fable primarily penned by New Riders of the Purple Sage founder John "Marmaduke" Dawson and Hunter (Garcia contributed the bridge). It's the story of a cad-on-the-run who is not only on a sheriff's bad side, but also married to two women. It's told so expertly that you don't know whether to root for the guy, feel sorry for him, or hope for society's sake that someone tracks him down. The story could perhaps serve as a Rorschach test to determine the state of mind of any given listener.

In all, *American Beauty* is an album that even non–Dead fans should own, a genuine classic that should be wedged into record collections (or playlists) right alongside *Revolver*, *Dark Side of the Moon*, and *Blonde on Blonde*.

American Beauty was released in November 1970 (November 1 has been said to be the exact release date). It entered the Billboard album chart on December 26 and rose to #30.

The 2003 Rhino reissue features as bonus tracks the single version of "Truckin'," as well as the single edit of its B-side, "Ripple," and a radio ad, the latter two of which are hidden tracks. The reissue does not include the studio outtake of "To Lay Me Down," which can be found on the *So Many Roads* box set (Garcia also recorded a version for his first solo album). Also included are five live cuts: "Friend of the Devil" is from the May 15, 1970, show at the Fillmore East in New York City; "Candyman" dates from April 15, 1970, at the Winterland Ballroom in San Francisco; "Till the Morning Comes" is from October 4, 1970, also from Winterland; "Attics of My Life" is from a June 6, 1970, gig at the Fillmore West in San Francisco; and "Truckin'," which is missing its opening chorus, comes from a December 26, 1970, show at Legion Stadium in Los Angeles.

Wake of the Flood

In the television special *A Charlie Brown Christmas*, Linus quotes Lucy, saying, "Of all the Charlie Browns in the world, you're the Charlie Browniest." That sentiment could be applied to the Dead's sixth studio album, *Wake of the Flood*, because of all the Grateful Dead albums, it's the "Grateful Deadiest." The record

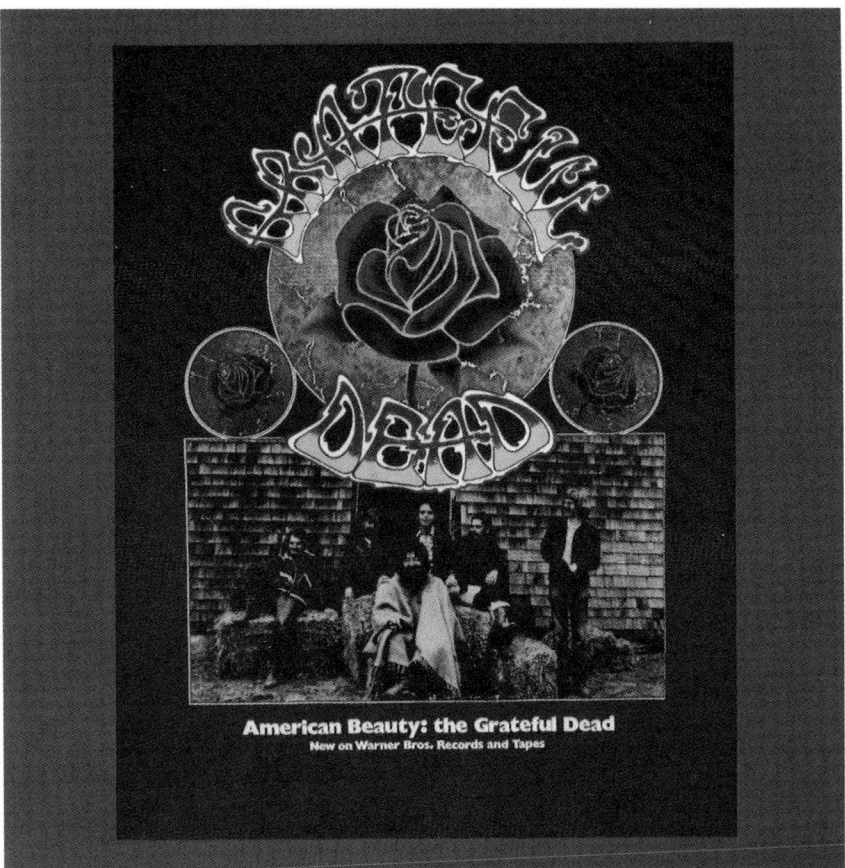

This advertisement for the *American Beauty* album was reproduced inside the booklet of the 2003 reissue CD. The album is one of the few in the band's catalog to garner widespread critical acclaim and in 2003 was ranked #258 on *Rolling Stone* magazine's list of the 500 greatest albums of all time.   *Author's collection*

was released in 1973 after the band put out two multi-disc live albums (*Skull and Roses* and *Europe '72*) and comes the closest to capturing both the sound and feel of the band's live shows. While not as consistently interesting as *American Beauty*, at least two of its songs, "Stella Blue" and "Eyes of the World," are arguably more powerful and mature compositions than is anything on that album.

Wake of the Flood also holds importance in the Dead's pantheon because it contains a number of "firsts" for the band. It's the first album they put out without Pigpen (who had died seven months prior to its release). It's also the first studio recording to feature new keyboardist Keith Godchaux along with new singer Donna Jean Godchaux-MacKay, who was then Keith's wife and billed as Donna Jean Godchaux. The album was also the Dead's first release on their own label, Grateful Dead Records (the band's other label, Round Records, was a subsidiary dedicated to solo projects and the works of other artists). Also, second drummer Mickey Hart was not onboard for this album or the next. He had temporarily left the band in 1971 after his father, Lenny Hart, who was also the band's manager, stole the band's advance money from their record company.

By the time *Wake of the Flood* was released, it had been almost three years since the Dead had last released a studio album. In the interim, they chose to place new songs on their preceding live albums. Because of that, expectations were probably a bit too high for the album, and it was bound to disappoint by virtue of not being *American Beauty, Part Two*. Although *Wake of the Flood* charted higher than any of the band's studio releases had up to that point, it never enjoyed much of a reputation. One reason for that might have been the negative review that appeared in the nation's premiere rock magazine at the time, *Rolling Stone*. Writing in the January 3, 1974, issue, reviewer Jim Miller all but dismissed the band as "professional amateurs" and said that the album's lyrics "plumb new depths of dull-witted, inbred, blissed-out hippy-dippyness." As for the vocals, he went on to claim that "the poor bastards still can barely sing," and described their voices as coming across as "generally sick, usually woozy, and often afflicted with perpetual head cold, twinges of sinus trouble, you name it."

Clearly the Dead no longer commanded the respect of *Rolling Stone*, although that would change in the next decade. Part of the problem might have been that the Dead weren't trendy anymore. The acoustic rock sound that the Dead helped pioneer was being pushed aside by glam rock and a more progressive brand of rhythm and blues that would evolve into disco. On top of that, hippies themselves were becoming passé, with punk rock being just around the corner (the Ramones played their first gig just five months after this album's release).

But time has vindicated *Wake of the Flood*. On this album, the Dead were artistically forward-thinking enough not to want to copy past glories, but assured enough of their artistry not to bow to any trends, although Weir's multi-part "Weather Report Suite" could be seen as a nod to progressive rock. The album's foreboding title and mysterious cover (depicting an old woman gathering wheat) weren't exactly designed with mass commercial appeal in mind, either—nor was the back cover, which contained no song titles or personnel credits.

The opening cut on the album, the stage favorite "Mississippi Half-Step Uptown Toodeloo," was the latest in a series of Hunter's shaggy dog tales about a misfit on the run. But it was more mature in conception and imagery than what had come before, alternating jaunty verses with a sobering, minor key chorus. That chorus is enlivened by the new male-female harmony sound the band was able to utilize with the addition of Godchaux-MacKay. A gorgeous fiddle counterpoint part by bluegrass legend Vassar Clements makes the finished mix sparkle. The song closes with an expansive-sounding coda, Garcia and Hunter's first since "Doin' That Rag." Besides being a powerful piece of music in its own right, it evokes both Hoagy Carmichael and Mark Twain with its reference to a "lazy river."

The album also has Keith Godchaux's only composition for the band, "Let Me Sing Your Blues Away." The song, which has lyrics by Hunter, manages to fit in well with the surrounding material, even though it's by a writer new to the band. The blend of music and words comes together almost uncannily at one point to create one of the most poignant moments on the bridge: "When I was a young man, I needed good luck / But I'm a little bit older now and I know my stuff." Released as a single, it didn't chart.

The molasses-slow, loping "Row Jimmy" is a quintessential Dead number, with mirage-like lyrics that always seem just a step away from becoming clear and making sense. The first side of the original vinyl record closed with "Stella Blue," another enigmatic ballad that over the years became one of the best loved Garcia-Hunter songs. Whether it's about a guitar, as some have said, or is just mood music, it's a song that sounds as though it simultaneously could almost be a jazz standard yet could only have been conceived by the Grateful Dead. Both songs have a wistfulness about them that's unique to Garcia and Hunter's writing; as on *American Beauty*, sad songs proved to be the pair's forte. The understated piano playing Godchaux displays on these cuts would become an important element of the Dead's sound and provided a surefooted foundation from which Garcia could launch his six-string excursions.

Side two's "Eyes of the World" is a danceable number with jazzy chords that the band used as a vehicle for some of their best jams over the ensuing decades. Hunter once described the song in an interview as being mystical, but his lyrics can also be read as an acknowledgment of self-awareness, especially when heard by fans in a live context. Again, this song contains a spot where music and lyrics come together to form a transcendent moment, specifically on the line "Sometimes the songs that we hear are just songs of our own," which sometimes drew cheers from audiences. Like several Dead singles during this period, "Eyes of the World" did not chart, even thought it was edited down for release on a 45 record.

If there's a weak link on the album, its "Here Comes Sunshine," which has a leaden chorus that doesn't quite live up to the perky riff that frames the song. The album closer, Weir's "Weather Report Suite," marks new territory for the band. The three-part song opens with a scored guitar prelude that serves as a preview of what they would do structurally on future multi-part suites such as the title tracks to *Blues for Allah* and *Terrapin Station*. A second section ("Part I") was co-written with folk singer Eric Anderson and is a ballad containing one of the most beautiful melodies Weir ever devised (perhaps too subtle for the concert stage, which is why it wasn't played more often). That serves as a transition to the third part, "Let It Grow," which has lyrics by Weir collaborator John Perry Barlow that use his real-life background in working the land on a farm as a metaphor for life itself. It became a staple of the band's live shows, like almost all the other songs on the album.

Wake of the Flood was released October 15, 1973. It entered the Billboard album chart on November 17, eventually rising to #18.

GD-4503

GRATEFUL DEAD

U.S. BLUES

"U.S. Blues" might have become an FM radio staple, but like many of the band's singles, it didn't make the Billboard Top 100. It was one of a handful of Dead 45s to come with a picture sleeve, however.   *Author's collection*

The 2004 reissue offers an early version of "China Doll," which would appear on the next Dead album, and the acoustic demo of "Weather Report Suite." Also included is a seventeen-minute live version of "Eyes of the World," performed on September 7, 1973, at the Nassau Coliseum in Uniondale, New York. Actor Peter Coyote also writes one section of the liner notes. The reissue does not include the 3:26 single edit of "Eyes of the World," nor the 4:15 edit of "Weather Report Suite—Part I" that was its B-side.

Grateful Dead from the Mars Hotel

By the time of 1974's *Mars Hotel*, as the album is colloquially known, the Dead felt comfortable enough with the sound they'd developed early in the decade to experiment with it a bit. Where *Wake of the Flood* is the album where the Dead sound the most like they did live, *Mars Hotel* has several songs with intricate, subtle arrangements that could only have been perfected in a recording studio. This dovetailed nicely with the increasing sophistication the next generation of rock artists were bringing to their music. For example, 1974 was the year of Steely Dan's *Pretzel Logic*, Genesis's *The Lamb Lies Down on Broadway*, David Bowie's *Diamond Dogs*, and Joni Mitchell's *Court and Spark*.

Some of the glossier, more intricately arranged songs on *Mars Hotel* fit right in with those albums, so it's not a surprise that the album became the Dead's highest charting effort to date, just missing the Top 10. It's also not a surprise that the album's lone single, "U.S. Blues," failed to chart at all. Although 1974 might have been a great year for albums, it was one of the worst years for singles, with gimmicky hits like Paper Lace's "The Night Chicago Died" and Bo Donaldson and the Heywoods' "Billy Don't Be a Hero" dominating the airwaves. "U.S. Blues," which leads off *Mars Hotel*, has one of Hunter's best lyrical premises. It casts the United States in a first-person role as a beleaguered and somewhat belligerent Uncle Sam, who wonders why he needs to dodge bullets when he has no qualms about stealing someone's wife. Like "Born in the U.S.A.," it's a protest song that can also be interpreted as a celebration of the country because of a rousing chorus (which in this case is "Wave that flag," the song's original title). Garcia's singing is more assured than ever, and the song's funky shuffle made it an FM standard and concert staple.

From there the album gets weird. But it's a good weird. The Dead had last experimented on *Anthem of the Sun*, obscuring some great songs with weird instrumentation and effects. This time around, odd instruments and studio trickery enhance the songs. On the chilling death ballad "China Doll" (originally called "The Suicide Song"), Keith Godchaux plays a haunting arpeggiated harpsichord part, while the background vocals are so bathed in echo that they sound like ghosts. As with "Box of Rain," this song piles on so many verses that by the time the chorus hits, it feels like a major emotional breakthrough Deadhead Elvis Costello later used this type of song structure on his *Imperial Bedroom* album.

"Unbroken Chain," which follows, sustains the moody vibe of the record. It's also a song by Phil Lesh, who hadn't been heard from as a composer since 1970's "Box of Rain." A poetic musing on life and love co-written with Lesh's longtime pal Bobby Peterson, it's also a feast for the ears, with swooshing synthesizer effects and a complicated mid-song jazz break (so complicated, in fact, that the band didn't attempt it on stage until more than twenty years after its release). If there's one Grateful Dead song that should be listened to on headphones, this one is it. Actually, that goes for the whole album, which is something of an aural wonderland with its clever production touches, proving the Dead could be a studio band when they wanted to be.

When it rains it pours: yet another Lesh composition shows up on the album, the bouncy "Pride of Cucamonga," an enjoyable country romp also co-written with Peterson. John McFee, who would later play with Costello (among others), sits in on pedal steel, an instrument Garcia felt he himself was too rusty to play properly at the time.

What Garcia may have lacked in pedal steel chops, he more than made up for in songwriting prowess. Two of his and Hunter's other tunes on the album, "Scarlet Begonias" and "Ship of Fools," rank among the best songs in the band's catalog. The first is a laid-back rocker about meeting an outré woman in England who is nonetheless a kindred spirit. It also has an odd, jerky rhythm that gives the underrated Kreutzmann a chance to shine and a coda that allows Godchaux-MacKay to really wail (one of her best moments). "Ship of Fools" is a mournful ballad with one of Garcia's best melodies and Hunter's most open-ended lyrics. Is it a political statement, a personal plea for sanity, or a letter to a parent from a frustrated now-grown child? The offhand subtlety and complexity of this type of Hunter lyrics was the band's secret weapon and gave their music a depth and sense of importance.

That leaves Bob Weir's "Money Money" and Garcia and Hunter's own "Loose Lucy" to fill out the album. Which leads one to think: maybe the Stones, not the Dead, were best suited to penning sarcastic and/or lascivious rock songs about women. Actually, both songs are credible enough rockers, although Weir's time signatures in "Money" get annoying. It's just that in the company of the other material, they can't help but sound run-of-the-mill. Other bands should have had such problems.

Finally, the album was named for an apparently real Mars Hotel. The cover, when held upside down in front of a mirror, appears to read "Ugly Rumors," a play on the phrase "ugly roomers," to which someone thought the residents of the hotel would take offense.

Grateful Dead from the Mars Hotel was released on June 27, 1974. It entered the Billboard album chart on September 20 and rose to #12.

The 2004 CD reissue has an alternate version of "Loose Lucy" and Lesh's acoustic demos of his two songs, "Unbroken Chain" and "Pride of Cucamonga." The most interesting live bonus cut is the early draft of "U.S. Blues," which was titled "Wave That Flag" and sported different lyrics when the Dead performed it on March 28, 1973, at the Springfield Civic Center in Springfield, Massachusetts. Other live cuts include a version of Chuck Berry's "Let It Rock," taped on June 23, 1974, at Jai-Alai Fronton in Miami, Florida; "Scarlet Begonias," recorded on October 16, 1973, at Winterland in San Francisco; and "Money Money," taped live on May 17, 1974, at PNE Coliseum in Vancouver, British Columbia. A 3:12 single edit was made for "U.S. Blues," which shortened the song considerably from its 4:37 length on the album. The edited version has not been issued on CD.

Blues for Allah

Anyone who thinks the Dead "went disco" with *Shakedown Street* in 1978 needs to take a closer listen to 1975's *Blues for Allah*, because none of the faster songs on this album use rock rhythms or even rock chords, à la "Loose Lucy" or "Money Money," and instead employ some of the funky beats that were in the air then. "Help on the Way," "Franklin's Tower," and "The Music Never Stopped" all draw from the syncopated proto-disco and rhythm and blues grooves that were being pioneered in 1974 and 1975 by Stevie Wonder ("You Haven't Done Nothin'"), George McCrae ("Rock Your Baby"), and even Earth, Wind & Fire ("Shining Star").

Elsewhere, the Dead wax experimental (the title track) or instrumental (Weir's "Sage & Spirit"), and the one classic ballad they perform, "Crazy Fingers," is based around a reggae beat. The Dead might have been in the vanguard of country rock six years earlier, but by the year before America's Bicentennial, they were temporarily leaving rock behind, judging by this album.

And yet, these songs are considered "rock" because they're played by a rock band and put across with rock energy. By this point the Dead had developed their own style, a musical stew that drew from a huge array of influences, one of which was rhythm and blues. And why not? In their live show, the band had already brought danceable blues into their repertoire ("Turn On Your Love Light"), as well as Motown ("Dancin' in the Streets"). So, it made sense that the Dead would be influenced, perhaps subconsciously, by the R&B sounds of the mid-1970s. The other option would have been for the Dead to stagnate, and record the same predictable album over and over again like the Rolling Stones ended up doing. Instead, in their own subtle way, the Dead helped pioneer the merging of African American rhythms and rock music, for which new wave bands such as Blondie and Talking Heads would later be credited.

So, while *Blues for Allah* might not be "classic" Dead in the sense that *American Beauty* is, it represented a big stylistic leap for the band, and an unpredictable one at that. The Dead were likely able to explore new styles of music in this period because they had more time to do it. The band had taken a year off from touring, which also gave them lots of time to work up songs together and put them in ornate musical settings (making *Blues for Allah* another good "headphones" album). Lyrics were also purportedly written on the fly, but they don't sound it. With Mickey Hart back in the fold and two drummers flailing away, it's little wonder that the Dead got more rhythmic.

The album opens with a trio of songs that became a mini–song suite when they were performed live on occasion: "Help on the Way">"Slipknot!">"Franklin's Tower." The syncopated backbeats and snaky guitars of "Help" and "Franklin" are what give these songs their life, so the sound of the vocals is almost more important than the lyrics themselves (something David Byrne and Brian Eno would learn when they juxtaposed spoken word samples with dance beats on their groundbreaking 1981 album *My Life in the Bush of Ghosts*). Still, "Help on the Way" is a plea for a lover to stick around that paints a vivid picture of a relationship despite its economy of words. "Franklin's Tower" is positively brimming with metaphor and is said by Hunter to have been inspired by both the birth of his son and the impending Bicentennial. It's the kind of song you can play for years and still draw meaning from but was probably too esoteric to expect to chart as a single, which it didn't.

"Slipknot!" is a guitar piece probably entitled as such for the intricate finger work it required (Garcia once likened playing leads to untying knots). The difficulty of playing this song might be the reason the "Help">"Slipknot!">"Franklin's" sequence was only played a few more than one hundred times. Weir and Barlow indulge in a bit of musical autobiography in "The Music Never Stopped," which was released as a single in edited form and hit #81, beginning its chart run on October 25, 1975. Weir's melody gives Godchaux-MacKay a solo spot on which to shine on the pre-chorus, while Barlow's story of a "band beyond description" seems to encapsulate the Dead experience in three words. "Crazy Fingers" is one of Garcia's finest ballads, a jazzy lullaby brightened by Godchaux-MacKay's harmonies.

The title track is the Dead taking the experimentation of both *Anthem* and some parts of *Mars Hotel* one giant step further. "Blues for Allah" is a three-part song that opens with a self-titled section that boasts the kind of odd melody you'd expect to find on an old King Crimson album. The second part, "Sand Castles and Glass Camels," is a freeform, band-written jam that pretty much defines weirdness and comes replete with cricket sound effects. The final part, "Unusual Occurrences in the Desert," is a blissful bit of Garcia-Hunter musical poetry, with its refrain of "under eternity" coming off like a mantra. As with "Slipknot!," the complexity of this composition was probably the reason it wasn't played much. In this case, it was performed a grand total of five times.

While the Dead's experimental works were mostly relegated to the studio, some of the numbers from the then-current Garcia and Weir solo projects were making it to the stage regularly. Including one or two here in lieu of the more experimental tracks would have made for a classic album, not just a really good one. Solo album stage favorites that might have worked on *Blues for Allah* include "It Must Have Been the Roses" and "They Love Each Other," from Garcia's 1976 album *Reflections*, and the "Lazy Lightnin'"/"Supplication" sequence from the debut album by Weir's side band, Kingfish. Although there were enough high-quality songs to go around at this point, that wouldn't always be the case. A lack of strong, original material would mar the band's next few albums and support any feelings people had that the band's main songwriters were starting to spread themselves too thin.

Blues for Allah was released on September 1, 1975. It entered the Billboard album chart on September 20, rising to #16.

Unlike all of the other Rhino Records CD reissues of Grateful Dead studio albums, the *Blues for Allah* reissue contains only unreleased studio recordings, most of which are jams credited to the whole band. "Groove #1" finds the band hitting a loose "Loose Lucy" vibe, while "Groove #2" has them sounding jazzy, with Keith Godchaux's electric keyboard playing staccato lead parts. "A to E Flat Jam" is a shuffle that sounds like the Doobie Brothers attempting "Ramble On Rose," while "Proto 18 Proper" has some mean wah-wah guitar by Garcia.

Also featured is an eight-minute Garcia-composed instrumental, "Distorto," that sounds like a warm-up for the next album's title track, "Terrapin Station," and the Hunter-Weir composition "Hollywood Cantata," which is essentially an early draft of "The Music Never Stopped" with different lyrics and title.

The 3:14 single edit of "The Music Never Stopped" was not issued on CD, nor was the 3:07 edit of "Franklin's Tower."

12

Now We Play for Clive

The Dead's Studio Recordings, 1977–89

S tarting with the Dead's Boston Music Hall gig on November 13, 1978, Bob Weir occasionally altered a line in "Jack Straw" to be "We used to play for silver, now we play for Clive." It was an in-joke referencing Clive Davis, the president of Arista Records, the major label to which the Dead signed in 1976. Weir might have been kidding around with his lyric alteration, but the Dead's signing to Davis's label and "playing for Clive" did have major ramifications on their studio work. They started working with producers and for the most part stopped making albums that reflected their live sound. This gave fans who came aboard at this important juncture in the Dead's career the unfortunate impression that their studio albums were a losing proposition, which wasn't the case previously.

Terrapin Station

If there is a dividing line as to when the Grateful Dead's albums took a turn for the worse, this rather schizoid 1977 album represents it. Although not a bad album by any means, *Terrapin Station*'s lack of focus keeps it from hitting the highs the Dead achieved on their previous half dozen releases. The album's first half showed the band trying out a bunch of different musical styles, some of which worked better than others. The second showcased the title song, which was a progressive rock–inspired epic that ran the length of the whole side of the original vinyl album. But never did the two album sides meet stylistically, and therein lies the problem with the album.

Like *Wake of the Flood*, *Terrapin Station* ushered in a bunch of "firsts" for the band. It was the first album released on Arista Records, after the Dead decided to forego running their own label. It was the first album since 1967 on which they brought in an outside producer. In this case, it was Keith Olsen, who was best known at the time for producing Fleetwood Mac's self-titled 1975 commercial breakthrough. And it was the first album to break the streak of first-rate Dead albums that started back in 1969 with *Aoxomoxoa*.

Bringing in an outside producer was one of Davis's "primary demands," according to Dennis McNally's biography *A Long Strange Trip: The Inside History of the Grateful Dead and the Making of Modern America*. Davis's request didn't meet with opposition from the group because they were never very comfortable in the studio to begin with and figured some outside ears couldn't hurt.

But hindsight has shown that having an extra pair of ears did, in fact, harm the band. For the first time in their career, the Dead became self-conscious. Instead of songs coming off as organic, they now sounded contrived, thanks to the intricate arrangements Olsen saddled them with. And instead of the band developing a consistent sound that reflected some element of their live presentation, they now seemed to dramatically lurch from style to style on different songs. This could never have happened had the band continued producing themselves: the Dead lacked the skills as producers to pull off such sonic sleight-of-hand. The Dead weren't a pop band that crafted singles, like Fleetwood Mac or the Beatles, so the idea of giving each song its own "environment" was pointless. Songs on Dead albums were meant to work together, not as singles taken out of context.

Olsen's approach is especially apparent on the album's first single, a remake of Martha and the Vandellas' "Dancing in the Street" (called "Dancin' in the Streets" here). The Dead played this song as early as 1966 and retired it after a 1971 New Year's Eve gig. They broke it out again on June 3, 1976, in Portland, Oregon, which is when they started giving it a brand new beat—a disco one. That wasn't so bad live, as it worked in the context of the groove-heavy material the Dead had just unleashed on *Blues for Allah*. But on record, Olsen adds incongruous horns and has the band sing an embarrassing opening chorus tag, making the whole affair sound more like a parody of a rock band doing disco than the real thing.

The single didn't chart, nor did the album's second 45, the Phil Lesh–Peter Monk rocker "Passenger." A riveting number live, "Passenger" comes off on *Terrapin Station* as pedestrian hard rock with all the rough edges sanded off. A few songs down sits Donna Godchaux-MacKay's first composition for the group, "Sunrise," a gospel-tinged ballad supposedly written for the Dead's late roadie and friend Rex Jackson. It's a nice enough song, especially during the build-up around the two-minute mark, but the slick production makes it sound like it was phoned in from a Christian rock album. There is a thin line between "eclectic" and "unfocused," and on this album, the Dead crossed it.

Luckily, *Terrapin Station* contains enough strong tracks to make it a passable record. Bob Weir and John Perry Barlow's opening cut, "Estimated Prophet," pits an ear-grabbing melody against an incongruous 7/4 beat and manages not only to work, but also to shine as one of the band's most innovative numbers. When Robert Fripp reconvened King Crimson at the dawn of the 1980s, he and drummer Bill Bruford were considered innovators for doing with time signatures what Weir had already done. The song's odd story, told from the point of view of a crazed fan, makes it all the more compelling as does its shimmering "California" chorus.

The prog-rock thrust of "Estimated Prophet" also fits in stylistically with the title track (officially called "Terrapin Station Part One"), one of the best pieces of music the band ever created. A sixteen-minute tour de force of luminous guitar hooks and cryptic-but-touching lyrics, it easily stands up to other long-form classics of the vinyl era, such as Genesis's "Supper's Ready" or Yes's "Close to the Edge." What is most surprising is that a band that had built its reputation on improvisational jams could pull off a seven-part, pre-arranged piece with such skill. The music unfolds artfully and perfectly underscores Hunter's (unresolved) story about a woman who makes two men compete for her affections.

A lot of noise has been made in Dead books about Olsen's erasing some timbale parts played by Hart to make room for the track's orchestration (performed by the Martyn Ford Orchestra) and chorus (the English Choral Choir). Olsen's sweetening did, in fact, remove some of the edge that the song had in concert—so did the completely pointless fade-in on "Samson and Delilah." Both are the kind of touches the Dead would never have brought to the proceedings had they produced this album themselves. So much for "playing for Clive."

Terrapin Station was released on July 27, 1977. It entered the Billboard album chart on September 10 and peaked at #28.

The expanded CD reissue from 2004 adds several studio outtakes. These include a vocal-less run through of the traditional stage favorite "Peggy-O"; a crunchy guitar-fueled instrumental called "The Ascent"; a cover of Johnny Russell's 1972 country hit "Catfish John"; a complex Lesh song called "Equinox"; and an early take of "Fire on the Mountain." Also included is a sixteen-minute version of "Dancin' in the Streets" that was performed at Cornell University's Barton Hall on May 8, 1977. Not included on the CD was the 3:17 edit of "Terrapin Station" that was used for the B-sides of both the "Dancin' in the Streets" and "Passenger" singles.

Shakedown Street

Oh no! It's disco Dead! Hide the kids and cover your ears! Actually, time has proven that the disco elements of *Shakedown Street* aren't even the album's biggest problem. As mentioned in the previous chapter, the Dead had been dancing around dance music since *Wake of the Flood*'s "Eyes of the World," and had moved deeper into it on segments of the *Blues for Allah* album. The Dead also jumped on the disco bandwagon with disastrous artistic and commercial results with their 1977 single "Dancin' in the Streets." So, the disco-fied title cut of *Shakedown Street* just made the band's embrace of dance music more explicit, which wasn't totally unexpected in 1978, the year that the Bee Gees dominated the pop charts.

This time around, the Dead enlisted as producer the founder and creative voice of Little Feat, Lowell George. Unlike on *Terrapin Station*, on *Shakedown Street*, George at least brings to the band some consistency of sound. All the songs here sound as though they're from the same album and done by the same band. Even the cover art works. Gilbert Shelton's painting, which depicts an imaginary Shakedown Street, is arguably one of the band's best cover designs.

And the title track of *Shakedown Street* is one of the band's best songs. Its souped-up disco arrangement compliments the tune, unlike on "Dancin' in the

Streets," where the rhythm detracts from the song. Also, the studio arrangement of "Shakedown Street" isn't that far off from how the Dead played it live. In fact, the way Garcia and Hunter match music with lyrics in this song might be one of the cleverest conceits that the band ever pulled off. It is, after all, a melancholy song about alienation set to a high-stepping dance beat. Hunter's line "Maybe the dark is from your eyes" is one of the most perceptive observations about depression any artist has come up with.

All that's the positive part. The not-so-good aspect of *Shakedown Street* is that the band simply didn't have enough top-notch material to create a fully memorable album. Wait, scratch that. The Dead did, in fact, have enough material for a truly great album. But Garcia and Weir chose to put that material on solo albums. Had *Shakedown Street* contained the title track to Weir's second solo album, *Heaven Help the Fool* (also released in 1978), it would have had a higher hit-to-miss ratio. Had Garcia contributed "Rubin and Cherise" or the title track of his 1978 release, *Cats Under the Stars*, then *Shakedown Street* might have been considered one of the Dead's best efforts.

What could have been removed to make room for those songs? Well, there was Weir and Barlow's make-work blues tune, "I Need a Miracle," which at least had some wicked Matt Kelly harp playing. There was Garcia and Hunter's none-too-interesting updating of the "Stagger Lee" myth, which was unlikely to make anyone forget Lloyd Price's firecracker 1959 hit of the same title. There was also the band's stiff take on the old Olympics and Young Rascals hit "Good Lovin'," which contained tons of keyboards and virtually no guitar. The Dead weren't so much bad writers as bad editors, not knowing which songs to put on which albums. It's debatable as to whether the Dead's covers of "Dancin' in the Streets" or "Good Lovin'" should have even been chosen to be recorded in the studio.

The Dead were never the most prolific composers, and fallout from side careers of the band's two main writers was bound to catch up with them at some point. It wound up affecting this album and the next one. The Dead weren't alone in this respect. A similar situation occurred with the Who a few years later, when main writer Pete Townshend started saving all his best songs for his solo albums. Garcia had played with a lot of other musicians by this point, and it may have been around this time that he began to have second thoughts about whether the Dead should have even been his first priority. A good argument can be made that *Cats Under the Stars* is superior to *Shakedown Street*, arguably the first instance of a Dead-related solo album eclipsing the artistic impact of the band's own album.

All that said, *Shakedown Street* is at least an interesting *sounding* album. By the time this album was recorded, George had created around a half dozen albums filled with funky, soulful rock for Little Feat. Although some Dead members later complained that George (who died less than a year after the sessions) was too strung out on cocaine to produce a cohesive record, their statements seem like a case of revisionist history. *Shakedown Street* sounds slick, not haphazard, and was totally in tune with what was going on in 1978. The idea of "disco Dead" wasn't as strange as it seemed back when other rock bands, such as the Electric Light Orchestra and the Rolling Stones, were copping trendy dance beats.

But in the Dead's case, commercial pandering didn't pay off. The opposite happened, in fact. Neither the title track nor the band's cover of "Good Lovin'" charted as singles, even though they were both released in more listener-friendly edited versions. The album became the first Dead studio album to miss the Top 40 since *Aoxomoxoa*—so much for the idea of bringing in producers to improve the Dead's commercial lot in life.

The biggest pleasures on *Shakedown Street*, besides the title song, are its most esoteric, not its most commercial. The rare Weir-Hunter-Hart collaboration "France," with its steel drums and lyrics about a fantasy version of a far-off land, sounds as though Jimmy Buffet served as musical consultant. But it sure makes for a fun listen and even looks ahead to the World Music trend of the 1980s. "Fire on the Mountain," by Hart and Hunter, is a successful foray into reggae that would have been even better at six minutes than at four. "If I Had the World to Give" might not be "Stella Blue" when it comes to deep ballads, but it does prove that Garcia and Hunter could have written conventional ballads for pop singers if only that whole Dead thing hadn't gotten in the way. And this time around, Godchaux-MacKay captures the Dead vibe convincingly with the mellow sway of her love lament, "From the Heart of Me." Sounding like the old Dead of the mid-1970s, it even made it to stage around a half dozen times. It would be the last hurrah for the Dead's only female member, who would leave the band along with her husband a few months after the release of this album.

Shakedown Street was released on November 15, 1978. It entered the Billboard album chart on December 9 and rose to #41.

The 2004 CD reissue contains one unreleased studio cut: a version of "Good Lovin'" with Lowell George on lead vocals. Also featured are two live recordings of "Fire on the Mountain" and the Nubian wedding song "Ollin Arageed," which was recorded on September 16, 1978, at the Gizah Sound and Light Theatre in Cairo, Egypt. There is also a version of "Stagger Lee" that was recorded at the same venue the next night. The disc also includes a version of "All New Minglewood Blues" from November 24, 1978, at the Capitol Theatre in Passaic, New Jersey. Neither the 3:46 single edit of "Shakedown Street" nor the 3:26 single edit of "Good Lovin'" was issued on the CD.

Go to Heaven

Go to Heaven was somewhat of a return to style, if not form, for the Grateful Dead. The disco high-hat beats and polished arrangements of the previous two albums were mostly gone. In their place were more punchy rock sounds, courtesy of yet another producer, Gary Lyons. Lyons was someone who definitely knew a thing or two about rock, having produced and engineered Aerosmith's *Night in the Ruts* album from 1979 and the first Foreigner album from 1977. Before that, he served as engineer on albums by the British rock acts Be-Bop Deluxe and Queen.

"Alabama Getaway" was the lead single from *Go to Heaven* and was also released in the United States with a picture sleeve. New member Brent Mydland's "Far from Me" was selected for B-side honors.   *Courtesy of Eric Schwartz*

But for fans, the pedigree of the album's producer was the least of their concerns. In early 1979, both Keith Godchaux and Donna Godchaux-MacKay left the group, and in their place the Dead hired a new keyboard player who could also handle the high-register vocals Godchaux-MacKay had sung. Enter Brent Mydland, whose best-known work had come as a member of the country rock band Silver. Silver was a genuine one-hit wonder act whose lone chart success came in 1976 with an admittedly catchy pop confection that got to #16 called "Wham Bam" (also called "Wham Bam Shang-A-Lang" on some copies of the single). Mydland had come into contact with Garcia when he'd played keyboards with Weir's offshoot band Bobby and the Midnites, who played on a bill with the Jerry Garcia Band. Garcia liked what he heard. Some fans weren't so sure at first.

Where the vocals of both Godchaux and Godchaux-MacKay fit in with the Dead right off the bat, Mydland's aggressive brand of blue-eyed soulful singing didn't seem to blend   not at first, anyway. Mydland's songs, though well-written, sounded more like they belonged on albums by artists like Michael McDonald,

Robbie Dupree, or even Christopher Cross, as opposed to the Dead. As time rolled on, Dead fans came to not only accept but also treasure Mydland's contribution. But when *Go to Heaven* was brand new, Mydland's two songs, "Far From Me" and "Easy to Love You," seemed to stand in stark contrast to the country and mainstream rock that formed the rest of the album.

Mydland's songs, along with the white suits the Dead wore on the album cover, seemed a signal to some that the band was losing its identity or "selling out" to the mainstream. Hindsight has shown that the suits were intended ironically, not as some sort of tribute to *Saturday Night Fever*. And Mydland's songs were as musically valid as any of the other numbers; they just came from a different place. But in the wake of *Shakedown Street* and the many stylistic shifts the band had made over the past half decade, *Go to Heaven* was seen by some Deadheads as the Dead moving still further away from their roots.

Mydland's situation mirrored that of Blondie Chaplin and Ricki Fataar, two South African musicians who were added to the Beach Boys lineup in 1971. Longtime fans were incensed that the pair of "outsiders" were writing and singing on Beach Boys albums. But a funny thing happened on the way to the future: just as Mydland is now appreciated by fans who have grown to love his work over the ensuing decades, so are Chaplin and Fataar among Beach Boys fans, who now consider Chaplin's lead vocals on "Sail On, Sailor" to be one of the band's best moments.

The most valued moments from *Go to Heaven*, though, were Garcia's, largely because there were so few of them. At this point, he had fallen into hard drug use and his writing had slowed down. Even his next (and last) solo record, *Run for the Roses* from 1982, would show a lack of inspiration. In a few years, his voice would deteriorate. *Go to Heaven* gives us the last of the "old" Garcia on the mere two originals he and Hunter contributed. "Alabama Getaway" comes off as another outlaw tale with lots of Old West imagery, but its fast tempo and quicksilver guitar licks are what made it an FM staple and took it to #68 on the pop charts in June 1980. "Althea" is a classic Dead slow rocker with a down-and-out protagonist who seeks a woman's advice about his confused life. Considering Garcia's personal situation at the time, it's little wonder he took to this Hunter lyric.

Weir's "Feel Like a Stranger" continued in the vein of the more rhythmic-heavy area he'd gotten into on the past few albums. Funk beat aside, its distorted guitar and synth bleeps took it closer to what rock bands such as Styx or Steely Dan were doing at the time. Its theme of alienation at a concert (or some musical setting) also seems to pick up where "Estimated Prophet" leaves off. "Lost Sailor" and "Saint of Circumstance," which were usually paired together in concert, are two of Weir's most powerful slower songs, building up tension with Zappa-like jazz chords and break sections that give newcomer Mydland a chance to shine a bit.

Go to Heaven closes with an oldie of sorts. Here, the Dead revive "Don't Ease Me In," the jaunty Henry Thomas number from the 1920s the band had cut as the B-side of their first single, "Stealin'" (Garcia and Weir had also performed it with Mother McCree's Uptown Jug Champions). This time around, it's given a tighter arrangement. Its outlaw story, which might have served as inspiration for "Friend of the Devil," is sweetened with enough layered harmonies to have made it an FM favorite in this incarnation, even though the single didn't chart.

Other than "Antwerp's Placebo (the Plumber)," a short, dissonant instrumental written by the two drummers (probably to nab some royalty money), that was all she wrote for the Dead for a long seven years. In the time between, Garcia fell into a coma, had to relearn how to play the guitar, and made a triumphant comeback. Had he died, the Dead's catalog would have begun and ended with "Don't Ease Me In," as the band's remake closed out *Go to Heaven*.

Go to Heaven was released on April 28, 1980. It entered the Billboard album chart on May 24 and rose to #23.

Bonus tracks on the 2003 CD reissue include three studio outtakes: another try at the traditional "Peggy-O"; Robert Hunter's "What'll You Raise" (later included on his 1986 album *Rock Columbia*); and the traditional "Jack-A-Roe." Live cuts include "Lost Sailor" and "Saint of Circumstance" from October 25 at New York's Radio City Music Hall and an undated rendition of "Althea," which sounds like it was recorded the next night. The very slight 3:29 single edit of "Alabama Getaway" was not issued on CD.

In the Dark

In the Dark was both the Dead's big comeback album and the group's biggest album ever. It also contains the surprise hit song "Touch of Grey," an edited version of which edged into the Billboard Top 10, hitting #9 in the summer of 1987. The album is arguably the best work the Dead released during the last part of their career as a recording act. All seven of the songs that make up the original album not only work on their own, but also compliment each other on disc.

This time around, Garcia produced the album himself with John Cutler, the band's in-house studio engineer. The pair crafted an atmosphere that stood halfway between what the Dead of the 1980s sounded like on stage and what radio in the 1980s sounded like. Garcia and Cutler also fully captured the richness of Lesh's bass sound on a few tracks, notably "West L.A. Fadeaway." In all, the band sounds like a glossier version of its concert self, which was a result achieved from recording the basic tracks for each song as a unit. This wouldn't be the case on the next album.

In the Dark was more than just a hit album. Its popularity catapulted the band from cult status into the upper ranks of rock royalty. For longtime fans, it also showed that Garcia was alive and well and back at the top of his game. He not only co-produced but also wrote the majority of the album's songs. His voice sounded more confident, if more frayed, than it had in years.

If there's any drawback to *In the Dark*, it's that the Dead had the misfortune to record it during a time period when rock music sounded artificial and was

If Deadheads were concerned that "Touch of Grey" going Top 10 signaled a new, commercial era for the band, they needn't have worried. The follow up single, "Throwing Stones," failed to chart on the Billboard Top 100.   *Courtesy of yesterdayandtodayrecords.com*

following pop music's lead in using now-dated effects such as digital echo, gated reverb, and treated voices. This lack of naturalism ran counter to the come-as-you-are aesthetic that served the Dead on their best albums. A few years down the road, the subgenre of grunge would explode, and its influence would prompt bands to re-emphasize their natural sound. The post-grunge period, which lasted roughly from 1992 through 1995, saw the rise of back-to-basics rock acts such as the Gin Blossoms, Blind Melon, the Spin Doctors, and Sheryl Crow. Had the Dead been recording during this period, they'd have been releasing records in a musical environment more in line with their own sound.

In the Dark begins with the now-familiar strains of "Touch of Grey," an ear-grabbing Garcia-Hunter song introduced in September 1982. Despite its contemplative verses about the dissolution of both a relationship and the world itself, the song nonetheless comes off as triumphant because it resolves in a fist-raising chorus that celebrates survival. Its use of the word "grey" was also probably a deliberate reference to grey hair, something the band's core audience (and some members of the band itself) were dealing with. It's little wonder that the song struck such a chord with audiences. A video that showed the band as skeletons didn't hurt either.

Two of the other Garcia-Hunter songs sported blues-based melodies, but they were done up with enough panache not to come off as stiff revivals. The swaggering "When Push Comes to Shove" has enough sex appeal in its shuffle to give Bonnie Raitt a run for her money. The downbeat "West L.A. Fadeaway" gave Garcia the chance to commit to vinyl the raunchiest lead guitar he'd played in years. The album's closing number, "Black Muddy River," has a hymn-like quality that compares favorably to the earlier "Attics of My Life." With its gospel imagery and rousing chorus, it's one of the band's most moving pieces of music, made all the more so because it was the final song Garcia ever sang on stage.

"Hell in a Bucket" and "Throwing Stones" saw Weir move away from the jazzy dance beats that had become his stock-in-trade on the group's three previous albums. Here, he gets back to good old rock 'n' roll music, a move probably precipitated by his involvement with his rock-oriented side project Bobby and the Midnites. "Bucket" is amusing because it's a Dead song with an aggressive edge that starts by broaching the topic of revenge. (So much for hippie peace-and-love stereotyping.) Weir and Barlow get political in the similarly rousing "Throwing Stones," which didn't chart as the follow-up single to "Touch of Grey," but always kept audiences singing along with its chorus of "Ashes, ashes all fall down."

Mydland's sole contribution to the album was "Tons of Steel," a song that uses train imagery as a metaphor to describe a life careening out of control. The Dead had introduced this back in 1984, but it dates from even earlier, having been originally cut for Mydland's unreleased solo album back in 1982.

Listening to *In the Dark* today, it actually sounds more dated than the records the band released in the early 1970s because of some of the production techniques Garcia and Cutler used. The high-pitched, cartoonish backing vocals on "West L.A. Fadeaway" and the ridiculous samples of whips and motorcycles on "Hell in a Bucket" are the most obvious examples of this. But you had to dazzle with production if you wanted a hit record in the 1980s, and at least this time around the Dead's attempts to catch the ear of the public managed to . . . catch the ear of the public.

In the Dark was released on July 6, 1987. It entered the Billboard album chart on August 1, eventually rising to #6.

The 2004 CD reissue adds Weir's "My Brother Esau," the flip side of the "Touch of Grey" single that was also on cassette copies of the album. There is also an alternate version of "West L.A. Fadeaway" from March 1984 and studio rehearsals of "Black Muddy River" and "When Push Comes to Shove," both from December 5, 1986. A studio rehearsal of "Touch of Grey" dates from as far back as August 1982, while a live version of "Throwing Stones" is from a 1987 Fourth of July show.

The reissue does not include the edited single version of "Touch of Grey" that shortens the song from 5:48 to 4:14. Also not included is the 45 edit of "Throwing Stones," which takes that song from 7:20 to 4:04.

Built to Last

Some of the early Dead albums, such as *Aoxomoxoa* and *Workingman's Dead*, came close to being Jerry Garcia solo albums because he dominated the proceedings to such a large degree. Few would have imagined in 1989 that there would be a Dead album that could almost be called a Brent Mydland solo album. But *Built to Last* is nearly such an album. It's got four songs co-written by Mydland, more than the three contributed by Garcia or the two offered by Weir. What's more, another one of Mydland's songs called "Gentlemen, Start Your Engines" was recorded for the album but didn't make the cut. Unfortunately, Mydland died from a drug overdose less than a year after the release of *Built to Last*. So, the album now reads like his personal swan song, right down to the sadly ironic title and house of cards illustration on the cover.

Mydland seemed to suffer from depression and had substance abuse problems. His mental anguish is reflected in his songs, which makes for an unnerving listening experience. Barlow, who wrote lyrics for Mydland, said one reason he wrote with the keyboardist was to give him a reason to want to live. According to Barlow, Mydland couldn't reconcile the low opinion he had of himself with the adulation he was getting from fans. So, Barlow's lyrics closely reflect Mydland's mental state on this record. As such, the four Mydland songs on *Built to Last* take the Dead into a place that it hadn't really gone before, which was into the realm of despondent music made by suicidal musicians such as Ian Curtis, Phil Ochs, and Nick Drake. Where Garcia's songs were melancholy, Mydland's were fatalistic.

All of this has only made these songs more powerful with the passage of time. In "Just a Little Light," Mydland muses about his own confusion and alienation, singing the now-famous couplet "I had a lot of dreams once, but some of them came true / the honey's sometimes bitter when fortune falls on you." The mid-tempo "Blow Away," which boasts one of Mydland's best melodies, characterizes love as a practical joke—and a temporary one at that. Only "I Will Take You Home," written as a lullaby for Mydland's daughters, has any semblance of positivity. Yet, no one would deny the song is a tearjerker, a designation it had even before its composer passed on. Steve Parish suggests, in his book *Home Before Daylight: My Life with the Grateful Dead*, that the poor reception Mydland's songs received in some quarters may have caused him to spiral further into depression. If that's true, it's an irony that's beyond sad.

Mydland's rawness is balanced by Garcia's detachment on this album. Here, the guitarist offers three nice enough melodies, but doesn't seem to connect with the material, some of which is questionably arranged. "Foolish Heart" offers advice to a would-be lover but sounds musically fractured, with the major chords of its introduction not quite setting up the minor key verses. Maybe this is one reason it didn't chart when it was released as a single. The title track's demand of "Show me something built to last" seems oddly self-referential, an idea that worked on "Touch of Grey" but comes off as arrogant here. Was the veteran

Brent Mydland, shown here performing at Virginia's Hampton Coliseum in 1988, was something of a secret weapon for the band in the 1980s. He didn't sing as many lead parts as Jerry Garcia or Bob Weir did, but he could bring down the house with his impassioned vocals, especially when he broke out the lullaby he wrote for his two daughters, "I Will Take You Home."   *Photo by Russ Grabski*

band clapping itself on the back while saying newcomers would come and go? Probably not, but it sounded that way. And the skeletal melody made it difficult not to pay attention to the words. With "Standing on the Moon," Garcia sounds like he was on the verge of a brilliant melody and chord scheme, but chose not to work any further on the song after getting the basic idea. The lyrics have Garcia surveying the world's troubles and sound as though they were influenced by Louis Armstrong's 1968 song "What a Wonderful World," which became a surprise hit after being used in the movie *Good Morning, Vietnam* in 1988—the year before the band debuted "Standing on the Moon" on stage.

That was it for Garcia for this album, although it wasn't the last of his studio recordings to be released. He came off more inspired and more in his element on two albums he recorded in the early 1990s with David Grisman, *Garcia/ Grisman* from 1991 and *Not for Kids Only* from 1993. His final recorded performance can be heard with the Jerry Garcia Band on the soundtrack of the 1995 film *Smoke*, director Wayne Wang's comic drama about a motley band of characters that frequent a Brooklyn tobacco shop. For the film, Garcia and company cut a version of Otis Redding's "Cigarettes and Coffee" and a rendition of the standard "Smoke Gets in Your Eyes," which was co-written by Garcia's namesake, Jerome Kern. It stands as one of the more uncanny moments in Dead history that one of the last studio recordings made by Garcia was a cover of a song written by the composer after whom he was named.

Built to Last is rounded out by two of Weir's most powerful songs, "Picasso Moon" and "Victim or the Crime." The first is a Chuck Berry–styled rocker, the second a tortured-sounding account of drug addiction with lyrics by the actor Gerrit Graham. With its ascending chord scheme and soul-baring lyrics, "Victim" is one of the most intense songs Weir ever sang, if not the most pleasant. The fact that its lyrics could have been directed at Garcia, who was falling back into hard drugs around this time, makes it all the more powerful.

Built to Last might have worked better as an album if it had captured at least some of the band's onstage power. The production, again by Garcia and Cutler, comes off as too quintessentially '80s, with its synthesizer plings and electronic percussion effects. The sound is so locked in that decade, in fact, that some of the songs seem as though they'd fit right in with the Reagan era one-hit wonder tunes collected on the *Living in Oblivion* compilations. The reason for the sonic spaciness, it was said, was that the band members mostly recorded their parts separately as overdubs and were rarely in the same room at the same time the album was recorded. But some of it was just that the band was trying to make a record that fit in with the times. The trouble was that "the times" back then meant hair bands and dance music, at least as far as Top 40 went.

By the early 1990s, bands that the Dead had inspired, such as Blues Traveler and Phish, were already making commercial inroads. Had the Dead conjured up an album of the material they'd penned after Mydland passed away, they might have been able to go out on a high note. *Built to Last* is a compelling album due to the power of Mydland's songs, but it was a lesser record than a band of the Dead's stature should have made.

Built to Last was released on October 31, 1989. It entered the Billboard album chart on November 25 and rose to #27.

The 2004 CD reissue offers three live recordings as bonus tracks. "Foolish Heart" and "Blown Away" date from July 19, 1989, while the band's cover of country artist Rodney Crowell's ballad "California Earthquake (Whole Lotta Shakin' Goin' On)" dates from October 20, 1989, just after San Francisco had experienced the traumatic Loma Prieta Earthquake, which left more than three thousand people injured.

Not included on the reissue is the Garcia-Hunter outtake "Believe It or Not," an early 1960s-styled ballad in 6/8 time that had been placed on the 1999 box set *So Many Roads (1965–1995)* and can be heard live on the *Spring 1990* box set. Also not included on the CD reissue but featured on *So Many Roads* is the Mydland outtake "Gentlemen, Start Your Engines," a song that's an allegory about drinking that was co-written with Barlow.

13

New Ones Comin' as the Old Ones Go

Why There Are Two *Aoxomoxoas*

C hange was in the air when the members of the Grateful Dead convened in late 1968 to record their third album, *Aoxomoxoa*. The Dead were looking to move away from the experimental approach of their previous album, *Anthem of the Sun*, and concentrate on a more song-oriented format, which was largely the result of Jerry Garcia's forming a strong songwriting partnership with his old friend and pre-Dead musical collaborator, Robert Hunter. The album's songs might have been more conventional, but their arrangements weren't. Bells, harpsichords, and all manner of unconventional percussion and vocal parts adorned the songs on *Aoxomoxoa*, and the shadow of psychedelic music still hung over the proceedings—all of which would come to seem awfully dated, quaint even, by 1970.

Perhaps this is one reason several members of the band went back into the studio two years after it was recorded to remix and re-edit this album and the one before it. Legend has it that the master tapes were lost (they've since been found), but if that was the only reason the Dead went back to remix the tapes, they could have just handed the job to a recording engineer with instructions to recreate the mixes they'd originally done. It certainly would have been simpler to do it that way.

Instead, Garcia and Phil Lesh went back into the studio sometime in 1971 and reworked significant portions of their second and third albums. With the second album, the remixing wasn't so drastic, and the remixed version of the album was only in print from the early 1970s until the CD era. But with *Aoxomoxoa*, the remix became the standard mix, with the original mix going on to become a rarity until it was reissued as part of a 2010 box set that contained the band's first five studio albums. So, what listeners get when they pop *Aoxomoxoa* into their CD players is revisionist history, courtesy of the Grateful Dead.

What's Become of the Album

To understand why the members of the Dead wanted to revise their own history, you have to look at the music scene at the time of *Aoxomoxoa*. You also have to examine the circumstances behind the recording of it and consider why it represents an important turning point in the band's recorded oeuvre—possibly *the* most important turning point.

When the Dead went into the recording studio to record *Aoxomoxoa*, musical trends were a-changin'. Big time. Lots of the groups that had sprung up in the wake of psychedelia had given up after an album or three (e.g., Clear Light, the Peanut Butter Conspiracy, Ultimate Spinach) or continued playing to diminished audiences (e.g., the Seeds, Love, the Blues Magoos). Psychedelic rock was yesterday's news, like Merseybeat or rockabilly. No one knew then that all these genres would get revived and then revived again in the next few decades, or that the artists who helped shape them would become legends. All the Dead knew then was that the genre they had helped pioneer had quickly become passé, putting the band's viability in danger. When it came to studio records, "going psychedelic" began to appear quaint, although some of the influence of that genre (such as longer songs and lots of jamming) would infuse live albums, such as the one the Dead would released in 1969, *Live/Dead*.

In 1968, though, a lot of rock's heavyweight acts, such as the Beatles and Bob Dylan, had moved away from their more unconventional music and lyrics and were crafting more roots-oriented songs and sounds. This was partially in response to some of the newer bands that had become popular in 1968, such as Creedence Clearwater Revival and the Band, both of whom eschewed psychedelic weirdness in favor of plainspoken lyrics and a more down-home sound. It was the last of these acts that the Grateful Dead seemed to be channeling for some of the songs on *Aoxomoxoa*, the first album on which the Dead start to sound like they represent an American experience, not just a San Francisco experience.

Aoxomoxoa is also significant because it showed a change in the power dynamic within the band, one that would remain in place until the band dissolved in the wake of Garcia's death in 1995. On the first two albums, compositions were group efforts, cover versions of old songs, or song sections divided among band members. But power struggles within the group, which saw a period of Bob Weir and Pigpen being asked to leave the band, led to Garcia and Hunter becoming the Dead's de facto composers for a while. Garcia's first bid for control was on *Aoxomoxoa*, where he co-wrote and sang lead on all the songs. His back-to-basics musical vision, coupled with Hunter's Americana-infused lyrics, can now be seen as a dry run for the country- and bluegrass-oriented albums the band would record and release in 1970, *Workingman's Dead* and *American Beauty*. Although Lesh is credited with co-writing the music on the original vinyl edition of *Aoxomoxoa*, on the CD releases he only gets co-composition for one track, the opening "St. Stephen," so maybe the original album's credit had to do with his help with arrangements. Songs by the Garcia-Hunter team would soon make up most of the Dead's repertoire and give it some of its most important songs, even though other band members would go on to write a lot of great tracks. So, with *Aoxomoxoa*, the idea of the Dead being Garcia's baby was firmly established on record.

Whether Garcia's power grab was good for the band's chemistry at the time is up for debate, because Pigpen and Weir were unhappy with having their musicianship called into question. But it turned out to be good for the music. Garcia pushed the band into new, more rootsy territory, which fit the group better since it did have roots as an acoustic jug band that played traditional tunes.

As much as the Dead wear the psychedelic tag, they never seemed comfortable experimenting with some of the hallmarks of psychedelic music, which included backward tapes, song suites with multiple sections, and songs with abrupt changes in texture or tempo. *Aoxomoxoa*, despite its trippy, palindrome title, is the first Dead album on which Garcia's country and bluegrass roots begin to show, and these roots would inform the band's music until its end. The Garcia-Hunter team seemed tailor-made for this type of music. The former's taut, sinewy melody lines were a perfect fit for a more homey, acoustic sound, while the latter could seemingly evoke all manner of Americana by writing just a few lines.

And yet they were still, like, the Dead from San Francisco, you know? They couldn't totally leave psychedelia behind. So, *Aoxomoxoa* became a musical compromise of sorts. Some of the eight songs were relatively conventional country rock tunes that wouldn't have been out of place on the two studio albums that followed. But they're given arrangements that still look back to the psychedelic era, sometimes making them sound weird for the sake of weirdness. This is very noticeable on the original version of the album, but is toned down considerably on the remix. *Aoxomoxoa* did contain one foray into total weirdness: the spooky, droning chant "What's Become of the Baby," which is sort of the Dead's own "Revolution 9." But that track is the exception here, not the rule.

One Man Gathers What Another Man Spills

Part of the reason for the musical oddness is that the band had added a new keyboardist, Tom Constanten, during the recording sessions for their previous album, *Anthem of the Sun*. Constanten, a modern classical composer, is credited on that release with playing prepared piano and "electronic tape" and was helping the band move beyond the garage rock sound that permeated its self-titled debut album. So, he remained for *Aoxomoxoa*, although this time around, Garcia (who you have to assume was calling the shots with Weir and Pigpen in abstentia) used him to color a bunch of regular tunes, not to spill his electronic weirdness wholesale onto the tapes. *Aoxomoxoa* would be Constanten's last studio effort with the group. There was little place for him as the Dead edged toward a more mainstream direction, and on stage, he "never got over a certain stiffness," as Lesh once said, and it's hard to imagine a less stiff band in concert than the Dead.

So the Dead were caught between two worlds for this crucial third release. On the one hand, they were a trippy psychedelic band. Yet on the other, they were the emerging country rock–oriented unit people came to know and love later on. Musically speaking, the latter role suited the Dead better. Their more

The original 1969 mix of *Aoxomoxoa* can be found on the 2010 box set *The Warner Bros. Studio Albums*, which also contained an illustrated booklet, a poster, and a re-pressing of the "Dark Star" single. *Courtesy of Rhino Records*

avant garde music was never as intelligent as that of Frank Zappa and their attempts to get freaky on *Anthem of the Sun* proved more annoying than revelatory. For that release, it sounded as though the band had taken a bunch of good songs and severely damaged them by messing around with tape splicing and speed alterations. Not surprisingly, that album wasn't very successful chartwise. But the Dead camp must have worried a bit when the more commercial *Aoxomoxoa* was a chart disappointment, getting to only Number 73 on the Billboard album chart.

The original version of the album explains why: Garcia simply doesn't sound confident yet. On "Dupree's Diamond Blues," his first vocals sound directed inward, as though he were uncomfortable singing Hunter's somewhat bawdy, blues-tinged lyrics about a man willing to rob a jewelry store and go to jail to get some "jelly roll" (a sexual expression that emanates from blues slang). On "Doin' That Rag," his singing can barely be heard because it is buried way down in the mix. Why so shy? The same goes for "Cosmic Charlie," which sounds far more unfocused the first time around.

That might have been the way *Aoxomoxoa* remained for the ages had the Dead not decided to pursue the country rock implicit in most of its tunes—and had the Dead not succeeded with that very style. A few years later, after *Workingman's Dead* and *American Beauty* brought the band a bigger audience and a few minor hit singles, *Aoxomoxoa* must have started to seem to the band like the little album that couldn't. This couldn't have sat well with its creators, as some of the songs are equally as good if not superior to what the band put on those hit albums, even if those hit albums were more consistent song-wise.

So, Garcia went back into the studio with Lesh and did something virtually unheard of in rock at that point. They decided to make like it was the 1980s (and beyond) and do a remix. But they weren't gearing up to make the album ready for the dance floor, as future remixers would. Instead, they went back to the original *Aoxomoxoa* sixteen-track tapes and recorded some new parts, removed some old parts, edited some songs here and there, and remixed the entire album. Then, they put the album out again with the same catalog number and a small legend on the back noting that there had been a remix. This retooling gave *Aoxomoxoa* a much-needed sonic upgrade. When fans bought the new edition in 1971 or later, they heard a sound that wasn't completely different from what they'd come to expect from the band in the early 1970s. In other words, the new-model *Aoxomoxoa* makes the album more palatable to fans who came aboard during the Dead's country-oriented phase. That was the good part.

The bad part was that the Dead and their co-conspirators, the record label, rewrote history by changing an album after the fact. Although people tamper with albums all the time these days, remixes come out on a separate album or a single, not a modified version of the original, unless that modification is appended to the album's title somewhere.

What would have happened if other bands from the 1960s had gone back to albums, done some tampering, and then slipped them out in the same jackets? Imagine, if you will, the Beatles returning to the 1965 release *Rubber Soul* in, say, 1967 and saying, "Hey, those last-minute background vocals we did on 'You Won't See Me' are kind of hoarse—let's re-sing 'em!" Beatles fans might just have started bonfires to torch the reissue copies they bought. Or imagine the Rolling Stones unearthing "(I Can't Get No) Satisfaction" two years later, and reworking the lead guitar line so that listeners no longer have to hear the awkward "click" that happens every time Keith Richards steps on his distortion pedal. How would the Stones' fans have taken this? It would have been considered an outright deception and a scandal might have ensued, with the band's musical integrity being called into question.

Decades later, in the mid-1980s, Frank Zappa took the Mothers of Invention's classic 1968 album *We're Only in It for the Money* and released it with re-recorded drums and bass. Howls of protest can still be heard if you listen long enough or peruse the Zappa message boards online. This sort of thing doesn't go over well with fans who get attached to the sound of a record as much as its songs. But not too many people had bought *Aoxomoxoa* to begin with, and it was never considered a classic on the level of the aforementioned Mothers of Invention album. So, not too many people complained about the reworking of *Aoxomoxoa*, if they noticed it at all.

Tell Me, What's the Matter?

But if the Dead's revisionist history resulted in a better album to listen to, well, what's the matter, really? Ethics aside, it's hard to listen to the retooled *Aoxomoxoa* and not think that Garcia and Lesh did the right thing. It especially sounds great if you compare it to the rather flaccid-sounding original. The second time around, guitars snap, keyboards crackle, and drums pop. With the first go-round, most of the mixes came off sounding rather dead, and not in the good, capital-letter sense of that word. By 1971, the group's mastery of their instruments and vocals had been sharpened after several years on the road. Their studio know-how was also much greater after recording two subsequent albums that became hits and were even celebrated by rock critics (who never much took to the band). And it shows in the way Garcia and Lesh messed with *Aoxomoxoa*.

The new vocals dubbed onto "Dupree's Diamond Blues" are far more confident; Garcia's impish delivery puts Hunter's story across far better. On the remix front, "St. Stephen" rocks harder and sounds clearer, and the jam at the end of "China Cat Sunflower" doesn't drone on beyond its welcome. The Dead were also liberal with re-editing some of the songs here; for example, "Doin' That Rag" loses its out-of-place a cappella tag the second time around.

Overall, the redone *Aoxomoxoa* features a brighter, more cohesive sound than its elder cousin does. Drums no longer have an unconvincing thud but jump out of the mix. Guitars chime instead of drone, and virtually all of the vocals sound punchier. Some of the strange percussion parts played by second drummer Mickey Hart are toned down or dropped from the mix entirely. But you can't please all of the people all of the time. On the *Grateful Breed* blog, some fans of the band seemed dismissive of Garcia's revision of the album, preferring the original. "This original mix seems like a completely different record, and IMHO much better," wrote one commenter.

People looking to hear the original mix of this LP can find it now as part of *The Warner Bros. Studio Albums* vinyl box set, a package containing the band's first five studio albums on 180-gram vinyl—plus a bonus single of the studio version of "Dark Star" backed with "Born Cross-Eyed" in a different mix. The current CD reissue of *Aoxomoxoa*, which is the widely available version, features the reworked album and also contains four live bonus cuts peripherally related to the studio songs.

If this album gets remastered again for CD, the compilers should think about ditching the bonus live cuts, which would work better if they were placed on a separate live album from this period in the Dead's career (a period that has relatively few live recordings, so a full album would be something fans would want). In place of the live cuts, the entire original mix of *Aoxomoxoa* could be added. Each version of the album runs fewer than forty minutes, and both could easily fit on an eighty-minute compact disc, which would give fans a chance to compare and contrast one version of the album with the other.

The following is a list of the alterations the Grateful Dead made when it reentered the recording studio in 1971 to rework *Aoxomoxoa*. These changes do not include equalization settings, which are drastically different throughout all the tracks and make the treble much brighter and the bass much deeper than on the original.

"St. Stephen"

◆ Garcia's lead vocals were re-recorded (the line "Now and then" stands out as particularly different) and moved from the left channel to the center.

◆ Bells were added on the bridge.

◆ Garcia's phased guitar was moved from left to right.

◆ Mickey Hart's percussion was removed from the guitar break before the first solo.

◆ Handclaps that start at 2:28 in the original are removed for the remix.

◆ Lesh's harmony vocals were moved from right to center and lowered.

"Dupree's Diamond Blues"

◆ Garcia's lead vocals were re-recorded.

◆ Lesh's bass part was re-recorded.

◆ Bill Kreutzmann's drum track was either redone or an alternate drum track on the master tape was used.

◆ A glockenspiel present on the original chorus was brought way down in the mix.

◆ Garcia's acoustic guitar was moved from left to right.

◆ Constanten's organ was moved from right to left.

◆ An extended bass note at the end was faded early, chopping the song's length.

"Rosemary"

◆ Garcia's vocals were brought up in the mix and more flanger effect was added.

◆ A new acoustic lead guitar was recorded (or was retrieved from the master tape) and used in the left channel.

◆ The song fades out a few seconds earlier.

"Doin' That Rag"

◆ The drum track was brought from the left to the center and given much more prominence.

◆ Mickey Hart's percussion track, heard originally on the left channel, was removed.

◆ The "Woo-hoo!" someone yells after the first half of the first chorus is removed in the remix.

◆ The remix fades out; the original resolves in an ending, followed by an a cappella mock-barbershop quartet coda.

"Mountains of the Moon"

◆ The remix moves Garcia's acoustic guitar from right to center.

◆ Constanten's harpsichord was moved to the left channel and given much less echo.

◆ The high-pitched, ghostly background vocals that start around forty seconds in were removed in the remix.

"China Cat Sunflower"

◆ The introduction starts in a different place.

◆ Garcia's vocal was flanged.

◆ Extra keyboard parts, including a glissando just before the second verse, were removed.

◆ The jam at the end of the remix is faded out early, shortening the track by a half minute.

"What's Become of the Baby"

◆ Introductory sound effect noises are removed for the remix.

◆ Backwards tapes and vocal effects on the original are removed for the remix.

◆ Garcia's lead vocals are mixed through a lot of echo.

◆ The sound effects that end the song were faded early, shortening it by a half minute.

"Cosmic Charlie"

◆   The introductory drumming and noises have been removed.

◆   Garcia's lead vocals were moved from left to center and brought way up in the mix.

◆   Lesh's harmony vocals were brought way down.

14

I Was There

Bob Weir on Haight-Ashbury and Monterey Pop

Bob Weir hadn't yet turned twenty when the Grateful Dead performed at the historic Monterey International Pop Music Festival on June 18, 1967. The event, which attracted up to ninety thousand people, was one of the high points of what the media later dubbed "The Summer of Love." Here, Weir speaks about that heady period in the Dead's history.

The Summer of Love was pretty much the death knell of what was happening, of the little renaissance that we had in San Francisco in the mid-1960s. If you ask anybody who lived in the Haight-Ashbury before the Summer of Love, they'll all tell you the same thing. I think that the summer before it and the year before it were special.

Before the Summer of Love, the Haight-Ashbury was a youth ghetto where the students who went to San Francisco State all stayed. It was a low-rent area where kids would flock to, and there were lots of artists and musicians and writers. And people who were studying and making art. It was sort of an artist's ghetto. It was a really, really fun place. The horizons were totally limitless there. The media just couldn't understand that. It was beyond them.

And so they sensationalized what they could understand: the drugs, the free love—all those aspects of what may or may not have been happening there. So then the area became immediately a magnet for all the riff raff and misfits and such who were rattling around the country. They just rattled on out to the coast and set up camp in the Haight-Ashbury. And it changed overnight, the complexion of the place. Suddenly the streets were full of speed freaks and drug addicts and it was just a very different place. We moved out.

I figured it was over. At the time I didn't want it to be over, but we had to call a spade a spade there. First, we moved further up the hill away from the Haight-Ashbury, but still stayed in the city. Then, as soon as we mustered the wherewithal, we got out of town entirely.

Down in Monterey

It was like stepping into a dream. It was a fairly spectacular dream, but it was sort of slow motion. Everything was there just like everybody expected it—all the big stars, all the excitement. But the excitement was sort of low-key excitement. I don't know how to describe it better than that.

My personal recollections are a couple. I was playing in the Guild Guitars exposition tent with a collection of guys. It just started off with me and a bass player and a drummer. The Guild Guitar folks sort of herded us together and got us in there and got us playing. One by one, a few other folks stepped in. I knew Paul Simon; he stepped up. We were plugged into amplifiers, but he was playing an acoustic guitar. I tried to make mention to him over the din that maybe he might want to grab an electric guitar and plug that in—I had an extra channel on my amplifier. And he said no, he was content to play the acoustic guitar—we might not hear him but we could feel the vibrations. So I sort of went with that; I figured, OK.

Then a couple of minutes later another kid came in. This guy was a tall, skinny black kid with a headband. And the last place for him to plug in was the other channel of my amplifier, which is where he plugged in. We had a lot of fun and played for a good long while. The jam devolved into a lot of feedback and your basic spooky noisemaking session. We were hanging off the amplifier like a couple of crazed monkeys, and anyway, I developed a friendship with the guy and it turned out to be Jimi Hendrix, unsurprisingly. I didn't know him at the time. So that's one recollection.

Another would be when I was onstage when the Who played. We played either right before or right after them, I can't remember which. They went into I guess it was "My Generation." They went into their demo derby routine, and there were guitar and amplifier parts flying everywhere. And a guitar came sailing over at me. I had to sort of fend myself off. I grabbed the neck. I was just holding it and I was about to hand it to a girl sitting next to me. (She was a fan of ours and the girl that ended up running our fan club for years—our oldest and best fan, a girl named Sue.) I was about to hand it to her, and one of the roadies ran up and grabbed it from me and said, "We put these back together"—which surprised me. It looked good and goddamned broken to me.

That Summer

It makes me put stock in what it was that we discovered back then that still makes sense—that sense of openness, that sense of anything is possible. I still retain that. Let me rephrase that. It makes me put stock in what it was that we discovered back then that still makes sense and that I still use in my life now: that sense of openness, that sense of anything is possible. I still retain that. I should probably employ that more, but I employ that in the music I play all the time.

The propensity to question authority is something that I've taken with me from that era. Kids by nature are given to questioning authority. They're a little bit on the rebellious side. There were so many of us. There was such a preponderance of us in society at that time on account of the Baby Boomers that rebelliousness became somewhere between the rock 'n' roll aesthetic and the basic human nature of kids. That rebellion became something of an institution. I've at least retained that. I question authority all the time. My own included.

Portions of this interview ran in the August, 17, 2007, issue of Goldmine *magazine.*

Bob Weir hadn't yet turned twenty when the Grateful Dead performed at the Monterey International Pop Music Festival on Sunday, June 18, 1967. The youngest Dead member (until Brent Mydland and Vince Welnick arrived later), Weir was considered the "kid" of the group early on, but ended up carrying the band on stage during their final years.

Courtesy of Relix Media Group

15

Looks Like Rain

Why the Dead Didn't Really Blow It at Woodstock

S ince the early 1970s, countless tapes of fan-recorded Grateful Dead concerts have changed hands. Since 1993, thirty-six soundboard recordings of Dead concerts have been released as part of the *Dick's Picks* series, and those CDs sometimes contain snippets of other concerts. On top of all that, there are two other concert series that have been issued on multi-CD sets, and the Dead have released a lot of live albums that have nothing to do with any series at all. It's not a stretch to say that they have put out more live recordings than any other band has.

But one live show that's not likely to ever see a CD release is the Grateful Dead's performance at the Woodstock Music and Art Fair on the evening of Saturday, August 16, 1969. Depending on which source you believe, the show was either bad, awful, or worse than anyone could have imagined. Why would a band who made their name with live performances, not albums, perform poorly at the biggest gig of its career up to that point? There were apparently several reasons. First, there was the weather, which was bad. Then, there were technical problems with the group's sound system. Finally, there were the drugs the band members were taking, which they may have been better off ingesting after they had played, not before.

The Dead's troubles at Woodstock are briefly touched upon in several books, but not really detailed fully anywhere. So, the best way to get a sense of what really went down on that historic night—which included performances by Creedence Clearwater Revival, Janis Joplin with the Kozmic Blues Band, and Sly and the Family Stone—is to listen to the actual tapes themselves. They're easily accessible and can be streamed on the website Archive.org. The site is an online digital library that allows users to access old web pages through its Wayback Machine and also allows Deadheads to listen to a lot of their favorite band's shows thanks to other Deadheads who upload old tapes.

In the case of the Woodstock gig, the fan responsible for letting the world hear how the Dead played is Bill Koucky, who recorded the group on a Panasonic SV-3700 eight-track machine at fifteen inches per second and then transferred his original reels to digital audio tape. (Note: Recordings at Archive.org are sometimes removed from the site; this is the recording that was uploaded to the website in 2008 and remains online as of this writing.)

Click the Play button on the page's embedded player, and what you hear is . . . actually not that bad. Granted, it's nowhere near a first-rate Dead gig. There's a false start to one song and a ten-minute interruption while the band's crew sorted out technical problems. But there are no out-of-tune guitars, embarrassing missed musical cues, or frighteningly bad vocals—all of which have been known to be heard on bootleg recordings of *other* bands who shall remain nameless.

The set list didn't flow well and wasn't really appropriate for a big crowd that was probably not very familiar with the band. But it won't sound odd to anyone who followed the Dead over the years and/or owns live CDs. The worst you can say about this show is that the group's playing is dull, their singing sounds disengaged, and their set list could have been better thought out.

As in a lot of cases like this one, the legend is more dramatic than the actual event. And as the decades have passed, the legend continues to grow. If the folks in Deadland put the Woodstock gig out as a CD, fans wouldn't exactly go wild over the performance, but they wouldn't be put off, either. Still, it makes for a better story for band members to lament how awful they were instead of saying that their playing was merely blah. Garcia definitely waxed dramatic in an interview published in Blair Jackson's book *Garcia: An American Life*. "Jeez, we were awful!" he said. "We were just plumb *atrocious!*"

The disconnect between what the band members remember about their performance and how it actually sounds to fans now makes for amusing reading on Archive.org, where most of the comments on the Woodstock gig are positive. Reviewer "TimothyHorrigan," for example, rates the recording "4.00 out of 5 stars" and notes that while the show is "legendary for being the worst show the Dead ever did," he's "already dug up much worse shows. (Like, for example, their last show in August 1995, sadly.)"

Where did he get the idea that the show was that bad? "I . . . heard Jerry Garcia refer to it as such on late night TV in the early 1980s," he writes. "It makes an amusingly ironic story that the Dead would play their worst show ever at Woodstock—but in fact the recording is quite listenable. The 'Mama Tried' is actually good. . . . Even the stage banter has a certain charm to it, although I am glad I wasn't a member of the crew who worked on this event."

As it turns out, it's the circumstances surrounding the Dead's performance that were the worst part of their Woodstock experience, and that's what seems to have colored the memories of the band members and their crew ever since.

By the Time They Got to Woodstock . . .

As many have noted, the weather at Woodstock was problematic, with enough rain to prompt the people in the crowd to go into an anti-rain chant at one point (it didn't work).

Bob Weir spoke about this in an August 1989 *Rolling Stone* article written to commemorate the twentieth anniversary of the event titled "Woodstock Remembered." Said Weir, "It was raining toads when we played. The rain was part of our nightmare." Weir went on to say that "the other part was our sound-man, who decided that the ground situation on the stage was all wrong. It took him about two hours to change it, which held up the show. He finally got it set the way he wanted it, but every time I touched my instrument I got a shock. The stage was wet and the electricity was coming through me."

When the Dead set up camp at Woodstock midway through the event, they were venturing into uncharted territory—an unnerving undertaking. Just before their Saturday performance got underway, the crowd was starting to swell to just under a half million people. Food started to become scarce. There was no precedent for a gathering as large as Woodstock, and the feeling was that disaster could happen at any time. It didn't, of course, but everyone's worst fear about festivals was realized several months later during a gathering at California's Altamont Speedway Free Festival, where the Dead refused to play because of the threat of impending violence.

When I interviewed the Dead's longtime sound engineer, Bob Matthews, in 2009 for an MSNBC.com article about the fortieth anniversary of Woodstock, he said that the Dead's crew was "overwhelmed" by the size and scope of the festival as well as the rain.

"It was more than we were prepared for as far as the enormity of the task, of the number of people who showed up, and the logistics of having that many people in a cow pasture," Matthews said.

Joey Reynolds, who was a Top 40 disc jockey at the time, told me in an interview for the same story that the massive amount of traffic leading into the festival created a chaotic situation like he'd never seen before: "There were all these roads leading to one road that had thousands of cars. At first, we thought there was a little weekend traffic that was going to stop somewhere—and it didn't. It just got worse and worse and bigger and bigger and there were more and more people."

Matthews notes that the traffic situation intimidated the people in the Dead's camp: "When we arrived there, just getting our rental cars from there to the performance area was sort of like Never Never Land. It was amazing to see all these cars and all these people. 'How do we get from point A to point B, because there's no way to drive?' It was an adventure."

In the book *The Road to Woodstock: From the Man Behind the Legendary Festival*, festival producer Michael Lang notes that more troubles came the Dead's way when their road crew started to unload their gear: "As [the Dead] were loading their heavy equipment onto the forty-foot turntable onstage, the platform wheels collapsed. This caused a delay, which was lengthened when the Dead insisted that their soundman Owsley Stanley rewire the stage for their set. Tinkering with the sound system and their hook-ups resulted in constant shocks from the guitars."

When I asked Matthews what he believed the worst thing about the Dead's time at Woodstock was, he replied, "The fact that it rained, and the mud that we had to deal with. The electrical grounding hadn't been thought through far

How bad were they? Not very. The Dead's Woodstock performance wasn't brilliant, but they did a decent enough job showcasing the talents of the two front men from the band's early era, Jerry Garcia and Pigpen, shown here on volume ten, issue number one of *Relix* magazine. Garcia sounds believably forlorn on the then-unreleased "High Time," while Pigpen rocks the house on a forty-seven-minute version of "Turn On Your Love Light."
Courtesy of Relix Media Group

enough to the point of what happens if it does rain and we do have all this mud. There were hums, buzzes, and lots of electrical shocks. I remember Bob Weir jumping back five feet when he went up to touch the microphone the first time."

The Music Sometimes Stopped

On the concert recording, the Dead's Woodstock segment doesn't start promisingly, as it kicks off with three minutes of stage announcements and fumbling about by the group. An unfamiliar voice keeps saying things that don't make much sense. Turns out the voice belongs to Ken Babbs, a member of the Merry Pranksters, the group that were friendly with the Dead and that made it their mission to promote psychedelic drug use. Now that makes sense.

Speaking of drugs, Garcia claimed in Jackson's book that substances impaired his playing that night: "I was high and I saw blue balls of electricity bouncing across the stage and leaping onto my guitar when I touched the strings." Drugs were also in the air, quite literally. As the Dead's then manager, Rock Scully, recounts in his 1996 book (co-written with David Dalton) *Living with the Dead: Twenty Years on the Bus with Garcia and the Grateful Dead*:

> In the middle of their very first number, "St. Stephen," this crazy guy we know runs out into the middle of the stage and started flinging LSD off the stage . . . Okay, his acid is *purple*, but it looks brown. Oh no, it's the brown acid—the acid you're . . . *not supposed to take*. When Garcia sees this mad, crazy guy throwing what looks like brown acid off the stage, something he might under normal circumstances have thought droll and antic now looks ominous. He is asking himself the question men zonked out of their minds on psychotropic substances should never ask themselves: "Why *me*?"

The Dead's first number at Woodstock was a truncated rendition of "St. Stephen," notable mostly because it barely passes the two-minute mark. Was the Dead pioneering the short song form that the Ramones would make famous a few years later? No, it's more like the Dead felt the song wasn't working, so they simply decided to cut it short. But it doesn't really sound all that bad, just a bit stiff. And according to Scully, the weather continued to pose a problem. He went on to say that the group played "horribly" and couldn't "get it right. Not one song." The sound, he said, was awful and the weather remained windy and unseasonably chilly.

Considering all that, maybe the Dead should have segued from "St. Stephen" into one of their favorite old covers, the traditional song "Cold Rain and Snow." Instead, they moved directly into Merle Haggard's "Mama Tried," which was not one of the smoothest transitions they ever attempted. Weir's voice sounds shaky, and they all sound like they're afraid to really lay into the music, but Garcia does throw in a few cool guitar leads. His harmonies don't come off too smoothly, but that's mostly because they're placed way up in the mix in front of the lead vocals, not behind them. Bad mixing does not a bad concert make.

But then the problems really start. After the Dead wrap up the Haggard number, the crowd gives up some enthusiastic applause, but then starts to chant, "Play louder!" This seems to get to the band, as Garcia then shakily asks, "You want it louder?" The Dead attempt to launch into the then-new tune "High Time," but it turns out to be a low time for them. What follows is a long break, where the band's crew members attempt to figure out why they can't turn the amps up to the proverbial eleven. It's never good to leave a crowd waiting, especially after you've already kept them waiting by taking forever to set up the stage, and this break couldn't have been good for the musicians' morale.

"It's a sinister plot," Weir says on the recording, referring either to the group's equipment problems or to the sheets of rain that were continuing to drench the crowd.

Next up is "Dark Star," which was given a rather upbeat and jazzy interpretation considering the downbeat circumstances. It runs around 20 minutes, which is a pretty normal length to anyone who has seen the band in concert and traded tapes. But it might have been a tad extensive for a crowd unfamiliar with the number, which wouldn't see an album release for a few months (a studio version had been released on 45, but it's unlikely that many in the crowd owned the record, which didn't chart).

Finally, the Dead get around to doing "High Time," but it's overshadowed by what comes next. And that's a forty-eight-minute rendition of their version of Bobby "Blue" Bland's "Turn On Your Love Light," with Pigpen on lead vocals. With Pigpen in the driver's seat, the Dead was always more aggressive, and that's no exception here. The Dead work up a good head of steam thanks to his enthusiasm, but it just might be too much of a good thing, what with the forty-five-minute-plus length.

Scully wasn't impressed with this performance. "Finally the Dead set finishes up with 'Lovelight,'" he writes. "But even Pigpen's sure-fire rabble-rouser can't quite pull it off."

Wanna Take You Higher—or Not

What's most disappointing about the Dead's Woodstock performance is something that fans and the band have danced around but never quite spoken about. The problem isn't what the Dead did at Woodstock, but what they failed to do. The Dead failed to make like Jimi Hendrix, or Janis Joplin, or Sly and the Family Stone, or the Who. In other words, the Dead failed at being transcendent and at pulling off a career-making or career-defining performance. It's unlikely that they picked up many new fans or even thrilled fans who were at the festival. Worst of all, it seems as if they disappointed themselves.

Granted, the festival is arguably the most famous rock-related event of all time and has become a cultural touchstone, so it's understandable why the Dead would beat themselves up about not being up to par on that particular night. Yet, all of this didn't matter for the band. Unlike the aforementioned performers, the Dead were a cult band and stayed a cult band for most of their career, and it's doubtful that even their best performance would have brought them to some imaginary "next level." The Dead didn't play the type of extroverted music that Hendrix and Joplin did or the Top 40 music performed by Creedence and Sly Stone. At that point in the band's history, they played the kind of music you had to contemplate to "get," and it's unlikely a festival audience would get what they were about with one listen. Also, the Dead hadn't yet written any of the crowd-pleasing numbers that would get fans up and dancing in the 1970s and beyond.

The Dead's performance at Woodstock didn't have any noticeable effect on their career at the time. In fact, the trio of albums they released just after the event—*Live/Dead*, *Workingman's Dead*, and *American Beauty*—all became the Dead's most successful albums to that date. So, a case could be made that just by getting their name out there, the Dead helped broaden their audience. And it's not as though the band failed to draw a concert audience following Woodstock, either.

The Grateful Dead didn't allow any of their set to be used for either the 1970 movie *Woodstock* or its accompanying soundtrack, *Woodstock: Music from the Original Soundtrack and More*. For years, the performance went unheard by anyone except Deadheads who knew where to look for it. But in August 2009, on the fortieth anniversary of the event, Rhino Records released a six-CD box set called *Woodstock—40 Years On: Back to Yasgur's Farm*, which contained the first officially released version of anything from the Dead's set. It featured "Dark Star."

Some live footage came out in 2009 on a multi-disc DVD set called *Woodstock 40th Anniversary Ultimate Collector's Edition* also released to cash in on (er, mark) the fortieth anniversary of the concert. At four hours long, it contains performances by acts not seen in the original release. It has previously unreleased footage of Creedence Clearwater Revival, Johnny Winter, Mountain, and . . . the Dead doing "Turn On Your Love Light." Writing in the *Examiner*, reviewer Shawn Perry was impressed with what he saw:

> There can be no doubt that Ron "Pigpen" McKernan's performance on "Turn On Your Love Light" was a highlight. If the surviving members of Grateful Dead can ever come to grips with what good came from their part in the festival, it should be the energy and soulfulness the late whisky-toting, R&B-singing organist brought to the party. The Dead would never be able to take this song to the same level of intensity after Pigpen's untimely passing in 1973.

But not everyone in the crowd took to what Pigpen was doing that evening. On Archive.org, a short segment titled "Applause, Stage Announcements" immediately follows the Dead's performance. A female voice is heard making a request in the middle, between announcements about "Richie who lost his chick" and "Dick Hyman of Westport" who needs to meet "Dr. French in the pink hospital tent." She makes the request twice: once in the middle, once at the end. What does she ask for? An encore of "Dark Star"? One more number sung by Pigpen? No, what she wants to know is, "Hey, when does Sly come on?"

Can't win 'em all.

Live/Dead

How the Dead Established the Double Live Rock Album

It was something you took for granted if you came of age during the 1970s: if a rock act wanted to stake a claim to importance and let people know it had *arrived*, that group had to release a live album somewhere along the way. And it had to be a double live album if anyone was going to take the band seriously.

Throughout the decade, double live albums were everywhere you looked, especially at the top of the charts. There was Peter Frampton's career-making two-fer *Frampton Comes Alive!*, which stayed at #1 for ten weeks in 1976 and had a fifty-five-week chart run. Kiddie metal purveyors KISS had only landed one album in the Top 40 charts until *Alive!* went gold after its 1975 release, hitting #9 and making the group a favorite with middle schoolers everywhere. Even the Bee Gees, who had turned their backs on rock for disco, went platinum with the 1977 double live release *Here at Last . . . Bee Gees . . . Live.*

Beyond being cash cows, double live albums were also artistic statements, a message that a band could cut it outside the confines of the increasingly high-tech studio world. The back-to-basics rock on Grand Funk Railroad's *Live Album*, from 1970, came off explosive even when played at a low volume. *At Fillmore East*, released the next year, showed that the Allman Brothers were a band whose instrumental prowess went far beyond what they'd shown on their two studio releases. Lynyrd Skynyrd's *One More from the Road*, from 1976, gave listeners four sides of proof that the pioneering Southern rockers were ten times more energetic in a live setting.

But the granddaddy of all these albums was the Grateful Dead's *Live/Dead*, a double album that came out November 10, 1969. The record was groundbreaking because it showed a wilder, more improvisational side of the band at which the group's three studio albums had barely hinted. Not only did *Live/Dead* help further the band's reputation as one of the premiere live acts of all time, but it made the live album itself a valid artistic and commercial entity—something it had never been in rock.

There had been double albums in rock before, with the most well known being Bob Dylan's *Blonde on Blonde*, the Mothers of Invention's *Freak Out*, the Beatles' self-titled 1968 effort, and Jimi Hendrix's *Electric Ladyland*. But the Dead were the first major band to put out a double live album, which was an especially audacious move when you consider that the live album was still in its infancy as a commercial force at that point.

Got Junk If You Want It

To understand why *Live/Dead* was such a game changer, we need to look back to the history of rock and see what live albums were before its release. For the most part, they weren't all that exciting. Usually live albums were considered cash-ins: a way for bands to put out some old songs, reap the rewards of their success, and not try anything much new.

In jazz, live albums had long been a viable artistic and commercial commodity because they were real-time demonstrations of musicians' skills. But rock was seen as a genre that was built on studio contrivances such as Sun Records' echo, Lesley Gore's double-tracked vocals, and the Beatles' massive overdubs, not improvisational brilliance, so live releases were usually considered an afterthought in any given artist's career.

This was also the case in rhythm and blues and soul. Even though James Brown's *Live at the Apollo* went to #2 in 1963 and now sits as part of the Library of Congress's collection, it didn't exactly inspire other performers to do the same. Sam Cooke's *Sam Cooke at the Copa* sounded like supper-club soul designed to appeal to a wary white audience. The more limited budgets of smaller rhythm and blues record labels may also have been a reason live albums didn't become popular among listeners of that style.

The best live disc from a rock 'n' roll band in the mid-1960s was probably the Beach Boys' *Beach Boys Concert*, which became the group's first #1 album shortly after it was released in October 1964. Although it's exciting to hear the California surf band at the top of its game on the LP, the record doesn't change the consensus that the group was ultimately a studio band.

Nor did it inspire a spate of similar albums. The Beatles didn't release a live album in the 1960s, claiming that the hordes of screaming tweenage girls at their concerts made recording anything of quality impossible (the Beatles did, however, agree to release those same concert tapes in 1977, after live albums became a commercial force). The Rolling Stones' sole live album of the 1960s, *Got Live If You Want It!* from 1966, is one of the worst concert albums ever, with embarrassing performances and obvious studio overdubbing. The Stones didn't even deem it worthy of release in England (although to be fair, they had released one of the record's songs on a UK-only live EP that was much better and less altered in the studio than the American album was).

In May 1970, the Who dropped their *Live at Leeds* album, and in September 1970, the Stones put out *Get Yer Ya-Ya's Out! The Rolling Stones in Concert*, a much better live release than their previous one. A few months before, the recently broken-up British blues group Cream had put out their first real live release, *Live Cream* (the group had previously released one disc of live material along with a disc of studio cuts on the double album *Wheels of Fire*). But with the possible exception of the Who, all of these records' designations as single albums made them appear as minor artistic statements, especially coming as they did in the shadow of *Live/Dead*.

Bring Out Your Dead

On *Live/Dead*, the Grateful Dead don't bother to acclimate you to the new, mysterious world you're about to enter. Instead, they plunge the unsuspecting listener directly into the abyss with the opening track, "Dark Star," the band's future signature jam tune that goes on for more than twenty minutes and is largely based around one chord. "Dark Star" draws as much from jazz as it does from rock and is unlike anything the band had put on an album to that point. Unlike the longer songs on the band's first two albums, its instrumental sections aren't an extrapolation of a melody established by vocals. It's the other way around: the instrumental jam is the tune itself, and the two vocal passages serve as adornment to the musical theme.

Back in the days of vinyl albums, the twenty-three-minute "Dark Star" took up the whole first side of the first disc. The second side at least put the listener back on familiar ground, as it starts with a live version of "St. Stephen," which had opened the previous album, *Aoxomoxoa*. Here its riff is expanded, a bridge is added (colloquially known as the "William Tell Bridge," after a lyric), and the song is joined with the long jam tune "The Eleven," named as such because of its tricky 11/8 time signature. Discussing this sequence with a Deadhead is like discussing the fact that the sun rises in the east and sets in the west. But to a new listener who hadn't gotten to see the Dead play by 1969, *Live/Dead* was a whole 'nother thing.

All of side three is devoted to Pigpen's fifteen-minute take on Bobby "Blue" Bland's "Turn On Your Love Light," while the fourth side has Jerry Garcia showing his bluesy side on a cover of the Reverend Gary Davis's "Death Don't Have No Mercy." Seven minutes of feedback and a short a cappella reading of the traditional "And We Bid You Goodnight" conclude the album. (The 2001 CD reissue adds the studio single version of "Dark Star," from April 1968, plus a radio ad.)

New Dead fans probably didn't quite know what to make of *Live/Dead*, except that it was like nothing they'd ever heard. Although the album only got to #64, it still charted higher than any previous Dead album, and its influence was far greater than its chart placement indicated. It also received critical praise. Robert Christgau, writing in his Consumer Guide column, gave the album a grade of A+ and said, "Side two of this four-sided set contains the finest rock improvisation ever recorded, and the rest is gently transcendent as usual. Beautifully recorded, too."

Lenny Kaye, who gave the album a positive write-up in *Rolling Stone*'s February 7, 1970, issue, opened his review on a praiseworthy note: "*Live/Dead*

"Dark Star" became known to most listeners in 1969 when it was featured as a side-long improvisational jam on *Live/Dead*. But it had been released as a single in April 1968, for which it was given an uncharacteristically fast studio arrangement. The single, which had a different mix of "Born Cross-Eyed" on the B-side, did not chart. *Courtesy of Sharon Balan*

explains why the Dead are one of the best performing bands in America, why their music touches on ground that most other groups don't even know exists."

Kaye was even more effusive about his fondness for the album in his closing paragraph. "I'm not going to end this by using some overworn phrase about how this is possibly the best live album ever a must for your record collection something no fan should be without etc. etc.," he wrote. "But if you'd like to visit a place where rock is likely to be in about five years, you might think of giving *Live/Dead* a listen or two."

In 2003, *Rolling Stone* would rank the album #247 in its list of the 500 Greatest Albums of All Time, making mention of how the Dead was in arrears to Warner Bros. after spending too much money recording studio albums: "After two expensive studio albums put them $100,000 in debt, this live set was more than just cheap, it was pivotal. For the Dead, the magic happened onstage, as demonstrated by the glorious 23-minute jam-outs on 'Dark Star' and a raging, 15-minute cover of Bobby Bland's '(Turn on Your) Love Light.'"

Around eight months after *Live/Dead*, the Dead's California contemporaries, the Doors, came out with their own double live set, *Absolutely Live*, and in November 1970, Grand Funk's aforementioned *Live Album* dropped. In July 1971, the Allman Brothers' live album was released. Humble Pie followed in November with the platinum-selling *Performance: Rockin' the Fillmore*, and all of a sudden the double live album was the album most every artist had to make (even if some bands did doctor up those albums in the studio, the Dead included). Before the '70s were out, it seemed every major rock act had to have one, including Aerosmith; the Beach Boys; Crosby, Stills, Nash and Young; Deep Purple; Genesis; Jethro Tull; Ted Nugent; Queen; and Bob Seger and the Silver Bullet Band. Bob Dylan released two: one by himself and one with the Band. So did KISS. Even non-rockers John Denver, Neil Diamond, and Barry Manilow got in on the act.

Double live albums had appeal beyond the music. They came in fold-out record jackets (called gatefolds) that opened up and let bands put extra photos or artwork on their inner folds. In the days before MTV and YouTube made seeing your favorite artist every day no big deal, extra photos of musicians who were usually only pictured once or twice on the front and back of albums seemed to be a gift. Sometimes double albums came with booklets inside that contained more photos or even a lyric sheet. *Live/Dead* had a book that contained the words to three of the group's originals on the album: "Saint Stephen," "The Eleven," and "Dark Star." All of this might seem trivial in the days of instant access to bands' multi-page websites, but during the time when rock albums were king, double live ones with extra art added up to a Big Statement on the part of artists.

It could even be argued that rock acts who released single-disc live LPs caused their careers to suffer. Fans had come to expect double albums because they approximated the running times of concerts more closely than single LPs did. Plus, double albums sent a sort of subconscious message to fans, telling them that the music of a given act was important enough to warrant two discs. First and foremost in this regard is Pat Travers, one of the best blues rockers of the late '70s, who dropped one of the hottest live albums of the decade in 1979 with *Live! Go for What You Know*. But as good as the album was, it was a one-disc set that probably had the unfortunate effect of making Travers seem more small-time than he actually was. Ditto Mott the Hoople and Laura Nyro, both innovate artists who dropped single-disc sets. And the same could be said to a lesser degree about Cheap Trick, whose 1978 release *Cheap Trick at Budokan* was a massive seller, but seemed a bit lacking in importance, clocking in at barely more than forty minutes.

The influence of the double live album resonated into the CD era, when country rocker Garth Brooks chose to call his 1998 concert album *Double Live*, just in case anybody missed the point.

But as the '70s rolled along, Garcia and company had one more trick up their collective sleeves when it came to setting the standard for live albums. And for their next move, they took a page out of the playbook of former Beatle George Harrison.

Go to Europe

In December 1971, Harrison upped the ante on live albums by coming out with a three-disc set made up of live performances done at an all-star charity concert he'd organized earlier in the year, the Concert for Bangladesh. It rose as high as #2 on the Billboard album chart. Harrison had already topped the charts when he released the first triple album in rock the year before with *All Things Must Pass*, his first solo album after leaving the Beatles. With the live triple album now a commercial entity, the Dead decided to try to do one too, with *Europe '72*, even though the Dead weren't quite the household name that any of the ex-Beatles were. Eventually, triple live albums would be released by Emerson, Lake and Palmer; Wings; and Yes. The triple live set never quite caught on like the double live album did, probably because it was expensive and teenagers only had so much money to spend.

But that didn't hold for the Dead. Not only did fans buy *Europe '72*, but it also became *the* Grateful Dead album to have, further establishing the live album as an almost mandatory release for any rock band that wanted to be taken seriously. After all, if the laid-back hippies in the Dead could come up with three albums of live material, surely other more commercially oriented bands should find a way to muster up two discs, right?

The Dead's three-disc live set had come on the heels of another two-disc live set, officially titled *Grateful Dead*, but called *Skull and Roses* because of the design on its cover. This album of mostly new material (most of which was cover songs) had followed the two country-rock efforts by the band, *Workingman's Dead* and *American Beauty*, that had brought them to a much wider audience. With seven discs of live material spread over three live albums, the Dead was clearly in the vanguard of the new live album craze, even if the band did let its studio side suffer in the process.

Skull and Roses got to #25 on the album chart, while *Europe '72* only notched one point higher but ended up eventually going platinum. Reviewing the album in the January 4, 1973, issue of *Rolling Stone*, Tom Dupree probably echoed the feeling of a lot of fans when he wrote, "I am convinced that God made the Grateful Dead so that they could be heard in concert." Concluded Dupree, "No record album can replace a live appearance by the Dead—but those who can't get enough of this exceptional band will be kept busy for a good little while with this one."

Europe '72 served a different function than *Live/Dead* did. Where *Live/Dead* showed how a rock band could use the double live set to push musical boundaries and surprise fans, *Europe '72* demonstrated how a live release could become a band's ultimate statement, meaning the type of album average rock music fans needed to own even if they had no other records by that particular band. *Europe '72* became the Dead release you had to have in much the way live albums by Skynyrd and Frampton became records everyone felt they needed to own. This is a situation that could never have happened in the 1960s, when studio creations such as *Sgt. Pepper's Lonely Hearts Club Band* and the Rolling Stones' *Let It Bleed* were considered "must-have" records.

The popularity of *Europe '72* in college dorms (and places beyond) ensured that the Dead never went with many seats unsold for live gigs and got to play bigger halls in the years following its release. It probably also spurred on fanatics of the band to start taping shows in hopes of recapturing lightning in a bottle. Decades after it came out, the album remained popular enough to warrant a sequel, *Europe '72 Volume 2*, a two-CD set that featured twenty tracks that were also recorded during the band's spring 1972 tour of Europe. The album's sequel came out in September 2011, the same month the seventy-three-CD mega box set, *Europe '72: The Complete Recordings*, dropped and became a near-instantaneous collector's item thanks to demand far outstripping supply. When it comes to anything *Europe '72*–related, it seems, Deadheads can't get enough.

The same can't be said for the rest of the world when it comes to live albums. Garth Brooks's 1998 CD set notwithstanding, the double live album became a relic of the 1970s when the music industry started to change in the 1980s. In the wake of the moving images offered by MTV, live albums started to seem static and old fashioned. Once concert videos hit the market in the form of VHS tapes and then DVDs, the idea of a live album where you couldn't actually see the band play seemed pointless.

In Deadland, though, things were different. The double live album continued to be popular, as the live show was considered the band's forte. But that didn't mean fans were indiscriminate about what the Dead put out. When the band released *Steal Your Face*, a 1976 set that Deadheads considered substandard, it quickly got nicknamed *Steal Your Money*. The group's subsequent double live releases, *Reckoning* and *Dead Set*, weren't met with the same amount of enthusiasm as the earlier live albums were. This was possibly because the element of surprise was gone and possibly because the massive amount of concert tape trading that was going on by 1981 made the albums seem anti-climactic.

But in its heyday, the double live album was the release you had to have if you were going to throw a party in your dorm room over the weekend, or if you just wanted to seriously rock out when there were no bands coming to town. The Dead and *Live/Dead* need to be given credit for this brief cultural phenomenon.

One Man Gathers

A Look at the *Dick's Picks* Live CD Series

T here's an old saying: "There is nothing like a Grateful Dead concert." That saying was proven right by the popularity of *Dick's Picks*, a thirty-six-volume series that showcased individual Dead concerts. The series, which was the first of its kind, proved so successful that it spawned several similar ones, all of which made the Dead the band with the most live releases in the history of rock.

The *Dick's Picks* series, which was named for the band's late tape archivist, Dick Latvala, who selected the shows to be released, was made up of unpolished, "soundboard" recordings directly captured to stereo tape without any studio polish or sweetening. Most recording acts would be lucky to be able to put out a handful of respectable-sounding concert tapes without having to do some remixing or editing in the recording studio. The fact that the Dead was able to drop three dozen such recordings on the market between 1993 and 2005 made a pretty good case to the outside world that the "tapers" at Dead shows had been right all along: most every gig this band played was worth hearing.

The series delivered some surprises to longtime Deadheads, the most prominent being the thirty-fifth volume, which saw the release of a show recorded on August 7, 1971, at Golden Hall in San Diego, California. The tapes of this show had previously been thought to be lost, and when they were found on a houseboat owned by the parents of the late Keith Godchaux, they became known as the "Houseboat Tapes."

Dick's Picks also gave a legitimate release to several of the most popular shows traded among fans on cassette in the 1970s and 1980s. Two examples include the December 19, 1973, show at the Curtis Hixon Hall in Tampa, Florida, which was selected for *Volume One*, and the May 2, 1970, show at Harpur College in Binghamton, New York, which became *Volume Eight*.

Here, finally, was a chance for everyone to experience what going to a classic Dead show was like. The CDs marked the first time that fans, especially new ones, were able to easily access recordings of legendary shows. Some of *Dick's Picks* may have sounded a little rough, but the sonic quality was a step up from most of the copies of tapes that average Deadheads were able to access.

Although non-professional archival recordings of rock bands are commonplace today, they were novel when *Dick's Picks* began. Few record companies or recording artists ever thought to document what artists were doing, because

The *Dick's Picks* CDs came with a standard maroon cover design for the first six volumes. With *Volume Seven*, unique designs showing ticket stubs began to be used for cover art. The CDs themselves sported designs that looked like tape reels.   *Author's collection*

few thought anyone would care in the distant future. The Dead sought to preserve their own legacy if only for themselves, so starting in the 1970s they began recording virtually all of their concerts through their mixing board (or soundboard) directly onto stereo tapes.

These tapes eventually came to be stored at the band's Club Front office inside temperature-controlled rooms that became known as the Vault and overseen by Latvala, who was appointed the band's official archivist in 1985. Before he came to work for the band, Latvala was a taper who had a private collection of more than a thousand tapes. He must have felt right at home in the Vault, as the Dead had tapes of most of the concerts they performed. It's hard to imagine any other rock group having a more extensive archive. According to Latvala's widow, Carol Latvala, it was Dead roadie and live recording engineer Bill "Kidd" Candelario who suggested putting the soundboard tapes out and naming the series *Dick's Picks*, because Latvala was overseeing the releases.

The releases turned out to be something of a true calling for Dick, according to Carol:

> He felt like finally he was getting to do the job he had come there to do, which is make this music available to the widest possible audience. When he first got his job as archivist, his job was mainly cataloging and listening to tapes. That was really fun, but mainly he liked to get the music out there to the fans because he had been a fan for so many years and knew that's what he lived for—another show that he was unaware of or something fantastic that he had never heard.

How did the Dead come to believe that non–professionally recorded concerts would find an audience? Two reasons: First, there was the popularity of the tapes of live recordings of the band. If Deadheads could enjoy tenth-generation cassettes with loads of tape hiss, then soundboard recordings on CD probably wouldn't be hard for them to accept. Second, there was also a history of releasing such recordings in rock. Funny enough, the first of such archival rock tapes to be released as an album seems to have been of the Dead themselves.

In 1971, the fly-by-night label Sunflower Records got hold of a tape of a June 1966 Avalon Ballroom show that preceded the band's contract with Warner Bros. Sunflower released the concert spread out over two albums, *Vintage Dead* and *Historic Dead*. The first of these, *Vintage Dead*, charted as high as #127, while *Historic Dead* got to #154. They weren't massive hits by any means, but they were popular enough to prove that there was a market for older live shows, especially when production costs for such releases were relatively inexpensive.

In 1972, Atlantic Records released a live Velvet Underground album, *Live at Max's Kansas City*, which formed part of a mono cassette tape recording of the band's last show with Lou Reed. In 1977, a former Beatles associate chanced upon an early tape of the group playing live in Germany and released it as *Live! at the Star-Club in Hamburg, Germany; 1962*. Both recordings were seriously rough-sounding, but both were prized by fans of each group because they lent insight into what these artists sounded like without any studio polish.

It took Frank Zappa to make whole series out of such things. In 1991, he officially released live bootleg recordings of his as part of a string of CDs all subtitled *Beat the Boots*. Chances are that someone in the Dead's camp noticed this series and sensed that there was a growing audience for old live recordings of classic rock acts that had cult followings.

Plundering the Vault

The Dead's first release of live recordings from their legendary Vault came on April 15, 1991, and was of a concert from August 13, 1975. Not surprisingly, it was titled *One from the Vault*. A second volume followed the next year, *Two from the Vault*, and featured performances from shows on August 23 and 24, 1968, at the Shrine Auditorium in Los Angeles. It took until 2007 for the third CD

Photographer and graphic designer Robert Minkin took over design duties for the *Dick's Picks* series starting with *Volume Twenty-Five*. His abstract images, created on computer software, were a hallmark of later releases, as seen here on the cover of *Volume Thirty-Four*.

Author's collection

in this series to be released (it was of a February 19, 1971, show at the Capitol Theater in Port Chester, New York). These three releases were recordings from multi-track tapes, though.

The first *Dick's Picks* was made available by mail order only in December 1993. The Dead were careful about making sure fans knew they were getting music that was recorded on the fly without being meant for release. The back of the CD bore the following legend:

> Caveat Emptor: This compact disc has been digitally remastered directly from the original half track 7 ½ ips analog tape. It is a snapshot of history, not a modern professional recording, and may therefore exhibit some technical anomalies and the unavoidable effects of the ravages of time.

All of the *Dick's Picks* CDs would come with such warnings, but most fans didn't have a problem with the sound quality, especially when compared to those old, hissy tapes. Before long, *Dick's Picks* had proven so popular that they began to pop up in stores. A small piece of paper was issued and slipped into these copies, explaining the band's intentions to unsuspecting fans:

THANK YOU for selecting *Dick's Picks Volume One*! This gem from the Grateful Dead tape vault was first issued in 1993, as a mail-order-only item for discerning Deadheads. It turned out to be so popular that we've decided to make it more widely available. *Dick's Picks* is a series of live releases carefully selected by the Grateful Dead's intrepid vault custodian, Dick Latvala, which are then edited and mastered to CD at the Dead's studio. This is the real, raw stuff, direct from the original two-track tapes. We don't always have complete tapes of shows, and sometimes what we do have isn't "just exactly perfect". But *Dick's Picks* is the next best thing to being there, a front row seat in history and most of all, a real good time!

DICK'S PICKS VOLUMES TWO AND THREE are now available via Grateful Dead Merchandising Mail Order (see reverse for details). You can cast your vote for shows you'd like Dick to Pick by visiting the official Grateful Dead site on the World Wide Web: http://www.dead.net.

As it turned out, sound quality and choice of shows was not a problem; the release of partial shows was. For example, the second volume, which came out in March 1995, contained an October 31, 1971, show at the Ohio Theatre in Columbus, Ohio, and featured a riveting "Dark Star" that surprisingly morphed into a jam based around the old Archie Bell and the Drells' hit "(Do the) Tighten Up." But the drawback of this release was that it contained only the second set of this show and even left out the encore, "Johnny B. Goode." The first release in the series had included fourteen of the twenty-six songs played that night and moved some of the songs out of their original running order. Fans who kept detailed records of set lists became frustrated, remembers Carol Latvala:

> One of the biggest arguments among the tape collectors was "whole show or not." There was a big prejudice for releasing a whole show. And in some cases some of the *Dick's Picks* were not whole shows. That, as I remember, was one of the biggest critiques. But there was little criticism as far as the sound quality went, because by the time they released them they sounded pretty good.

Leaving off songs or entire sets wasn't Latvala's idea, though. According to Carol, band members often expressed dissatisfaction with their performances and held veto power over what made it out of the Vault:

> That was the biggest obstacle he faced: one of them wouldn't like their performance or think that the show had sucked or this and that. So it was very difficult to get the initial go ahead to do any of the releases. Artists are very prickly about their particular performances and none of these tapes were meant to be released.

All that changed, she notes, when the series ended up giving the band an income stream after the money from concerts stopped coming in following Garcia's death in 1995. The first edition of *Dick's Picks* to offer a full concert was *Volume Five*, which came out in May 1996. It contained the band's December 26, 1979, show at the Oakland Auditorium Arena in Oakland, California, which was spread over three discs. It clocked in at a whopping 176 minutes, almost three hours' playing time.

Leaving a Legacy

In an interview with *Rolling Stone* that was published on December 8, 1998, Dick Latvala said he also came in for some criticism regarding his preference for releasing shows from the 1970s:

> I represent Deadheads so to speak—sometimes not so well, from others' points of view. I hear: "That old fart Latvala, he can't even get into the Eighties and Nineties." I've been using shows from the Seventies, and I will get into shows from the Eighties, I just drag my feet on that one. There are great shows from many years and our goal is to represent all the eras. It's gonna take about thirty or forty releases before we even get a basic foundation—an introduction to Grateful Dead music. Then it can get refined. We're just beginning.

Dick Latvala unfortunately never lived to see how integral to the Dead's legacy his series became. He died on August 6, 1999, at age fifty-six after he'd had a heart attack and slipped into a coma. At the time, *Dick's Picks Volume Fourteen* had just come out. The release showcased highlights of the

Weir, Kreutzmann, Hart, and Garcia get their jam on at a 1990 show at the Shoreline Amphitheatre in Mountain View, California. Only two *Dick's Picks* volumes covered the 1990s: *Volume Nine* and *Volume Twenty-Seven*.   *Photo by Russ Grabski*

band's performances at the Boston Music Hall in Boston, Massachusetts, on November 30 and December 2, 1973. Rather than stop the series, Grateful Dead Productions opted to continue it under the direction of David Lemieux, who was named archivist after Latvala's passing. A native of Canada, Lemieux boasts some impressive credentials, as he worked as a film archivist and holds a master's degree in film archiving from the University of East Anglia in Norwich, United Kingdom.

Over the next half decade or so, Lemieux continued to oversee the series until Rhino Records, who had bought the Dead's Vault, decided to end it in October 2005 with *Volume Thirty-Six*. By then, the series had become something of an institution because it offered a window into the band's live shows unknown to anyone not in tapers' circles. *Dick's Picks* let the average Dead fan (or the curious) hear how songs such as "Friend of the Devil" evolved on stage or how the jams in songs such as "Eyes of the World" sometimes spiraled into twenty-minute extravaganzas (as on *Volume Seventeen*).

The series, which averaged three releases a year, not only kept the Dead's legacy alive after Garcia's passing, but also enhanced it. Where most bands only had a few unreleased studio cuts or a concert or two to posthumously offer fans, the Dead seemingly had their entire recorded legacy to tap into. It came as a surprise to casual fans of the band just how much high-quality material was out there. And in the world of the Dead, the success of *Dick's Picks* signaled that the market for unreleased recordings was bigger than perhaps anyone had thought.

The Unheard Music

One of the most interesting aspects of *Dick's Picks* was that it featured songs the band played but never put on studio albums, solo albums, singles, or live albums. The first volume had a cover of the traditional blues "Nobody's Fault but Mine," the second had the aforementioned "Tighten Up Jam," and the fourth had a live version of "Mason's Children," a song recorded for *Workingman's Dead* but left off the album. *Volume Five* had a Ma Rainey blues in "C.C. Rider" (later a hit for Chuck Willis and Mitch Ryder), while the sixth volume, which featured a 1983 concert, had "Keep Your Day Job," a Garcia-Hunter song that had made its debut the year before. The eighth volume offered two previously unreleased songs in the traditional "Cold Jordan" and the band's reworking of James Brown's "It's a Man's Man's Man's World," which was sung by Pigpen.

Volume Twelve had a short instrumental cover version of the World War II–era hit "Beer Barrel Polka," as well as "Seastones," a dissonant, experimental track that Phil Lesh co-wrote with avant garde keyboardist Ned Lagin, who released an album by the same name on the Dead's Round Records label. *Volume Fourteen* contained a bit of the big band–era tune "The Merry-Go-Round Broke Down" as part of a medley. The seventeenth volume had Garcia singing "That Would Be Something," from Paul McCartney's first solo album. *Volume Twenty* had Weir tackling a Bobby Womack song that the Rolling Stones made famous, "It's All Over Now."

Volume Twenty-One marked the CD debut of the Dead's cover of Willie Dixon's blues classic "Spoonful." On *Volume Twenty-Five*, the band showed their sense of humor by covering Warren Zevon's 1978 hit, "Werewolves of London," and on *Volume Twenty-Six*, the band returned to the work of laid-back bluesman Jimmy Reed ("Big Boss Man") by covering his "I Know It's a Sin" with Garcia on lead vocals and Pigpen on blues harp. The twenty-seventh volume had covers of the Who's "Baba O'Riley" and the Beatles' "Tomorrow Never Knows" played as an encore at the band's December 17, 1992, show at the Oakland Coliseum.

Volume Thirty had a host of previously unheard songs, as it featured pioneering rock 'n' roller Bo Diddley as a guest during a March 25, 1972, gig at New York's Academy of Music. Songs both acts played include "Hey! Bo Diddley," "I'm a Man (Mannish Boy)," "I've Seen Them All," and "Mona." Other songs unheard elsewhere include the Dead's cover of Marvin Gaye's "How Sweet It Is (To Be Loved by You)," soul singer Freddie Scott's "Are You Lonely for Me Baby?," and an instrumental version of the nineteenth-century standard "The Sidewalks of New York."

Volume Thirty-Four has a Phil Lesh bass solo (called "Bass Solo"), and *Volume Thirty-Five* includes the only released recording of Pigpen's "Empty Pages."

The releases also gave amusing names to the sections of improvised music that served as segues between songs. A jam connecting "He's Gone" to "Drums" on *Volume Nine*, for example, was titled "No MSG Jam." On *Volume Seven*, the jam that melded "Dark Star" with "Morning Dew" was called "Spam Jam," the title perhaps a nod to Monty Python's Spam song, as the concert in question was recorded in England. Other interestingly titled jams include "Spinach Jam," "Wood Green Jam," and "Lunatic Preserve." In all, there were so many new, old songs and jams scattered around on the various *Dick's Picks* collections that a CD set could have been compiled from those tracks alone.

Sons of *Dick's Picks*

Just before *Dick's Picks* ended its run, Grateful Dead Productions announced it was putting out a new cycle of releases that wouldn't be put on CDs. Called the *Grateful Dead Download Series*, these sets allowed fans to digitally access full concerts without having to deal with them being chopped up and put onto separate CDs. The first release in the series, which appeared in May 2005, featured the April 30, 1977, show at the Palladium in New York City. The second came out the next month and featured a concert from January 18, 1970, at Springer's Inn in Portland, Oregon. In all, the series offered twelve volumes of shows that were sometimes supplemented with rehearsal performances. An example of this is the last one, *Volume Twelve*, which came out in 2006 and delivered the April 17, 1969, show that the band played at Washington University in St. Louis, Missouri.

The Dead camp went in the opposite direction with the soundboard series that followed, *Road Trips*. The series made its debut in November 2007. Not only did the band go back to putting out hard copy editions of their releases, but each one came with a lavish booklet that featured an essay as well as rare or previously unseen photos. Also, *Road Trips* didn't focus on full concerts, but instead offered highlights from various tours. The first one spotlighted the band's fall 1979 tour of the East Coast.

Two problems plagued the series. First, it didn't offer full shows, which caused the same grumbling among Deadheads that *Dick's Picks* did when it went the same route. To this end, the series begat a downloadable sub-series, *Road Trips Full Show*, which addressed that issue. The other problem *Road Trips* had was that it was confusingly numbered. Instead of having sequential numbers, like the *Dick's Picks* series, each volume had a subset of numbers (*Volume 1 Number 1, Volume 1 Number 2*, etc.) which made it hard to remember which ones were which.

The idea behind the series was explained on the band's website: "*Road Trips* is something a little different. We want to plug in a few more pieces of the Grateful Dead puzzle by putting the spotlight on different tours and series of shows that have been neglected through the years."

According to Lemieux, who produced *Road Trips* along with fellow Dead authority Blair Jackson, the series "wasn't all that well received. That was largely because people said they weren't all that interested in compilations. I'm sure some people are, but we certainly got a lot of feedback, so I moved the series toward complete shows."

Road Trips ended in 2011 after its seventeenth release. The *Road Trips Full Show* series comprised two downloadable releases, both of which were originally made available in 2008. The first was a complete show of the Dead's November 5, 1979, gig at the Spectrum in Philadelphia, the second a complete show from the following night.

The newest soundboard CD series as of this writing is *Dave's Picks*, which was named for Lemieux by Rhino Records. Lemieux serves as producer for this series, which so far has only featured complete shows. The first volume offered the May 25, 1977, show at the Mosque in Richmond, Virginia; the second the July 31, 1974, gig at Dillon Stadium in Hartford, Connecticut; the third the October 22, 1971, show at the Auditorium Theatre in Chicago, Illinois; and the fourth the September 24, 1976, show at the College of William and Mary in Williamsburg, Virginia.

All of the aforementioned soundboard series are a testament to the influence and popularity of *Dick's Picks* within the world of the Grateful Dead. But the series was almost as important outside of the realm of the Dead, because its popularity showed that documenting concerts was important for both historical and commercial reasons. Many of the jam bands who were influenced by the Dead started to supplement their studio releases with live CDs of entire shows, some of which came out in box sets. But *Dick's Picks* was there first, making the Dead's documented legacy available to anyone interested in exploring it.

Further information about Dick Latvala can be found on the website maintained by his son Richie Latvala at www.dicklatvala.com.

18

I Was There

David Lemieux on Archiving the Dead's Catalog

As the Grateful Dead's official archivist since 1999, David Lemieux has brought his experience and considerable knowledge to his role, overseeing countless reissues of the band's studio albums, putting together live CDs, and, most recently, picking soundboard concerts for release for the new series that bears his name, Dave's Picks. *Here, he speaks about what he does day to day and how he came to work in the Dead's fabled Vault, which was located at the Dead's old Club Front studio and rehearsal hall and held the band's massive archive of tapes.*

I'll preface all this by saying I'm a huge Deadhead and it's been a huge part of who I am since I was about fourteen or fifteen.

I got into archiving when I went to college and studied history and then film studies. Around the time I graduated with a second degree in film studies in 1997, I started hearing about film preservation and film archiving. So, I went to the University of East Anglia in Norwich for my master's degree in film archiving.

I came back to Canada and did an internship as part of my master's at the British Columbia Archives, which collects everything related to government agencies and anything that's orally or culturally important to the Province of British Columbia. In the meantime, I'd written Dick Latvala an e-mail in the spring of 1998. When I wrote Dick, I said, "I'd love to do an overview of your Grateful Dead archives but specifically look at your film and video, which you really haven't done much of." There had been a couple of DVDs at the time, but they really hadn't been delving into the film and video archive the way they had with audio, with *Dick's Picks* and the *From the Vault* releases. I sent the e-mail, but did not expect a reply. And Dick happened to respond. He called me about three months later. Dick asked if I was going to be in California anytime soon. He happened to have called me the day before I was flying down to California to go see the Other Ones, so I said, "Yeah, I'm going to be there tomorrow." So he said, "Well you've got to come by in a couple of days."

I went to the Vault about two days later and spent about three or four hours with Dick there. And then John Cutler, who was the head of the Vault and head of the studio, came in. At first he has this attitude like "What are you doing

The *Road Trips* series was criticized for not offering complete shows, but *Volume 2, Number 2* contained the Dead's full February 14, 1968, concert at Carousel Ballroom, some of which was used for the live sections of *Anthem of the Sun*. The set also contained a significant amount of bonus material. *Author's collection*

letting [a stranger] into the Vault?" The Vault is a very secure place. It's not like it's open to the public, and at the time there were only a couple of keys. But John and I hit it off because I think John realized that I was legitimate in what I did. He asked, "What makes you a film archivist?" I said I'd studied film archiving and got a master's in it and I worked at a film archive. I don't think you can be more legitimate than that. I certainly didn't mention that I was a Deadhead.

We talked for a while and, like any Deadhead, I thought it was all shockingly cool. A month or two went by after that, and I wrote both Dick and John letters—on paper. Dick's was more of a Deadhead letter: "Hey, man that was awesome—thank you!" John's was a little more professional. I told him how going to the Vault was very helpful for my master's and wrote a little bit about the Dead's archive and how they preserve film as an example of a non-film archive. In that letter I also wrote a PS saying, "If you need somebody to help catalog and help organize your film and video collections, let me know," because I knew that Dick was so overwhelmed with the audio. Dick wasn't all that big on the video stuff, and I knew that he really didn't have time or the interest in it from what he'd told me. I wrote the PS and then I deleted it. I said, "That's cheesy." They were so generous with their time that the last thing they'd want to hear is "Oh, by the way, do you have a job for me?"

And then I said, "You know what? You get nothing in life if you don't take a chance." So I put the PS back in. A couple of days later, Cutler called me and said, "Hey, were you serious about that?" I told him yes, so he asked me to come back. I flew down a couple of weeks later and gave them my vision of what I would do with the collection. I figured it was a three-month job. They hired me on February 1, 1999, so I went down for a three-month contract and cataloged their entire video collection, created a database, created a preservation plan for which tapes I thought needed preservation the most, and gave them a few other ideas that I had.

A Workingman with the Dead

In the summer of 1999, Phil had started playing with his rotating cast of Phil Lesh and Friends. He was playing at the Warfield Theater once a month and he wanted to record the shows, so he put Cutler in charge of building a recording truck every time he did a run of shows. I'd go to the Warfield and help build the recording truck, which was real cool. So I kept coming down, and then in August 1999, John said, "This new DVD thing is becoming quite popular and we want to do *The Grateful Dead Movie* on DVD and include a little bit of bonus footage, so we need you to come and sort through the archives." So I took another leave of absence from my British Columbia job, and literally as I was packing up my car, I got a call from John saying that Dick had gone into a coma the night before. I was devastated because he had become a good friend. I told John to let me know when Dick gets better and I would come down then, but he said, "No, we've got to get this project done." In typical rock 'n' roll tradition, "the show must go on and even though tragedy happens we must push forward."

I came down the next day, and while I was there Dick passed away. The CEO of Grateful Dead Productions sat me down and asked if I wanted to stick around and do Dick's job, and I said, "I'd love to." So that's how I got the job. In September 1999, I moved down there and I've been doing it since.

My first order of business was continuing *Dick's Picks*. The first couple were—I won't say they were easy—but they were most certainly a tribute to Dick because they were things he really wanted to get out. He passed away right after *Volume Fourteen* came out, and then *Volume Fifteen* almost immediately went into production. He was really high on the Boston Garden run from '91, so we made that show *Volume Seventeen*. We made sure that what we were doing was hopefully continuing his vision.

Eileen Law became the project manager right around this time, so she was in charge of dealing with the record pressing plants for the CDs, and she dealt directly with artists and photographers in terms of negotiating contracts and things like that. My job is primarily listening to music and then overseeing the production of things. I also sequence the compilation CDs, such as the *Road Trips* series. In the case of compilations, you're not just picking a show, you're picking the best versions of the same songs from a five-night run or something.

For full show releases, once a show is picked for release, the master tapes get sent to mixing engineer Jeffrey Norman. He and I work closely together to make sure that it's right. Jeffrey does all the engineering and makes the sound decisions. Where I come in is to make sure that the song indexes are at the right points and that the fade out is at the right point at the end of each CD.

When I'm pretty sure that a show is going to be picked for release, I'll listen to it every day. I'll listen to it in the car, I'll listen to it at home, I'll listen to it with headphones—whatever it takes. Then maybe after three months of hearing it, I'll say, "You know, as high as I am on this show and as much work as I've put into this show, it's just not good enough." So it gets nixed or I'll personally nix it. It's the kind of thing where a moment of inspiration on a show is not good enough—the whole show has to work. But if a show turns out not to work, I luckily always have a bunch of good ideas and other directions I can head in.

More Skeletons from the Closet

People above me make the decision on ending a CD series and starting a new one, so when the *Dick's Picks* series ended at *Volume Thirty-Six*, I didn't know that it was going to be the last one. But it was perfect poetic justice that that one turned out to be the last, because that was one of the shows Dick put up to the band in 1992 or '93 as a potential *Volume One*. It was something he really not only wanted, but also wanted as *Volume One*. That's how strong he thought it was and I agree.

After it came out I remember calling over to Rhino, and they said, "We might take a little break from *Dick's Picks*." And, you know, I don't question why—if that's what they want to do, it's fine. A couple of months later they decided they were going to go in a new direction with the *Road Trips* series. They explained what the vision was for that, and I worked within those parameters for a little while. By 2011, they had decided they were going to end the *Road Trips* series. When a lot of the personnel at Rhino changed in late 2010, the new senior vice president, Mark Pincus, and I sat down, and he asked what I thought of the *Road Trips* series. I said, "Well, I think the sets with full shows are fine, but I think the problem is it really suffered from a poor launch. I don't think it was well received from the beginning. Even though we moved to full shows, I don't think a lot of people got past what the original conception of the *Road Trips* was." So he said, "What do you think about ending it and starting over?" I said, "Yeah, let's go back to *Dick's Picks* or something." They came up with the idea of *Dave's Picks*. It wasn't like they asked me for my input on it, but of course I'm flattered and I'm humbled they did that.

With *Road Trips*, there was a conscious decision to move away from the personal side of things. *Dick's Picks* was largely about the personal side of things. It

With *Dave's Picks*, the Dead's audio and video archivist, David Lemieux, was given free reign to select his favorite concerts for release. The third volume, released in August 2012, featured a show performed on October 22, 1971, at the Auditorium Theatre in Chicago.
Author's collection

was people getting to know Dick. Dick was absolutely used in the promotion of these things because they wanted people to know a real person was picking this stuff. So with the new series, they realized there was a value to having a personal connection, whoever the person was. And people have responded. Certainly the interest is there. Sales are up. People seem to dig it. And Rhino seems very happy with it. I'm pretty sure it's going to continue for quite some time.

Managing a Legacy

All of that is really just the tip of the iceberg of what I do. I do so much more outside of just listening to shows for *Dave's Picks* and other releases. I was made the band's legacy manager about a year and a half ago. What that means is I oversee Rhino's activities on the non-music stuff. I make sure the band is aware of all activities and make sure the band has the ability to comment on, approve, or deny the use of things. So I'm the liaison and the conduit between Rhino and the band members. It keeps it busy and interesting. I also have a one-hour radio show on SiriusXM seven days a week.

But you know, Rhino is really helming all the activity now, so they're the ones who come up with these great ideas. And then it's really just a matter of making sure the band is onboard with things. And generally Rhino and Mark have a very good sense of the Dead's legacy.

We don't have a Vault anymore. Grateful Dead Productions shut down in 2006. The physical tapes went to the Warner Music Group, and the merchandising was outsourced, although the merch development and licensing stayed in the house. By 2006, we were down to about eight to ten people. And then, although Grateful Dead Productions closed as an entity, there still obviously is a Grateful Dead production company. It's the business arm of the Dead, so I still do work for them, but I don't work in the Vault anymore. I work from home. When we need music, if I don't already have a reference copy of it, or if it's not obtainable, it's a very simple call to the archives down at Warner Bros., and we get a transfer made.

The archives, from which we used to draw a lot of our newspaper clippings and photos, have all gone to the University of California at Santa Cruz, so we work very closely with [Dead archivist] Nicholas Meriwether there. When we're picking a show for release, we'll call up Nick and say, "OK, here's the show date, pull everything you can." Within a couple of weeks, Nick will send us loads of scans of newspaper clippings, gig contracts, photos, and other memorabilia from that show or that tour that we can then put in our CD booklet. So not a lot has changed in terms of the process. We're still doing four releases a year, and we still do one big box set a year.

Friends ask, "How many versions of 'Sugar Magnolia' can you listen to?" And I say, "All of 'em, man!"

19

He's Gone

The majority of the Grateful Dead's fan base hopped aboard the bus sometime in the late 1970s, after the group had established its live dual-singer approach. Concerts would start with either Jerry Garcia or Bob Weir singing a number, then more or less alternate until they ended. Once in a while, Keith Godchaux or Brent Mydland would chime in with vocals from behind their keyboards, and in 1977 and 1978, backing singer Donna Jean Godchaux-MacKay sang her composition "Sunrise" nearly thirty times. But mostly the Dead's vocal presentation was the Jerry and Bobby show.

So, it's sometimes a surprise for newbie Deadheads to listen to old recordings and discover that once upon a time the group had a dedicated lead singer—one who didn't stand behind a guitar or keyboard but held the microphone center stage in the tradition of Mick Jagger, Robert Plant, and Axl Rose. That singer was the late Ron "Pigpen" McKernan, who was a driving force during the band's start-up days, but whose role gradually decreased and eventually faded away altogether as the years passed.

Being a lead singer with the Dead didn't mean that Pigpen sang entire sets or albums. But it meant that on the occasions when Pigpen did grab the mic to do his thing, the tone of the proceedings totally changed. He sang aggressively, egged on the crowd, and sometimes waded into the crowd and exhorted men and women to pair up.

All of this came about because the types of songs Pigpen sang were markedly different from those Garcia or Weir sang. Pigpen had been a blues fan since his younger days and was said to be something of an authority on the genre because his father was a disc jockey who played rhythm and blues records on a Berkeley radio station in the early 1950s (back then blues fell under the category of R&B, which was also known as "race music"). The songs Pigpen brought to the band didn't exactly work as stage pieces with him sitting behind his organ and quietly intoning the words. They were rabble-rousing, high-spirited songs, such as Bobby "Blue" Bland's "Turn On Your Love Light," which called for a singer to really emote—so that's what Pigpen did. Although he did sing from behind his organ, his most interesting live performances have him fronting the band.

Listening to early concert tapes of the Grateful Dead and hearing Pigpen sing, two things are evident. First, his vocal disposition gave the band a much harder edge. With Pigpen at the helm, no one would ever accuse the Dead of being too "laid back," which was a charge leveled at them by their critics in the band's later years. In fact, when Pigpen fronted the Dead, they sounded about as dangerous as they looked in photos of the time, and that look largely came from Pigpen's penchant for wearing biker-type clothing.

The second thing that hearing Pigpen in concert shows is that his music didn't really fit into what the Dead were all about. Sure, he could get the crowd going, and he definitely sounded "authentic" in copying the African American singers he loved. But he also sounds like a guest vocalist in his own band, someone being given a spotlight to do his thing before being ushered back onto the sidelines so the main show could resume.

When Things Go Wrong …

At this point, a neophyte Dead fan might ask, "So why was Pigpen there to begin with if he was the odd man out?" Well, because he helped start the whole thing off. Long before there was a Grateful Dead, Pigpen and Garcia became the first two band members to meet. This was back in 1961, and Pigpen was interested in Garcia's acoustic treatments of blues songs. Pigpen was a budding guitarist as well as a keyboardist and blues harp player, so he had Garcia show him some six-string licks. Because Garcia also tutored Weir on guitar, the balance of power in the band tipping toward Garcia was already set in motion back then.

The three future Dead men formed an acoustic jug band called Mother McCree's Uptown Jug Champions. According to Garcia, it was Pigpen's idea to move the band onto electric instruments. For decades it was assumed that nothing by Mother McCree was ever recorded, but a tape of the band playing live was found and can be heard on a self-titled CD recorded in 1964 and put out in 1999. It features Pigpen, Garcia, and Weir with three other musicians all playing on around a dozen and a half traditional numbers. The album, though not particularly inspired, should be heard by anyone seeking insight into the roots of the Dead. Behind the kazoo and comb-and-paper percussion is a somewhat goofy folk group that would soon morph into one of the most important rock bands ever.

Pigpen's high time with the band came when they decided to get an electric group together (at his behest), which became known as the Warlocks. Garcia explained the importance of Pigpen at this stage of the band in a 1994 video interview that's made the rounds on YouTube: "We had one strong suit. We had Pigpen in the band. And he was this guy from Palo Alto whose father had been a rhythm and blues disc jockey. So . . . for him the blues was very natural, and he played harmonica and he sang really well. He really had no real wish to be a performer. We sort of forced him into it because we knew he could do it. So he was sort of the front man for the band. He was our powerhouse guy. And the rest

By 1966, Ron "Pigpen" McKernan already sported the biker look that would become his trademark with the Grateful Dead, as shown by this photo taken at Olompali State Historic Park in Novato, California.   *Photo by Rosie McGee*

of us could play better than him, but he could sing better than us or anybody else. So he got to be the front man for the band. It worked well."

But by the time the Warlocks had become the Grateful Dead, Garcia had begun to assert himself as the artistic leader, so there wasn't a whole lot of Pigpen to be heard on the Dead's early albums. On the group's self-titled debut, he only sings lead on one song, a cover of Sonny Boy Williamson's blues favorite, "Good Morning Little School Girl." On the second album, *Anthem of the Sun*, he dominates the second side, singing "Alligator" and "Caution (Do Not Stop on Tracks)," both of which he co-wrote. But he doesn't sing anything on the group's third effort, *Aoxomoxoa*, nor is he credited with playing any instruments on it. He sings a version of "Love Light" on *Live/Dead* and Robert Hunter's "Easy Wind" on *Workingman's Dead*, and his own "Operator" on *American Beauty*. On the self-titled 1971 album (aka *Skull and Roses*), he takes the lead vocals on a cover of the Jimmy Reed blues tune "Big Boss Man."

The Pigpen-Hunter collaboration "Mr. Charlie" and Pigpen's cover of the Elmore James–associated blues standard "It Hurts Me Too" (retitled "Hurts Me Too") are highlights of the band's landmark live LP, *Europe '72*. It was the last group album on which he appeared, not counting concert CDs released after his death. Pigpen's best song is arguably the moving "The Stranger (Two Souls in Communion)," a track that was added to the box set version(s) of *Europe '72*. (More information about "The Stranger" can be found in chapter 26.)

As CDs from the *Dick's Picks* series began to trickle out in the 1990s and 2000s, more and more of Pigpen's contributions to the band came to the fore. Pigpen passed away in 1973, but if you comb through enough live shows recorded before then, you can find Pig at his best. A good place to start is the *Road Trips Volume 2, Number 2* set (confusingly, the sixth set in the series), which is a two-disc set featuring a concert recorded on Valentine's Day 1968, plus some bonus material recorded earlier in the year. It showcases Pigpen on two versions of "Love Light" and has organ featured prominently in the mix on some songs, which wasn't usually the case.

Hard to Handle

A lot has already been written about what caused Pigpen's early death, but some of it bears repeating because it's pertinent to the topic of why his role in the band gradually became smaller and smaller. Pigpen was a heavy drinker, and from all accounts his alcohol intake caused serious damage to his liver by the time he was in his mid-twenties. His preference for alcohol over the hallucinogens preferred by the rest of the band made him the odd man out both personally and, eventually, musically (it was apparently harder to get into freeform jams when not tripping on LSD). When they wanted to expand their sound to reflect their trippy states of mind in 1968, they started to feel that Pigpen's organ playing was lacking. So they brought in another keyboardist, Tom Constanten, a classically trained player who was an old friend of Phil Lesh's. Consequently, *Aoxomoxoa* features a host of classically infused Constanten keyboard parts, not Pigpen's organ pumping, making it a big departure from what the band did on vinyl previously.

Pigpen is revered in retrospect more for his singing than for his keyboard playing anyway, but there are places his keyboards are prominent. His work on organ is best heard on the 2001 double CD *Birth of the Dead*, which is made up of studio recordings the band made for Autumn and Scorpio Records as well as live cuts. On tracks such as Garcia and Lesh's "Mindbender (Confusion's Prince)" and the cover of Gordon Lightfoot's "Early Morning Rain" (a hit for Marty Robbins), Pigpen's playing sounds similar to the keyboard work of the garage bands of the time. Such groups included Question Mark & the Mysterians ("96 Tears"), the Blues Magoos ("We Ain't Got Nothin' Yet"), and the Castaways ("Liar Liar"). Both discs are not only filled with Pigpen's organ playing, but also have him blowing harmonica and singing lead on several tracks, including his own composition "Tastebud." Another version of this song can be found as a bonus track on the CD reissue of the first album. Pigpen's rudimentary keyboard playing worked for the band early on, but it didn't quite evolve with the band and hence never found a place in the new music the Dead was forging in 1968 and 1969.

More of Pigpen in his prime can be heard on the 2005 release *Rare Cuts and Oddities*, a collection of rare live and studio tracks from 1966 on which Pigpen is showcased as lead singer on more than a half dozen tracks. Highlights include his rendition of Rufus Thomas's "Walking the Dog" and Slim Harpo's "I'm a King Bee" (both also covered by the Rolling Stones), the Stones' "Empty Heart," Fontella Bass and Bobby McClure's "Don't Mess Up a Good Thing," and an early version of "Caution (Do Not Stop on Tracks)."

It's been written that around the time the Dead finished their second album, Garcia and Lesh began to feel that the musicianship of both Pigpen and Weir was holding the band back during its experimental jams and sometimes even during the onstage execution of regular songs. Both musicians were asked to leave the band, but eventually found their way back into the fold. Several accounts have Pigpen relegated to playing percussion instruments on stage during this period.

In this light, Pigpen's story resembles that of the late Brian Jones of the Rolling Stones, who passed away four years before Pigpen did. Both men co-founded their respective groups but soon found their talents eclipsed by two other bandmates who stepped into lead roles. Both struggled with substance abuse, which seemed to impair their musical abilities. Both participated less and less musically when their bands moved beyond the music they were capable of playing at the time. Both played a pretty mean blues harp. And both died at the age of twenty-seven.

The difference between Jones's and Pigpen's stories is twofold. Jones got neither a song on a Stones album nor lead vocals—although his harmony on the Stones' cover of Rufus Thomas's "Walking the Dog" is mixed so loud that it comes close to being a lead vocal. Pigpen at least was able to have his say on several Dead albums. Also, Pigpen got a second life with the Dead, so to speak. Even though it was clear that things were going dreadfully wrong for him health-wise in the early 1970s, the Dead still made room for him in concert sets and on albums. By contrast, the Stones fired the clearly troubled Jones in the summer of 1969, shortly before he died.

Pigpen's dissolution into a life of alcohol abuse may have been hastened by a schism that developed between his personal and professional lives. He just might not have been cut out for a life in the demanding pop music world. In Phil Lesh's autobiography *Searching for the Sound: My Life with the Dead*, he intimates that the extroverted Pigpen whom audiences saw on stage was something of a front for the introverted "real" Pigpen. Writes Lesh,

Pig was the perfect front man for the band; intense, commanding, comforting; but I don't think he enjoyed doing that quite as much as sitting on a couch with a guitar. . . . Never was Pigpen more at home than with a bottle of wine and a guitar, at home or at some party, improvising epic blues rant lyrics, playing Lightnin' Hopkins songs . . .

Did Pigpen use alcohol to cope with the stresses of life as a public figure that he wasn't otherwise prepared to deal with? That's not easy to answer without an in-depth look at the man. Such a look may be coming to a theater near you.

Influence and Legacy

Deadheads should get ready because there's probably going to be a movie about one of the band's least known members. It's called *Pigpen . . . A Blues Singer*. It's interesting that a biopic would be made about one of the Dead's lesser-recognized members before one was done about any of their well-known members (a film about Garcia's early life was in the works as of 2010, but hit a snag when Garcia's estate refused the filmmakers the use of his music). But a cult of personality has sprung up around the Dead's resident blues enthusiast, and it seems that now there's a growing interest in his story. The film's website, Pigpenblues.com, said the film was "slated for release in 2013," but the date has since been pushed back to 2014 or beyond.

Relix magazine reported on April 13, 2012, that the film was being produced by the team of Terry Allen Fraser and Diana Raquel Sainz (*The Encore of Tony Duran*) and will be a biopic that "follows the life of Pigpen from his start as a young blues musician to his time as the Grateful Dead's frontman." Sainz was quoted in the piece as saying:

> The world of the Grateful Dead continues to be huge. It's still a strong international community of creative fans and loyal followers. Pigpen was part of the big picture, but met an early and untimely death at the age of 27. We are still in the development stages of this project, but the response, support, and feedback has been overwhelming. With the story transforming into what will entertain and illuminate music fans everywhere, the film will honor a talent that remains forever in the hearts of many—and is unknown to many more.

Although some of Pigpen's music seems anomalous when surveying the rest of the Dead's work, he did leave his mark on the band. One example of him doing this is that he was the one who made the Dead's cover of the Olympics/ Young Rascals hit "Good Lovin'," an important live showcase long before it was designated as the lead-off track on the *Shakedown Street* album. After he passed away, the band handed the vocals over to Bob Weir, who sang the song much like Pigpen did and not like Garcia, who had sometimes sung it early on. Another forward-looking Pigpen number was "Mr. Charlie," which had the kind of funky, syncopated beat the Dead would later make a regular feature of their music on tracks such as "Eyes of the World," "Franklin's Tower," and "The Music Never Stopped."

Pigpen's cover of Howlin' Wolf's "Smokestack Lightning" may also have influenced one of the band's most important songs, "Truckin'." "Smokestack Lightning" was a blues standard covered by the Yardbirds and loosely rewritten as "Graveyard Train" by John Fogerty of Creedence Clearwater Revival. When the Dead performed a twenty-minute version of the song in February 1970 with Pigpen at the helm, they kicked it off with its signature riff, but toward the end, they moved into a bluesy shuffle that sounds a lot like the main riff to "Truckin'," which the Dead wouldn't debut live until August of that year. This version of "Smokestack Lightning" can be heard on the 1973 album *History of the Grateful Dead, Volume One (Bear's Choice)*. Pigpen brought a convincing weightiness to the blues numbers he sang, such as "Katie Mae" on the aforementioned *Bear's Choice*, where he sounds uncannily like the song's author, Lightnin' Hopkins. The band's takes on blues numbers weren't nearly as convincing after Pigpen wasn't around to sing lead on them.

Pigpen was also a minor celebrity of sorts in his day. He and Janis Joplin dated, and a poster of the two was even made showing the pair on the steps of the Grateful Dead house at 710 Ashbury Street. Around the time of *Aoxomoxoa*, Warner Bros. Records created a promotion called the "Pigpen Look-Alike Contest," where the company solicited photos from fans who attempted to cop his biker chic style.

A cache of unreleased recordings was found in Pigpen's apartment after his death, but there's no clear date for when they were recorded. Some sources say 1966, others 1970. This collection of songs has made the rounds of fans and has even shown up on YouTube on occasion, with fans stringing the songs together and using photos of Pigpen to create videos. One of Pigpen's more affecting originals from this batch of recordings, the song "No Time," was featured on the *Pigpen . . . A Blues Singer* movie's website as of this writing.

The unreleased Pigpen songs on the "apartment tapes" have gone under various titles, but the ones that have circulated the most include "Two Women," "Michael," "Katie Mae" (also heard on *Bear's Choice*), "New Orleans/That Train," "Instrumental," "Bring Me My Shotgun," "C.C. Rider," "Hitchhiking Woman," and "When I Was a Boy," which are said to date from 1970. "I Believe," "She's Mine," and "Like a Long Time" (aka "No Time") are reportedly the final recordings he made, and the version of "Sweet Georgia Brown/Betty and Dupree" features Pigpen with Jorma Kaukonen of Jefferson Airplane in 1964. On such a tape that was uploaded to YouTube, several of the songs appear in two versions. There are also other unreleased Pigpen songs that have been issued on rare bootlegs or written about in various places, but the above ones are the recordings that have been the most accessible to fans looking to find out more about Pigpen.

The recordings offer a fascinating look at a different, gentler side of Pigpen. For one thing, they showcase his skills on acoustic guitar and piano, which weren't heard much within the context of the Grateful Dead. For another, the songs show that, as tough as Pigpen could sound when he was in front of an audience, he could sound that much sweeter when seated alone with only his acoustic guitar for accompaniment. Maybe Lesh was right about Pigpen's being most comfortable playing at home on an old acoustic guitar.

Pigpen's story has resonance beyond the Dead's because he embodied the archetype of the type of artist who came to change the world of pop music. He was a white kid who found his voice in African American music and brought a credible version of that music to a wider audience. Garcia, Weir, and Lesh didn't really fit this archetype because they never immersed themselves in any African American music form as deeply as Pigpen immersed himself in the blues (rock 'n' roll doesn't count, as it was played by white folks almost from the beginning).

In this light, Pigpen's story fits in with that of such early rock artists as Elvis Presley and Mick Jagger and, oddly enough, with such recent artists as the Beastie Boys, Eminem, and Madonna (enjoy that sentence because it's probably the only place you'll ever see Pigpen's and Madonna's names that close to each other). Since the 1990s, the Dead have been pretty generous with releasing old recordings on CD, and the Internet has given music fans a convenient way to upload unreleased recordings that they would have had to press into bootlegs in years past in order for the public to hear them. Who knows what tapes will turn up next unexpectedly? We may not have heard the last of Pigpen yet.

20

Dark Star

What Place Did Tom Constanten Have in the Dead's Music?

I f you spend enough time listening to the Grateful Dead's music and reading about the band members, one thing that becomes evident is the group's openness to new ideas and experiences. That collective mindset is what let the band hop aboard Ken Kesey's acid trip bus and later on allowed audio engineer Owsley "Bear" Stanley, Dan Healy, and others to design the gigantic sound system known as the "Wall of Sound."

But the Dead's most peculiar move might just have been bringing in Tom Constanten as a full-fledged band member in late 1968. Constanten is arguably the least-known member of the Dead because he stayed for the shortest amount of time—less than a year and a half, with his first concert being November 23, 1968, at Ohio University in Athens, Ohio, and his last coming January 26, 1970, at the Civic Auditorium in Honolulu, Hawaii. During that time, he played on two studio albums, *Anthem of the Sun* and *Aoxomoxoa*, and the *Live/Dead* album. He can also be heard on several live CDs recorded during the years he was with the band and released after the band broke up.

Why bring a keyboardist into a band that already had one? And why bring a seventh member into a group that already had a pretty busy sound? The answer to these questions can be found by going back through a part of the Dead's history that's rarely discussed: the temporary firing of Pigpen and Bob Weir just after the July release of *Anthem of the Sun*.

During this period, Garcia, Lesh and the drummers were evolving rapidly as musicians, pushing the improvisational jams they'd always done to the nth degree on several songs, notably the pivotal "Dark Star," which the band added to their live repertoire sometime in mid-1967. When Garcia and Lesh began to sense that their musical capabilities were starting to outshine those of Weir and Pigpen, they led the charge to vote them out of the band, at least temporarily, with the idea that maybe they'd improve. Weir, for his part, evolved into a first-rate rhythm guitarist. Pigpen, who was a guitarist and singer as well as a keyboardist, tried to improve his technique by taking lessons (reportedly from the mother of Quicksilver Messenger guitarist John Cipollina).

But Pigpen's work on keyboards was always rudimentary, and even a lot of improvement in a short time wouldn't have brought his musicianship up to par.

So, by the fall of 1968, when it looked like Pigpen and Weir were going to stay in the band after all, Lesh suggested bringing in his college friend and roommate Constanten on a permanent basis.

Constanten, who was nicknamed "T.C.," was no stranger to the band. In Constanten's 1992 autobiography, *Between Rock and Hard Places: A Musical Autobiodyssey*, he mentions that Lesh introduced him early on to Garcia, whom Lesh had met at a party in 1961. Constanten also met Hunter around this time, so it's not as though he were going in as a stranger when he first made inroads into joining the band when he added piano and other effects to the *Anthem of the Sun* album in late 1967 and early 1968. But what exactly did the Dead hope to achieve by adding a classically trained keyboardist to the mix instead of, say, a rock 'n' roll piano-pounder or Hammond organ expert? They probably didn't exactly know the answer to that—and maybe the "what if?" element even appealed to them. At the time, "Dark Star" was practically evolving by the night, and Constanten had proven that he could think in terms of out-of-the-box musical ideas with the work he did on *Anthem*. One such move included throwing a children's toy gyroscope at the soundboard and strings of a piano to create a crashing glissando sound.

According to Phil Lesh, in his book *Searching for the Sound: My Life with the Grateful Dead*:

> Even though we knew that the band worked best with all of us playing, Jerry and I thought it would be a good idea to add another element. We decided to ask T.C. to come in and augment the keyboard slot, thus freeing up Pigpen to concentrate more on singing and the harp. T.C. joined us on our next tour, and he and Pig shared the organ seat, giving the band a rich, strange sound. It was very stimulating to have a new voice providing a running commentary on the music from such oblique and wonderful perspectives.

In the world of the Grateful Dead circa 1968, the weirder things were, the better. The band's focus would soon change, but during that period, Constanten proved to be the right man for a difficult job—so who was he, anyway?

A Man upon the Scene

Tom Constanten was born Thomas Charles Hills on March 19, 1944, in Long Branch, New Jersey, a city located on the fabled Jersey Shore about seven miles north of Asbury Park, the town Bruce Springsteen immortalized with the title of his first album. His parents split up when he was four years old, and he was given the surname Constanten after being adopted by his stepfather, Frank Constanten (it's pronounced with the accent on the "tan," not the "con"). He started in music at age nine, taking his first piano lesson then. But his family soon relocated to the then–relatively new town of Las Vegas, where he went through what he called "a mixed bag of instructors." He also studied classical violin.

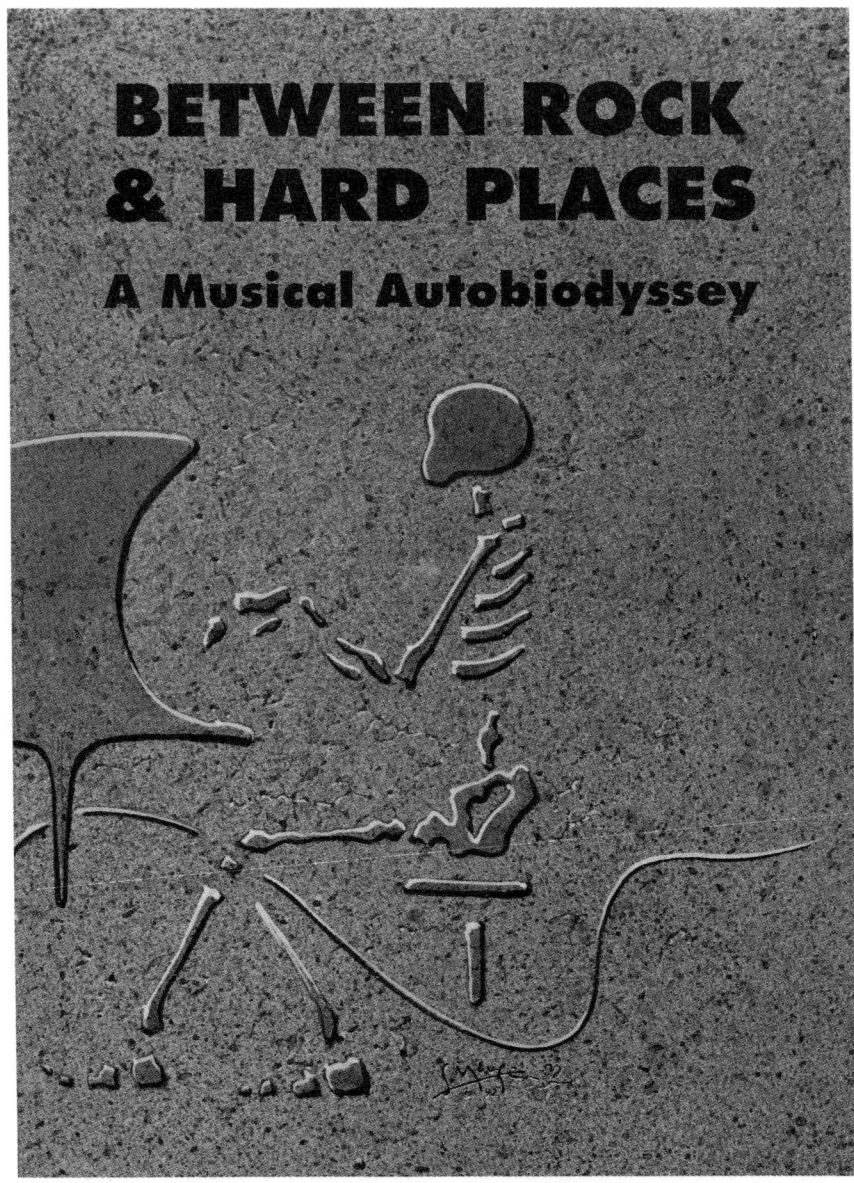

Tom Constanten's book *Between Rock and Hard Places: A Musical Autobiodyssey* contains a chapter about how he came to join the Dead and what times were like during his short, strange trip with the group.   *Hulogosi 1992; cover illustration © Stanley Mouse*

Unlike most of the other Dead members who first stepped onto a performance stage in coffeehouses or rock clubs, Constanten's concert debut outside of high school took place on a concert stage with a symphony orchestra. After successfully performing one of his original piano compositions at a high school talent show, he was encouraged by his music teacher to write a piece that could be performed during a concert by the Las Vegas Pops Orchestra. They accepted his work, and on May 28, 1961, he performed his composition, *Conversation Piece*, before an audience at the Las Vegas Convention Center. After graduating from high school, Constanten started college in the fall of 1961 at the University of California, Berkeley, where he lasted only one semester. But that was long enough to meet a fellow classical music buff, Phil Lesh, who would change his life several years later. The pair's like-mindedness is emphasized in the way they met, a story that could not be told any better than the way Constanten relates it in his book:

> During a break I got caught up in a conversation about music in general with Margie Panofsky (yet to attain distinction in early music). A rather intense discussion was joined by a third party. When I said, with teenage conviction, that music might have stopped in 1750 but it started up again in 1950, this blond-haired guy spontaneously reached across and heartily shook hands with me. He subsequently invited me to share his apartment, a block off of the U.C. campus. Compared to my humble room in a house in the Berkeley Hills, it seemed too good a deal to pass up. His name was Phil Lesh. Phil introduced me to a fascinating array of music and people. As a volunteer at [listener-supported radio station] KPFA, he had access to the latest tapes of a European festival performance of Stockhausen, Boulez, and more.

The pair found out that the pioneering experimental/electronic composer Luciano Berio just happened to be teaching a course at nearby Mills College, so they signed up. Among the students in the class was Steve Reich, who would make his name as a minimalist composer in the 1970s and be awarded the Pulitzer Prize for Music in 2009. In a 2003 talk Constanten had with the website Digital Interviews, he said that around this period there was also talk of a Lesh-Constanten band that Reich was in on as well. All three musicians played a series of concerts at the San Francisco Mime Troupe in May 1964, after which Lesh and Constanten joined Reich's improvisation ensemble, which included several other members.

Constanten writes that, during this period, the apartment he shared with Lesh "had become an avant garde music factory." At the time Lesh was working on his much–remarked about composition for four orchestras, *Foci*. Constanten was composing his own works, including a piece for chamber orchestra titled *Phrases* and a work for pianists called *Three Pieces for Two Pianos*. The pair's taste in music also encompassed the pioneering jazz trumpet work of Miles Davis and the instrumental experiments of the Stan Kenton Orchestra.

It was interesting stuff, but a world apart from the traditional music that Garcia was playing just a few miles away in Palo Alto at the time. But when Garcia and Lesh began playing together in 1965, worlds didn't collide so much as mesh. Lesh was a trumpet player who'd never played the bass. Garcia sensed his innate musicality and encouraged him to take up the electric bass guitar so they could play together. Lesh brought some of his classical training to the bass, where he often played lead lines and counterpoint parts in relation to what the other musicians were doing.

After college didn't work out, Constanten joined the Air Force and was stationed in Denver, Colorado. The reason he didn't officially join the Dead during the recording of the *Anthem* album was that he had military duties to fulfill. When his obligations to Uncle Sam were done with, he boarded a plane and headed off to Ohio where the Dead were playing. He purportedly caught the Dead live at the Columbus Veterans Hall in Columbus on November 22, 1968, and was on stage playing in the band the next night. But Constanten and the Dead weren't an easy a fit for several reasons.

The main reason was that the group already had several years playing together as a professional unit, and any additional player was going to have to work twice as hard to blend in. In his book, Constanten says that he "felt like a rookie joining a championship team when I joined the band," even though he'd played before large crowds in Vegas previously. He mentions that "there's a reluctance to mess with a winning formula," meaning that the Dead weren't about to reconfigure themselves to suit his playing; the opposite would have to happen. To that end, Constanten began searching for a style that would work within the context of the Dead's music. It wasn't easy:

> I figured that this configuration deserved nothing less than an original groundbreaking approach, such as Phil was doing with his bass work. Slowly—too slowly some might contend—that was what I set out to do at the keyboard. One of the band members suggested that I'd've been better advised to imitate someone who was already "doing it." Aside from any philosophical disagreements I might have with the premise that it was based on, I couldn't make that advice work. Patterns that I'd appropriated from [Santana's] Gregg Rolie or [the Band's] Garth Hudson wouldn't fly in rehearsals.

Studio Versus Live

Constanten learned that what worked in a studio setting didn't necessarily fly when the band played live. Part of the problem was the equipment he was given to work with. On *Aoxomoxoa*, Constanten was able to bring a wide variety of keyboard textures to the table, including harpsichord on "Mountains of the Moon," old-fashioned organ on "Dupree's Diamond Blues," and bells on "St. Stephen." On the road, he was placed behind Pigpen's old Vox Super-Continental organ because the new Hammond B-3 Pigpen had been playing had gotten repossessed. The results were underwhelming—and that's when he could even be heard.

Although his bread and butter is modern classical music, Tom Constanten has returned to the music of the Grateful Dead, jamming with bands such as Terrapin Flyer and releasing CDs such as 2000's *Grateful Dreams*, where he reinterprets several Dead classics on piano.

Author's collection

For example, on the version of "St. Stephen" from *Live/Dead*, an organ fanfare by Constanten introduces the "William Tell" bridge section. The playing is impressive, but the actual sound of the organ comes across with all the power of a children's toy keyboard. Constanten says he was "chronically underamplified" and couldn't hear himself. "Seeking relief from being positioned stage right, directly in front of four Jerry Garcia twin reverbs turned up to 10, I moved across the stage, there to be greeted by Mickey's cannons," he writes.

When he pointed out his amplification problems to the band's sound engineer at the time, Owsley Stanley, he was told that "a good worker never blames his tools." Still, it's frustrating to hear Constanten come up with interesting keyboard lines as "Dark Star" grew into a monster jam, only to be drowned out as soon as Garcia's guitar and voice take center stage (a good example being around the five-minute mark of the November 7, 1969, performance at the Fillmore Auditorium).

But other sources say Constanten's style just never quite jelled with the Dead's. In manager Rock Scully's account of his time with the band, *Living with the Dead: Twenty Years on the Bus with Garcia and the Grateful Dead* (co-written with David Dalton), he states that Constanten "can handle the cadenzas all right, but he has a hard time with the funky chicken," meaning that Constanten couldn't loosen up from his classical style enough to blend in with the Dead's improvisational ethos. David Gans says that Lesh once told him that "the rap on T.C. was that he could jam, but he couldn't swing." In *A Long Strange Trip: The Inside History of the Grateful Dead*, Dennis McNally says that personality issues also came between Constanten and the other musicians. Writes McNally, "He felt that at times he became a pawn in the run-of-the mill bickering, wherein a complaint about T.C. could mean a complaint about his sponsors Phil and Jerry. Hunter found him holier than thou because of his devotion to Scientology and his resulting refusal to take LSD alienated him from Owsley among others."

The one place where trouble didn't arise was, oddly enough, in the relationship between Constanten and the Dead member he was brought in to partially replace, Pigpen. From all accounts, the classical student got along quite well with the harp-blowing blues aficionado, and the musicians ended up sharing a house in Novato and rooming together on the road. Pigpen also reportedly served as best man at Constanten's first wedding.

In the End There's Still That Song

Analysis by Deadheads regarding Constanten's contributions varies. On an Archive.org page devoted to the subject, the opinion of commenters ranges from the joking ("Tom who?") to the personal ("a look at Scientology itself") to the thoughtful. The latter comes courtesy of a commenter who goes by the moniker "ghostofpig," who attended the band's shows almost from the beginning. He writes:

> The leap from my first shows in 1967 to the Constanten era is astonishing. The band I encountered on 6-14-68 was light years ahead of the one from the summer before. . . . I believe that [Constanten's] catalytic energy pushed Phil who in turn pushed Garcia during 1968. His swirling playing allowed the organ to become an energizing force for the ongoing, nascent psychedelia that Jerry and Phil were seeking out. His expressiveness is perhaps best heard on the many "Dark Stars" of 1969 that floated on the wings of his eerily incandescent playing.

But by 1969 it was clear that the Dead were moving in another direction: away from psychedelic experiments and back to the rootsy, acoustic-based American music Garcia was playing back when Constanten was learning all about modern classical music concepts like dissonance and minimalism. He ended up parting ways amicably with the band just before they began work on *Workingman's Dead* in February 1970.

According to Lesh's book, Constanten was notified around that time that he'd been offered the chance to become both the composer and musical director for a musical called *Tarot*. The band and Constanten agreed that the time was as good as any for them to part ways, so Constanten left and became the only former Dead keyboardist to escape the "curse" and not die prematurely.

Constanten went on to form the band Touchstone, which performed the music for the original cast album from *Tarot*, released in 1972. It was an instrumental album of progressive rock that has now become a collectible among vinyl buffs. The band included Gary "Chicken" Hirsh, who was previously with Country Joe and the Fish, and Paul Dresher, who worked with Steve Reich and Terry Riley.

Constanten stayed active in music, performing regularly and recording sporadically. From 1974 through 1984, he served as a professor of music for SUNY Buffalo and the San Francisco Art Institute. In 1986, he was named an artist-in-residence at Harvard University.

In 1988, Constanten ventured back into the world of recorded music, and back into the land of the Dead. He collaborated with Robert Hunter for a cassette-only album release called *Duino Elegies*. It features Constanten playing selections from Brahms and Chopin while Hunter read his translations of the poetry of Rainer Maria Rilke. In 1989, Constanten released an album of solo piano pieces, *Fresh Tracks in Real Time*, which included a rendition of "Dark Star." He also began a working relationship with Dead keyboard tech and keyboard player Bob Bralove. In 1997, they released their first album under the moniker Dose Hermanos; several more followed. Most recently, Constanten and Bralove have been playing with the Chicago-based Dead-inspired band Terrapin Flyer. Constanten remarried in 1993 and now has two daughters.

One of the most interesting aspects of his short time with the Dead is that Constanten was inducted into the Rock and Roll Hall of Fame with the band in 1994. The Rock Hall often excludes musicians who weren't band founders or were in groups for short periods of time. The most prominent example of this is the Velvet Underground's Doug Yule, who sang lead on several key tracks and led the group after Lou Reed defected. Constanten had said that the Rock Hall induction is part of what has given him what his friend Peter Coyote called "a comfortable level of fame": enough to be positive without the constant glare of the spotlight becoming a nuisance.

21

Ship of Fools

The Dead's Ten Worst Decisions

E very recording act, no matter how great, makes its share of bad moves. The Clash fired drummer Topper Headon and destroyed their delicate chemistry. The Who decided to play a general admission concert at a venue where such events were known to get out of control. The Rolling Stones kept releasing albums long after their songwriting muse went missing. Here, in chronological order, are some of the Dead's worst choices.

The Way They Handled Altamont

As Phil Lesh admits in his book, *Searching for the Sound: My Life with the Grateful Dead*, the Dead made several bad decisions when it came to being involved with the Altamont Speedway Free Festival, which took place December 6, 1969. The band probably shouldn't have agreed to be involved at all. The idea for staging a free concert was conceived to foster goodwill by and for the Rolling Stones, which the Stones decided they needed after rock critic Ralph J. Gleason called them out for setting the price of their concert tickets too high. This wasn't the Dead's problem, as they'd played free concerts and kept their ticket prices reasonable. Yet their manager, Rock Scully, seemed to want the Dead to be on a bill with the Stones, so the Dead signed on. Strike one.

The concert's original location at Golden Gate Park was supposed to be a secret until twenty-four hours before the concert so that too many people wouldn't show up. But Mick Jagger blabbed about it to the press, so another venue had to be quickly found, which meant no bathroom facilities or medical supplies. Strike two. Then, the Stones' camp decided the Hells Angels motorcycle gang should work security, as the Stones had gone that route with the (apparently mellower) British chapter. Strike three! The Dead should be out! But the Dead didn't walk away just yet; instead, they decided to fly by helicopter into the heart of mayhem, only to decide not to perform, while the Stones kept the crowd waiting until dark so they could better shoot the movie they were making, which turned out to be *Gimme Shelter*. Would a set by the Dead perhaps have mellowed out the crowd? We'll never know. But the Dead put themselves in a damned-if-you-do-and-damned-if-you-don't position with Altamont, and the problem should have been averted long before it got to that stage.

Not Releasing a Studio Album in 1972

The Dead were on something of a songwriting streak starting with 1969's *Aoxomoxoa* and dropped two of their best studio albums in 1970. After that, they decided to release two multi-disc live albums of new material, not coming out with a new studio release until 1973. Commercial considerations aside, this blunted this impact of the Dead's artistic power and robbed the world of what might have been the ultimate Dead album. (For a complete rundown of what this album might have been like, see chapter 26, "One Old Score: The Great Lost Grateful Dead Studio Album of 1972.")

Having Garcia Direct *The Grateful Dead* Movie

Phil Lesh has gone on record as saying the idea for *The Grateful Dead* movie was brought to the band by director Leon Gast, who wanted to make a simple documentary about the band. Gast walked off the project when he didn't get along with Garcia, though, and pretty soon that left Garcia to not only make the artistic decisions about what the film should be, but also to spend hours doing tedious editing. On the artistic front, Garcia's instincts weren't as sound as his musical decisions. Although the movie is interesting, the editing is static, and the pacing is slow, with the opening animated sequencing going on too long. That sequence purportedly cost $25,000, adding to the $600,000 it cost to make the movie. In all, it took from late 1964 to June 1977 to get the movie out.

Not surprisingly, this pushed Garcia beyond his limits personally, and he moved into the harder drug use that would plague him for the rest of his life. There was cocaine for when he needed to stay up all hours of the night plowing through frame after frame, and heroin when he needed to come down. In *A Long Strange Trip: The Inside History of the Grateful Dead*, author Dennis McNally says that the film became an obsession of Garcia's, and Garcia is quoted as saying, "Every time I thought about something, my mind would come back to the film and I'd get depressed." The movie is definitely worth seeing, especially when it's given theatrical screenings, as it was in 2012 on the day that would have been Garcia's seventieth birthday. But it's not as much fun to watch when you think about the toll it took on Garcia.

Not Releasing a Studio Album Between 1980 and 1987

Go to Heaven, which was released in late April 1980, was simultaneously a return to form for the Dead and a musical step forward. It was a return to form because some of the music harkened back to the Dead's earlier work, especially coming on the heels of the dance-oriented *Shakedown Street*. And it was a step into the 1980s because it introduced the songs and singing of new keyboardist Brent Mydland. The album was also reasonably successful, peaking at #23, higher than the band's previous two albums had placed. *Go to Heaven*'s lead single, "Alabama Getaway," received substantial FM radio play and climbed to #68. A second single, "Don't Ease Me In," didn't chart, but also got heavy FM rotation. At this point, the Dead should have been armed and ready to go into the '80s, especially since they introduced a bunch of great songs during the next few years, including the future hit "Touch of Grey." The Dead also left a trio of release-able cuts off *Go to Heaven* that later came out as bonus cuts on the reissue CD.

So what happened? Garcia fell into addiction using a potent form of heroin known as Persian. The Dead dropped two double live albums in 1981 and then . . . nothing. Nothing from the group, anyway. Garcia dropped his final solo studio album in 1982, and Bob Weir released two albums with his side band Bobby and the Midnites in 1981 and 1984, respectively. As nice as it was to see the group in concert so many times in the early 1980s, the lack of a new studio album was a sign of artistic stagnation. It also set the Dead up to implode in the 1990s when, unlike every other band, they couldn't seem to take a break from touring to give serious attention to their new material, virtually all of which was worthy of immortalizing on disc. Had the band insisted on recording a new project in the early 1980s, might that have been the impetus Garcia needed to pull him away from his demons? It's hard to say, but the Dead's aversion to the recording studio and preference for the road wasn't really for the best, no matter how many great shows they played after *Go to Heaven*.

Dylan and the Dead

Spaghetti sauce and chocolate. Drinking and driving. Television and the radio. All are great on their own, but not so wonderful when paired together. So it was with Bob Dylan and the Grateful Dead, two of the best rock acts ever to walk the face of the earth and two entities that should never have performed together, except maybe for a guest spot or two. The reasons for this are easy to suss out: the Dead had developed an intuitive sense of how to play together for two decades, and bringing Dylan's notoriously freewheeling style into the mix made the whole thing sound like less than the sum of its parts. Yes, the Band played well with Dylan, but that combination worked because, at the time, Dylan was just getting his feet wet playing rock, and the Band were helping to create his live style. By the time Dylan joined up with the Dead in July 1987, the styles of both groups were as good as engraved in stone, and they didn't mesh, making great songs like "I Want You" and "All Along the Watchtower" sound more rocky than rocking.

Even worse, the pairing of these two rock giants seemed to outsiders like something of a cash-in, making the Dead appear crass, something they never were. The subsequent live album, *Dylan and the Dead*, just seemed to drive that home as it garnered near-universal negative reviews even from Dead-friendly critics such as Robert Christgau. The kicker was that for a "superstar" album, it didn't even sell all that well, only getting to #37 and staying on the Billboard album chart's Top 40 for three weeks. Had Bob Dylan and the Grateful Dead convened to work up a real super group album like the Traveling Wilburys did, maybe they'd have come up with something brilliant. But a bunch of hastily rehearsed summer gigs did not great art make.

Agreeing to Participate in MTV's "Day of the Dead"

By August 1987, the Dead had a hit single, a hit album, and had played a round of shows with Dylan. Concert parking lots were overflowing with new fans who came to party, not to hear music, and the laid-back scene of the early 1980s seemed all but gone. Enter MTV, the cable music channel known for capitalizing on trends of the moment. Because the Grateful Dead had become trendy in summer of 1987, the music channel decided to devote a whole day's programming to the band, showing old footage, the "Touch of Grey" video, and interviews with Garcia and Hart.

The channel broadcast live outside the band's July 12 show at the Meadowlands Sports Complex (aka Giants Stadium) in New Jersey. And it was this that sent the message to MTV's young, impressionable viewers that Dead concerts were a big party everyone should try attending at least once. Interviewers Carolyne Heldman and Ritch Shydner talked to Deadheads in various states of inebriation, some of whom sang impromptu, off-key renditions of "Touch of Grey." "It's the whole thing: it's the concert, it's the party, it's the band," says a Deadhead at one point. Had the Dead gotten security to usher MTV's trendy video jockeys out of the parking lot and not agreed to be interviewed, "Day of the Dead" might not have happened at all. What also might not have happened could have been all of the open drug dealing, arrests, and gate crashings that plagued the band during their final years.

Not Following Up the *Built to Last* Album

The Dead's final studio effort, *Built to Last*, might not have been on par with *American Beauty* when it came to artistic brilliance, but it was a solid enough effort. After the death of Brent Mydland, who had written more songs than any other band member had on that album, it might have appeared to casual listeners as though the Dead's songwriting flame had gone out, because no new album seemed to be forthcoming anytime soon. But that was far from the truth. As the 1990s wore on, both the Garcia-Hunter team and Phil Lesh underwent something of a creative renaissance, coming up with their best songs in years. But the band never could get it together enough to put these songs on a proper album, and that was unfortunate. For a complete rundown of what the last Dead album would have sounded like, see chapter 35, "Days Between: The Final Dead Album That Never Was."

Not Getting Help for (Fill in the Blank)

The reason that the Grateful Dead had a hands-off policy when it came to interventions for drug and alcohol abuse came from Garcia. Garcia didn't like to play the role of police officer, telling others what they should or shouldn't do with their lives. Nor did he like people playing the cop when it came to his own excessive behavior. But when your band members and associates begin to pass away, one by one, and your own health begins to fail you, maybe it's time to change your philosophy. It seems as though Garcia took steps toward doing that toward the end of his life when he owned up to his addiction and checked into the Betty Ford Clinic, then the Serenity Knolls drug treatment center. But by then, it was too late and the damage had been done. Even more unfortunately, the damage had also been done to several of the band's associates and other members who'd preceded Garcia in death.

Garcia and the band members who followed his philosophy went wrong thinking that the use of alcohol and harder drugs could be tolerated the same way as the non-addictive drugs the band members favored earlier in their careers. They couldn't. It's unfortunate that Garcia didn't turn to the recovery industry for help earlier and set a different example. He might have come to realize that his ideas about not micromanaging human behavior were relics of an earlier era, when the drugs were different and the musicians were younger and stronger.

Some say that Jerry Garcia's insistence on directing *The Grateful Dead Movie* nudged him toward using harder drugs, which helped him get through the endless hours of editing. The film is still occasionally screened and was brought back to select theaters on August 1, 2012—which would have been Garcia's seventieth birthday.

Author's collection

Nitpicking About the *Dick's Picks* Series

When the *Dick's Picks* series was started in 1993, it was cause for celebration, because it finally made high-quality recordings of everyone's favorite concerts easily available. Sure, the recordings were from two-track tapes recorded directly from the mixing board and didn't quite have the polish of professionally made live recordings. But they sounded cleaner than did the cassette tapes most people were able to access, which had usually been copied several times over.

That was the good news. The bad news was that the band members had gone through the concert tapes and asked that certain songs be removed because they considered their performances not to be up to snuff. Why the worry? Real fans had these tapes already and had already heard those performances. A nadir of sorts was reached on the second *Dick's Picks*, a one-disc set that included a mere six songs out of the twenty-two the Dead had played the night of October 31, 1971, at the Ohio Theatre. The problem of truncating concerts was resolved as the series went on, with *Volume Five* being the first to include a full show. But *Dick's Picks* was supposed to be a clean-up, not a cover-up, of the band's tapes, and there are entire segments of shows still sitting on the cutting room floor that should have been put on these discs.

Going Out on the 1994 and 1995 Tours

Deadheads sometimes talk about seeing concerts near the end of the band's career where they were on fire. This might have been true when judging those concerts against other recent concerts. But compared to the band's golden era in the 1970s, the Grateful Dead that went out on tour starting in 1994 wasn't quite the same band. Most of that had to do with Garcia. In his book *Garcia: An American Life*, biographer Blair Jackson emphatically states that Garcia was "in no condition to be onstage." To late-stage Deadheads, this might not have been evident at the time. The shows not only were selling out, but also were in stadiums, and everyone seemed to be having a good time.

But when you listen back to recordings from the leg of the 1994 tour that started June 8 at the Cal Expo Amphitheatre, it's clear that all was not well in Deadland. By that fall, Garcia was no longer leading the band, but being carried, especially on "off" nights such as October 9 at the USAir Arena in Maryland. The next year wasn't much different, and examples of Garcia being "off" abound, with the June 18 performance of "Wharf Rat" being a particularly sad example. Although live recordings have been released that cover virtually all the stages of the Dead's career, none of the shows the band played during their last few years have been released on CD as of this writing. They can be heard on the Archive. org website, however, and are mostly interesting because of the disconnect between the cheering stadium crowds and the lackluster final performances by Garcia.

22

I'll Sing to Them This Story

The Significance of Donna Jean Godchaux-MacKay

In the 1970s, rock bands such as the Rolling Stones, Humble Pie, and Pink Floyd liberally employed the use of female singers. But only the Grateful Dead officially admitted one such singer as a member of the band: Donna Jean Godchaux-MacKay, who was the only woman ever to become a member of the band. Donna Jean Godchaux-MacKay was married to the late Dead keyboardist Keith Godchaux during her time with the Dead (and was known as Donna Jean Godchaux), and she has since remarried and now goes by Donna Jean Godchaux-MacKay.

The addition of Godchaux-MacKay expanded the band's musical range significantly. With her onboard, the Dead could add high harmonies, backing vocal exhortations, or entire sections of songs that would have been out of the vocal range of the male band members (e.g., "The Music Never Stopped").

But adding Godchaux-MacKay as a member was more than just a musical move for the Dead. She might have only left her mark on a few Dead songs as a vocalist and/or a songwriter, but her admittance to the band is also among the most important things they ever did for non-musical reasons. By counting a woman in their ranks, the band made good on their promises of being open to new ideas and progressive thinking. And with Godchaux-MacKay in tow, the Dead were able to position themselves as a band in tune with the changing times as more and more women began to enter the rock world.

A Thing (or Two) of the Past

To fully understand why Godchaux-MacKay being made a member of the Dead was a significant factor for the band as well as for the larger rock culture of the 1970s, we have to go back to the early days of rock 'n' roll, when the genre emerged in the mid-1950s. Like several other musical genres that would liberate music (the British Invasion and rap, for example), rock 'n' roll had an ironically anti-liberating effect on women in music. Around the time rock 'n' roll was born, female singers in both the pop and country genres were plentiful. But rock

Marathon gigs such as the Dead's thirty-song concert at the University of California, Santa Barbara, in 1973 would prove to be a baptism by fire for Donna Jean Godchaux-MacKay, who had been a studio singer before she joined the Grateful Dead.   *Photo by Rosie McGee*

'n' roll became a boys' club, probably because of its aggressiveness, so its early female adherents, such as Wanda Jackson and Janis Martin, didn't make much large-scale commercial impact.

Women were not to be dissuaded, though, and some did find a way to make their mark in the late 1950s. Connie Francis was a schmaltzy pop vocalist all the way, but she sometimes employed rock's instrumentation and rhythms (e.g., "Stupid Cupid," "Lipstick on Your Collar"). Brenda Lee hit it big in 1959 with the hard-hitting countrified rock of "Sweet Nothin's," penned by rockabilly wild man Ronnie Self.

Over on the rhythm and blues side of the tracks, the Shirelles' first hit in 1958 with "I Met Him on a Sunday (Ronde-Ronde)" and made a huge impact, launching what came to be known as the "girl group era." That lasted roughly from 1959 to 1963 and brought together strains of rock 'n' roll, pop, and R&B under one umbrella. Groups such as the Cookies ("Don't Say Nothin' Bad (About My Baby)"), the Orlons ("South Street," "Cross Fire!"), the Ronettes ("Be My Baby," "Baby, I Love You"), and (especially) the Shangri-Las ("Leader of the Pack") might not have had the raw sound of the early rock 'n' rollers, but they made up for it with lots of attitude.

The girl group era also helped launch Motown Records, the African American–run Detroit-based label that went from indie start up to international powerhouse in less than a decade's time. Motown's first female hit was Mary Wells's "Bye Bye Baby" in 1961; later that year, the Marvelettes would follow with "Please Mr. Postman," and from there on out, Motown almost always kept a female presence on the pop charts. By 1963, there were enough women on the charts to make up for the almost total lack of them five years before. The African American girl groups brought a more soulful sound to the mainstream, with their call-and-response vocals and ad-libbed exhortations coming straight out of gospel music. For a brief moment in 1962 and 1963, it seemed as though popular music were becoming the culmination of the dream many had of America becoming a "melting pot."

And then the dream came crashing down.

Almost as soon as the Beatles hit America in early 1964, girl groups became yesterday's news. Girl groups would continue to have hits until 1965, but after 1964, their impact was dulled considerably. Trends drive what music fans listen to, and in that period, groups of women singing were out, while guys with long hair strumming electric guitars were in.

One irony was that a lot of the new wave of bands had been influenced by girl groups and even covered their songs. Examples include the Beatles doing the aforementioned Marvelettes hit and the Shirelles' "Baby It's You," the Zombies covering the Supremes' "When the Lovelight Starts Shining through His Eyes," and the Searchers covering the Orlons' "Don't Throw Your Love Away," among others. The Beatles and the groups that followed them also made rock 'n' roll as a genre passé, creating a new, more progressive style of music that came to be known solely as "rock."

British Invasion bands had made female singing groups seem as dated as those singers had made early rock 'n' rollers look. Out of all the groups that came over from England, only one of them, the Honeycombs, had a female member, and they didn't make much of an impact on America, save one very poppish song, "Have I the Right?" So much for the British bands ushering in a new era of "progressivism." In terms of gender equality in music, the Beatles, the Rolling Stones, and the Animals actually blasted listeners back decades, to before singers such as Rosemary Clooney and Doris Day made inroads into the pop realm in the late 1940s. The lack of women in post–British Invasion rock led to the misconception that rock was a boys' club. This point of view would last well past the Dead's prime era and would influence some people's negative feelings toward Godchaux-MacKay's role in the band.

Women did flourish in another area, though: soul music. The death of the girl group era didn't spell the end of girl groups for African American female singers, and throughout the 1960s, the Supremes, Martha and the Vandellas, and the Marvelettes made some of the best music and scored some of the biggest hits of the decade.

Women were also welcomed into rock in the city of San Francisco, the Dead's home base. Jefferson Airplane had front women in Signe Anderson and then Grace Slick, who previously had sung for the Great Society. Big Brother and the Holding Company adopted Janis Joplin as a singer and then Kathi McDonald. It's a Beautiful Day had singer-keyboardist Linda LaFlamme onboard. There was also Linda Tillery, the co-lead singer in the Loading Zone; Lynne Hughes, who sang for Tongue & Grove; and Jan Errico, who both drummed and sang for the Vejtables, a band from nearby Millbrae. Women were in pop groups such as the Mamas and the Papas and Spanky and Our Gang, but in San Francisco they rocked alongside the men. All of this probably influenced the Dead's decision to bring Godchaux-MacKay on as a permanent member throughout most of the 1970s. She wailed in the tradition of the girl group soul singers, but she was also rock-oriented like the female vocalists from San Francisco.

Beyond Rock 'N' Roll

When rock historians assess the early days of rock 'n' roll, they usually speak of the music coming about because of the melding of two genres: rhythm and blues music and country music, then known as "hillbilly music." The Grateful Dead drew from both of these styles when it came to creating their own music. When girl group music merged with soul music, it brought forth a powerful new sound, one that would come to dominate popular music after Aretha Franklin hit big in the late 1960s. Female soul singers pushed pop music into a dynamic area previously unknown to either rock 'n' roll or pop, and they broadened the emotional range of both styles by letting female voices take center stage. This was one area of American popular music that the Dead could not hope to tap into without a female member, though, until they brought in Godchaux-MacKay.

By the end of the 1960s, though, soulful girl groups had also lost their commercial cachet, with established ones struggling and fewer and fewer new ones appearing. But when musical genres become unpopular, they don't usually disappear altogether. They tend to go underground and reappear in a different form. So, by the late 1960s, when girl groups had a hard time getting work, some found they could get steady gigs singing backup for the new acts that had become the de facto mainstream of rock.

The gospel-oriented Sweet Inspirations, which featured Whitney Houston's mother, Cissy, found work backing Elvis Presley and Jimi Hendrix. A trio of session singers called the Blackberries joined Humble Pie for a tour and before that sang in various configurations on records by the Rolling Stones and others (the Blackberries' own Motown album went unreleased, however). The Bluebelles renamed themselves Labelle and backed singer-songwriter Laura Nyro on an album of oldies before striking out on their own (sparking a mini–girl group revival that encompassed themselves, the Pointer Sisters, and the now-forgotten Three Degrees).

Enter Godchaux-MacKay, who by the late 1960s was singing in a female vocal group called Southern Comfort and doing backing vocals on records by Elvis Presley and Cher. When she and her husband, Keith, moved to California and she met Garcia, worlds collided. The Dead had been able to incorporate roots music such as the blues and country into their repertoire, but after Godchaux-MacKay came onboard, they were also able to bring some elements from the rich heritage of girl groups into their musical arsenal. The addition of Godchaux-MacKay allowed the Dead to tap into the energy of female soul music, which had been with rock 'n' roll almost since its beginning but had not been part of rock culture, which had become almost exclusively white since the British Invasion.

Godchaux-MacKay's addition to the band made musical sense, considering the depth of musical knowledge of the band members, especially Garcia, who as a solo act would cover one of the best girl group hits, the Marvelettes' "The Hunter Gets Captured by the Game" on a 1974 album. But to the general rock audience, who had grown up thinking of a rock band as a unit showcasing the talents of men who played instruments, the addition of a "chick singer" was a mystery, if not a downright annoyance. The Dead were still largely an underground FM radio phenomenon at that point, and the band tying themselves to a musical genre that was associated with the then–commercially oriented AM stations seemed to either make little sense to people or be viewed as a "sellout move." "What's this got to do with rock?" you can imagine skeptical fans rhetorically asking.

But adding Godchaux-MacKay's vocals to the mix was not so much a bid to expand the band's commercial base as it was to enlarge their musical vocabulary. There was a subtle richness to the band's sound when Godchaux-MacKay was onboard, and that allowed the Dead to go into areas they otherwise couldn't.

For example, when the band covered the Martha and the Vandellas hit "Dancing in the Street" (titled "Dancin' in the Streets" on *Terrapin Station* and the 45 record), Godchaux-MacKay's backing vocals gave the cover an authenticity, because male-female vocal interplay was one of the hallmarks of Motown's production style. A similar dynamic was at play when the Godchaux-MacKay-era band covered "Iko Iko," a traditional New Orleans chant that didn't become widely known until it was covered by a girl group, the Dixie Cups, who took it to #20 in 1965. On stage, Godchaux-MacKay's harmonies with Garcia on the Dolly Parton–Porter Wagoner ballad "Tomorrow Is Forever" brought the band closer than ever to an authentic country sound.

Like Mickey Hart's additional percussion, Godchaux-MacKay's vocals were not a primary element of the Dead's sound, but an enhancement to it. Both broadened the scope of what the band did. When Hart played, he tied the band's music into the traditions of world music. When Godchaux-MacKay sang, she provided a link between the Dead's music and all of the music that the girl group era connoted, including gospel, Motown, pure pop, and Southern soul. When Godchaux-MacKay left in 1979, the Dead's connection to these subgenres of early rock 'n' roll went with her in much the way the Dead's connection to traditional blues was largely lost when Pigpen passed on.

Studio to Stage

Godchaux-MacKay was born Donna Jean Thatcher and raised in the musical city of Muscle Shoals, Alabama. As a teenager, she took to singing and later joined the vocal group Southern Comfort, made up of Mary Holliday, Ginger Holliday, and Jeanie Greene. The group worked in such studios as the Norala Sound Studio, where they sang on the Percy Sledge chart-topper "When a Man Loves a Woman" and at producer Chips Moman's American Sound Studios, where they recorded vocals for Elvis Presley's #1 hit "Suspicious Minds."

In 1970, Southern Comfort came out with its lone release, a 45 on the Cotillion label of a song called "Milk and Honey," backed with the track "Don't Take Your Sweet Love Away." The record did not chart.

Afterwards, Donna Jean Thatcher moved to San Francisco where, in the space of about a year, she met her husband, Keith, and became a member of the Grateful Dead. It was she who corralled Garcia after a show at the Keystone and convinced him to let Keith audition for the band. When he passed the audition and became a member in October of 1971, she was asked to join as well. She deferred at first, but did come out for one number, "One More Saturday Night," on New Year's Eve 1971. She officially signed on five months later, on March 25, 1972, at the Academy of Music in New York.

The first song she sang that evening was the second set opener that night. It was, appropriately enough, a cover of Marvin Gaye's "How Sweet It Is (to Be Loved by You)," an old Motown tune that had prominently used female backing vocals. The song was a Top 10 hit in 1964, and its female voices had been provided by a group called the Andantes, who provided female session vocals at Motown Studios much the way Southern Comfort did at studios in Alabama.

Godchaux-MacKay sang backup to Garcia's lead vocals when the Dead played "How Sweet It Is" live for the first (and only) time at the Academy of Music, and although the performance has never been released, it can easily be heard at Archive.org.

And with that one song, a whole new world of musical possibilities opened up to the band. Godchaux-MacKay appeared on Dead albums starting with *Europe '72* and running through *Wake of the Flood, From the Mars Hotel, Blues for Allah, Steal Your Face, Terrapin Station*, and *Shakedown Street*. During that time, she wrote two songs for the band, "Sunrise" and "From the Heart of Me," and sang lead and backup vocals that sometimes had a transformative effect on songs. Her wordless wailing on the coda of "Scarlet Begonias" gave it an otherworldly edge; her vocals on the chorus of "The Music Never Stopped" grounded it in soulfulness. There's a lilt that her harmonies bring to "Crazy Fingers," a soulfulness she lends to "Passenger," and a jazz sensibility her co-lead vocals add to "France."

In concert, things weren't always so smooth. Her singing could sometimes come off as shrill and off-key, a situation purportedly caused by the fact that she had trouble hearing herself in the band's monitor mixes (keyboardist Tom Constanten also complained about not being able to hear himself on stage).

Part of the problem was also her inexperience in the live arena. Although Godchaux-MacKay had spent a lot of time in studios, the first time she ever performed in a live situation was with the Grateful Dead, a fact she shared with several interviewers over the years, including Ann Marie Svilar in a 2008 interview with Jambase.com. "A lot of my years in the Grateful Dead were really acclimating to the live situation," she said.

Godchaux-MacKay's voice usually came across fine during her solo passages, but could be problematic when the band sang harmonies together, like on the chorus of "Playing in the Band." According to David Gans, who hosts *The Grateful Dead Hour* radio show, the off-key harmonies originated with Bob Weir, who insisted on singing vocal parts too high for his range, which either threw off Godchaux-MacKay or made her singing seem off key by comparison. Gans says that close listening to concert recordings will reveal this, and it's "received wisdom" among Dead fans that Godchaux-MacKay was out of tune much of the time.

Such received wisdom is similar to the assessment of latter-day Beatles fans who believe that Ringo Starr's drumming was substandard. If that was the case, then why did all three other Beatles (among others) tap him for drum duties after the band split up? Similarly, if Godchaux-MacKay's vocals didn't cut it, then why did Garcia also have her sing in his side project, the Jerry Garcia Band? Because other members of the band were known to sing off key on occasion, Gans says, there was likely an element of misogyny in the fact that some fans chose to single out Godchaux-MacKay when it came to complaints in the vocal department. Fans who had grown up with post–British Invasion rock and its almost total lack of female participants probably weren't comfortable with seeing a woman in a formerly all-male rock band.

After the Dead founded their own label, Round Records, the band had enough faith in Godchaux-MacKay's vocals to tap her and Keith to do a solo album for the label. The 1975 album, titled *Keith and Donna* (not *Keith and Donna Godchaux*, as some discographies claim), features Garcia as both a guitarist and backup singer. Alongside seven self-penned songs and one traditional number ("Who Was John"), Godchaux-MacKay takes an impressive vocal turn on Ike and Tina Turner's "River Deep, Mountain High," a song co-written by girl group

The Keith and Donna years, which lasted throughout most of the 1970s, are regarded by many Deadheads as the Dead's best era, especially when it came to live shows. The married musical team left the fold in 1979, after they grew disillusioned with band politics and decided that they wanted to spend more time with their young son, Zion, who was born in 1974. Keith Godchaux died in a car accident shortly after the duo formed the Heart of Gold Band in 1980.   *Author's collection*

songwriters and producers Phil Spector, Jeff Barry, and Ellie Greenwich, the last of whom was also a member of a girl group, the Raindrops.

Expanding the Audience

The addition of Godchaux-MacKay may well have expanded the band's audience, making it more female friendly, although there is no way to quantify that. One thing that can be stated factually, however, is that 1970s-era rock bands that relied on guitar solos didn't usually have very big female audiences.

Back in the 1970s, members of the progressive rock band King Crimson used to joke that their audience was made up of so few women that they could count them while viewing the audience from the wings of the stage before shows. For various reasons, progressive rock appealed mostly to a male audience back in the 1970s, although that situation changed somewhat in the 2000s with the rise of such female guitar heroes as Orianthi, Kaki King, and Ana Popovic.

And although the Dead weren't a progressive rock band, they did share some musical qualities with progressive bands, such as the propensity to concentrate on long instrumental passages. The Dead probably saw the same demographic change in their audience after adding Godchaux-MacKay as Fleetwood Mac did after they added Christine McVie and then Stevie Nicks to their lineup. Both performers gave female listeners someone with whom they could closely identify.

Godchaux-MacKay's long, flowing hair and penchant for wearing flowing dresses were also a reflection of the look of a lot of female Deadheads in much the way Pigpen's biker image mirrored the look of many male Dead fans. In both cases, each performer displayed a persona that gave him or her an instant identity to which Deadheads could relate.

As mentioned previously, there weren't a whole lot of women in rock bands back in the post-Joplin era of the early 1970s. There were female solo performers, such as Carole King and Carly Simon, but they were more pop than rock. And there were women in pop groups like the 5th Dimension, Pickettywitch, and Smith (whose dynamic front woman Gayle McCormick would have been a major star in any other era). The first all-female band signed to a major record label was Fanny, in 1970; they were followed a few months later by Joy of Cooking, a band from the Dead's backyard of Marin County who weren't all female, but were led by two women. Neither group had much success despite the high quality of the music both created.

That situation started to change, if only slightly, when Heart emerged as a national act in 1975, which was the same year Nicks joined Fleetwood Mac and gave the band their first significant US hit. Although Fleetwood Mac had added McVie in 1970, the group wasn't the big act they would become later on. Conversely, the Dead were coming off a trio of hit albums when they invited Godchaux-MacKay to join, sending the message (however subtle or unintentional) that in the Dead's world, women were being admitted to the boys' club of rock. As much as some critics liked to paint the Dead as a throwback during the 1970s, this move was actually very forward-looking and likely inspired a lot of young female audience members to become involved in music as participants, not just observers.

End of an Era

The problems Godchaux-MacKay ultimately had with the Dead ended up being as much personal as professional. According to Dennis McNally's band bio, *A Long Strange Trip: The Inside History of the Grateful Dead and the Making of Modern America*, Godchaux-MacKay had become dependent on alcohol while Keith had become hooked on drugs. She was also tired of dealing with the band's internal politics, where musicians and roadies would form their own cliques and bad-mouth the other cliques. She also longed for a more stable home environment in which to raise their son, Zion, who had been born in 1974. The pair's final show was on February 17, 1979, and they exited the band by mutual agreement after a band meeting held at their house.

The couple then formed a group called the Ghosts, which was later renamed the Heart of Gold Band when they reformed with a slightly different lineup. The band ended in tragedy, though, when Keith was killed in a car accident on July 23, 1980. After his death, Godchaux-MacKay decided to leave the music business and became a Christian after marrying the group's bassist, David MacKay, a pastor. The group's recording sessions were compiled on the 1984 album *The Ghosts Playing in the Heart of Gold Band*, a little-known album that's become rare, but can still be found cheaply on eBay.

In the late 1990s, David and Donna Jean formed a new group, the Donna Jean Band, and decided to revive the Heart of Gold Band four years later, along with her sons Zion and Kinsman, and Keith's brother Brian. Her new career in music kicked into high gear after she performed at the Gathering of the Vibes in 2005 (held to commemorate the tenth anniversary of Garcia's death), and the Dead cover group the Zen Tricksters asked her to sit in on a few numbers. She ended up fronting the group under the moniker Donna Jean and the Tricksters (minus the "Zen"), and they released a self-titled CD in 2008 that garnered positive reviews on AllMusic.com and JamBands.com. The CD contained a song co-written with Keith Godchaux, "Farewell Jack."

In 2009, she branched off with that band's guitarist to form a new unit, the Donna Jean Godchaux Band featuring Jeff Mattson. The lineup also features MacKay on bass, as well as Joe Chirco on drums and Freeman White on keyboards. Since then, Godchaux-MacKay has experienced a newfound appreciation among jam band fans, getting regular write-ups in the pages of *Relix* magazine and in regional newspapers when her band plays live.

Donna Jean Godchaux-MacKay was inducted into the Rock and Roll Hall of Fame in 1994, along with the other members of the Grateful Dead. In the summer of 2012, she appeared as part of the Rock and Roll Hall of Fame's (redundantly titled) Hall of Fame series, where she spoke candidly about moving to San Francisco, meeting Keith, and joining up with the Grateful Dead. Her interview was conducted to promote an exhibit devoted to the group, *Grateful Dead: The Long, Strange Trip*, which was on display from April 12 through December 2012.

23

I Was There

Dean Grabski's Tales of a Taper

If you once traded concert tapes or spent time listening to shows on Archive.org, chances are you've heard a tape made by Dean Grabski. The New York native, who is now a West Coast taper of everything from classical music to jam bands, talks here about his days on tour.

For me, what happened was I started to go to shows and became aware of recording concerts and collecting tapes in the late 1970s when I was in high school. Some of my friends had older brothers who were Deadheads, and they would travel out to Red Rocks and other infamous venues for all these great shows and bring home recordings. They would give them to their brothers, and then their brothers would bring them into school and we'd trade them. So I started that way. I think the first show I taped was Halloween 1979 at Nassau Coliseum after I'd attended a bunch of other shows.

When I graduated from high school, I was one of those relatively aimless souls who didn't have a good, solid direction as to what I wanted to do. So I ended up working in the ski business, which was perfect because it was seasonal and allowed me to go on the road during the warmer months. During the winter, we'd get ready for touring by designing and printing up T-shirts to help pay our way for the spring and summer tours, when getting off work was easy in the ski business. Because the Dead weren't busy in the wintertime, it really worked out kind of perfectly, and I got stuck in that continuous tour cycle for a number of years, 1981 through 1985.

I first started recording shows with a boom box, which left me disappointed with the results of my recordings. So I bought an Aiwa portable tape deck and started to patch out of other people's setups. Patch taping consists of sneaking your tape deck, cables, and tapes into the venue, and then finding another taper's setup and plugging or "patching" your tape deck out of that taper's deck. Usually someone else would come in and they'd run theirs off of yours, and you'd end up with this string of tape decks all patched together with everybody flipping over their cassettes at the same time! Eventually, I bought a pair of my own microphones, starting with Sonys and then upgrading to Sennheisers and other brands as my finances would allow.

I never taped from the soundboard. The soundboard thing was elusive. We would ask. I remember at Red Rocks in 1983, we were set up behind the board, and I asked Dan Healy if I could patch out. He replied, "Not in a venue like this where the sound is so terrific." So the few times I would approach them I'd always get turned down, and you don't want to keep barking up the wrong tree. And, to be honest, unless it's a really well mixed board recording, I prefer a really great audience recording anyway and enjoy trying to replicate the concert experience, which is in large part hearing the sound of the venue.

Sneakin'

When I started taping in the 1970s, there wasn't a Tapers' Section yet, but it was so easy to bring in gear because security was just completely lax. They would maybe pat you down once in a while. If you got it in the door, then you were pretty much gonna be ignored inside. The band let people get away with it. The band obviously let people get away with it. Eventually, security started tightening up, and they'd look for weapons and glass and things that clueless fans started binging in. So it became more and more difficult to smuggle in the gear, and then next thing you knew there was a Tapers' Section.

But we did everything to sneak in back then. We had false casts: you'd put a cast on your arm and put as much gear in it as you could, and you'd get inside and take the cast off. I had a friend who had a false leg cast, and he would go in with crutches. Once inside, his false leg cast would come off, and inside it he had his whole rig. People would smuggle in taping gear in people's wheelchairs, because usually security wouldn't search the handicapped. I wasn't really comfortable smuggling stuff in, but I did it for a while. Eventually, though, I started copying this other guy's idea to get the gear in: I'd walk in, open up my bag, and say it was my electronic test gear from work. I'd say something like, "I just

Before *Dick's Picks* and Archive.org, tapers documented which songs the Grateful Dead played on the j-cards of cassette tapes and often had to guess the names of songs that the band hadn't put on albums yet. Here, Dean Grabski wonders if "Hell in a Bucket" might be called "Enjoying the Ride" when the Dead played it during their first set on June 20, 1983, at Merriweather Post Pavilion.   *Courtesy of Dean Grabski*

got off work and I couldn't leave my work tools in my car, so I really have to take it in with me." Usually they'd look through the stuff briefly and go, "All right! Go ahead!"

Before file sharing and digital recordings, you'd make copies of your tapes for friends. Often one copy might sound a little muddier than the other, or one of the decks might be running a little faster, which would alter the recordings. I got to the point where I purchased two of the exact same cassette decks, which helped insure that when I brought my master tapes home and made copies for people, they were as close to the master recordings as they possibly could be. I was trying to get as many people the low-generation recordings as possible. And then hopefully once you got those tapes to them, they'd do the same thing when they made their copies.

Sometimes we'd have tape copying parties. Everyone would come over with their tape decks and we'd make tapes, listen to music, play cards, and that sort of thing.

If the Thunder Don't Get You Then the Lightning Will

Being a Deadhead meant lots of miles and crazy, insane drives. Like in the fall of 1981, instead of doing the normal East Coast tour, the band did a shortened three-show weekend because they were getting ready to go to Europe. The first night, Friday, was in Lehigh, Pennsylvania, but Saturday night was all the way up in Buffalo, and Sunday was in Washington, DC. I drove to all of them from my home base in New York—a pretty long weekend with 1,150 miles of driving along with going to shows.

At a Merriweather Post Pavilion show in 1983 (June 20), there was a huge thunderstorm, and our microphones were ten feet in the air on an aluminum stand with the deck inside my shirt so it wouldn't get wet. It was strapped to my chest. I remember thinking, "Well, if the stand gets hit, I'm going down hard!" When you listen to that recording, one of the crazy things about it is that there are a couple of spots where the power momentarily drops out. You can hear all the amplifiers shut down, leaving just the echo and the crowd going insane. Then the power goes back on, and you can hear all the amplifiers turn back on with a loud "thump" and the music comes blaring out. The thunder, rain, and power outages all just seemed to make the band and especially Phil play harder and harder. It was totally insane.

When I went to see the band in Europe in 1990, I remember nervously flying into Paris with a duffle bag full of T-shirts along with my taping gear and all my clothes. Hoping the shirts wouldn't be confiscated as a commercial product, I went through customs and they didn't even look at anything. No search at all. They just stamped the passport, and it was as though I were waiting for the other shoe to drop but it never did. Airport security made up for it when I left London after the last show, as they went through all of my stuff. They ran through everything. It took them more than an hour to go through all my stuff.

Today, a lot of people I'm friendly with are also tapers. We meet at shows, have a brew, and talk about music, recording, cables, and microphones, and generally geek out together. Two of my best taper friends are in the high-end audio business. We tape together and listen together, making the shared experiences and relationships a really big part of my taping scene.

I did feel this power and this aura from the music. I was drawn in by it and soon found myself compelled to document that magic. Recording with friends was my scene, and that was always a much stronger draw than what became the whole parking lot party and all that went along with it. The parking lot party was the demise of the whole scene as far as I'm concerned. I've traveled to Asia six times in the last ten years, and it doesn't even sit on the list of being as high as being a Deadhead. And I love going to Asia.

24

Playing in the Band

A List of Significant Dead Concerts

E very fan has a favorite Grateful Dead show they either attended or heard on tape. But beyond that, there are a lot of concerts that hold historical significance in the band's history for one reason or another. According to the 1999 book *DeadBase X: The Complete Guide to Grateful Dead Song Lists*, the band played 2,318 shows between 1965 and 1995. What follows are some of the most important ones. This list excludes dates that marked various band members' entrances and exits from the band, which are covered elsewhere in this book.

Magoo's Pizza Parlor, Palo Alto, California; May 5, 1965

The Dead's first gig as a group was performed under their original name, the Warlocks, and with Dana Morgan, Jr. on bass guitar. Phil Lesh wouldn't officially join until around a month later, with the June 18 gig said to be the first show he played with the band.

Big Nig's Acid Test, San Jose, California; December 4, 1965

The second Acid Test and the first show played under the moniker "Grateful Dead" was held at a house owned by an African American man given a now–politically incorrect nickname by Ken Kesey. Admission was reportedly $1. Needless to say, no set list survives, much less a tape. For an idea of what the band might have sounded like at this juncture, check out the Acid Test shows that can be heard on the bootleg *Grateful Dead & Merry Pranksters: The Acid Test Reels (1965–1967)*.

Monterey International Pop Music Festival, Monterey, California; June 18, 1967

This was not the most transcendent performance, mostly due to a mysterious, unknown harmonica player who sat in with the band. Still, Monterey will always rank among the Dead's most important gigs because it put them in front of their first massive audience while placing them shoulder-to-shoulder with such future legends of 1960s rock as Jimi Hendrix, Janis Joplin, and the Who. The band wouldn't allow footage from their set to be used in the subsequent concert movie *Monterey Pop*, but fellow performers Eric Burdon and the Animals still immortalized it in song with a line from their hit "Monterey": "The Grateful Dead blew everybody's minds."

Shrine Auditorium, Los Angeles, California; December 13, 1967

This was reportedly the first time the band played "Dark Star" live. The song, which became the band's signature jam tune, had been written in September of that year when Robert Hunter heard the Dead rehearse an instrumental version of the song and wrote words to it. No recording of this show is known to exist, but an embryonic version of "Dark Star" from a few months later (February 14, 1968) found its way onto *Road Trips Volume 2, Number 2*.

The Quick and the Dead Tour, Northwest United States; January–February 1968

Starting with a gig at the Eureka Municipal Auditorium on January 20, 1968, the Grateful Dead and Quicksilver Messenger Service embarked on a tour of the Pacific Northwest called The Quick and the Dead. It was an important step for the Dead because it was their first full-scale, out-of-state tour. The tour, which lasted through February 4, included three dates in Seattle, Washington, followed by five shows in three cities in Oregon: Seattle, Portland, and Eugene.

Fillmore West, San Francisco, California; June 7, 1969

In June 1970, the Dead would surprise listeners by releasing an album of largely acoustic music, *Workingman's Dead*. But anyone who was at this concert wouldn't have been that surprised, because it marked the band's first acoustic set. Make that a mini–acoustic set, as the band played only the first three songs unplugged: "Dire Wolf," "Dupree's Diamond Blues," and "Mountains of the Moon." This gig also paved the way for the acoustic sets that would become a regular part of the Dead's concerts for the next few years.

Woodstock Music and Art Fair, Woodstock, New York; August 17, 1969

As with the Monterey festival, the Dead found themselves in front of their largest audience to date and didn't play their best, mostly because of equipment problems and bad weather. Still, the band became part of history by playing what's become the most well-known music festival of all time.

Europe '72 Tour, Europe; April–May 1972

The Dead's first sojourn abroad not only brought out the best in their playing, but also brought forth a wealth of first-rate new material from the band's composers, much of which made its way onto the landmark live set *Europe '72*. By

Before the Dead's now-legendary encore jam with the Allman Brothers at the Summer Jam at Watkins Glen, the bands had played and socialized together. This 1972 shot shows Garcia hanging out with the Allman Brothers' Berry Oakley a few months before the bassist died in a motorcycle crash.   *Courtesy of BigHouse Archives*

this point, the Dead had acquired a new keyboardist in Keith Godchaux, which rejuvenated the band musically, and it showed in their playing. Their mixture of American musical genres was potent enough to keep even the cynical British begging for more, with the group wrapping the tour with a four-night run at London's Strand Lyceum.

Hollywood Bowl, Los Angeles, California; June 17, 1972

The Hollywood Bowl, which seats nearly 18,000, is the largest amphitheater in the United States. With their first show at this venue, the Dead made the leap from playing small halls to larger performances. This show was also Pigpen's last, although he took no lead vocals.

Summer Jam at Watkins Glen, Watkins Glen, New York; July 28, 1973

The third time was the charm for the Grateful Dead when it came to playing large festivals. And for this one, they not only got to play two long sets in front of an estimated six hundred thousand people, but the band also played a sound check that wowed the early-bird crowd, a segment of which was released on the *So Many Roads* box set. The Dead also joined the other acts on the bill, the Allman Brothers Band and the Band, for an encore of "Not Fade Away," "Mountain Jam," and "Johnny B. Goode."

Winterland Arena, San Francisco, California; October 20, 1974

Known colloquially as "the last one," this was the band's final show with its Wall of Sound system and the last show the band played before taking a hiatus from touring in 1975. The show also marked the return of Mickey Hart to the fold. It was filmed and became the basis for *The Grateful Dead Movie*.

Cornell University's Barton Hall, Ithaca, New York; May 8, 1977

Many consider this to be the finest show the Dead ever played because of the quality of the tapes circulated. Although it's less revered now, since Archive.org has allowed Deadheads to compare it with other shows of the era, it does contain some of Garcia's best playing on "Row Jimmy" and "Brown-Eyed Women." Surprisingly, it never came out as a *Dick's Picks*. According to Dead.net commenter "Wiilybru," when he asked Dick Latvala why, Latvala's response was, "Hell, everybody and his brother has that!"

Raceway Park, Englishtown, New Jersey; September 3, 1977

According to Dead historian David Gans, this outdoor show is significant because several hundred thousand people attended. As many of those attendees were first-time concertgoers, this show became the one where a lot of people hopped on the bus and spread the word. The concert was released in 1999 as *Volume Fifteen* of the *Dick's Picks* series. The Marshall Tucker Band and New Riders of the Purple Sage were also on the bill.

Gizah Sound and Light Theater, Cairo, Egypt; September 14, 1978

With this concert and two that followed in the two days after, the Grateful Dead became the first rock band to play the ancient pyramids. The band's trip to the cradle of civilization came at the behest of Lesh, who wanted them to perform at an ancient "place of power." A planned live album never panned out at the time, but in 2008, segments of the September 15 and 16 shows were released as the CD/DVD set *Rocking the Cradle: Egypt 1978.*

Radio City Music Hall, New York, New York; October 1980

The Dead's eight-night run at the historic New York venue showed that new member Brent Mydland had given them something of a second wind as his masterful keyboard playing breathed life into neglected favorites such as "China Doll," among others. The band produced the first-ever live rock telecast for their October 31 show, which closed the run and was broadcast to select movie theaters equipped with high-end sound systems. Segments of that show and the two before it were later released on the *Dead Ahead* videotape/laserdisc from 1981 and the expanded DVD that came out in 2005.

Warfield Theater, San Francisco, California; September–October 1980

The Dead re-introduced their acoustic side at this series of shows, all of which opened with the band playing in an unplugged format. This set-up gave the group license to bring back songs they hadn't played in years, such as the solo Garcia track "Bird Song" (the first song played at the first show), the old bluegrass song "Rosalie McFall," and the traditional folk song "I've Been All Around This World." Some of these performances made it onto the double live 1981 album *Reckoning.*

US Festival, Devore, California; September 5, 1982

The US Festival was a would-be version of Woodstock that took place in September 1982 and again in the spring of 1983. The 1982 edition began September 3 and opened with a host of new wave and punk acts such as the Ramones, Oingo Boingo, and Talking Heads. So what in the holy hell were the Dead doing there? Playing a surprisingly energetic "breakfast set" at 9:30 a.m. on the third day. As the group ran through "Playing in the Band," "Truckin'," and other favorites, they exposed themselves to a whole new audience (live and through a radio simulcast), perhaps planting the seeds for their popularity later in the decade.

Berkeley Community Theatre, Berkeley, California; October 27, 1984

At this show, the Grateful Dead became the first major label band to officially sanction a Tapers' Section, thereby giving their blessing to fans who wanted to circulate live recordings among themselves. It wasn't a bad show to get on tape either, as the band rocked out with a raucous version of the Willie Dixon-Koko Taylor blues "Wang Dang Doodle," and broke out the non-LP early '80s rarity "Keep Your Day Job" for an encore.

Oakland Coliseum Arena, Oakland, California; December 15, 1986

This was Garcia's comeback show after coming out of the diabetic coma he had fallen into six months earlier. A rejuvenated Grateful Dead opened with a rendition of "Touch of Grey" that had the crowd on its feet before the song was even a hit. The moment that went down in Dead lore, though, was when the audience went wild during "Candyman," right after Garcia sang the line "Won't you tell everybody you meet that the Candyman's in town?"

Brendan Byrne Arena, East Rutherford, New Jersey; October 14, 1989

This was a notorious show, but not for a good reason. It was after this show that concertgoer Adam Katz, nineteen, was found severely beaten on a traffic island on Route 120 and died the next day. Katz's murder was never solved and has become one of the most infamous fan deaths in rock history. After an FBI investigation that implicated the venue's security team, Katz's family sued both the arena and the state of New Jersey for attempting to cover up the murder. Katz's death was a harbinger of the violence and unrest that would mar Dead concerts in the coming years.

Oakland Coliseum Arena, Oakland, California; December 31, 1991

With their closing concert of 1991, the Dead wrapped up a year in which they ascended to being the top-grossing touring act around for the first time, according to Pollstar. According to a June 11, 1992, *New York Times* article, "Pop Concerts Shake Off Last Summer's Malaise," the Dead "brought in $34.7 million for their approximately 75 North American dates in 1991" and were "virtually the only act to play stadiums." The Dead topped Pollstar's list again in 1993.

Soldier Field, Chicago, Illinois; July 9, 1995

This was the final Grateful Dead concert, although no one knew it then, and also the last concert of a difficult tour, and it shows in the roughness of Garcia's singing. He sang his final lead vocal on the mournful "Black Muddy River," which prompted Lesh to break out the more upbeat "Box of Rain" for the encore. The 1970 song, which was co-written by Hunter and Lesh as something Lesh could sing to his then-dying father, became the last one the band ever played on stage.

25

Ace

A Dead Album with Weir as the Leader of the Band

In much the way *Aoxomoxoa* and *Workingman's Dead* are Grateful Dead albums with Garcia as the artistic leader of the band, *Ace* is a Grateful Dead album with Bob Weir in charge. The difference is that where *Aoxomoxoa* and *Workingman's Dead* were billed as Grateful Dead albums, *Ace* came out as a Bob Weir album. The question is why, and there are two answers.

The first is simple: the album came into existence because of a new recording contract. In 1971, the Grateful Dead had signed a second deal with their record company, Warner Bros., and the deal allowed for band members to make solo albums as part of the package. In January of that year, Jerry Garcia put out his first solo album, *Garcia*. The same month *Ace* was released, Mickey Hart dropped his first solo album, *Rolling Thunder*, a wildly eclectic album that ran the gamut from big band jazz to electronic music to straight up rock songs.

But where *Garcia* was performed almost solely by Garcia himself and *Rolling Thunder* featured a rolling cast of musicians, *Ace* featured almost every member of the Dead, even new recruits Keith Godchaux and Donna Godchaux-MacKay. Essentially, Weir had made a Dead album in all but name. The band even acknowledged as much by putting one of *Ace*'s cuts, "Mexicali Blues," on the "best of" album, *Skeletons from the Closet*, a 1974 release that contained no tunes from Garcia's first solo outing even though the band had performed several of them live on a regular basis by that point.

If people thought *Ace* meant there was dissent in the land of the Dead, a quick glance at the album credits on the back cover put an end to that. Not only does Weir prominently credit all his bandmates, but he also shares production credit with them, acknowledging that the production duties were done by "everyone involved." Weir even throws in a nickname for drummer Bill Kreutzmann (who's listed as William "Fairplay" Kreutzmann) and makes sure to note that it's Phil Lesh on harmony vocals on "Mexicali Blues," as opposed to one of the other singers-for-hire. In the future, there would be other solo albums by Dead members that featured the band, but *Ace* started the tradition.

Beyond the lead vocals, *Ace* differs from a Dead studio release in another significant way: Weir co-wrote all of the eight songs. The songs on *Ace* are either by Weir with Robert Hunter, by Weir and his longtime pal and then-new lyricist

John Perry Barlow, or by Weir himself. (Although Mickey Hart gets co-credit for "Playing in the Band" and "Greatest Story Ever Told" on various Dead releases, the original green label vinyl pressing of *Ace* does not credit him on either song, possibly because he'd left the band in February 1971 after his father was accused of pocketing the band's advance money from Warner Bros.).

Weir also didn't take to the road with an off-shoot band after going solo. He simply melded his songs with the Dead's as though they had always been part of the Dead's repertoire. In the coming years, both the pair of Keith and Donna and Kreutzmann would play in the Jerry Garcia Band, and Garcia would play on Keith and Donna's 1975 album, but the idea of offshoot projects involving band members was novel at the time of *Ace*.

At the time, the album probably left some fans scratching their heads as to why Weir would strike out on his own only to play with the same musicians he was supposedly striking out from—most band members make solo recordings to define themselves apart from their bands, not as part of them. That leads to the second reason for *Ace*'s existence, and it involves a chapter in the band's history that's rarely written about.

Bob Weir, whose photo as a high school freshman was included in the *Mother McCree's Uptown Jug Champions* CD booklet, met future lyricist John Perry Barlow while still in high school. Together, the pair would go on to write the bulk of the *Ace* album and several Dead standards.

Author's collection

Lose Your Step, Fall out of Grace

Sometime in 1968, just after the release of *Anthem of the Sun*, Bob Weir and Pigpen were asked to leave the Grateful Dead. Neither musician was keeping up with the rest of the band when it came to the new, more freeform psychedelic jams the group wanted to explore. In Pigpen's case, this was because the Dead were moving further and further away from the blues and roots music he favored. In Weir's case, it was because his rhythm guitar playing on electric guitar wasn't really evolving: he still flailed away as if he were playing acoustic guitar.

Neither firing was really enforced, and both musicians were back in the band within a few months, if not weeks (the band has never spoken much about this incident, and evidence from concert tapes is spotty). But there was some fallout. Some of the other musicians played a couple of shows without Pigpen or Weir under the names Jerry Garrceeah and His Friends and Mickey and the Hartbeats. The group canceled a proposed fall European tour. Pigpen doesn't appear on the album that was recorded around this time, *Aoxomoxoa*. On that album, Weir gets no lead vocals for the first time on a Dead album, not even on the bridge of "Cosmic Charlie" ("Say you'll come back . . ."), which he sang live early on. Evidence of this can be heard on the *Fillmore West 1969: Complete Recordings* box set, which features one of the earliest performances of the song dating from February 27, 1969.

To supplement Pigpen's playing, the band brought in Phil Lesh's old music pal, Tom Constanten, as a second keyboardist. Weir simply worked harder at his craft and his songwriting: the first song he got primary credit on after his return was "Sugar Magnolia," one of the band's best songs. But the psychological effects of being ousted must have lingered.

This is likely one reason that Weir decided to sign the contract for a solo album, even though he'd composed only a few songs for the band. The album was validation of his talent and a chance to up his standing within the band without having to deal with the band's politics. When it came to that, Weir had always been the George Harrison of the group. Like Harrison, Weir was the youngest member of his band who was often treated like a kid because he pretty much was a kid when the band coalesced. And, like Harrison, Weir wrote songs in the shadow of a formidable songwriting duo. *Ace* cast off that shadow, at least partially.

Playing Outside the Band

There's a confidence on *Ace* that Weir hadn't quite shown on vinyl with his mothership band. Sure, his lead vocals on "Sugar Magnolia" were fiery, but there's a newfound assurance on *Ace*'s tracks that put them vocally above the way Weir usually sang in the studio.

What's more impressive is that the normally non-prolific Weir managed to get a solo album out as quickly as he did. His next effort, *Heaven Help the Fool*, wouldn't be released until 1978, and in the interim, he would only contribute six original tracks to Dead albums and two to the first Kingfish album, plus a collaborative track. In *The Grateful Dead Movie*, Barlow says that to get Weir to write songs, you practically had to put a gun to his head. So Weir getting a solo album out by age twenty-four was a definite achievement, made all the more so because the quality of the songs was so high.

The eight originals that make up *Ace* are so strong that virtually all of them became live staples of the Dead's act. According to DeadBase.com, "Greatest Story Ever Told" made it to 280 shows, "Black-Throated Wind" to 158, and "Playing in the Band" to 602. From side two, "Looks Like Rain" was featured in 417 shows, "Mexicali Blues" in 436, "One More Saturday Night" in 340, and "Cassidy" in 334. Only the upbeat shuffle "Walk in the Sunshine" was never played live, probably because its bounciness was a bit too pop-oriented to fit in with the Dead's style.

Several of these songs made their live debuts with the Dead before the album's May 1972 release, including "Greatest Story Ever Told" and "Playing in the Band" (which were introduced February 18, 1971), "Black-Throated Wind"

(March 5, 1972), "Looks Like Rain" (March 21, 1972), and "Mexicali Blues" and "One More Saturday Night" (October 19, 1971).

How did Weir manage to crank out some of his best songs in the space of about a year? For the early ones, it was inspiration and Weir's hitting his stride as a composer. But for the later tunes, deadlines loomed and he had to come up with something. According to a source close to the band, Weir had signed the contract to do his solo album in late 1971, and pressure was mounting on him and Barlow to get moving. "In December they realize, 'Well, we've got two songs and we need ten.' So they start writing songs like crazy," says the source. "They were writing songs right through the sessions, because that's the way Bobby works. He needs a gun drawn."

Because Weir had to move quickly on a lot of the tunes, there was little time for his musical focus to become diffuse or for him to want his songs to be unconventional or "*outside* at the get-go," as Barlow later characterized them. On the album, he presents a succession of rockers and ballads that sound both organic and heartfelt. Nothing on the album comes off as contrived or forced. Both Barlow and Hunter offer lyrics that Weir sounds comfortable singing, and the arrangements delivered by the shifting ensemble are full of ideas, but never overwhelm the singer.

All of this is easy to take for granted until you hear Weir's next solo effort, which doesn't quite fire on all cylinders. The production by Keith Olsen (Fleetwood Mac, Heart, many others) is too saccharine, the arrangements don't suit the songs well, and Weir himself sounds disengaged—a guest at his own party. *Ace* is so emotionally engaging that you almost don't notice the production could be a bit tighter in spots.

Not everyone was impressed with the album, and it was a stroke of bad luck that one such person happened to reside in a high place: the reviewer's chair at *Rolling Stone*. In his review of *Ace*, writer Bud Scoppa starts off admitting that he has no special love for the band, but then praises *Ace* because it boasts "some vitality." Then, after calling Weir's voice lively but not distinguished (and trashing Garcia's singing in the process), he dismisses half the album.

"*Ace* is the best Grateful Dead album to appear since *Live Dead* [*sic*]," writes Scoppa. "This is not to say it's any kind of outstanding achievement: there isn't a single memorable song on the whole first side, and Weir displays more enthusiasm and general likeableness than stylistic clarity or consistency in a good many instances." Scoppa also opines that the performances by Grateful Dead members on the record outshone the material.

Although only a small segment of the record-buying public allows reviews to determine what records they buy, it couldn't have helped to have a reviewer in such a widely respected magazine as *Rolling Stone* give a lukewarm response to the album. If there was one record that could have appealed to people outside the Dead camp, *Ace* was it. But readers were unlikely to get that from the review.

Time has a way of righting wrongs, though, and *Ace* is now widely seen as not only Bob Weir's finest moment on record, but also one of the best Dead solo projects. A breakdown of its tracks reveals why each one not only works on its own, but also contributes to making the album more than the sum of its parts.

Ace in the Whole

The following is a rundown of the eight tracks that make up the *Ace* album.

"Greatest Story Ever Told"

Unlike a lot of Grateful Dead albums, *Ace* doesn't quietly slink into existence; rather, it explodes right from the get-go, with a holler from Weir. It launches one of his best rockers, which sports a killer riff that's somewhat similar to Mitch Ryder's hit 1966 cover of "Devil with a Blue Dress On." In 1987, the Dead acknowledged this connection by segueing "Story" into "Devil" at their September 9 and 16 shows.

This co-write with Hunter has one of the wordsmith's most clever lyrical conceits: positing religious figures as outlaws. It's a bit like a more comedic version of the Band's "The Weight," with religious caricatures replacing composer Robbie Robertson's quasi-religious characters. By the end, Hunter is intimating that it's all showbiz: "You get what you come for, you're ready to go / It's one in ten thousand just come for the show."

Musically, Weir's melody is a near-perfect match for Hunter's words, especially on the line "You can't close the door when the wall's caved in," which both musically and lyrically recalls Eddie Cochran's famous line "You can't use the car if you didn't work late" from his 1958 hit "Summertime Blues." The song ends with some tasty interplay between Keith Godchaux's piano and Garcia's guitar.

"Black-Throated Wind"

Barlow penned the lyrics to this ballad, and they're a pretty convincing lament from a lovelorn hitchhiker. But it's Weir's exquisite melody and chord progression that makes the song memorable, with its solemn minor key verses giving way to a sunnier major key chorus. High-pitched horns give the story a sense of drama, a feeling driven home by the guilt-riddled lyrics of the chorus: "It's forced me to see that you've done better by me / Better by me than I've done by you."

Despite the song being a ballad, Weir seems to get caught up in the moment and starts to push his voice to the limit as the song draws to its close. So, when his voice breaks on the final chorus, it comes off as sincerity, not inept singing. This is the kind of moment that would have been "corrected" had the voice processing software Auto-Tune been around in 1972, and it's a good thing such technology didn't exist when this was recorded, because Weir's blemishes-and-all performance drives the song's message home that much more powerfully.

"Walk in the Sunshine"

As the only song on the album never played live by the Dead, "Walk in the Sunshine" merits special attention. The song is reflective of its title because it's the closest Weir (or possibly any Dead member, ever) came to the giddy subgenre of the late '60s and early '70s known as sunshine pop. This genre was popularized by such groups as the Sunshine Company ("Happy"), Harpers Bizarre ("Feelin' Groovy"), the Peppermint Rainbow, ("Will You Be Staying After Sunday"), and the Association.

In fact, "Walk in the Sunshine" bears a passing resemblance, in both its music and words, to the Association's "Time for Livin'" (#39 in the spring of 1968). But Weir's tune is too gritty to come off as fluffy pop. Donna Godchaux-MacKay's harmony vocals ground it in soulfulness, and Barlow's lyrics become cunningly subversive after a few verses. The song might start out exhorting listeners to toss away their wristwatches (also a line in the Association song), but it takes that sentiment a big step further by slipping in the lines "You got to burn down all the buildings, you got to throw out all the laws." So much for Weir going sunshine pop on listeners!

"Playing in the Band"

"Playing in the Band" is arguably the best song on *Ace*. It also became one of the Dead's most enduring live staples. It takes a more generalized, philosophical view of life as a musician than does its thematic predecessor, "Truckin'," which made its point with vignettes. It also rocks pretty hard considering its odd 10/4 time signature (on Hart's *Rolling Thunder* album, it's called "The Main Ten (Playing in the Band)" with the "ten" referencing its time signature).

The *Ace* band really cooks during the instrumental break where they get to stretch out. And they stretch out for seven and a half minutes, not long by the standards of a Dead concert, but long enough to give the album track some heft. And it's a good thing they do, because they were competing with themselves on this track. "Playing in the Band" made its live debut when the Dead performed it on February 18, 1971, but listeners at the time were likely to be most familiar with the version that the band put on the *Skull and Roses* album eight months later. That four-minute version comes off as a warm up for the *Ace* version, which rocks harder and more convincingly since the musicians had become more familiar with it.

"Looks Like Rain"

Weir gets orchestral with the original version of this melancholy acoustic ballad about loss. Just before the four-minute mark, weepy strings enter, driving home the bittersweet melody, which skillfully evokes the anxiety of parting with a loved one by alternating between major and minor key modes within its verses. Garcia checks in with a pedal steel guitar part that adds to the song's poignancy, while Barlow's lyrics are as good a goodbye letter as anyone has come up with.

"Mexicali Blues"

This jaunty number was one of the original "cowboy songs" that Weir regularly sang live with the Dead. This original effort, which was co-written with Barlow, sounds authentic enough to sit alongside the kind of songs it was derived from, such as Marty Robbins's "Big Iron" (#26 in 1960), which Weir covered on the first Kingfish album.

"Mexicali Blues" is also noteworthy for its political incorrectness. It's doubtful that any artist after 1990 or so could have gotten away with lyrics like "So instead I've got a bottle and a girl who's just fourteen / And a damn good case of the Mexicali Blues" without someone, somewhere, protesting. By the end, the protagonist of this song shoots and kills a law man who might or might not be the teenager's boyfriend. Who said the Dead didn't edge close to gangsta rap in its lyrics from time to time?

"One More Saturday Night"

This is the only number on the album for which Weir takes sole credit, and it's as close to authentic early rock 'n' roll as he would ever get. As a mock '50s rocker, it's pretty impressive, with its insistent guitar riff and driving rhythm. In his *Rolling Stone* review, Scoppa calls the song "a solid Chuck Berry-style rouser." Not quite. If "One More Saturday Night" is a "rouser" in anyone's style, it's the style Little Richard developed for "Good Golly Miss Molly" and Creedence Clearwater Revival copped for "Travelin' Band," as it bears some similarities to both of those hits (the Dead also covered "Good Golly Miss Molly" in 1987, as it's part of Ryder's "Devil With a Blue Dress On" medley).

According to Dennis McNally's biography of the band, *A Long Strange Trip: The Inside History of the Grateful Dead*, Weir and Hunter fought over the lyrics to this song, with Hunter refusing co-credit because of Weir's major rewriting of his work. If Weir is responsible for the majority of the lyrics of "One More Saturday Night," he did an impressive job with lyrics such as "I turn on Channel Six, the President comes on the news / Says I got no satisfaction, that's why I sing the blues." Lines like that are both humorous and to the point, two elements that were also present in the songs that served as antecedents to this one.

"Cassidy"

Ace closes on a pensive note with "Cassidy," one of Weir's best songs and one of his most complex. The words, by Barlow, reference Beat Generation scenester Neal Cassady, who had already been namechecked by the Dead in "That's It for the Other One." But the words also allude to birth and a child and have been interpreted as also being written for Cassidy Law, the recently born daughter of the Dead's then–fan club organizer, Eileen Law.

Musically, Weir again moves between major and minor modes within his verses, conjuring an anxiety-riddled, happy-confused vibe that virtually everyone has felt when they have a child on the way. Just when the song starts to seem a little too mellow, Weir snaps listeners to attention with a hard-hitting bridge (the part that begins "Quick beats in an icy heart").

As the years went on and the Dead began to perform virtually all of the *Ace* cuts live on a regular basis, it became second nature to think of Weir as a first-rate songwriter whose tunes could rival those of Garcia when he was on. But in its time, *Ace* was something of a surprise to Dead fans, most of whom probably didn't think Weir had it in him. As it stands now, *Ace* remains one of the strongest studio albums to feature the band, and it doesn't even bear the Dead's name.

26

One Old Score

The Great Lost Grateful Dead Studio Album of 1972

I f you listened to rock radio back in the 1970s or early 1980s, you'd have regularly heard a song called "Playing in the Band" by the Grateful Dead. It was one of their signature songs, along with "Truckin'," "Sugar Magnolia," and "Uncle John's Band," and it was one of their most-played songs in concert.

The live version could be found on the group's 1971 album called *Grateful Dead*, also known as *Skull and Roses* (because of the art on the cover) or *Skullfuck* (the band's original title, which was nixed by the record company for obvious reasons). But back then, like now, people usually wanted to buy the version they heard on the radio, which, as in this case, was often the studio version.

The problem was that if you wanted the studio version of "Playing in the Band," you'd have learned that it was nowhere to be found on any Grateful Dead album. Instead, it closed side one of Bob Weir's first solo album, *Ace*, which came out in 1972. You'd have wondered why such an important track was placed on a solo album when it could have benefited the band to place it on a group effort.

Why, indeed. The reason behind that move—and several other questionable ones by the band around that time period—is why we're metaphorically gathered here today. Let's go back in time a bit, shall we? It's 1971. The Grateful Dead has just come off of two fantastic albums, *Workingman's Dead* and *American Beauty*, both from the previous year. Not only were these albums given high marks by critics—who weren't always effusive in their praise of the band—but they brought the band their first real commercial success, both peaking within the Top 40 and eventually going platinum. For the record, *Workingman's* got to #27 and *American Beauty* peaked at #30.

So, what did the Dead do next? Did they capitalize on their success and come out with one of the all-time ultimate albums, which they definitely had in them? No. They threw up a dust cloud, dropping a live album, a semi-live one, and a spate of solo albums, thereby stretching out all their best songs over eight (count 'em) separate vinyl discs and five albums per se. The live releases included the aforementioned double album and the classic triple album *Europe '72*. Both charted higher than the studio releases did, coming in at #24 and #25, respectively. The solo releases included the debut album by Jerry Garcia, *Garcia*; the previously mentioned *Ace*; and Mickey Hart's *Rolling Thunder*, which Lindsay Planer called "criminally overlooked" in an AllMusic Guide review of *Garcia*.

Some of this was for artistic reasons. At this stage of the game, Garcia was itching to stretch artistically, having already performed with New Riders of the Purple Sage and Crosby, Stills and Nash. So, a solo album was a logical next step. Weir, too, had something to prove, after having been temporarily ejected from the band a few years back. But the reason band members wanted to ink solo deals went beyond the artistic, as former manager Rock Scully recounts in *Living with the Dead: Twenty Years on the Bus with Garcia and the Grateful Dead* (co-written with David Dalton).

"We get a separate deal for Jerry—extra money!" writes Scully.

No matter the motive, what Deadheads got out of all this was a lot of new music. What they didn't get—and what the world didn't get—was a knockout album that would have rivaled anything the band ever put to tape as being among their best. It would have also given new members Keith Godchaux and Donna Godchaux-MacKay a chance to show off a bit in a studio setting. Yet no such album was ever made. On the one hand, you have to admire the Dead for not pandering to the public and taking the strictly commercial route. On the other, anyone who has followed this band's career and wondered why there were no studio albums released from November 1970 until October 1973 is left asking, "Dude, where's your album?"

Scully's book explains the feeling inside the Dead camp: "Garcia and [lyricist Robert] Hunter regret that some of the new songs on the album—which could have been tuned up in the studio—are buried among the covers and live versions of earlier songs."

He then goes on to quote Hunter: "To me, all that material was the kicker follow-up album to *American Beauty*. Instead, we put out this three-album thing that sounds good, but it spreads out the material so thin we never get to hear what those songs might have sounded like on an album of their own."

Some Assembly Required

What would that album have sounded like? It's easy enough to figure that out. The band's new tracks are all there on the various group and solo efforts. It's just a matter of cherry-picking them and assembling them into a coherent running order. First, let's figure out what to leave out. Let's scrap most cuts from *Skull and Roses*, because there are only a few originals among the many cover versions, and the band couldn't be expected to put out an album of all covers at that juncture of their career. Those originals include three of the songs most played live, according to DeadBase.com: "Bertha" and "Wharf Rat" (played 394 times each) and "Me and My Uncle," the band's most-played live song ever, (616 live plays on that one). "Playing in the Band," however, was too important a song not to give a group studio treatment, so that one definitely should have been considered for a non-live album release.

We also have to leave out the tracks on the Mickey Hart album. He wasn't technically a member of the band then, having taken a sabbatical because he took personally the money troubles involving his father, Lenny Hart, who had taken over as the band's manager and been arrested on charges that he embezzled from the band. That's a shame, because it's fun to imagine a Dead record with his song "Blind John," which was sung by Jefferson Airplane's Grace Slick, Paul Kantner, and David Freiberg on Hart's album. We'll also leave aside the various cover tunes the band was doing that turned up on later live albums such as *History of the Grateful Dead, Volume One (Bear's Choice)* or *Ladies and Gentlemen . . . the Grateful Dead*, because it's unlikely the group would have brought songs like "Katie Mae" or "Ain't It Crazy (The Rub)" into the studio.

That leaves *Europe '72, Garcia,* and *Ace* to choose from. Let's take a moment to discuss *Europe '72.* Although purportedly a live album, it was doctored in the studio, according to Scully, who says in his book that "*Europe '72* is the Dead (mostly) live at their furry finest, but it isn't a purely live album. The 'live' sound is partially re-created in the studio by playing studio tracks back over the same equipment that the live stuff was originally recorded on, thus generating an approximation of the original ambience. Got that?"

For many, *Europe '72* was the album that connected them to the Dead, making the fact that the Dead didn't release a studio album that year irrelevant. In 2001, Rhino Records released a "mega box set" titled *Europe '72: The Complete Recordings,* for which the above promotional image was designed. The package offered fans all twenty-two of the band's spring 1972 European shows on seventy-three CDs and sold out its limited run of seventy-two hundred copies in fewer than four days, according to Dead.net.   *Courtesy of Rhino Records*

So, as much as that album is beloved by Deadheads (and even non-Dead-heads), it's not hard to imagine everyone being better served by some of the newer songs appearing on a studio album and the empty space created by their omission being filled by more examples of the band's current jamming prowess than were showcased on the album as it was released. If you have a band that's legendary for its jamming, why not show it off more? The Allman Brothers sure did on both *At the Fillmore* and *Eat a Peach*, and the triple album format of *Europe '72* gave the Grateful Dead the chance to do the same.

Garcia used to like to talk to interviewers about the ever-evolving nature of "Dark Star," so my vote goes to the inclusion of an up-to-date version of "Dark Star." There was one included on the *Europe '72 Volume 2* set the band put out in 2011, so the group definitely had a version in the can. In fact, considering all the new recordings on that release and the box set *Europe '72: The Complete Recordings*, there were a lot of tracks the band could have used to fill out *Europe '72*, had they chosen to omit some of their new songs.

Getting back to what might have been included in the Dead's great lost studio album of 1972, one way to pick tracks is to look at which of the new, self-penned songs were played the most live. All together, there were twenty tunes. But let's include Pigpen's "The Stranger (Two Souls in Communion)," included on the expanded *Europe '72* and in the *Golden Road (1965–1973)* box set, and let's not include "The Yellow Dog Story" from the same set, as it's a spoken word piece that was intended as filler while the band tuned up. There were also two more Pigpen tunes the band was performing at the time: "Empty Pages," which was played live just a few times and can only be found officially on the thirty-fifth *Dick's Picks*, and "Chinatown Shuffle," which was included on the second volume of *Europe '72*. That release also includes a version of the Hunter-Garcia original "Loser," which made it onto Garcia's debut long player.

Because time was tight on single albums, and because the band didn't prioritize those cuts, neither will we. So those cuts won't make the cut here.

The band's priorities can be discerned from looking at the top ten most-played new songs from this era. According to Deadbase.com, they are "Playing in the Band" (602 performances), "Jack Straw" (474), "Mexicali Blues" (436), "Tennessee Jed" (433), "Deal" (423), "Looks Like Rain" (417), "Sugaree" (358), "Loser" (345), "Brown-Eyed Women" (348), and "Cassidy" (334).

The bottom ten, meanwhile, includes "One More Saturday Night" (340 plays), "He's Gone" (327), "Ramble On Rose" (316), "Bird Song" (296), "Greatest Story Ever Told" (280), "The Wheel" (258), "Black-Throated Wind" (158), "To Lay Me Down" (63), "Mr. Charlie" (48), and "The Stranger (Two Souls in Communion)" (12).

Eight Songs in Communion

Considering that Dead studio cuts usually run around five minutes or more, these tracks yield more than two albums. But you have to figure that Garcia and

Weir would have wanted to release solo albums anyway, so most of the cuts in the "bottom ten" here would have been kept for solo projects. And because Pigpen's health was fading fast and his days were numbered, they'd have probably given him one or two spots on the album, so one of his songs will be featured. Pigpen's songs rank among the least-played tunes of the bunch not because they're disliked, but because of the singer's absence from the stage after 1972. In exchange for those songs, we'll give Garcia and Weir back a few tracks for each of their solo albums, notably "Deal," because it led off Garcia's album, and "Cassidy," because it closed Weir's. Also going to Weir will be his "Mexicali Blues," because it's unlike anything the Dead were doing on their LPs at the time.

Excluding other solo cuts such as "Bird Song" and "Greatest Story Ever Told" leaves us ten songs to work with. Those songs, and their running times from their respective albums, now include "Sugaree" (5:54), "Jack Straw" (4:48), "He's Gone" (6:53), "Tennessee Jed" (7:10), "Looks Like Rain" (6:12), "Loser" (4:10), "Brown-Eyed Women" (4:38), "Mr. Charlie" (3:39), "The Stranger (Two Souls in Communion)" (6:50), and "Playing in the Band" (7:38). These add up to a grand total of 55:52, which would have worked great for a CD, but was a bit too long for an album back then. Individual sides of vinyl albums could only hold around twenty-five minutes of music without a reduction in volume and sound quality, and while certain bands and artists did like to push that limit (Todd Rundgren comes to mind), the Dead's expansive, loose sound wouldn't have taken well to being sonically constricted—so a few songs still need to go. Because "Mr. Charlie" was a live Pigpen showcase, that's best left for the live album, and because "Loser" would tip the album's balance too much toward Garcia, it goes too. (Laugh if you will, but from evidence gathered from hundreds of rock books, this is all very close to the way album running orders were actually decided back in the day before artists had eighty minutes to play with.)

When you divide the songs up so that they work time-wise on an album side and play in a coherent fashion, they look like this:

Side One

◆ "Sugaree" (5:54)

◆ "Jack Straw" (4:48)

◆ "Tennessee Jed" (7:10)

◆ "The Stranger (Two Souls in Communion)" (6:50)

◆ Total time: 24:02

Side Two

◆ "He's Gone" (6:53)

◆ "Brown-Eyed Women" (4:38)

◆ "Looks Like Rain" (6:12)

- "Playing in the Band" (7:38)
- Total time: 24:41

Those running times push each side just past the twenty-minute mark, which is about as long as most actual Grateful Dead albums ran. Plus, you have to figure that some of the live cuts we're pulling from *Europe '72* would have been a minute or two shorter if they'd ever gotten studio incarnations. So, more or less, you now have twenty-minute sides and an album that's pretty damned impressive. Here's a track-by-track look at the songs.

"Sugaree"

The Dead were never a singles band, although according to Scully's book, their management did make a big push to get "Uncle John's Band" some airplay (it missed the Top 40, stalling out at #69). Had "Sugaree" been on a Dead album,

Garcia's "Sugaree" was released with a picture sleeve for the German market. The song eventually became a regular part of the Dead's live repertoire and probably would have been a candidate for a Dead single had the band cut a studio version.

Courtesy of Eric Schwartz

it might have been another chance at getting on the radio a bit more. First, the title was somewhat familiar since rockabilly singer Rusty York had a minor hit with a Marty Robbins song of the same name in 1959 (it got to #77 in July). Second, the song's blend of a sweet melody with ominous lyrics was a prevailing trend in 1970s music and can be heard in hits as disparate as R. Dean Taylor's "Indiana Wants Me," Michael Martin Murphey's "Wildfire," Edward Bear's "Last Song," Terry Jacks's "Seasons in the Sun," and even the Vicki Lawrence chart topper "The Night the Lights Went Out in Georgia."

Third, Hunter's paraphrasing of the lyrics of the lullaby "Hush, Little Baby" in the bridge is the stuff of which popular songs are made. And finally, in 1976, Rod Stewart had a #1 with a song that's similar in both melody and rhythm to "Sugaree," "Tonight's the Night (Gonna Be Alright)." Granted, "Sugaree" isn't as commercial as that sleazy seduction anthem, but because the public loved the "remake," they'd probably have gone for the original, too, even if it doesn't have a "virgin child" cooing in French at the end.

"Jack Straw"

We can share the women, we can share the wine, we can share the lead vocals: "Jack Straw" holds a unique place in the Dead's catalog in that the vocals were originally sung by Bob Weir, and then eventually co-sung with Garcia's singing the opening of the verses. No matter who sings it, it's one of Hunter's most affecting lyrics, possibly referencing a European peasants' revolt, but with the couplet "We used to play for silver / Now we play for life" as a metaphor for growing up. A studio rendition probably would have rivaled "Uncle John's Band" in the harmony department and then some, considering that the band had Donna Godchaux-MacKay's voice at its disposal by that point.

"Tennessee Jed"

This is a bouncy little number with deceptively downbeat lyrics. But beyond the imagery of the "ball and chain" and "iron shackles" is a clever titular conceit. When you see the title, you think that "Tennessee Jed" is a nickname, but when hearing the lyrics, it's used as an instruction to the title character. Several years later, country singer Jim Stafford would mine this same idea for high comedy with his song "My Girl Bill." A studio version might have brought Hunter's evocative-but-disturbing lyrics to the fore in the way the late Levon Helm did when he covered this song on the last album he released in his lifetime, *Electric Dirt*.

"The Stranger (Two Souls in Communion)"

It's a shame that the majority of Dead fans had to wait until 2001 to hear this Pigpen number, because it's probably the best thing he did. It's a ballad that gets philosophical, and it's not hard to see a seriously confessional aspect to the lyrics. "Did I take a wrong turn on life's winding road?" sings Pigpen. "Won't somebody help me find the right way to go?" It's also got a nice melody, and Pigpen sings it in a style that's far more vulnerable and sweet than his rough 'n' ready vocals on the blues tunes he usually covered. The song got a surprising revival in 2010, when it was played live at Phil Lesh's seventieth birthday celebration during a Furthur concert featuring several guest stars. Black Crowes singer Chris Robinson took the lead vocals and received an ecstatic review from Deadheadland.com for his effort.

"He's Gone"

Side two would begin with this live favorite. According to the online resource the Annotated Grateful Dead Lyrics, Hunter supposedly wrote this song about the disappearance of Mickey Hart's father, Lenny. As a song, it also bears some similarities to the old chain gang song "Long John," later popularized by Pete Seeger. This may have been in the back of the minds of traditionally minded Hunter and Garcia. Whatever the case, the song's intention never matched the way it was interpreted by fans, which was as a send-off to those departed. A studio version of this would have amounted to a eulogy for Pigpen, no matter the intention of the lyricist.

"Brown-Eyed Women"

This unassuming mid-tempo rocker has a way of creeping up on you. It's never been one of the songs that fans seem to clamor for, yet it appears on a lot of *Dick's Picks* and always sounds good because the band falls into its rhythm so well. Would a studio version have bested any of the live takes we've come to know and love? Maybe, maybe not, but it might have given the Dead a chance to emphasize the rhythms a bit more, like they did with the material on *Grateful Dead from the Mars Hotel*. Another thing it might have done is brought out Hunter's lyrics, sung from the point of view of a kid who grew up among bootleggers during the Prohibition era. How's that for a history lesson?

"Looks Like Rain"

This early collaboration between Weir and his school friend-turned-lyricist John Perry Barlow might have been a contender for a single had it been a Dead track rather than a solo song. Promoting an established band to radio stations would have been much easier than promoting a new solo artist, after all. The song has got a killer guitar hook that was appropriated—consciously or not—by Bob Seger for his hit "Main Street." Someone on the Furthur discussionboard posted about "Main Street" being a good cover for Weir—it might make a better segue into or out of "Looks Like Rain."

"Playing in the Band"

This is one of the quintessential Dead numbers and a rare collaboration between Weir and Hunter, who didn't work much together after this because the lyricist had issues with the singer's altering his lines. You'd never know that by the way Weir breezily sings Hunter's verses as the band plays in the absurd 10/4 time signature, which shouldn't work, but somehow does. The song was also a great set closer that the band sometimes extended to twenty minutes when the mood struck. Hunter's words wax philosophical but not didactic, culminating in one of the best choruses of any song the band played.

So, that's it for the hypothetical great lost Grateful Dead album. If you put these tracks together from their respective sources, you can get a pretty good approximation of what such an LP would have sounded like. And don't worry that a few of the cuts are from solo albums. As Scully points out in his book, Garcia's album is all him and Kreutzmann, while Weir's *Ace* features every member of the band save Pigpen.

Had fans of "Playing in the Band" found it on this album, they'd have probably bought it. And the title? Well, why not take a cue from *Wake of the Flood* and grab part of a line from one of the songs? One good phrase is "Meet you at the jubilee" from "Sugaree," but that's a bit too upbeat for this collection. Hey, how about the phrase "Steal your face" from "He's Gone?" That way, there would be at least one good album with that title.

27

Sing Me a Song of My Own

Dead-Related Solo Albums and Record Labels

T o get a larger sense of where the members of the Grateful Dead were coming from as musicians, it's essential to listen to the solo projects in which they were involved. Often, the musicians of the Dead brought songs from their outside excursions back to the band, where they were performed on stage. Sometimes other Dead musicians would assist their fellow band members with outside projects.

The following is a list of solo recordings that Dead members made at the same time they were involved with the band. These recordings provide insight into what musicians were doing when they weren't doing it with the Dead, and what influences they may have brought back to the band during its existence. As such, solo projects done after the Grateful Dead ceased to exist or after a musician had left the group are not included (e.g., Tom Constanten's solo albums and Bob Weir's work with RatDog). Also not included are guest appearances by Dead members on albums by outside bands (such as Jefferson Airplane), because that information could fill a book by itself. Most of the following recordings were solo records; when a band or collaboration was involved, the names of the band or collaborators are listed following the album's title.

Jerry Garcia

Many of Garcia's best studio moments came on his solo albums. His earliest efforts are as important as Grateful Dead albums are for anyone seriously interested in the band.

New Riders of the Purple Sage, New Riders of the Purple Sage (1971)

Garcia didn't write any songs for this country rock band's debut album, but he was both a founding member of this group and a full-fledged one, at least for a brief period. On this album, he plays either pedal steel or banjo throughout, and

NEW RIDERS OF THE PURPLE SAGE

Garcia appeared on the New Riders of the Purple Sage's self-titled 1971 debut album as a full-fledged member of the group, chiming in with banjo and pedal steel. When Grateful Dead obligations caused him to leave the group, he was replaced by steel guitar whiz Buddy Cage, a session musician who had played on albums by Anne Murray and Brewer and Shipley (with whom Garcia also played).   *Courtesy of Sharon Balan*

his speedy pedal steel runs on "Panama Red" especially stand out. Two tracks also feature Mickey Hart on drums.

Garcia (1972)

Garcia's first solo album includes six Dead concert staples: "Deal," "Bird Song," "Sugaree," "Loser," "To Lay Me Down," and "The Wheel." He also forays into the world of atonal avant garde piano music with two songs, "Late for Supper" and "Spidergawd," and he showcases his prowess on synthesizer on a third, "EEP Hour." *Garcia* was recorded alone with only Bill Kreutzmann's musical assistance. Essential listening.

Live at Keystone, Merl Saunders, Jerry Garcia, John Kahn, Bill Vitt (1973)

Garcia gets to show off his chops in playing alongside musicians who would become longtime compatriots. Several CDs of additional performances from these July 10 and 11 shows would follow, and in 2012, a comprehensive box set was issued as *Keystone Companions: The Complete 1973 Fantasy Recordings*.

Garcia (Compliments of Garcia) (1974)

Garcia lays his influences bare with an album of cover versions, tipping the hat to composers as diverse as Chuck Berry, Irving Berlin, and Dr. John. The CD reissue contained in the *All Good Things* box set (see below) adds ten extra tracks, essentially doubling the length of the original album.

Old & In the Way, Old & In the Way (1975)

David Grisman, John Kahn, Vassar Clements, and Peter Rowan played in this traditional bluegrass group, which featured Garcia on banjo and harmony vocals

The bluegrass supergroup Old & In the Way gave Jerry Garcia a way to return to playing banjo, an instrument he'd mastered long before the Grateful Dead formed. The group only released one album during Garcia's lifetime: their self-titled debut on the Dead's Round Records label.   *Courtesy of Sharon Balan*

(and lead vocals on one song, the traditional "Pig in a Pen"). This album was recorded at San Francisco's Boarding House in 1973. Three more live CDs of Old & In the Way featuring Garcia were released after Garcia's death: *That High Lonesome Sound*, *Breakdown*, and *Live at the Boarding House.*

Reflections (1976)

Another essential Garcia album that features such Dead concert staples as "Might As Well," "Mission in the Rain," "It Must Have Been the Roses," and "They Love Each Other," *Reflections* also includes musical assistance by all the members of the Dead.

Cats Under the Stars, Jerry Garcia Band (1978)

Some (including Garcia himself) consider the first album done under the moniker of the Jerry Garcia Band to be Garcia's best solo outing. It's definitely his most varied, with reggae ("Love in the Afternoon"), hard rock ("Rhapsody in Red"), a mournful ballad ("Palm Sunday"), and classic Dead-sounding numbers ("Rubin and Cherise").

Run for the Roses, Jerry Garcia Band (1982)

A weak album recorded as Garcia was slipping into drug addiction, it nonetheless offered the only opportunity for anyone to hear him in a studio setting during the early 1980s, when the Dead had stopped recording studio albums. Only the title track and the underrated "Valerie" are indispensable, but the six bonus tracks added on the CD reissue in the *All Good Things* box set at least add some much-needed heft to the original paltry seven-song lineup.

Almost Acoustic, Jerry Garcia Acoustic Band (1988)

This live CD was recorded at New York's Lunt-Fontanne Theatre in the fall of 1987. It finds Garcia successfully giving acoustic treatments to traditional songs such as "Swing Low, Sweet Chariot" and "Deep Elem Blues" in much the way he did during the Dead's acoustic sets at the Warfield Theatre and Radio City Music Hall in 1980.

Garcia/Grisman, Jerry Garcia and David Grisman (1991)

With just guitar, mandolin, and minimal percussion, the two veteran pickers create an intimate acoustic album miles away from what the Dead were going for at the time. Garcia is in fine voice on his lead vocals (including a cover of B.B. King's "The Thrill Is Gone"), and the four instrumentals are absolutely compelling.

Jerry Garcia Band, Jerry Garcia Band (1991)

Recorded at the Warfield in San Francisco in the spring of 1990, this album finds Garcia tackling covers by artists ranging from Bruce Cockburn ("Waiting for a Miracle") to Peter Tosh ("Stop That Train"). Not groundbreaking, but contains first-rate performances.

Not for Kids Only, Jerry Garcia and David Grisman (1993)

Garcia and Grisman return with their second studio album in three years, an entertaining romp through traditional children's songs ("Teddy Bear's Picnic," "When First unto This Country") that can also be enjoyed by adults, as the title suggests.

All Good Things: Jerry Garcia Studio Sessions (2004)

This six-CD set compiles all five of the Garcia and Jerry Garcia Band studio albums, along with bonus tracks plus an extra CD of previously unreleased material called *Outtakes, Jams & Alternates.*

Bob Weir

With his solo and collaborative efforts, the Grateful Dead's rhythm guitarist got to try on musical styles beyond his work with the motherband.

Ace (1972)

A Grateful Dead album with Weir as leader and featuring the studio debuts of "Greatest Story Ever Told," "Playing in the Band," "One More Saturday Night," and "Cassidy," among others, *Ace* is essential listening.

Kingfish, Kingfish (1976)

Weir appears as a full-fledged band member on this country rock band's debut. His "Lazy Lightnin'" and "Supplication" are featured, and he sings lead on a cover of Marty Robbins's "Big Iron."

Live 'N' Kickin', Kingfish (1977)

Weir's country rocking side project gets bluesy on this live release, which has Weir taking lead vocals on a cover of Chuck Berry's "Around and Around."

Heaven Help the Fool (1978)

Keith Olsen, who had produced *Terrapin Station* for the Dead, took the production reins for Weir's second solo effort. The eight-song album was criticized at the time for being too slick, but it's held up better than the reputation it's gotten, mostly because of strong material such as the title song and "Bombs Away."

Bobby and the Midnites, Bobby and the Midnites (1981)

This side project of Weir's also featured Brent Mydland for its first album. Unlike with Kingfish, Weir is the bandleader here: only his face is pictured on the inner sleeve, and he sings lead throughout. "Festival" is the strongest cut, but everything would have sounded better if it hadn't been drowned in cavernous '80s reverb by producer Gary Lyons, who had previously worked on *Go to Heaven*.

Where the Beat Meets the Street, Bobby and the Midnites (1984)

Weir's second record by this side project fares better sound-wise, thanks to the detailed production work of Jeff Baxter (Steely Dan), but is more notable for guest appearances by the likes of guitar whizzes Brian Setzer and Steve Cropper than for its songs.

Keith Godchaux and Donna Godchaux-MacKay

The Dead's resident married couple also worked as a pair outside the realm of the band.

Keith and Donna Godchaux (1975)

Good singin' and good playin', as the saying goes, but there's not much good songwriting on this pair's only album together. The choice to cover the most overrated single in history, "River Deep, Mountain High," was also ill-conceived.

Robert Hunter

Hunter's solo albums are a treasure trove for fans of his lyrics, as his renditions of Dead tunes often contain extra verses or alternate lyrics.

Tales of the Great Rum Runners (1974)

The Dead lyricist's debut sets the tone for his career: his songs are often first-rate, but his voice is just as often inexpressive or off-pitch. This unplugged effort isn't too far away from what the Dead were doing during their *American Beauty* era. This album includes a bluegrassy version of "It Must Have Been the Roses" that runs at a much quicker clip than Garcia's version does.

Tiger Rose (1975)

Garcia produced Hunter's second solo effort, which features not only Garcia but also Hart and Donna Jean Godchaux-MacKay. The arrangements bring out the best in Hunter's voice, especially the slinky synth-reggae backing of "One Thing to Try."

Jack O'Roses (1980)

Jack O'Roses is an essential listen because it includes Hunter's own version of "Terrapin Station" (here called "Terrapin"), which includes some sections left out of the Dead's version, one of which gives the album its title. Also featured are his folkie renderings of "Box of Rain," "Friend of the Devil," and "Rubin and Cherise," here titled "Ruben and Cerise." Hard to find, as it wasn't released in the United States.

The *Keith and Donna* album was one of ten long-players released by the Dead's Round Records label, an imprint that was dedicated to solo and solo-related works by the band's members. The album has never been reissued on CD. *Author's collection*

Amagamalin Street (1984)

Hunter's first album of all-new material in nine years was originally issued as a double vinyl album and featured interrelated songs that examined the relationships among four troubled characters. John Cipollina plays guitar.

Live 85 (1985)

This one comes with Hunter's own renditions of four Dead songs: "Jack Straw," "Easy Wind," "Franklin's Tower," and "It Must Have Been the Roses."

Flight of the Marie Helena (1985)

This album is not quite songs, but a poetry reading in seven parts, each part denoted by a different day.

Rock Columbia (1986)

Rock Columbia contains a version of his own "What'll You Raise," recorded by the Dead for *Go to Heaven* but not released at the time.

Duino Elegies (1988)

This forty-minute cassette-only release features Hunter's reading of his translations of German language poet Rainer Maria Rilke's ten-poem cycle inspired by his visit to an Italian castle in 1912. Tom Constanten provides piano. Reissued in 1992 in longer form as *Duino Elegies/The Sonnets to Orpheus*.

Liberty (1988)

This '80s-oriented pop rock effort features Garcia on guitar. The title track is an early (and arguably better) version of a song Garcia later rewrote for the Dead.

Box of Rain (1990)

A live album mostly featuring Dead classics, *Box of Rain* was scheduled to coincide with the publication of Hunter's book of lyrics, which had the same title.

Sentinel (1993)

This spoken word collection features Hunter reading twenty-three of his poems.

Mickey Hart

Most solo albums by drummers are vanity projects. Hart's works, however, were groundbreaking enough to earn him soundtrack work and a job compiling music from around the world for the Smithsonian Folkways label, which released *The Mickey Hart Collection* in 2011.

Rolling Thunder (1972)

A precursor to world music, Hart's percussion-heavy first solo album features Garcia, Lesh, and Weir, among other all-star talent such as Grace Slick. Recorded around the same time as Weir's *Ace*, Weir took two of its songs, "The Main Ten" and "Pump Song," and respectively rewrote them as "Playing in the Band" and "Greatest Story Ever Told."

Diga, Diga Rhythm Band (1976)

Diga's a surprisingly tuneful album considering it's almost all percussion. Garcia guests on "Razooli" and "Happiness Is Drumming," the latter of which formed the basis for "Fire on the Mountain."

The Rhythm Devils Play River Music, The Rhythm Devils (1980)

Hart produced and co-composed this album's worth of percussion-oriented music that formed the acclaimed soundtrack to Francis Ford Coppola's epic war movie *Apocalypse Now*. Kreutzmann and Phil Lesh contribute. Reissued in expanded form on CD in 1991 with the added subtitle *The Apocalypse Now Sessions*.

Dafos, Mickey Hart, Airto Moreira, Flora Purim (1983)

Dafos is more percussive songs with Hart serving as co-producer with Brazilian drummer Moreira, who would become a regular collaborator.

Yamantaka, Mickey Hart, Henry Wolff & Nancy Hennings (1983)

Hart co-wrote all six of the album's tracks with Wolff and Hennings, who helped invent new age music with their groundbreaking *Tibetan Bells* album in 1971. All tracks on this album were based on traditional Tibetan music.

Music to Be Born By (1989)

Hart self-produced and co-engineered this seventy-minute soundscape, which he put together in anticipation of the birth of his son, Taro, whose fetal heartbeat was used as the basis of the recording.

At the Edge (1990)

Hart is listed as playing more than two dozen instruments on this self-produced effort, released along with a book, *Drumming at the Edge of Magic*. Garcia guests on guitar on "Sky Water" and guitar synth on "The Eliminators," and plays samples of crickets (called a "forest zone") on "#4 for Gaia."

Planet Drum (1991)

Winner of the first-ever Best World Music Grammy Award, this all-percussion album was released in conjunction with Hart's 1991 book, *Planet Drum*.

The Dead's Own Record Labels

In 1973, the Dead left Warner Bros., the company that originally signed the band back in 1967. Tired of dealing with record executives and what the band considered faulty distribution of their records, the Dead decided to found their own record label. Actually, they founded two labels. The first was Grateful Dead Records, a label that released a total of four original albums (not counting reissues), all of which were by the band, including *Wake of the Flood*, *Grateful Dead from the Mars Hotel*, *Blues for Allah*, and *Steal Your Face*.

The group also started a label called Round Records, which released records by band members and records by outside musicians affiliated with the group, many of which were mentioned previously in this chapter. It wasn't that big an endeavor. In all, Round Records only released a total of ten albums.

Eight Round Records releases were either solo albums by Dead members or albums by groups in which they were involved. These include Hunter's *Tales of The Great Rum Runners* and *Tiger Rose*, Garcia's *Garcia* (aka *Compliments of Garcia*) and *Reflections*, Old & In the Way's self-titled debut, Keith Godchaux and Donna Godchaux-MacKay's self-titled album, the debut album by Kingfish, and Diga Rhythm Band's *Diga* featuring Mickey Hart.

Two records had less direct involvement from the Dead. The first was Ned Lagin's experimental synthesizer work *Seastones*, a 1975 album made up of an improvised nine-part modern composition that ran for more than forty minutes. Lagin is the main instrumentalist on the cut (which features him on piano, clavichord, synthesizers, and computers, among other things). But Garcia, Hart, and Lesh also chime in on their usual instruments, with Garcia also chipping in with some vocals. (When a CD of this album was released in 1991, it added a thirty-one-minute demo version of Lagin's composition as a bonus track).

The second Round Records release with minimal Dead input was Pistol Packin' Mama's 1976 album *The Good Old Boys*. Pistol Packin' Mama was a bluegrass quintet that featured Dave Nelson of New Riders of the Purple Sage on guitar and vocals. Garcia did produce this album, though, and also sings harmony on "Leave Well Enough Alone."

After three years in the record business, the Dead started to find the tasks of having to be executives, distributors, and promoters to be a bit much. The band shuttered the label in early 1976 and signed with Arista Records later in the year.

28

Sunshine Daydreams

Rare Films, DVDs, and TV Programs

It's pretty easy to see the Grateful Dead on video these days. In April 2012, Shout! Factory and Rhino Entertainment released a "definitive visual anthology" of the band's oeuvre in the form of a fourteen-DVD set called *All the Years Combine: The DVD Collection*. The set includes *The Grateful Dead Movie*, the *Dead Ahead* Radio City Music Hall television special, the *Closing of Winterland* concert, the *So Far* documentary, the *Ticket to New Year's* Pay-Per-View special, the *Truckin' Up to Buffalo* and *Downhill from Here* concerts, and four *View from the Vault* concerts. There's also a bonus disc of backstage footage and unreleased live performances. Two other live DVD releases have hit the market, too: *Rocking the Cradle: Egypt 1978* and the DVD that comes with the three-DC set *Crimson, White & Indigo: Philadelphia, July, 7, 1989*.

Because these releases are easily accessible and have been reviewed at length elsewhere, this chapter will look at the long-form films, TV programs, and DVD releases that aren't officially part of "the cannon." Films listed include movies about both the Dead and Deadheads. Television programs listed are just that: entire programs devoted to the Dead and not shows where the Dead appeared for one or two songs or interview snippets (such as *Saturday Night Live*). For a complete listing of all the Dead's TV appearances, consult the online Grateful Dead Family Discography.

And Miles to Go Before I Sleep: On Tour with the Grateful Dead Summer 1993

This hour-long documentary was put together by Peter Shapiro when he was an undergraduate student at Northwestern University, ostensibly to look at the lives of Deadheads during summer tour. But it ended up going far beyond that and interpolating interviews with a wide variety of people associated with the band in one way or another, including John Perry Barlow, Ken Kesey, Timothy Leary, and Wavy Gravy. Viewed today, the film offers a vivid snapshot of the Dead in their final phase, when the group's influence and audience were still expanding and few people sensed that the end was near.

The documentary, which was originally screened only as a student film, made its debut for a wide audience on February 22, 2013, when *Relix* magazine put it online. It was seen early on, though, by the makers of the documentary

Tie-Died: Rock 'n Roll's Most Deadicated Fans (see entry later in this chapter), who invited Shapiro to work as an associate producer for that effort. Shapiro has since gone on to become an independent filmmaker and major player in the jam band scene, having owned the Wetlands Preserve rock club and founded the Jammy Awards.

Can't Take It with You: "Jerry Garcia"

England's BBC2 produced this half-hour documentary in 2003 as part of its *Can't Take It with You* series, which investigated legal ramifications caused by incomplete or nonexistent wills of the rich and famous. This one looks at the battle that ensued over Garcia's will. It's a reasonably balanced program in that pretty much no one involved comes out looking good, save maybe Garcia's daughter, Annabelle Garcia-McLean, who serves as a proxy spokesperson for her mother, Carolyn "Mountain Girl" Adams Garcia, who does not appear.

Much of the episode is devoted to Garcia's official widow, Deborah Koons Garcia, who speaks about how Garcia's estate was able to better monetize his music-related products posthumously. "What's interesting is the ties and the ice cream make more money than the music," she says at one point. Then there's Doug Irwin, who crafted custom-made guitars for Garcia that were returned to him in Garcia's will, which was legally challenged by the other band members. Irwin ended up being allowed to keep two creations, Wolf and Tiger, which he then auctioned off, after which he tried to bill the estate for taxes. The episode is revealing in an unfortunately sobering way, with the narrator, Colin Murray, providing blow-by-blow commentary. The program has never been for sale, but it circulates on bootleg DVDs and is easily findable online.

Classic Albums: "The Grateful Dead: Anthem to Beauty"

This documentary about the Dead's recording career was part of a series called *Classic Albums* that aired on VH1, among several other channels. The program was originally an hour long when it aired in 1997, but it was expanded to an hour and fifteen minutes when it came out on DVD via Eagle Rock Entertainment. It looks at the making of both the *Anthem of the Sun* and *American Beauty* albums in terms of both songwriting and the recording process. Details are provided by interviews with Bob Weir, Robert Hunter, Mickey Hart, Dennis McNally, Tom Constanten, David Crosby, and Phil Lesh (who also narrates). One of the more amusing interview segments is with former Warner Bros. executive Joe Smith, who speaks on how the Dead's recording sessions differed drastically from those of artists the label had previously worked with because of "the element of chemicals involved."

There's also a lot of Garcia in the form of vintage interview footage. Other highlights include Lesh in the recording studio, playing individual tracks from the master tapes of "Born Cross-Eyed" and explaining which instruments went on which track and how they contributed to the full mix. One of the more interesting segments shows the band playing live on an episode of the short-lived TV show *Playboy After Dark*. That episode, from January 18, 1969, can be found on the 2007 DVD *Playboy After Dark—2nd Collection* and features performances of "Mountains of the Moon," "St. Stephen," and "Turn On Your Love Light."

Dawn of the Dead

The Sexy Intellectual production company, which has produced DVDs about a range of artists, including Nick Drake and Rage Against the Machine, produced this illuminating 2012 made-for-DVD documentary subtitled *The Grateful Dead & the Rise of the San Francisco Underground*. As the subtitle suggests, the film charts both the Dead's rise to national prominence during their formative years as well as their hometown's ascension to hippie hotspot of the moment. Peter Albin of Big Brother and the Holding Company discusses Garcia's involvement in the Palo Alto folk and bluegrass scene of the early '60s, and former Dead manager Rock Scully explains how the band's paltry album sales didn't quite cover the large budgets for their second and third albums. *Rolling Stone*'s Anthony DeCurtis puts things into a larger sociological context by speaking about how the consciousness of the counterculture changed in 1968.

The Scully interview is unique to this DVD, as are several other interviews, including ones with Tom Constanten, Dennis McNally, and David Gans. The release also looks at the history of other acts of the time, including Big Brother and the Holding Company, Jefferson Airplane, and Quicksilver Messenger Service. It's all put into context with narration by Thomas Arnold, an English-accented graduate of the Royal Academy of Dramatic Art, not the guy best known as Roseanne's former husband. And at two hours and eighteen minutes, no one leaves any stones unturned, and you definitely get your money's worth.

Dead Heads—An American Subculture

This twenty-eight-minute documentary isn't the place to go if you're looking for music, as it's more about sociology than about songs (in fact, no Dead songs or band members are even featured). But it still offers an interesting look at what makes Deadheads Deadheads. Most of the explaining is done by Rebecca G. Adams, PhD, a sociologist from the University of North Carolina at Greensboro, and Michael Kaern, PhD, from Boston University. The pair kick things off by talking about social theorist Georg Simmel and how his ideas about humanity relate to Deadhead subculture.

Several questions are raised and answered, including why the subculture continued to exist throughout the 1980s, how Deadheads continued to use '60s-style drugs, and why the better-heeled members of the community are willing to give away "miracle tickets" to those who show up without any. There are also many interviews with fans, presumably filmed outside concerts in 1989,

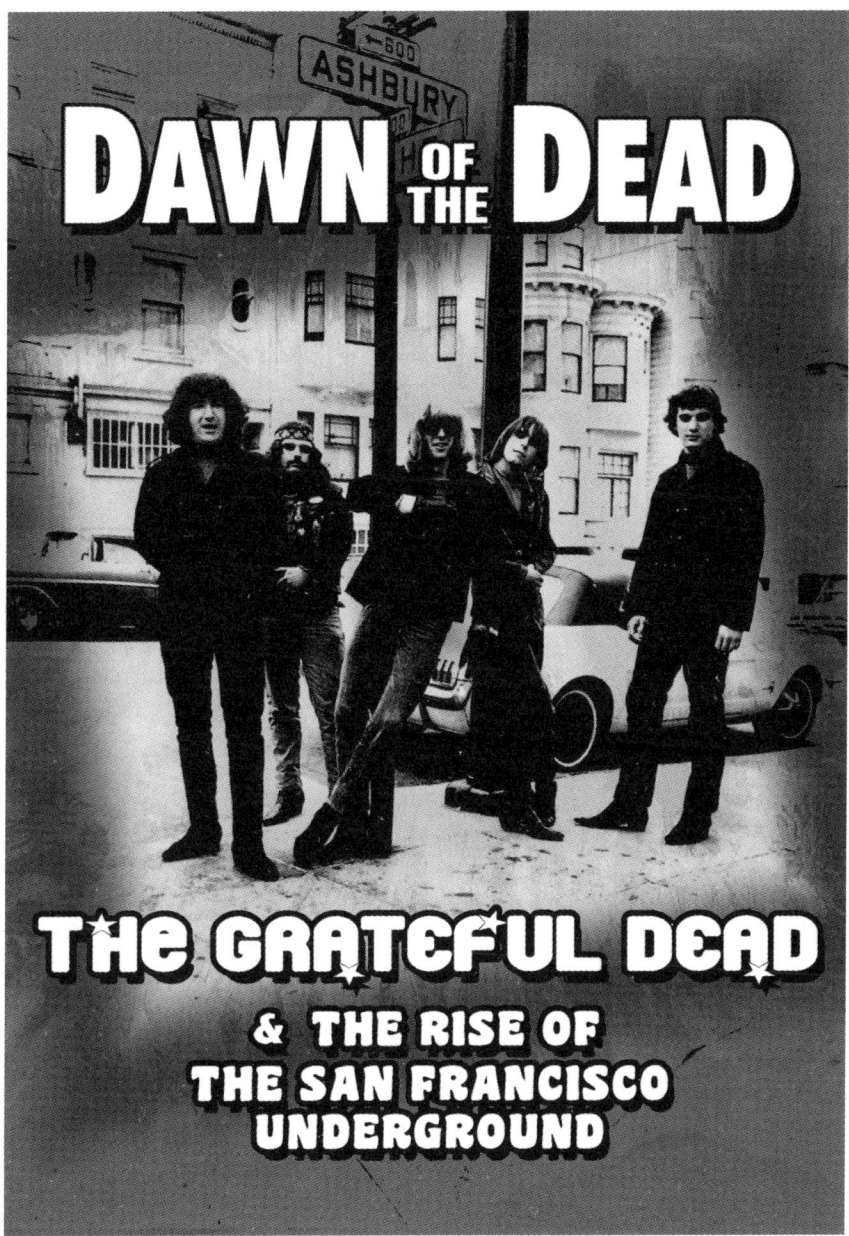

Jokey title aside, *Dawn of the Dead* is one of the most noteworthy documentaries about the Grateful Dead because it focuses on one very specific area of the band: their formation. By zeroing in on the time in which the Haight-Ashbury scene was just blossoming and almost anything seemed possible, the DVD successfully conjures the musical and social atmosphere that gave rise to the Dead.   *Courtesy of Chrome Dreams/Sexy Intellectual*

as this short film was published in 1990 and initially ran on PBS on January 13, 1991. It's available on DVD and online stream by the Films Media Group.

Dead Ringers: The Making of Touch of Grey

Justin Kreutzmann, the son of drummer Bill Kreutzmann, was just seventeen when he directed this half-hour behind-the-scenes documentary. The video looks at how director Gary Gutierrez put together the Dead's first official music video, and it features footage of the live audience brought in for the end of the video (from the May 9, 1987, gig at the Laguna Seca Raceway in Monterey), as well as interviews and the video itself. Originally released in 1987 in VCR format, it's long out of print and has never come out on DVD. It's not even listed as part of the résumé of Justin Kreutzmann, who is now a seasoned filmmaker and working as chief creative officer for Bob Weir's TRI Studios.

The End of the Road—The Final Tour '95

When director Brent Meeske set out to make a documentary about Deadheads starting in the spring of 1995, he had no idea that the band's tour would be their last. As such, his film, which came out in 2001, ended up being a final look at the end of the Dead's career as well. Because of that, his film is more engaging than the two other "Deadhead films" (*Dead Heads—An American Subculture* and *Tie-Died: Rock 'n Roll's Most Deadicated Fans*). As Meeske ended up essaying one of the Dead's most tumultuous tours, his film examines some of the more controversial elements of the scene, such as gate crashing and the huge disconnect that developed between veteran Deadheads and the new generation of rowdier fans.

It's not always pleasant viewing, and Meeske has taken some flak for portraying Deadheads in a negative light by interviewing some of the more troubled souls who populated the parking lot scene. But it is consistently interesting and, in hindsight, does capture the feel of the Dead scene in the summer of 1995, right down to its ending, which documents Garcia's memorial service in Golden Gate Park. The film, which has soundtrack music by Merl Saunders and Jerry Garcia, was released on DVD in 2005.

Festival Express

The Festival Express was the name of a rock 'n' roll tour that had a bunch of rock acts traveling through parts of Canada by train in the summer of 1970. One of those acts was the Dead, another was the Band, and another was Janis Joplin. Also onboard was a film crew, and lots of performances and informal jam sessions were captured, but no film was ever released at the time. But around thirty years later, folks started realizing that they had a piece of history on their hands, so a company called THINKFilm got together with the son of the original producer, and they all put together a film.

And what a film. The theatrical print has the Dead's performing "Don't Ease Me In," "Friend of the Devil," and "New Speedway Boogie." One of the best segments has Garcia's playing acoustic guitar and jamming with a very inebriated Rick Danko (of the Band) and Joplin on the traditional Band favorite "Ain't No More Cane." The DVD edition has three additional Dead performances, including "Casey Jones," "Easy Wind," and "Hard to Handle." There was no accompanying soundtrack released, so the DVD is now the only way to hear these songs.

The Grateful and the Dead

"For several years, composers or their families in many parts of Britain have been secretly supported by an infamous American rock band about which most of them knew nothing." That's the way this BBC special from January 22, 1993, begins as it tells the story of Phil Lesh, who has supported a host of modern classical composers in the United Kingdom through the Dead's in-house charitable organization, the Rex Foundation. This is one of the more compelling Dead-related documentaries because the BBC production is so well put together. It features an in-depth interview with Lesh, plus shorter interview segments with Garcia and Weir, the latter of whom says of the Dead's patronage, "It's always been our feeling that if you get some you give some back." The Dead are also seen performing several songs, including "Tennessee Jed," "Stagger Lee," and "Estimated Prophet." The program runs an hour and has never come out on DVD, although it's easy to find online.

Jerry Garcia Interview 1994

This forty-five-minute video interview with Garcia showed up on YouTube out of the blue and with no information about who conducted it or what it was going to be used for. Messages to the video's source went unanswered, but a commenter on YouTube claimed it was used for a documentary on the history of rock 'n' roll. Whatever the intent behind it, the interview offers a fascinating and unadulterated glimpse into Garcia's views on everything from what made him take up electric guitar, to how he feels about drugs, to what he thinks about rap music. Throughout it all, Garcia is relaxed and loquacious, looking more like a mad professor than like a rock star with his bushy white hair and beard. Judging by the date on the clapperboard, Garcia sat for this interview on May 2, 1994.

The Making of Built to Last

Not a DVD, not a movie, not even a segment from a television show—this hour-and-a-half video consists of rough footage of the band rehearsing several numbers for their final album, including "Picasso Moon," "Blow Away," and "Just a Little Light." A good portion of the video consists of a static camera placed beside Kreutzmann's drum set, and from that vantage point, we hear Garcia giving the drummer detailed instructions on precisely which tom toms and cymbals to use during the verses and choruses of Mydland's "Blow Away." And you thought the Dead just winged it!

Other segments show Weir running through "Picasso Moon" and Garcia rehearsing some guitar runs by himself. Toward the end, the members of the band sit listening to playbacks, and Mydland walks in with one of his daughters, who sits down next to Lesh unacknowledged. The video concludes with a slideshow of vintage photos of various band members. This video has also been circulated as an audio-only file titled *The Grateful Dead Live at Club Front—Grateful Dead Studio on 1989-03-01 (March 1, 1989)*. It's really only for hardcore fanatics, but those who can't get enough will get a window into a rarely-seen side of the group during its later years.

Sunshine Daydream

This 1972 concert film is a period piece in the best sense of that phrase. It captures both band and audience at an outdoor benefit the Dead did for the Springfield Creamery in Oregon during the daytime hours on August 27 of that year, and it looks pretty much exactly like you'd imagine (or remember) a Dead concert of that era would look like. There are lots of hippies, colorful vintage clothing, and tons of nudity, including nude shots of kids (which apparently wasn't as taboo back then).

There's also the Dead, whose three sets that day (and evening) are cherry-picked. Songs featured include "Promised Land," "I Know You Rider," "Jack Straw," "Dark Star," "El Paso," "Greatest Story Ever Told," and "China Cat Sunflower">"I Know You Rider." The movie was shot by Phil DeGuere, who later became a television writer and director, working on such shows as the '80s remake of *The Twilight Zone*, for which he invited the Dead to contribute a title theme that ran throughout its 1985–1988 run, as well as incidental music that was showcased the first season. The concert is co-emceed by Ken Kesey, whose brother owned the creamery (and still does). *Sunshine Daydream* is easy enough to find online, and a release was imminent as this book went to press.

Tie-Died: Rock 'n Roll's Most Deadicated Fans

Director Andrew Behar filmed this documentary on Deadheads during the 1994 summer tour, and it showcases an awful lot of Deadheads talking, playing music, or just milling around. But that's pretty much all it features. As a slice of life, it's interesting, but as an in-depth look into "the scene," it's less successful because it offers no historical perspective and lacks a much-needed narrative voice.

Some of the Deadheads do have fascinating stories, though. There's a girl who started touring at age fourteen and says she came to feel at home in the Dead's family after the dissolution of her own. There are several interviewees who bring their kids on tour, one of whom says his child's school understands his child's missed classes because "his three main teachers are Deadheads." Variety is provided by the Deadheads who perform their own songs, the best of which is an a cappella chant that goes "The river she is flowing, flowing and growing / The river she is flowing down to the sea." Released in theaters in 1995 and on DVD in 1999.

The Tomorrow Show

In 1981, *The Tomorrow Show* was just about the only place you could see some of the more outré rock acts of the day, such as the Clash, the Plasmatics, and Public Image, Ltd. The reason for this was the show's host, the late Tom Snyder, who made a serious (and commendable) effort to push boundaries when it came to commercial television. Such was the case on May 7, 1981, when Snyder devoted an entire episode of his program to all things Dead-related. The program featured an interview with Garcia and Ken Kesey; another interview with Garcia, Weir, and the band's drummers; and the group playing four songs, "On The Road Again," "Cassidy," "Dire Wolf," and "Deep Elem Blues." The Dead's episode can be found along with three others on the 2006 DVD *The Tomorrow Show: Tom Snyder's Electric Kool-Aid Talk Show.*

The Will: Family Secrets Revealed: "The Estate of Jerry Garcia"

Discovery Communications' cable channel Investigation Discovery devotes itself to documentary-style programs that pander to Americans' obsession with "true crime" stories. In 2010, the channel started running the show *The Will: Family Secrets Revealed*, which, according to the channel's website, "shows the outrageousness that abounds when the famous depart." The show produced episodes about Andy Warhol, Ritchie Valens, and Jimi Hendrix, and on January 18, 2013, it came out with one about Jerry Garcia. The program followed the schematic of the BBC2 show *Can't Take It With You* from years earlier: it looked at the battle over Garcia's will, which mostly involved Deborah Koons Garcia and Carolyn "Mountain Girl" Adams Garcia.

The difference is that, unlike the BBC2 program, this one comes off as exploitative and contrived. The interview subjects are dramatically backlit, making them look like criminals getting ready for mug shots, while most of the story is told with "re-enactments" that use actresses who look nothing like either of Garcia's wives (Mountain Girl as a blonde?!). Even the voice-over monologues are bothersome, with the macho-sounding narrator making it sound as if the battle over Garcia's will was the crime of the century. The program is about Garcia, guys, not Charles Manson. Ferret out the BBC2 documentary if you feel the need to watch this whole drama play out again.

29

Eyes of the World

A Roundup of Unreleased Live Dead Footage

I n the age of YouTube and Dailymotion, concert footage is becoming what cassette tapes were to an older generation of Deadheads: a way to share the experience and connect with fellow Deadheads. The following is an inventory of concerts or partial concerts that have been uploaded at some point to video-sharing websites. Most were recorded by fans, a few are professional recordings, and none have been officially released. This list is limited to concerts that were recorded in a reasonably proficient way, but some hard-to-watch videos were included when they were historically important. All videos have stereo sound unless otherwise noted.

Fillmore East, New York, New York; February 14, 1970

This grainy black-and-white footage is shot with a shaky handheld camera, but it's invaluable for presenting a rare look at the early Dead (it's excellently synched with high-quality sound, too).

- Set: "Dark Star," "Hard to Handle," "I've Been All Around This World," "Me and My Uncle," "Not Fade Away," "Mason's Children."

KQED Studios, San Francisco, California; August 30, 1970

A thirty-minute color performance from a program called *Calibration*, originally simulcast on the San Francisco FM station KSAN.

- Set: "Easy Wind," "Candyman," "Casey Jones," "Brokedown Palace," "Uncle John's Band."

Chateau d'Herouville, Herouville, France; June 21, 1971

A first-rate, hour-long performance originally broadcast on public television in France.

- Set: "Morning Dew" (partial version), "Hard to Handle," "China Cat Sunflower," "I Know You Rider," "Deal," "Black Peter," "Sugar Magnolia," "Sing Me Back Home."

Tivoli Concert Hall, Copenhagen, Denmark; April 17, 1972

Europe '72 footage, replete with the band wearing the clown masks seen on the inside of that album. Some segments were supposedly broadcast on TV in Denmark at the time, and the performance of "Truckin'" was used for the program *Classic Albums*: "The Grateful Dead: Anthem to Beauty."

◆ Set: "Me and Bobby McGee," "Chinatown Shuffle," "China Cat Sunflower," "I Know You Rider," "Jack Straw," "He's Gone," "Next Time You See Me," "One More Saturday Night," "It Hurts Me Too," "Ramble On Rose," "El Paso," "Big Railroad Blues," "Truckin'."

Orpheum Theater, San Francisco, California (Soundcheck); July 12, 1976

An hour of casual run-throughs with the band looking relaxed and happy. In mono.

◆ Set: "Dancin' in the Streets," "They Love Each Other," "The Music Never Stopped," "Stella Blue," "Let It Shine," "Stella Blue," "Eyes of the World."

Roosevelt Stadium, Jersey City, New Jersey; August 4, 1976

Fuzzy and in black and white, but the band cooks, especially Garcia, who sports uncharacteristically short hair.

◆ Set: "Sugaree," "New Minglewood Blues," "Row Jimmy," "Big River," "Loser," "Looks Like Rain," "They Love Each Other," "The Music Never Stopped," "Scarlet Begonias."

Capitol Theater, Passaic, New Jersey; April 27, 1977

A must-see black-and-white recording of a partial but rocking first set, and the rest is pretty good, too. The audio was broadcast on WNEW-FM in New York.

◆ First set: "New Minglewood Blues," "Loser," "The Music Never Stopped."

◆ Second set: "Estimated Prophet," "Scarlet Begonias," "Fire on the Mountain," "Ramble On Rose," "Samson and Delilah."

◆ Encore: "Johnny B. Goode."

Winterland Arena, San Francisco, California; December 30, 1977

Even a distant, blurry, fan-shot video with mono sound can't make the Dead in their prime any less exciting.

- First set: "Mississippi Half-Step Uptown Toodeloo," "Me and My Uncle," "Dire Wolf," "Looks Like Rain," "Row Jimmy," "Big River," "Peggy-O," "Passenger," "Ramble On Rose," "Let It Grow."
- Second set: "Samson and Delilah," "Ship of Fools," "Estimated Prophet," "Eyes of the World," "St. Stephen," "Sugar Magnolia."
- Encore: "U.S. Blues," "Good Lovin'."

Winterland Arena, San Francisco, California; December 31, 1977

The same type of murky, fan-shot video as the previous entry and an equally compelling show with much better sound.

- First set: "The Music Never Stopped," "Tennessee Jed," "Funiculi Funicula," "Me and My Uncle," "Loser," "Jack Straw," "Friend of the Devil," "Lazy Lightnin'," "Supplication."
- Second set: New Year's Eve countdown, "Sugar Magnolia," "Scarlet Begonias," "Fire on the Mountain," "Truckin'," "Wharf Rat," "Drums," "Not Fade Away," "Around and Around."
- Encore: "One More Saturday Night," "Casey Jones."

Cameron Indoor Stadium at Duke University, Durham, North Carolina; April 12, 1978

A black-and-white tape, but professionally shot and made essential by some killer second set performances.

- First set: "Jack Straw," "Dire Wolf," "Beat It on Down the Line," "Peggy-O," "Mama Tried," "Mexicali Blues," "Funiculi Funicula," "Row Jimmy," "New Minglewood Blues," "Loser," "Lazy Lightnin'," "Supplication."
- Second set: "Bertha," "Good Lovin'," "It Must Have Been the Roses," "Estimated Prophet," "Eyes of the World," "Drums," "Truckin'," "Wharf Rat," "Around and Around."
- Encore: "U.S. Blues."

Capitol Theater, Passaic, New Jersey; November 24, 1978

A dark video with a purple tinge, probably due to the stage lights. Hamza El Din guests on percussion and vocals on "Ollin Arageed."

- First set: Opening announcement, "Jack Straw," "Sugaree," "Me and My Uncle," "Big River," "Stagger Lee," "Passenger," "Candyman," "New Minglewood Blues," "From the Heart of Me," "Loser," "Promised Land."

◆ Second set: "I Need a Miracle," "Good Lovin'," "Friend of the Devil," "Estimated Prophet," "Shakedown Street," "Drums," "Ollin Arageed," "Fire on the Mountain," "Sugar Magnolia."

◆ Encore: "Johnny B. Goode."

Seattle Center Coliseum, Seattle, Washington; July 1, 1979

A hazy recording of part of the second set of an early Brent Mydland gig.

◆ Set: "Terrapin Station," "Playing in the Band," "Drums," "Space," "Stella Blue," "Truckin'," "Around and Around," "Shakedown Street."

Oakland Auditorium Arena, Oakland, California; August 5, 1979

An unprofessional fan recording, yet essential viewing because it's a full film of a "killer" show, to quote a YouTube commenter.

◆ First set: "Mississippi Half-Step Uptown Toodeloo," "Franklin's Tower," "Me and My Uncle," "Big River," "Candyman," "It's All Over Now," "Brown-Eyed Women," "Lost Sailor," "Althea," "Promised Land."

◆ Second set: "Scarlet Begonias," "Fire on the Mountain," "Estimated Prophet," "Eyes of the World," "Drums," "Ollin Arageed" (with Hamza El Din), "Not Fade Away," "Wharf Rat," "Around and Around."

◆ Encore: "Bertha," "Good Lovin'."

Like a lot of artists who opened for the Dead, Maria Muldaur had connections to the band. In the mid-1960s, she performed (as Maria D'Amato) with Jim Kweskin & the Jug Band, a group that influenced the Dead. Later on, she dated John Kahn, one of Garcia's closest friends and the bassist for the Jerry Garcia Band. *Courtesy of Michael Valentine Smith*

Oakland Auditorium Arena, Oakland, California; December 31, 1980

Four hours! A full show! What more could anyone want? How about an acoustic first set and then two electric sets? Matt Kelly blows harmonica on "Little Red Rooster," and John Cipollina plays guitar on "Fire on the Mountain" and the final three songs from the third set.

- First set: "Dire Wolf," "Thank You Uncle Bobo," "On the Road Again," "To Lay Me Down," "Monkey and the Engineer," "Jack-A-Roe," "Cassidy," "I've Been All Around This World," "The Race Is On," "Bird Song," "Ripple."

- Second set: "Alabama Getaway," "Greatest Story Ever Told," "They Love Each Other," "Little Red Rooster," "China Cat Sunflower," "I Know You Rider," "Looks Like Rain," "Althea," "Lost Sailor," "Saint of Circumstance," "Deal."

- Third set: New Year's Eve countdown, "Sugar Magnolia," "Scarlet Begonias," "Fire on the Mountain," "Estimated Prophet," "Drums," "Space," "The Other One," "Wharf Rat," "Around and Around," "Sunshine Daydream."

- Encore: "(I Can't Get No) Satisfaction," "Brokedown Palace."

Gruga Halle, Essen, Germany (Rockpalast Festival); March 28, 1981

A beautiful-looking tape of an exciting festival gig at which the Who was also on the bill. An animated Pete Townshend guests on guitar on "Not Fade Away," "Wharf Rat," and "Around and Around."

- First set: "Alabama Getaway," "Greatest Story Ever Told," "Sugaree," "Me and My Uncle," "Mexicali Blues," "Shakedown Street," "Little Red Rooster," "Althea," "Looks Like Rain," "Deal."

- Second set: "Samson and Delilah," "Ship of Fools," "Estimated Prophet," "He's Gone," "The Other One," "Drums," "Not Fade Away," "Wharf Rat," "Around and Around," "Good Lovin'."

- Encore: "One More Saturday Night."

Club Melk Weg, Amsterdam, Netherlands; October 16, 1981

Dark and murky with some jarring yelling by fans, but worth it to see the band play a tight acoustic first set.

- First set: "On the Road Again," "Dire Wolf," "Monkey and the Engineer," "Bird Song," "Cassidy," "Oh Babe It Ain't No Lie," "The Race Is On," "Ripple."

- Electric second set: "Playing in the Band," "Hully Gully," "The Wheel," "Samson and Delilah," "Gloria," "Turn On Your Love Light," "Goin' Down the Road Feeling Bad," "Playing in the Band," "Black Peter."

♦ Encore: "Sugar Magnolia."

Dane County Coliseum, Madison, Wisconsin; December 3, 1981

A muddy fan recording, but a now-legendary show performed in a blizzard.

♦ First set: "Jack Straw," "They Love Each Other," "Me and My Uncle," "Big River," "Loser," "C.C. Rider," "Althea," "Beat It on Down the Line," "Cassidy," "Deep Elem Blues," "I Need a Miracle," "Bertha."

♦ Second set: "Scarlet Begonias," "Fire on the Mountain," "Estimated Prophet," "He's Gone," "Drums," "Truckin'," "Black Peter," "Around and Around," "Johnny B. Goode."

♦ Encore: "It's All Over Now, Baby Blue."

Considering what concert tickets cost today, $40 for a round-trip bus ride to see the Dead (show tickets included) seems almost surreal. But that's the deal offered on this 1978 handbill, which advertised a trip that went from Long Island to the College of William and Mary in Virginia and back again. Party favors were even included.

Courtesy of Rob Bleetstein

Moscone Center, San Francisco, California; May 28, 1982

Dark video and mono sound. The second set and encore feature John Cipollina on guitar and Boz Scaggs on vocals.

♦ First set: "Alabama Getaway," "Greatest Story Ever Told," "Althea," "Little Red Rooster," "Tennessee Jed," "Truckin'."

♦ Second set: "Walkin' Blues," "A Mind to Give Up Livin'," "Turn On Your Love Light."

♦ Encore: "Johnny B. Goode."

Seattle Center Coliseum, Seattle, Washington; August 29, 1982

An above-average fan-shot video with tweezy sound that sometimes goes to mono.

- ◆ First set: "Jack Straw," "Big Railroad Blues," "Mama Tried," "Mexicali Blues," "West L.A. Fadeaway," "Little Red Rooster," "Loser," "Cassidy," "It Must Have Been the Roses," "Let It Grow."
- ◆ Second set: "Keep Your Day Job," "Samson and Delilah," "He's Gone," "Drums," "Not Fade Away."

Oakland Auditorium Arena, Oakland, California; December 31, 1982

A good-quality show recorded by the in-house multi-camera feed. Matt Kelly plays harmonica on "C.C. Rider" and "Baby What You Want Me to Do," and John Cipollina plays guitar on "Not Fade Away" and "Deal." The third set is performed with Etta James and the Tower of Power Horns.

- ◆ First set: "Cold Rain and Snow," "C.C. Rider," "Cumberland Blues," "Far from Me," "Cassidy," "Ramble On Rose," "Looks Like Rain," "Keep Your Day Job."
- ◆ Second set: New Year's Eve countdown, "Sugar Magnolia," "Sugaree," "Man Smart (Woman Smarter)," "Ship of Fools," "Playing in the Band," "Drums," "Not Fade Away," "Deal," "Sunshine Daydream."
- ◆ Third set: "Turn On Your Love Light," "Tell Mama," "Baby What You Want Me to Do," "Hard to Handle," "In the Midnight Hour."
- ◆ Encore: "Brokedown Palace."

Merriweather Post Pavilion, Columbia, Maryland; June 21, 1983

Another above-average fan recording for a first-rate outdoor gig.

- ◆ First set: "Alabama Getaway," "Greatest Story Ever Told," "Dire Wolf," "Me and My Uncle," "Cumberland Blues," "Cassidy," "Big Railroad Blues," "It's All Over Now," "Loser," "Looks Like Rain," "Might as Well."
- ◆ Second set: "Touch of Grey," "Man Smart (Woman Smarter)," "Terrapin Station," "Estimated Prophet," "Eyes of the World," "Drums," "Space," "Throwing Stones," "Black Peter," "Around and Around," "Good Lovin'."
- ◆ Encore: "U.S. Blues."

Manor Downs, Austin, Texas; September 13, 1983

So-so video, but it's a full show and Garcia is on fire, especially on "Scarlet Begonias."

STEREO WB P-1172W

20世紀フォックス映画《フィルモア最後のコンサート》オリジナル・サウンド・トラック

〈ジョニー・B・グッド〉

JOHNNY B. GOODE

歌・演奏：グレイトフル・デッド
GRATEFUL DEAD

ソー・ファイン／エルヴィン・ビショップ・グループ
SO FINE - ELVIN BISHOP GROUP

45 RPM
¥500

Chuck Berry's "Johnny B. Goode" was a stage favorite for the Dead, who performed it 284 times, according to Deadbase.com. A version from the 1972 film *Fillmore: The Last Days* was issued as a single in Japan with a B-side featuring Elvin Bishop's "So Fine," which was also in the film.   *Courtesy of Eric Schwartz*

- First set: "Bertha," "Little Red Rooster," "Loser," "Cassidy," "Don't Ease Me In," "My Brother Esau," "Brown-Eyed Women," "The Music Never Stopped," "Might as Well."
- Second set: "Scarlet Begonias," "Fire on the Mountain," "Truckin'," "Drums," "Spanish Jam," "Space," "The Wheel," "Throwing Stones," "Not Fade Away."
- Encore: "Brokedown Palace."

Merriweather Post Pavilion, Columbia, Maryland; June 27, 1984

Muddy video, rocking band, first set only.

- Set: "Jack Straw," "Friend of the Devil," "Little Red Rooster," "Cumberland Blues," "My Brother Esau," "Loser," "Let It Grow."

Augusta Civic Center, Augusta, Maine; October 12, 1984

Both visuals and sound leave a lot to be desired, but it features Mydland's "Don't Need Love," played only sixteen times and never recorded for an album.

- First set: "Feel Like A Stranger," "It Must Have Been the Roses," "On the Road Again," "Jack-A-Roe," "It's All Over Now," "Cumberland Blues," "The Music Never Stopped."

- Second set: "Cold Rain and Snow," "Lost Sailor," "Saint of Circumstance," "Don't Need Love," "Uncle John's Band," "Drums," "Space," "Playing in the Band (Reprise)," "Uncle John's Band (Reprise)," "Morning Dew."

- Encore: "Good Lovin'."

Nassau Coliseum, Uniondale, New York; March 29, 1985

Blurry video with barely passable sound, but interesting because Matt Kelly guests on harmonica on the second and third songs.

- First set: "Cold Rain and Snow," "Down in the Bottom," "I Ain't Superstitious," "Friend of the Devil," "Supplication Jam," "My Brother Esau," "Tennessee Jed," "New Minglewood Blues," "Don't Ease Me In."

- Second set: "Terrapin Station," "Man Smart (Woman Smarter)," "Goin' Down the Road Feeling Bad," "Baby What You Want Me to Do," "Drums," "Space," "Wharf Rat," "Throwing Stones," "Johnny B. Goode."

- Encore: "Brokedown Palace."

Cumberland County Civic Center, Portland, Maine; March 31, 1985

Hazy video of the second set only.

- Set: "Iko Iko," "Samson and Delilah," "He's Gone," "I Need a Miracle," "China Doll," "Jam," "Drums," "Space," "The Wheel," "Playing in the Band," "Day Tripper."

- Encore: "U.S. Blues."

War Memorial Auditorium, Rochester, New York; November 8, 1985

Shot from a long distance away, but the show has a rare cover of Jimmy Reed's "Baby What You Want Me to Do," played for the fifth and final time.

- First set: "Iko Iko," "Little Red Rooster," "Peggy-O," "My Brother Esau," "Brown-Eyed Women," "Baby What You Want Me to Do," "Jack Straw," "Might as Well."
- Second set: "Revolution," "Estimated Prophet," "Eyes of the World," "Drums," "Space," "The Other One," "I Need a Miracle," "She Belongs to Me," "Sugar Magnolia."
- Encore: "(I Can't Get No) Satisfaction."

Brendan Byrne Arena, East Rutherford, New Jersey; November 11, 1985

Average quality recording of the first set only, with graphics to fill out missing video on the first song.

- Set: "Hell in a Bucket," "Sugaree," "Cassidy," "Stagger Lee," "It's All Over Now," "Row Jimmy," "Feel Like a Stranger."

Kaiser Convention Center, Oakland, California; November 21, 1985

Blurry visuals and a rough-sounding Garcia, but a rare cover of the Olympics' "Big Boy Pete," played here the last of eight times.

- First set: "Big Boy Pete," "Dire Wolf," "Little Red Rooster," "Brown-Eyed Women," "Me and My Uncle," "Mexicali Blues," "Ramble On Rose," "Looks Like Rain," "Might as Well."
- Second set: "Shakedown Street," "Crazy Fingers," "Playing in the Band," "She Belongs to Me," "Drums," "Space," "The Other One," "Wharf Rat," "Playing in the Band," "Gimme Some Lovin'," "Midnight Hour."

Rich Stadium, Orchard Park, New York; July 4, 1986

Great looking outdoor footage of the first part of the second set.

- Set: "Cold Rain and Snow," "Fire on the Mountain," "Samson and Delilah," "The Wheel," "I Need a Miracle," "Uncle John's Band," "Drums," "Space," "Gimme Some Lovin'."

Meadowlands Arena, East Rutherford, New Jersey; April 6, 1987

Notable because it has the final "Dancin' in the Streets," otherwise a bit too gauzy to enjoy.

- First set: "Dancin' in the Streets," "Franklin's Tower," "Little Red Rooster," "Peggy-O," "Me and My Uncle," "Mexicali Blues," "When Push Comes to Shove," "Jack Straw," "Deal."

- Second set: "Feel Like a Stranger," "Cumberland Blues," "Tons of Steel," "Saint of Circumstance," "Drums," "Space," "Terrapin Station," "The Other One," "Stella Blue," "Sugar Magnolia."

- Encore: "Black Muddy River."

Giants Stadium, East Rutherford, New Jersey; July 12, 1987

The third set and encore feature Bob Dylan in performances not featured on *Dylan and the Dead.*

- First set: "Loser," "Tons of Steel," "Take a Step Back," "Ramble On Rose," "When I Paint My Masterpiece," "When Push Comes to Shove," "Promised Land," "Bertha."

- Second set: "Morning Dew," "Playing in the Band," "Drums," "Space," "The Other One," "Stella Blue," "Throwing Stones," "Not Fade Away."

- Third set: "Slow Train Coming," "Stuck Inside of Mobile with the Memphis Blues Again," "Tomorrow Is a Long Time," "Highway 61 Revisited," "It's All Over Now, Baby Blue," "Ballad of a Thin Man," "John Brown," "The Wicked Messenger," "Queen Jane Approximately," "Chimes of Freedom," "Joey," "All Along the Watchtower," "The Times They Are a-Changin'."

- Encore: "Touch of Grey," "Knockin' on Heaven's Door."

Madison Square Garden, New York, New York; September 18, 1987

Poorly lit, but made up for by Garcia's rocking take on "La Bamba," the third of only four times the band plays it.

- First set: "Hell in a Bucket," "Sugaree," "Walkin' Blues," "Candyman," "When I Paint My Masterpiece," "Bird Song."

- Second set: "Shakedown Street," "Terrapin Station," "Space," "Goin' Down the Road Feeling Bad," "All Along the Watchtower," "Morning Dew," "Good Lovin'," "La Bamba," "Good Lovin'."

- Encore: "Knockin' on Heaven's Door."

Oxford Plains Speedway, Oxford, Maine; July 2, 1988

A shaky handheld camera rendering of the second set and encore. Close enough to make for interesting watching, though.

- Set: "Crazy Fingers," "Playing in the Band," "Uncle John's Band," "Terrapin Station," "Drums," "Space," "The Wheel," "Gimme Some Lovin'," "All Along the Watchtower," "Morning Dew," "Sugar Magnolia."
- Encore: "The Mighty Quinn (Quinn the Eskimo)."

Madison Square Garden, New York, New York; September 20, 1988

Ragged-but-right video, awesome sound. A slightly better recording than the previous night's concert, which shows up online sometimes, too.

- First set: "Jack Straw," "Althea," "Mama Tried," "Big River," "Peggy-O," "When I Paint My Masterpiece," "Louie Louie," "The Music Never Stopped."
- Second set: "Bertha," "Cumberland Blues," "Looks Like Rain," "Terrapin Station," "Truckin'," "Goin' Down the Road Feeling Bad," "Morning Dew."
- Encore: "Johnny B. Goode."

Freedom Hall, Louisville, Kentucky; April 9, 1989

Darkly lit, but with lots of close-up shots. Features the last of nine "Louie Louies" the band did.

- First set: "Hell in a Bucket," "Sugaree," "Walkin' Blues," "It Must Have Been the Roses," "Me and My Uncle," "Big River," "Ramble On Rose," "Desolation Row," "Foolish Heart."
- Second set: "Louie Louie," "Man Smart (Woman Smarter)," "Ship of Fools," "Estimated Prophet," "Uncle John's Band," "Drums," "Space," "The Other One," "Stella Blue," "Sugar Magnolia."
- Encore: "Knockin' on Heaven's Door."

Shoreline Amphitheatre, Mountain View, California; June 21, 1989

Fantastic close-up footage, stellar sound, and fascinating shots of the pre-show crowd. Branford Marsalis guests on "Hell in a Bucket," "Ship of Fools," "Estimated Prophet," "Eyes of the World," and from "Truckin'" through the second set's end.

- First set: "Hide Away," "Touch of Grey," "New Minglewood Blues," "Ramble On Rose," "Box of Rain," "Dire Wolf," "When I Paint My Masterpiece," "Row Jimmy," "Cassidy," "Deal."
- Second set: "Scarlet Begonias," "Hell in a Bucket," "Ship of Fools," "Estimated Prophet," "Eyes of the World," "Drums," "Space," "Truckin'," "The Other One," "Morning Dew," "Turn On Your Love Light."
- Encore: "Brokedown Palace."

Giants Stadium, East Rutherford, New Jersey; July 10, 1989

Featuring the Neville Brothers from "Iko Iko" onward (including the encore) and Willie Green on "Drums" and the song that follows.

- ◆ First set: "Feel Like a Stranger," "Franklin's Tower," "Walking Blues," "Jack-A-Roe," "When I Paint My Masterpiece," "Tennessee Jed," "The Music Never Stopped," "Don't Ease Me In."

- ◆ Second set: "Foolish Heart," "Just a Little Light," "Playing in the Band," "Uncle John's Band," "Drums," "Post-Modern Highrise Table Top Stomp," "Iko Iko," "All Along the Watchtower," "Morning Dew," "Sugar Magnolia."

- ◆ Encore: "Knockin' on Heaven's Door."

Greek Theater, Berkeley, California; August 19, 1989

If you missed the Dead's last-ever Greek Theater show, you can experience it through this beautifully shot footage. An especially hot gig for Mydland.

- ◆ First set: "Let the Good Times Roll," "Jack Straw," "We Can Run," "Tennessee Jed," "It's All Over Now," "Loser," "Stuck Inside of Mobile with the Memphis Blues Again," "Box of Rain."

- ◆ Second set: "China Cat Sunflower," "I Know You Rider," "Playing in the Band," "Uncle John's Band," "Playing in the Band," "Drums," "Space," "The Other One," "Wharf Rat," "Not Fade Away."

- ◆ Encore: "Foolish Heart."

Shoreline Amphitheater, Mountain View, California; September 30, 1989

Professional-quality footage of an energetic gig. Garcia, who dominates the audio mix, breaks out his Wolf guitar, and Weir sports a pony tail.

- ◆ First set: "Bertha," "Greatest Story Ever Told," "West L.A. Fadeaway," "Queen Jane Approximately," "Row Jimmy," "Let It Grow."

- ◆ Second set: "Iko Iko," "Estimated Prophet," "Truckin'," "Smokestack Lightnin'," "Drums," "Space," "I Will Take You Home," "The Wheel," "All Along the Watchtower," "Touch of Grey."

- ◆ Encore: "U.S. Blues."

Meadowlands Arena, East Rutherford, New Jersey; October 12, 1989

The first song is missing and the video could be sharper and brighter, but the band is in good form, save Garcia's hoarse voice. Fan videos also circulate for the October 14 and 15 shows at the same venue, but they are very poorly lit.

◆ First set: "Sugaree," "Blow Away," "Tennessee Jed," "Queen Jane Approximately," "Bird Song," "Jack Straw."

◆ Second set: "Hey Pocky Way," "Cumberland Blues," "Looks Like Rain," "He's Gone," "Drums," "Space," "The Other One," "Wharf Rat," "Sugar Magnolia."

◆ Encore: "Brokedown Palace."

Meadowlands Arena, East Rutherford, New Jersey; October 16, 1989

Fan video to the 2001 double live CD *Nightfall of Diamonds*. Listed as the Brendan Byrne Arena, but the Meadowlands didn't change its name to that until 1996.

◆ First set: "Picasso Moon," "Mississippi Half-Step Uptown Toodeloo," "Feel Like a Stranger," "Good Time Blues," "Built to Last," "Stuck Inside of Mobile with the Memphis Blues Again," "Let It Grow," "Deal."

◆ Second set: "Dark Star," "Playing in the Band," "Uncle John's Band," "Playing in the Band," "Drums," "Space," "I Will Take You Home," "I Need a Miracle," "Dark Star," "Attics of My Life," "Playing in the Band (Reprise)."

◆ Encore: "And We Bid You Goodnight."

Oakland Coliseum, Oakland, California; December 31, 1989

Dim video of a rather rough New Year's show. Bonnie Raitt guests on slide guitar on "Big Boss Man."

◆ First set: "Sugar Magnolia," "Touch of Grey," "Man Smart (Woman Smarter)," "Big Boss Man," "Stuck Inside of Mobile with the Memphis Blues Again," "Shakedown Street."

◆ Second set: New Year's Eve countdown, "Iko Iko," "Victim or the Crime," "Dark Star," "Drums," "Space," "Dear Mr. Fantasy," "Hey Jude (Reprise)," "Goin' Down the Road Feeling Bad," "Throwing Stones," "Not Fade Away," "Brokedown Palace," "Sunshine Daydream."

◆ Encore: "In the Midnight Hour."

Hartford Civic Center, Hartford, Connecticut; March 19, 1990

Above average quality; included here because it's slightly better quality than the recordings of the March 16, 28, and 29 shows.

◆ First set: "Hell in a Bucket," "Bertha," "We Can Run," "Jack-A-Roe," "Picasso Moon," "Brown-Eyed Women," "It's All Over Now," "Deal."

◆ Second set: "Box of Rain," "Foolish Heart," "Playing in the Band," "Eyes of the World," "Drums," "Space," "China Doll," "Gimme Some Lovin'," "Goin' Down the Road Feeling Bad," "Around and Around."

◆ Encore: "Brokedown Palace."

World Music Theatre, Tinley Park, Illinois; July 23, 1990

Special effects visuals fill out the blank spots on this recording, but it's essential viewing because it's Brent Mydland's final show.

◆ First set: "Cold Rain and Snow," "Picasso Moon," "Good Time Blues," "Stagger Lee," "Cassidy," "Truckin'," "Nobody's Fault Jam," "Smokestack Lightnin'."

◆ Second set: "Victim or the Crime," "Foolish Heart," "Man Smart (Woman Smarter)," "Terrapin Station," "Drums," "Space," "All Along the Watchtower," "Standing on the Moon," "Around and Around," "Good Lovin'."

◆ Encore: "The Weight."

Ice Stadium, Stockholm, Sweden; October 13, 1990

Poor lighting and missing video sections (plastered over with graphics) mar this otherwise fine document of the band overseas.

◆ First set: "Cold Rain and Snow," "Feel Like a Stranger," "Candyman," "Walkin' Blues," "Loser," "Queen Jane Approximately."

◆ Second set: "Touch of Grey," "Estimated Prophet," "Crazy Fingers," "Playing in the Band," "Drums," "Space," "All Along the Watchtower," "Stella Blue," "Throwing Stones," "Not Fade Away."

◆ Encore: "One More Saturday Night."

Wembley Arena, London, England; October 31, 1990

More than three hours long and up close and personal, but parts of the second set are lost in darkness. With Bruce Hornsby.

◆ First set: "Help on the Way," "Slipknot!," "Franklin's Tower," "Little Red Rooster," "Loose Lucy," "Me and My Uncle," "Big River," "It Must Have Been the Roses," "When I Paint My Masterpiece."

- Second set: "Bird Song," "Promised Land," "Scarlet Begonias," "Fire on the Mountain," "Truckin'," "He's Gone," "Drums," "Space," "All Along the Watchtower," "Stella Blue," "Around and Around," "Good Lovin'."
- Encore: "Werewolves of London."

Knickerbocker Arena, Albany, New York; March 24, 1991

Average quality video, split between sets into two online files.

- First set: "Help on the Way," "Slipknot!," "Franklin's Tower," "Wang Dang Doodle," "Jack-A-Roe," "Beat It on Down the Line," "Brown-Eyed Women," "Desolation Row," "Deal."
- Second set: "Samson and Delilah," "China Cat Sunflower," "I Know You Rider," "Looks Like Rain," "He's Gone," "Jam," "Drums," "Space," "The Wheel," "I Need a Miracle," "Standing on the Moon," "Good Lovin'."
- Encore: "U.S. Blues."

Sam Boyd Silver Bowl, Las Vegas, Nevada; April 28, 1991

The third-generation video being posted online is blurry, but turn up the brightness (and the sharpness) and it's killer, especially the version of "Bird Song" with some hot licks by Carlos Santana.

- First set: "Jack Straw," "Candyman," "Wang Dang Doodle," "Althea," "Me and My Uncle," "Big River," "Bird Song" (with Carlos Santana).
- Second set: "Foolish Heart," "Saint of Circumstance," "Crazy Fingers," "Truckin'," "Deal," "Drums," "Space," "The Other One," "Wharf Rat," "Around and Around," "Sunshine Daydream."
- Encore: "Box of Rain."

Madison Square Garden, New York, New York; September 9, 1991

Average video, stellar sound. With Bruce Hornsby.

- First set: "Picasso Moon," "Sugaree," "Me and My Uncle," "Mexicali Blues," "They Love Each Other," "Stuck Inside of Mobile with the Memphis Blues Again," "Loose Lucy," "The Music Never Stopped."
- Second set: "Iko Iko," "Looks Like Rain," "New Speedway Boogie," "Playing in the Band (Reprise)," "Uncle John's Band," "Drums," "Space," "The Last Time," "Morning Dew."
- Encore: "The Mighty Quinn (Quinn the Eskimo)."

Polo Field at Golden Gate Park, San Francisco, California; November 3, 1991

Great outdoor footage featuring the Dead's segment of the memorial concert for Bill Graham. John Popper played harmonics on "Wang Dang Doodle"; the Dead backed John Fogerty on four Creedence Clearwater Revival tunes and also backed Neil Young on "Forever Young."

◆ Set: "Hell in a Bucket," "China Cat Sunflower," "I Know You Rider," "Wang Dang Doodle," "Born on the Bayou," "Green River," "Bad Moon Rising," "Proud Mary," "Truckin'," "The Other One," "Wharf Rat," "Sunshine Daydream."

◆ Encore: "Forever Young," "Touch of Grey."

Sam Boyd Silver Bowl, Las Vegas, Nevada; May 29, 1992

Bright, beautiful outdoor daylight footage; one of the best-looking fan videos in existence.

The *Spring 1990* box set was a limited edition item that featured six complete shows, a twenty-fifth anniversary tour program, ticket stubs, backstage passes, and a publicity photo, among other goodies. As of this writing, it's sold out, but an abridged two-CD version of the set, subtitled *So Glad You Made It*, can still be found easily.   *Courtesy of Rhino Records*

- First set: "Mississippi Half-Step Uptown Toodeloo," "Walkin' Blues," "Peggy-O," "Black-Throated Wind," "They Love Each Other," "Stuck Inside of Mobile with the Memphis Blues Again," "Jack-A-Roe," "Promised Land."
- Second set: "China Cat Sunflower," "I Know You Rider," "Looks Like Rain," "Crazy Fingers," "Playing in the Band," "Drums," "Space," "All Along the Watchtower," "Sugar Magnolia."
- Encore: "The Weight."

Sam Boyd Silver Bowl, Las Vegas, Nevada; May 30, 1992

Same fantastic outdoor video as the previous entry, but arguably a more exciting show.

- First set: "Jack Straw," "Sugaree," "Wang Dang Doodle," "High Time," "Maggie's Farm," "Cumberland Blues," "Cassidy," "Don't Ease Me In."
- Second set: "Eyes of the World," "Way to Go Home," "Truckin'," "Smokestack Lightnin'," "Terrapin Station," "Drums," "Space," "Spanish Jam," "I Need a Miracle," "Standing on the Moon," "One More Saturday Night."
- Encore: "Knockin' on Heaven's Door."

Sam Boyd Silver Bowl, Las Vegas, Nevada; May 31, 1992

The video is murkier than the last two shows of this run. Steve Miller plays on the last three songs of the second set and the two encore numbers.

- First set: "Help on the Way," "Slipknot!," "Franklin's Tower," "New Minglewood Blues," "It Must Have Been the Roses," "Queen Jane Approximately," "Bird Song," "Picasso Moon."
- Second set: "Scarlet Begonias," "Fire on the Mountain," "Man Smart (Woman Smarter)," "So Many Roads," "Saint of Circumstance," "He's Gone," "Drums," "Space," "Attics of My Life," "Spoonful," "The Other One," "Morning Dew."
- Encore: "Baba O'Riley," "Tomorrow Never Knows."

Knickerbocker Arena, Albany, New York; June 12, 1992

Great sound, but prepare to turn up your brightness setting.

- First set: "Jack Straw," "Sugaree," "Mexicali Blues," "Maggie's Farm," "Brown-Eyed Women," "Black-Throated Wind," "New Speedway Boogie," "Promised Land."
- Second set: "Scarlet Begonias," "Fire on the Mountain," "Way to Go Home," "Truckin'," "Smokestack Lightnin'," "Drums," "Space," "The Last Time," "China Doll," "Sugar Magnolia."
- Encore: "Attics of My Life."

Giants Stadium, East Rutherford, New Jersey; June 15, 1992

Scads of great close-ups. Steve Miller guests from "Space" through "Not Fade Away."

◆ First set: "Hell in a Bucket," "Sugaree," "The Same Thing," "Tennessee Jed," "When I Paint My Masterpiece," "Bird Song."

◆ Second set: "Box of Rain," "Saint of Circumstance," "So Many Roads," "Terrapin Station," "Drums," "Space," "I Need a Miracle," "Standing on the Moon," "Throwing Stones," "Not Fade Away."

McNichols Sports Arena, Denver, Colorado; December 3, 1992

Average video of an above-average show, especially the second set.

◆ First set: "Touch of Grey," "Little Red Rooster," "Peggy-O," "Queen Jane Approximately," "Ramble On Rose," "Cassidy," "Don't Ease Me In."

◆ Second set: "Playing in the Band," "Eyes of the World," "Corrina," "Terrapin Station," "Drums," "Space," "The Other One," "Morning Dew."

◆ Encore: "Gloria."

Oakland Coliseum Arena, Oakland, California; January 26, 1993

Murky video made interesting by Carlos Santana's guitar playing, which starts at "Drums" and continues through the encore.

◆ Second set only: "Shangri-La" (Vince keyboard solo), "Man Smart (Woman Smarter)," "Eyes of the World," "Estimated Prophet," "Terrapin Station," "Drums," "The Other One," "Stella Blue," "Turn On Your Love Light."

◆ Encore: "Gloria."

Richfield Coliseum, Richfield, Ohio; March 14, 1993

Up-close-and-personal fan video that mostly centers on Garcia and Weir. Missing the first two songs of the first set.

◆ First set: "Brown-Eyed Women," "Just Like Tom Thumb's Blues," "Lazy River Road," "Eternity," "Don't Ease Me In."

◆ Second set: "Touch of Grey," "Samson and Delilah," "Long Way to Go Home," "Corrina," "Terrapin Station," "Drums," "I Need a Miracle," "Stella Blue," "Throwing Stones," "Turn On Your Love Light."

◆ Encore: "I Fought the Law."

Knickerbocker Arena, Albany, New York; March, 28, 1993

The video is way too dark (prepare to turn up your brightness setting), but one of the best shows of the year.

- First set: "Mississippi Half-Step Uptown Toodeloo," "Walkin' Blues," "So Many Roads," "When I Paint My Masterpiece," "High Time," "Eternity," "Deal."

- Second set: "Scarlet Begonias," "Fire on the Mountain," "Samson and Delilah," "Ship of Fools," "Wave to the Wind," "Truckin'," "Drums," "Space," "Way to Go Home," "Attics of My Life," "Turn On Your Love Light."

- Encore: "Knockin' on Heaven's Door."

Robert F. Kennedy Memorial Stadium, Washington, DC; June 25, 1993

A truncated second set, but a gorgeous-looking video with lots of great close-ups and especially crisp sound.

- First set: "Mississippi Half-Step Uptown Toodeloo," "Little Red Rooster," "Just Like Tom Thumb's Blues," "Althea," "Cassidy," "Cumberland Blues," "Promised Land,"

- Second set: "China Cat Sunflower," "I Know You Rider," "Saint of Circumstance," "Uncle John's Band."

The Spectrum, Philadelphia, Pennsylvania; September 13, 1993

Below-average video of a below-average show, notable mainly for the acoustic tone on Garcia's "Lightning Bolt" guitar, which can barely be seen.

- First set: "Stagger Lee," "Black-Throated Wind," "Dire Wolf," "Let It Grow."

- Second set: "Scarlet Begonias," "Fire on the Mountain," "Playing in the Band," "Dark Star," "Terrapin Station," "Jam," "Drums," "Space," "Easy Answers," "Days Between," "Good Lovin'."

- Encore: "I Fought the Law."

Boston Garden, Boston, Massachusetts; September 26 1993

Excellent sound and inspired playing, but the band can barely be seen in the darkness.

- First set: "Jack Straw," "Althea," "Walkin' Blues," "High Time," "Me and My Uncle," "Maggie's Farm," "Lazy River Road," "Easy Answers," "Don't Ease Me In."

- Second set: "Iko Iko," "Saint of Circumstance," "Ship of Fools," "Truckin'," "Drums," "Space," "I Need a Miracle," "Standing on the Moon."
- Encore: "Rain."

Sam Boyd Silver Bowl, Las Vegas, Nevada; June 26, 1994

First-rate video of the first set, the better of the two. In mono.

- First set: "Hell in a Bucket," "Peggy-O," "New Minglewood Blues," "Ramble On Rose," "El Paso," "So Many Roads," "The Music Never Stopped."

Buckeye Lake Music Center, Hebron, Ohio; July 29, 1994

A video of the video screens. Average sound, lots of shots of fans in the rain.

- First set: "Rain," "Feel Like a Stranger," "Bertha," "Wang Dang Doodle," "Loser," "El Paso," "Althea," "Eternity," "Deal."
- Second set: "Foolish Heart," "I Want to Tell You," "Looks Like Rain," "Samba in the Rain," "Uncle John's Band," "Saint of Circumstance," "Drums," "Space," "I Need a Miracle," "Standing on the Moon," "Turn On Your Love Light."
- Encore: "The Mighty Quinn (Quinn the Eskimo)."

Boston Garden, Boston, Massachusetts; October 1, 1994

An up-close, eminently watchable fan video, marred only by occasionally shaky camera work.

- First set: "Help on the Way," "Slipknot!," "Franklin's Tower," "Walkin' Blues," "Althea," "Me and My Uncle," "Big River," "Just Like Tom Thumb's Blues," "So Many Roads," "Promised Land."
- Second set: "Scarlet Begonias," "Fire on the Mountain," "Way to Go Home," "Saint of Circumstance," "Terrapin Station," "Drums," "Space," "The Last Time," "Stella Blue," "One More Saturday Night."
- Encore: "Liberty."

Madison Square Garden, New York, New York; October 14, 1994

Very dimly lit, but the sound quality is excellent.

- First set: "Jack Straw," "West L.A. Fadeaway," "Queen Jane Approximately," "Lazy River Road," "El Paso," "Ramble On Rose," "Box of Rain."

- Second set: "Scarlet Begonias," "Fire on the Mountain," "Looks Like Rain," "Samba in the Rain," "Corrina," "Drums," "Space," "I Need a Miracle," "Attics of My Life," "Turn On Your Love Light."
- Encore: "Liberty."

Los Angeles Sports Arena, Los Angeles, California; December 16, 1994

Branford Marsalis sits in on trumpet for this whole show.

- First set: "Hell in a Bucket," "Cold Rain and Snow," "All New Minglewood Blues," "So Many Roads," "Childhood's End," "Eternity," "Don't Ease Me In."
- Second set: "Eyes of the World," "Samba in the Rain," "Estimated Prophet," "He's Gone," "Drums," "The Other One," "Wharf Rat," "Good Lovin'."
- Encore: "Lucy in the Sky with Diamonds."

Pyramid Arena, Memphis, Tennessee; April 2, 1995

Lots of graphics cover up the many blank spots in this video of a less-than-inspired, uncharacteristically short show.

- First set: "Shakedown Street," "The Same Thing," "Althea," "Stuck Inside of Mobile with the Memphis Blues Again," "Tennessee Jed," "Promised Land."
- Second set: "Here Comes Sunshine," "Eternity," "Crazy Fingers," "Estimated Prophet," "Drums," "Space," "The Last Time," "Wharf Rat," "Not Fade Away."
- Encore: "Unbroken Chain."

Knickerbocker Arena, Albany, New York; June 21, 1995

One of the better 1995 shows. Weir wears a tank top and leads the band; Garcia barely looks up.

- First set: "Hell in a Bucket," "Loser," "Take Me to the River," "Row Jimmy," "Broken Arrow," "Promised Land."
- Second set: "Scarlet Begonias," "Fire on the Mountain," "Man Smart (Woman Smarter)," "It's All Too Much," "Playing in the Band," "Drums," "Space," "Easy Answers," "Morning Dew."
- Encore: "U.S. Blues."

Three Rivers Stadium, Pittsburgh, Pennsylvania; June 30, 1995

The band's rain-themed second set was commentary on the torrential downpours that evening.

- First set: "Hell in a Bucket," "West L.A. Fadeaway," "Take Me to the River," "Bird Song," "Promised Land."
- Second Set: "Rain," "Box of Rain," "Samba in the Rain," "Looks Like Rain," "Terrapin Station," "Drums," "Space," "I Need a Miracle," "Standing on the Moon."
- Encore: "Gloria."

Soldier Field, Chicago, Illinois; July 9, 1995

The final show. Only an hour and fifteen minutes of the first part of the second set has surfaced on video so far.

- Second set (partial): "Shakedown Street," "Samson and Delilah," "So Many Roads," "Samba in the Rain," "Corrina," "Drums," "Space."

30

For the Faithful

A Dozen Essential Bootlegs

Because of all the taping done at Grateful Dead concerts, unreleased live recordings of the band have always been easy to come by. What's been circulated a lot less are unreleased studio recordings, such as outtakes, rehearsals, and recordings of Jerry Garcia's pre–Grateful Dead bluegrass groups. This chapter will round up a dozen such unreleased recordings, leaving aside the recordings of Dead concerts most everyone knows about. Some of these lost artifacts are available on bootleg CDs, but most have been made accessible for free by fans as downloads or online streams. All lend a deeper insight into what made the band tick beyond the legitimate studio releases.

Aoxomoxoa Outtakes

Bob Dylan scholar Clinton Heylin once wrote that the trouble with Dylan's 1980s albums wasn't that he didn't have enough good songs to fill them, but that he chose the wrong takes of songs to release. Dead fans might feel the same way after getting an earful of these early *Aoxomoxoa* recordings. Lesh has said that the album was recorded twice, and some of these rawer takes seem to be from the first version of it. The set leads off with an absolutely ripping version of "St. Stephen," which is structured more like the way the band usually played it live. The song goes into the classic riff after its short introduction, unlike the standard studio version, which bypasses the riff and goes right into the vocals. The singing is stronger, too, with Bob Weir's harmonizing coming off more aggressively.

"St. Stephen" leads into "The Eleven," which wasn't included on the studio album (it's also not on the reissue CD; what is included is called "The Eleven Jam" and is different altogether). "The Eleven" is a pretty rocking version, exploding with powerful double drumming (with each drummer panned to each side of the stereo field) and Garcia and Phil Lesh furiously riffing. Why leave something this good off an album? Even an experimental noise track, "The Barbed Wire Whipping Party," is amusing, with its truly freaky montage of stomped beats, yelling, and chanting.

Elsewhere, there are versions of "Doin' That Rag" and "Dupree's Diamond Blues" that show the songs in rougher, more sparse arrangements even though they sound like they're dragging in tempo a bit. But the biggest surprise is the more listener-friendly version of the experimental "What's Become of the Baby." Here Garcia's voice is unadorned with the vocal processing it was bathed in on the released recording. The song's swirling sound effects are also missing. With just Garcia and an acoustic guitar, the song is exposed as something of a haunting folk ballad, the type of song that might have had real potential if they'd played up its acoustic side. Speaking of which, one of the versions of "Mountains of the Moon" here features Garcia alone, backed by his acoustic guitars, and is arguably better than the released version. In all, it's a fascinating listen, even if the sound quality is less than desirable.

Black Mountain Boys at the Top of the Tangent

Garcia was in a host of acoustic groups before the formation of Mother McCree's Uptown Jug Champions, which led to the formation of the Warlocks and then the Grateful Dead. The final Garcia group before Mother McCree's looks to be this quartet, which sported the lineup of Garcia on banjo, Eric Thompson on guitar, future New Riders of the Purple Sage member Dave Nelson on mandolin, and Jim Beemis.

The main recording in circulation by this group is a performance dating from March 3, 1964, at Palo Alto's Top of the Tangent, a smallish folk club located above a pizza parlor called the Tangent. The sound is very bluegrass, with little of the folk affectations Garcia showed during his stint as Jerry and Sara, the duo he had formed with his wife, Sara Ruppenthal, about a year earlier. Captured on tape are nine traditional songs, including "Katie Mine," "Homestead on the Farm," "Barefoot Nellie," "She's More to be Pitied Than Scolded," "They Can Lock Me Up for Loving You," "The Hand of the Lord," "Who'll Sing for Me," and "Darling Aller Lee." Another tape circulates from September 16 of that year.

Blues Ruffs

Also known as *Blues for Allah Rehearsals*, these four CDs (!) of recordings date from March and June of 1975 and are mostly run-throughs of songs that would make it onto the album, released in September of that year. The sound is surprisingly clear and intimate for a non-legitimate release. If you're into working versions of songs, there's a lot here to wrap your head around: fifty-five songs in all. Some of the highlights include eight-minute workouts of "Franklin's Tower" and a take of "Help on the Way" sans vocals and leading into "Slipknot!" The band stretches out on these versions far more than they do on the album, when they had to rein things in because of the length constrictions inherent in the vinyl format.

Also of interest are two takes of Weir's "Lazy Lightnin'," which made it onto his side project Kingfish's self-titled debut album, released in 1976. Was the Dead planning on putting the song on *Blues for Allah* or rehearsing it for future live shows? There's also lots of untitled studio jams, which are a fascinating peek into the Dead's studio modus operandi, as some, like "Staccato Jam," sound like they could have been sculpted into songs. The idle chatter throughout, especially by Garcia, is also a lot of fun.

Brent Mydland's Unreleased Solo Album

Sometime around 1982, the late Brent Mydland recorded eight tracks for a proposed solo album. It never saw the light of day, although one song, "Tons of Steel," was later cut by the Dead for the *In the Dark* album. Anyone who enjoyed Mydland's soulful singing and songwriting on the Dead's final three studio albums will take to this effort, which was recorded by Betty Cantor. Those who are less enamored with the band's 1980s sound and how Mydland contributed to it should steer clear, because this is an '80s record through and through, and it has very little about it that connects it to the Dead, stylistically speaking.

The album is made up of the following songs, all of which appear to be original compositions: "Inlay It in Your Heart," "Tons of Steel," "Dreams," "Maybe You Know," "Nobody's," "See the Other Side," "Long Way to Go," and "Take One." In the second volume of *The Deadhead's Taping Compendium*, Cantor speaks briefly about Mydland's solo album, saying it was worked on "for a year, in between everything else." She goes on to say that Lesh used to visit the studio nightly and listen "with a big grin on his face. He loved it." Cantor also called the record "the best of Brent and the best of me" and said, "Someday I'd really like to put it out."

Like a lot of rock-oriented '80s efforts, Mydland's album sounds a bit generic at first. But with repeated listening, it reveals several standout songs and a bunch of Mydland vocal performances that are both impassioned and technically impressive. Mydland rocks out with abandon on "Maybe You Know," which comes close to the blues rock-cum-metal Pat Travers was doing at the time. Eddie Money guitarist and David Lee Roth collaborator Monty Byron reportedly plays a crunchy guitar part on "Tons of Steel," making it much heavier than the Dead's version, and the song arguably works better in this style. "Long Way to Go" is a power ballad that showcases the toppermost part of Mydland's vocal range.

Maybe the reason this record never came out is because it's so removed from anything the Grateful Dead did that someone was worried fans wouldn't accept it. Or maybe Mydland felt it was unfinished, as its running time is only a little more than half an hour. Whatever the case, it's a well-produced album that's a definite testament to Mydland's talent as both a composer and a singer. It's findable if you look hard enough online. And if it ever comes out on CD, an ideal bonus track would be the lost Mydland number "Only a Fool," performed only once by the band (April 23, 1984) and never recorded for an album or officially released as a live cut.

Grateful Dead & Merry Pranksters: The Acid Test Reels (1965–1967)

Poor sound quality, way too much rambling by Ken Kesey, and not enough music—but this collection is fascinating nonetheless, because you get to hear the very beginnings of the Dead. This box set is available in both four-disc and six-disc configurations. Of special interest is the six-disc set because disc five is composed of a "Watts Acid Test" gig from February 12, 1966, at the Youth Opportunities Center in Compton, California, that hasn't shown up on Archive. org. But even if most of the material has appeared elsewhere, it's nice to have it all in one place, if only for historic purposes.

This set starts with a January 8, 1966, gig at a "Fillmore Acid Test," which shows that some of the Dead's later repertoire was in place at this early a date. Both "Caution (Do Not Stop on Tracks)" and "Death Don't Have No Mercy" put in appearances, with the latter coming across as especially forceful. A January 29, 1966, gig pairs the Dead with the Pranksters and includes such tunes as "Peggy the Pistol," which contains the immortal couplet "Did you ever hear the story about Peggy the Pistol? / She didn't shoot a gun, but she shot a lot of crystal." The songs are interspersed with a Ken Kesey interview, among other snippets of non-Dead material.

Disc two has the Dead playing at the "Pico Acid Test" held at the Los Angeles Danish Center on March 12, 1966, and the "San Francisco State Acid Test" (aka the Whatever It Is Festival) held on October 2, 1966. The first includes classic Dead run-throughs of "Viola Lee Blues" and "In the Midnight Hour," while the second has a lot of trippy Prankster spoken word sections. Disc three continues the "San Francisco State Acid Test" with a lot of spoken word sections with Ken Kesey and Wavy Gravy. There's also a jam session from Halloween 1966, taken from the *World of Acid* film soundtrack. Listen with colored lights in the room and feel like you've taken a trip back in time. Or some kind of a trip, at least.

Disc four puts the listener back in time chronologically by opening with a studio recording of Neal Cassady and the Warlocks circa 1965. The rest of the CD is mostly a hodge-podge of Cassady raps and Garcia interviews. The hour-long Garcia interview dates from the summer of 1967 and has him speaking on a variety of subjects, such as why the band signed with Warner Bros. ("We have control over our product. It's not gonna be chopped or changed," he says.) If you plan on tracking down the six-disc set, CD five has an expanded version of the aforementioned "Watts Acid Test" with more songs. These include several future Dead staples such as "Beat It on Down the Line" and "Next Time You See Me." The sixth disc is an alternate version of the "San Francisco State Acid Test" with different edits and interview segments added in.

The Grateful Dead with the Beach Boys, Fillmore East, 1971

Talk about a culture clash. When the Beach Boys trucked through New York City to play a set with the Dead on April 27, 1971, the early '60s California surf heroes were desperately trying to reinvent themselves to appeal to the late '60s generation of hippie rock fans. It's probably not a stretch to say that the Beach Boys were trying to gain some hippie cred by association with the Dead. The idea for this pairing likely came about when both groups played together at Duke University three days before. The Beach Boys weren't on the Fillmore bill on April 27, but they were passing through New York on their way to a gig in Massachusetts.

And so it came to pass that during the third Dead set, the Beach Boys jammed on five numbers with the Dead and played two songs on their own. The

The Beach Boys–Grateful Dead set that took place at the Fillmore East has never come out on CD, but it can be heard on downloadable bootlegs such as this one.

Courtesy of bootlegtunzworld.org

set starts with both groups performing the Coasters' "Searchin'" and the Robins' "Riot in Cell Block #9." The Beach Boys then go it alone for "Good Vibrations," before which lead singer Mike Love attempts to score points with the Dead's audience by saying, "We did this on the bus with the Buffalo Springfield all stoned and drunk and everything. It sounded great." The ploy didn't work. After the song ends, calls of "Bring back the Dead!" and "We want the Dead!" rise up from the crowd.

The Beach Boys are clearly rattled, and bassist/keyboardist Bruce Johnston responds, "We're very grateful that there's something called the Grateful Dead, believe me, because they're ALL RIGHT! We've tried for two years to get together and it finally happened in the best place." The Beach Boys win back the crowd a bit with a somewhat ramshackle rendition of "I Get Around," after which the Dead come back out on stage and jam with the Beach Boys on their 1965 #1 hit "Help Me, Rhonda." It's the best joint performance of the set, with Bill Kreutzmann kicking the song into a "Truckin'" groove and Garcia's lead lines answering the vocals of Carl Wilson, who sings lead in place of Al Jardine. Wilson's changing of the line "She was gonna be my wife" to "She was gonna be my woman" shows how self-conscious the band was of being in a whole new world culturally (it was a lyric change they kept for years afterward).

"Rhonda" is followed by a tongue-in-cheek version of a then-current Beach Boys stage favorite, Merle Haggard's "Okie from Muskogee," which has some ripping Garcia leads. Weir and Wilson then harmonize on "Johnny B. Goode" before the Beach Boys leave the Dead to wrap their set with "Sing Me Back Home," "Uncle John's Band," and "Turn On Your Lovelight." "Sing Me Back Home" and "Lovelight" from this same night are included in the four-CD set *Ladies and Gentlemen . . . the Grateful Dead*, which collects together forty performances from the Dead's Fillmore run at that time, which lasted from April 25 to April 29.

Jerry Garcia, Marshall Leicester and Robert Hunter at the Boar's Head Coffeehouse

Is this the earliest Garcia performance circulating? This twenty-three-minute recording was said to be made in July 1961 and shows him playing guitar alongside Marshall Leicester on banjo and Robert Hunter on bass. The recording was made at the Boar's Head Coffeehouse, which was located in the Carlos Bookstall in San Carlos, California.

It's not quite as entertaining as some of the other early Garcia tapes, as Garcia seems to be playing a strictly supporting role here, taking no lead vocals. But it does hold some historical interest. Songs featured include "Poor Ellen Smith," "Wildwood Flower," "Brown's Ferry Blues," "Jesse James," "No One Will Stand by Me," "All the Good Times Are Past and Gone," and "Darling Corey." The last two are rambunctious audience sing-alongs.

Jerry and Sara at the Top of the Tangent

After playing with the bluegrass/old-time music trio the Sleepy Hollow Hog Stompers, Garcia formed a folk duo with his first wife, Sara Ruppenthal. The two had met in early 1963 when she was a sophomore at Stanford University in Palo Alto. They took to singing soon after as a duo called Jerry and Sara. Ruppenthal had a background in folk music, which blended well with the twenty-year-old Garcia's fixation on traditional music.

Shortly after they were married, the duo played a gig at the Top of the Tangent. Their performance that night was recorded and it shows the duo harmonizing on nine songs, with what sounds like Ruppenthal on guitar and Garcia on mandolin, at least most of the time. Their set list included "Deep Elem Blues," which the Dead would later play, as well as "The Long Black Veil," which was popularized by the Band on their first album and was later performed by Garcia and David Grisman.

Other songs include "The Weaver," "Heart No Longer Mine," "All Good Times Are Past," "Never Was a Married Man," "Mean as He Could Be," "Said the World," and "Foggy Mountain Top." The performance shows that long before *Workingman's Dead*, Garcia's acoustic style was in full bloom. So was his laconic stage banter: "We had a request to do a song called 'Long Black Veil,' which is a modern country song," he says. "But it's pretty anyway, even at that." The date attributed to this gig is sometimes February 2, 1963, but it probably took place around May 4 of that year, as Garcia mentions that the pair "got married last week" before dryly introducing "Never Was a Married Man."

Mars Hotel Outtakes

This double CD set boasts seventeen cuts and multiple takes of some songs such as "Unbroken Chain," which shows up four times, and "Pride of Cucamonga," which is featured three times. No matter, though: since the first of these was only played live a handful of times and the second never made it to the stage at all, these run-throughs are revelatory. Here, we get to hear the songs in rough-hewn renditions, minus the studio polish of the album versions. In other words, they sound like they're being performed live but without an audience, making them the next best thing to actual concert recordings.

There are also mixes of "U.S. Blues," "Scarlet Begonias," "Money Money," and "Loose Lucy" without any vocals—perfect for anyone who ever wanted to sing the Dead at karaoke night at their neighborhood bar. "Crazy Fingers" also puts in an appearance without any vocals, and it already sounds like it would when the band would re-record it for *Blues for Allah*, except it has a somewhat harder edge. These music-only tracks give listeners a chance to examine the Dead's studio sound on its own, and the interplay between band members comes through loud and clear. Lesh's solo acoustic demo of "Unbroken Chain" was later added as a bonus track to the CD reissue of *From the Mars Hotel*, but without the reverb heard here.

The Sleepy Hollow Hog Stompers at the New Boar's Head Coffeehouse

This eccentrically named trio was one of Garcia's earliest groups and played traditional acoustic old-time music. This is a recording of a performance dating from November 6, 1962, at a café housed by the Jewish Community Center in San Carlos. Garcia performs on guitar and banjo along with Marshall Leicester on banjo and guitar, and Dick Arnold on fiddle. All three sing. Interestingly, Garcia's vocals have the homespun, down-to-earth style he'd bring to the Dead, while the other singers emote in a more formal folkie style that would fall out of favor as soon as Bob Dylan appeared on the scene.

Although the quality of the recording is passable, it's sometimes maddening to listen to because so many songs cut off abruptly. Was the taper trying to conserve tape? The forty-minute recording includes eighteen numbers. One, "Buck Dancer's Choice," was later referenced in "Uncle John's Band." The others are "Run Mountain," "Billy Grimes the Rover," "Cannonball Blues," "Devilish Mary," "Little Birdie," "Sally Goodin'," "Hold the Woodpile Down," "Crow Black Children," "The Johnson Boys," "Shady Grove," "Hop High Ladies," "Sweet Sunny South," "All Go Hungry," "Hash House," "Rabbit Chase," "Three Men Went a-Hunting," and "Man of Constant Sorrow," which had appeared on Dylan's first album, released in March of that year.

Like the Jerry and Sara tape, this performance gives some context to the abrupt stylistic change the Dead appeared to make around 1970 when they moved away from psychedelic rock and took a turn toward traditional sounds. In Garcia's case, he wasn't so much following the lead of Bob Dylan and others in adopting a roots sound as he was bringing it all back home.

Wake of the Flood Outtakes

This set of fourteen tracks shows the Dead working up the numbers that would form their sixth studio album. Several numbers are here in multiple renditions, such as "Here Comes Sunshine," which gets four run-throughs, the first of which has new keyboardist Keith Godchaux experimenting with a harmonium-type sound. Speaking of Godchaux, his "Let Me Sing Your Blues Away" shows up twice, and the first version is especially interesting because it has an alternate saxophone line and rough vocals that are single-tracked and not overlaid with harmonies as they are on the released version—Keith unplugged, so to speak.

If you've ever wondered what the band would sound like sans lead guitar, check out the "Eyes of the World" included here, which is the basic track with vocals before Garcia dubbed in his lead parts. "Row Jimmy" is a rough take with Garcia's lone voice and no vocal harmonies. "Let It Grow" has an

August, 1973

Wake Of The Flood
OUTTAKES

® © 1973 GRATEFUL DEAD RECORDS

Bootlegs such as this are essential listening for anyone who wants to understand how the Dead worked up songs in the studio. In the case of *Wake of the Flood*, the songs were nearly fully formed by the time the Dead committed them to tape.   *Courtesy of bootlegtunzworld.org*

interesting bit of instrumentation that was left out of the final mix: a high-pitched sax solo similar to the one on the Doors' "Touch Me." The version of the first part of "Weather Report Suite" is a stripped-down early mix, not the demo included as a bonus track on the *Wake of the Flood* CD reissue.

The Wildwood Boys at the Top of the Tangent

If you've read the entries on the Black Mountain Boys, Jerry and Sara, and the Sleepy Hollow Hog Stompers, you already know the drill here: it's Garcia with a pre-Dead bluegrass group, in this case dating from early 1963. This six-song tape is said to date from February 23, 1963, and has Norman Van Maastricht on bass, Dave Nelson on guitar, and "honest" Jerry Garcia, as he's called during the introduction, on banjo. A droll Robert Hunter does the introduction, and he'd had to have moved from bass to guitar by this point.

This is easily the best of Garcia's pre-Dead bluegrass outfits because of the way he rocks the banjo on tunes such as the opening number, "Rollin' in My Sweet Baby's Arms." He also chimes in with an original instrumental, "Jerry's Breakdown." Equally as entertaining is the cover of Jimmie Rodgers's "Mule

Skinner Blues," which in 1960 had gotten a raucous cover by the Fendermen, who took it into the Top 5. Other numbers include "Standing in Need of a Prayer," "Pike County Breakdown," and a Dave Nelson guitar solo. A few months later, a version of this group with a slightly different lineup played at the Monterey Folk Festival.

31

Searching for the Sounds

Fifteen Obscure Dead Collectibles

L ike every other artist in the pop music world, the Grateful Dead has issued singles, albums, and special edition records that have become hard to find as the years have passed. The band have also appeared on soundtrack albums and in movies, so there are performances that have been released, but are not really well known. This is a list of such releases. It's not intended to be a comprehensive list—that could take up a book by itself—but rather a roundup of some of the more interesting releases either in the band's back catalog or having to do with it.

Deadheads might have only general ideas of what these items are about, so I've tried to provide explanations of what makes each of these releases unique and why each release might be of interest to casual fans or hardcore collectors. This list doesn't include the myriad of impossible-to-find foreign singles and the like (go to the *Lone Star Dead* web page to see some of these). Rather, I've limited this chapter to items released in the United States that have oddball appeal.

American Beauty EP

When Warner Bros. Records released the Grateful Dead's *American Beauty* in the fall of 1970, they also put out a five-song EP that showcased the album's most commercial cuts. An EP was an "extended play" record that was usually the size of a 7-inch 45 record, but that included more than two songs and usually played at the slower album speed of 33 and 1/3 to accommodate the extra music. That's the case here. EPs never quite caught on with the American public, but the Dead's mini-version of *American Beauty* wasn't really designed for the public. It was meant for jukeboxes, and if you track down a copy that was kept in good condition, it just might come with those little labels (called "strips") they used to use to mark off individual songs in jukeboxes.

The EP includes "Sugar Magnolia," "Operator," and "Till the Morning Comes" on side one and "Truckin'" and "Friend of the Devil" on the second side. All songs are full-length versions taken from the original album, unlike the versions used when "Truckin'" and "Ripple" were prepared for release as a single (see the entry further along in this chapter for more details on that).

"Dark Star"/"Born Cross-Eyed" Single

Hard as it is to believe, the Grateful Dead once recorded a 2:50 studio version of a song that could run as long as forty-five minutes when they performed it live. Their performance on the single version of "Dark Star" runs at such a speedy pace that you might think you have the single playing at too fast a speed when you first hear it. It's a lot more upbeat than the way the Dead came to play it in concert, that's for sure, although it's similar to the version from January 23, 1968, as found on the *Road Trips Volume 2, Number 2* bonus disc. But in the studio, this "Dark Star" comes off like a jangle pop version of the tune, if you can imagine that.

The single was almost impossible to find for decades, but Rhino Records made it a bit less rare when they dropped a reissue 45 of the single into the 2010 box set *The Warner Bros. Studio Albums*, which gathers together vinyl editions of the group's first five albums. Granted, this set might be a bit pricey, but at least it makes the single officially available somewhere. The set also includes the original mixes of the first three albums (see chapter 10 for more details). The B-side of the single is a non-LP mix of "Born Cross-Eyed," a longer version that's become a lot less rare since it was put on the latest CD reissue of *Anthem of the Sun*. Both the original single and the reissue come with a picture sleeve.

Deadicated Tribute CD

OK, so this is cheating because it's not a Grateful Dead disc we're talking about. But it is a CD that fans of the band are apparently interested in, because once it fell out of print, it started going for crazy prices. To recap: *Deadicated* was a CD that came out in 1991 on which fourteen artists covered fifteen Dead songs (Suzanne Vega got two songs). Like most CDs of this nature, the quality is wildly uneven, but it's unfair to claim which artist did which song justice, because in cases like this, it's really in the ears of the beholder. One person's idea of bliss just might be Lyle Lovett tackling "Friend of the Devil." But that also might be another's idea of audio torture.

What's funny about this CD is that for years after its release, you'd see it in used record stores going for just a few bucks. That's definitely no longer the case. Maybe the death of Warren Zevon, who performs "Casey Jones," drummed up interest just as the CD happened to go out of print. Other featured artists include Bruce Hornsby and the Range, Indigo Girls, Cowboy Junkies, Burning Spear, Dr. John, and Jane's Addiction.

Fillmore: The Last Days Soundtrack

Fillmore: The Last Days was a 1972 movie that centered on concert footage shot in late June and early July of 1971 at the Fillmore West, the San Francisco concert hall owned by promoter Bill Graham. The now-legendary venue served as a hometown launching pad for the Dead, Jefferson Airplane, Quicksilver Messenger Service, and others. It also hosted countless acts from out of town. The film was nearly forgotten until Rhino Records released it on DVD in 2009.

The soundtrack, which was issued on vinyl in 1972 and on CD in 1991, is not easy to come by. It should interest Deadheads because it's got two performances by the group that are otherwise unavailable on legitimate releases. Those performances include renditions of "Casey Jones" and "Johnny B. Goode" from July 2, 1971. The original vinyl edition of the soundtrack is a three-album set with a bonus 45 and includes music from all the aforementioned groups, plus Hot Tuna, It's a Beautiful Day, Santana, and others.

Mother McCree's Uptown Jug Champions CD

Back before there was a Grateful Dead, there was Jerry Garcia, Pigpen, and a high school kid named Bob Weir who played with a couple of other guys in a folk-related revival band playing traditional music. This was that band, and as luck would have it, they were recorded one night in 1964 while performing at a coffee house in Palo Alto, California. Mother McCree's Uptown Jug Champions played an acoustic style of music called jug band music (immortalized in a Lovin' Spoonful song of the same name), and that music featured such semi-instruments as kazoos, washboards, and washtub bass. All of that doesn't exactly make for easy listening, but this CD does lend insight into the roots of the Dead because it showcases some songs the band would regularly perform, notably "Beat It on Down the Line."

So why is it being mentioned in this section of the book? Because the CD, which came out in 1999, is now out of print and goes for prices on Amazon and eBay that are truly frightening. The CD's backstory is similar to the tale behind the Beatles' Hamburg tapes: someone recorded the band, forgot about the tapes, and then found them years later tucked away in an odd corner of a house. For years, this CD was recognized for its historic importance, but because it's no longer being manufactured, it's got collectible importance as well.

Road Trips Bonus Discs

The *Road Trips* live CD series was only discontinued in late 2011, but it's already becoming the stuff of legend—at least the bonus discs are, anyway. *Road Trips* was a series of soundboard recordings that compiled the best performances by the Dead during a multi-night run in a given city. According to the band's archivist, David Lemieux, the series wasn't as popular as the series that preceded it, *Dick's Picks*, because Deadheads prefer to hear full shows. So, you'd think that there would be even less interest in the bonus discs that were offered during early runs of most of these CD sets, because a lot of them don't even come close to offering entire shows.

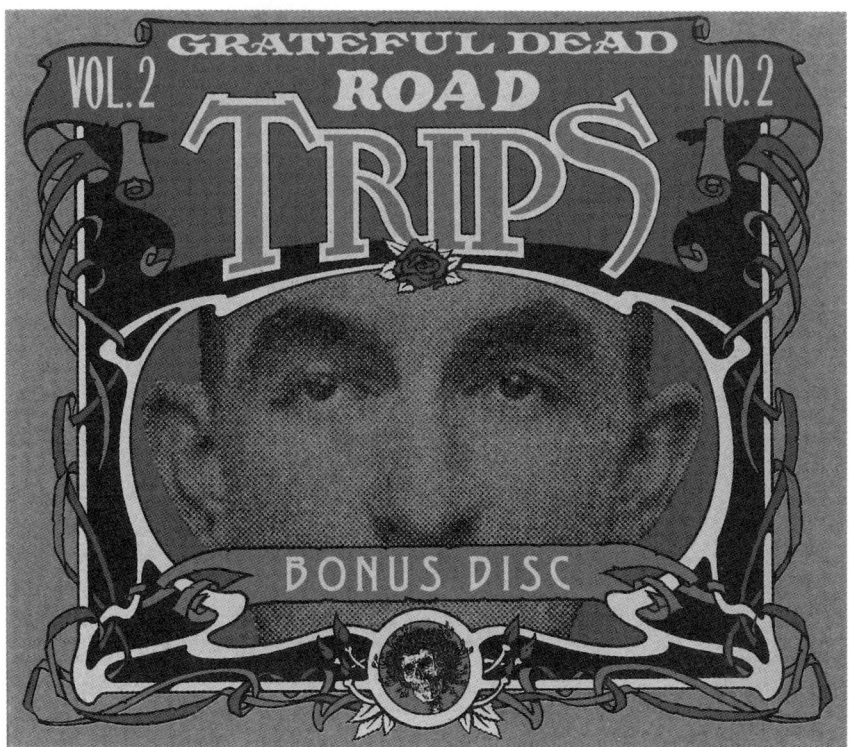

The bonus disc that came with *Road Trips Volume 2, Number 2* contained concert material recorded in January 1968, including a brief seven-minute version of "Dark Star." The disc is now out of print and sells for well more than $100 on eBay—when it can be found at all.

Author's collection

You'd be wrong. As time has gone by and these discs have become harder to find, they've started going for higher and higher prices on eBay. Maybe it's the "sold out" notice that graces the pages about some of these CD sets on Dead. net that's caused Deadheads to want these discs. Whatever the case, almost all of the CD sets in this series came with a bonus disc, the exceptions being *Volume 3, Number 4* and *Volume 4, Numbers 1–2* and *4–5*.

"Stealin'"/"Don't Ease Me In" Single

Before the band singed with Warner Bros. Records in 1966, it had auditioned for two other record companies based in the San Francisco area: Autumn Records and Scorpio Records. The Autumn sessions, which were co-produced by the disc jockey Tom Donahue, did not result in any releases at the time (although the tracks would turn up in the 2001 collection *Birth of the Dead*). Scorpio Records, which was a subsidiary of Fantasy Records, did release a single, although it came out in limited quantities.

That 45, which comprises a cover of the Gus Cannon jug band tune "Stealin'" and is backed with a cover of "Don't Ease Me In," was the first record to bear the name of the Grateful Dead. As such, it's become a collector's item. Interestingly, the 45 credits both songs to Garcia. Both were properly credited years later when they appeared on *Birth of the Dead* and *Go to Heaven*, respectively.

"Truckin'"/"Ripple" Single

Both "Truckin'" and "Ripple" were given separate mono mixes and edits when they were released as a single in late 1970. This was relatively standard for the era. In fact, songs are still edited and remixed for release as singles, just not in mono. The single version of "Truckin'" appears on the *American Beauty* reissue CD put out by Rhino Records in 2003. It surprised a lot of people who'd never heard it, as the balance of instruments is markedly different and it also contains a different vocal take on one of the verses. But also on that CD reissue are two hidden tracks: One is a promotional radio spot. The other is the single edit of "Ripple."

This version of "Ripple" is chopped down to 3:01 from 4:10 on the original LP. And what a weird edit it is. Instead of cutting out some of the introduction, they remove the second part of the first verse and all of the first chorus, so the song jumps from the line "Would you hold it near as it were your own?" to "There is a road, no simple highway." One assumes that Robert Hunter, who didn't like having his lyrics altered, did not get the final say on this edit. You wonder why they bothered to edit this B-side at all, as even the A-sides of singles back then had gone on as long as seven minutes. Had they forgotten about "Hey Jude" and "MacArthur Park?"

Spirit of '76–Live at the Cow Palace Bonus Disc

Rhino Records put out the Grateful Dead's 1976 New Year's Eve show as a triple disc live album that was mixed from sixteen-track tapes originally recorded by Bob Matthews and Betty Cantor at the Cow Palace in Daly City, California. But people who pre-ordered the release got some extra music: a bonus disc of eight tracks that contained "more than an hour of previously unreleased music from 1976, produced especially for this release," according to the press release put out at the time. Although the material was available on tapes swapped by fans, the bonus disc featured better sound.

Tracks included "The Music Never Stopped" and "Crazy Fingers," both recorded at Boston Music Hall in Boston, Massachusetts, on June 6, 1976; "Let It Grow" and "Might as Well," both taped at Riverfront Coliseum in Cincinnati, Ohio, on October 2, 1976; the medley of "Playing in the Band," "Supplication," and "Playing in the Band," recorded at the College of William and Mary in Williamsburg, Virginia, on September 24, 1976; and "Scarlet Begonias," recorded at the Mershon Auditorium in Columbus, Ohio, on September 30, 1976.

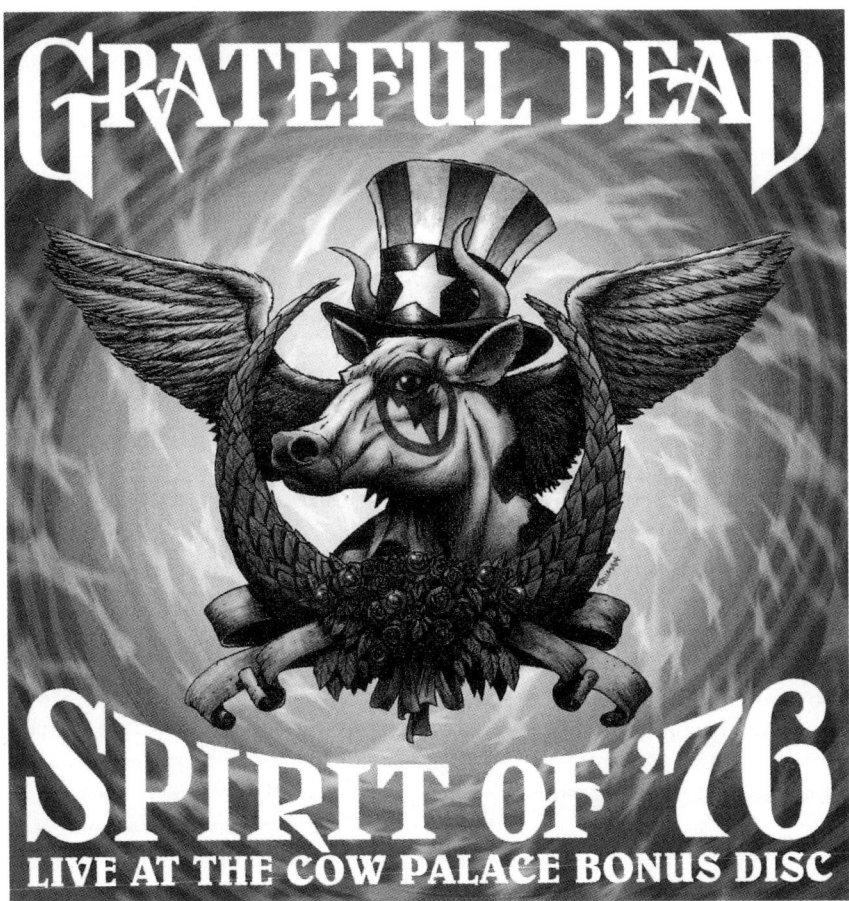

Early editions of the 2007 release *Live at the Cow Palace: New Year's Eve 1976* came with a bonus disc that had more than an hour of additional music. It contains performances recorded the same year and, like other bonus CDs, has become increasingly harder to find.   *Author's collection*

"Touch of Grey"/"My Brother Esau" Single (Colored Vinyl)

Sure, you've heard the Dead's first (and only) Top 10 hit enough times to last you a few lifetimes. But have you heard the B-side, which only came out at the time on cassette copies of the album? OK, so you've heard that too from all the times they played it in concert. But here's something that you might have missed. This record was released on colored vinyl with a picture sleeve that folds out into a poster.

"That's nice," you say. Actually, it is pretty nice. In Record Collector Land, where oddities and special editions are highly valued, this special issue of the Dead's biggest-selling single should be a hot number, considering how much rarity value it's got going for it. But it's not. The "record collecting community" has certain artists whose records they treasure and ones they don't, and the Dead fall into the latter category. But their loss is the Deadheads' potential gain. You can find this limited edition of "Touch of Grey" for just a few dollars more than what it sold for way back in 1987, and those copies are usually in near-mint condition—not a bad deal for a rarity that should be fetching quite a few bucks and maybe will someday if the Dead ever find favor with collectors.

"Uncle John's Band"/"New Speedway Boogie" Single

It's not often that the opening of a record will get you chuckling, but anyone hearing the edited version of the A-side of this single is likely to break into gales of laughter at the way this single starts. Thanks to a very awkward edit, the song abruptly cuts in during the acoustic guitar riff that begins around seven seconds into the standard studio version, removing the introductory guitar strumming. But the fun really starts at the 1:10 mark. Whoever edited this chopped out the second verse (the one about the "buck dancer's choice") and went directly to the third. The only trouble is that the third verse begins with the words "God damn," and Warner Bros. believed that wasn't appropriate back then, so the company removed those words.

But Warner Bros. didn't replace them with anything. What the company did was edit in a few bars of the song's non-vocal section into their place, so what you hear goes something like this: Pause, strum . . . "I declare! Have you seen the like?" Again, unintentional hilarity. After this verse, the song skips over the chorus and heads straight into the following verse ("It's the same story . . ."). Um, isn't the chorus the crux of the song and the part you'd want to emphasize on the single, not remove? Garcia reportedly hated this edit, saying that the folks at Warner didn't follow his instructions. That's believable. In all, good ol' Uncle John gets chopped down from his original 4:42 length to 3:07. For obvious reasons, this one wasn't added to the 2003 CD reissue of *Workingman's Dead*, making it a real rarity. Still, the Dead could have stuck it at the end as a hidden track for historical purposes. Or should that be "hysterical purposes"?

"U.S. Blues" Disc Jockey Single

OK, so "U.S. Blues" is a bit overplayed in Deadland, but have you heard the mono mix? Disc jockeys got to hear it, because the single was sent to them by Grateful Dead Records as part of a DJ single with a mono A-side and a stereo flip side. Several websites say that the stereo version is the A-side, but the copy I own that's sitting right in front of me clearly states "SIDE A" on the right side of the label underneath the word "MONO." As that side also plays as mono, we'll go with mono as the A-side. The mix really isn't all that different than it is on the standard version, although at times it sounds like Garcia's lead vocals are somewhat more prominent in the mix.

What's really interesting about this single is that it came with a picture sleeve that bore the title of the song in the middle and a specially designed "logo" related to the song in the bottom left-hand corner. Over the years, this sleeve has become pretty rare, and it hardly ever turns up on eBay. Standard copies of the single, which aren't plentiful either these days, have "Loose Lucy" as the B-side.

Arista went all out in promoting the Grateful Dead's 1987 single, "Touch of Grey." Some editions of the 45 record came in a picture sleeve that also contained a fold-out poster featuring photos of each band member. The record itself was pressed on grey vinyl.   *Courtesy of yesterdayandtodayrecords.com*

Vintage Dead and Historic Dead Albums

Not bootlegs, but not releases put out by the band, either, *Vintage Dead* and *Historic Dead* are two long-forgotten albums from 1970 and 1971 that came out on the independent Sunflower label. How did that happen if the Dead had a contract with Warner Bros. at the time? It's because these albums feature segments of a concert that was recorded before the Dead signed with Warner Bros. The concert was recorded at San Francisco's Avalon Ballroom in the fall of 1966. Deadheads have traced its origin to the Dead's show on September 16 of that year, which can be streamed on the Archive.org website as of this writing.

It's amusing to see how the record's producers attempted to fit the show onto four sides of vinyl by chopping it up and moving the songs out of order. The original set was as follows: "I Know You Rider," "It Hurts Me Too," "It's All Over Now, Baby Blue," "Good Morning Little School Girl," "Lindy," "Dancing in the Street," "In the Midnight Hour," "Stealin'," and an encore of "The Same Thing." The *Vintage* album puts the first three songs on the first side along with "Dancing in the Street" and relegates the eighteen-minute "Midnight Hour" to side two. (Proof that the Dead weren't involved in the Sunflower releases can be found in the label's use of the title "Dancing in the Street." The band always referenced the song as "Dancin' in the Streets.") The *Historic* album starts in the middle of the show with "Good Morning Little School Girl" and "Lindy" and places "Stealin'" and "The Same Thing" on side two. Neither album has ever been issued on CD, nor was the concert ever issued as part of the *Dick's Picks* series or any other, which is why it's still on Archive.org.

The Warner Bros. Sampler Albums

Back in the 1970s, Warner Bros. Records would issue "sampler" albums to showcase what were presumably the most interesting tracks from artists on its roster. These releases, which were usually double LPs, came with clever titles such as *The 1969 Warner/Reprise Record Show, Looney Tunes Merrie Melodies*, and *The Whole Burbank Catalog*. These were put out at discount prices and presumably offered listeners a way to try new music on the cheap in the days before Spotify and YouTube. Whether all that worked is up for debate, but what matters for our purposes is that several of these albums feature edited versions of Dead tracks.

The *1969 Warner/Reprise Record Show* has a shortened version of "Doin' That Rag" from *Aoxomoxoa*, while the one called *The Big Ball* has an edited version of "Turn On Your Love Light" from *Live/Dead*. Others have full versions of Dead tunes or complete tracks from Garcia's and Weir's solo outings. While not essential to anyone but the most avid Dead collectors, these albums nonetheless are fun to listen to and usually don't go for much on the used vinyl market. Plus, they provide an easy way for the curious to pick up some of the hits of the day by Van Morrison and the Faces or get introduced to now-obscure artists such as Lovecraft, Pearls Before Swine, Savage Grace, and Turley Richards.

Zabriskie Point Soundtrack Album and CD

Zabriskie Point was a 1970 film by Italian director Michelangelo Antonioni that was meant as a look into the counterculture with its portrayal of a young couple's political struggles (she's a do-gooder, he's a suspected cop killer). It's pretty much forgotten about today because it was a total failure in its own day, impressing neither the audiences nor critics. Its soundtrack also isn't remembered much except by Pink Floyd fans, because that band had a bunch of songs on it. The Grateful Dead had one and Jerry Garcia had one, making it his first outing as a solo artist. As this isn't a book about Pink Floyd, let's look at the Dead's contribution.

Actually, all the Dead contribute is "Dark Star," but it's an edit of the version from *Live/Dead* that you can't get anywhere else, and it runs 2:30. More interesting is the track by Jerry Garcia that leads off side two of the original vinyl edition. It's a song called "Love Scene" billed as "Jerry Garcia (Grateful Dead)," on the back cover, which probably led more than one Deadhead to pick up the soundtrack, thinking they were getting a rare cut by the band. In actuality, it's a solo acoustic number penned and performed by Garcia—not really essential, but still nice to hear. The 1997 CD reissue of the soundtrack has Garcia performing four improvisational renditions of the tune in addition to the original cut.

32

Ripple in Still Water

What Happened When Deadheads Invaded a Town?

By the early 1980s, the Grateful Dead's traveling band of fans known as Deadheads had started to grow in number. Enough people were following the band around that when the Dead played a few nights in any given place, that locale would transform overnight from a typical city involved in a typical daydream into a Day-Glo fantasyland out of the Summer of Love. Brightly dressed Heads would camp out overnight, take up residence in hotels, and hang out at shopping centers or restaurants. If you didn't know what Deadheads were before they came trucking into town, you learned quickly when you suddenly found yourself in a sea of tie-dye, headbands, and flying Frisbees.

When the Dead's popularity exploded after their 1987 hit "Touch of Grey," the band played bigger venues in more urban areas, so when troublesome incidents or arrests inevitably happened, they were usually reported in the daily papers or on local television news. But during the Dead's pre-celebrity "cult period," the smaller towns that held the mid-sized arenas the band played also felt the ramifications of Deadhead visits. The difference was that in the pre-Internet age, the news didn't travel much beyond the local papers. Today, the idea of having a bunch of latter-day hippies traipsing through town for a few days might seem amusing if not downright quaint. But back in the Reagan era, it was Cause for Alarm for the guardians of those two mainstays of suburban life, peace and quiet.

This chapter tells the story of how one particular town, Columbia, Maryland, reacted when Deadheads invaded its sphere three years in a row in the 1980s when the band performed at the outdoor concert spot Merriweather Post Pavilion. The band played two-night stands each year, so this meant that Deadheads camped out, hung out, and otherwise made Columbia's downtown area their own personal playground.

Even though this chapter looks at one particular town during one specific time period, it's really an allegorical story about what happened in Anytown, USA, when Deadheads arrived and created a "ripple in still water," to quote one of the Dead's lyrics. Why Columbia, Maryland? Because this writer lived there, attended his first Dead show there, and kept up with the town's growing dread of Deadheads in the community newspaper.

Sometimes We Live No Particular Way but Our Own

If anyone in the Dead camp thought much about Merriweather at all before their arrival, they probably knew it from its history. The outdoor concert hall, which seats just fewer than ten thousand, made a name for itself in the late 1960s and early 1970s, hosting pioneering rock acts such as Jimi Hendrix, Janis Joplin, and the Who. Jackson Browne also recorded a few songs there that wound up on his 1977 album *Running on Empty*, including the title track, which got to #11 on the pop charts in early 1978.

Why did the Dead play Merriweather instead of the Baltimore Civic Center and Capital Center, as they did the year before? They wanted a change of pace, said their publicist at the time, Dennis McNally: "It was a pleasant outdoor venue versus Civic Center concrete. And the audience didn't absolutely yet mandate civic centers."

It's unlikely any Dead people knew many details about Columbia, but you have to assume they figured it was a rock-friendly town considering it housed Merriweather. The Deadheads who were following the band in the early 1980s might have looked forward to stopping in Columbia, as it was considered a town with liberal political leanings that was founded on the very principles of tolerance. Columbia was dreamed up by pioneering urban planner James Rouse as a place where people of different races, beliefs, and incomes could live side by side. The city's ideas and ideals are reflected in its diverse demographics, interfaith centers, and neighborhoods, most of which contain a mix of both upper- and lower-income housing. In a 2012 *New York Times* editorial, Pulitzer Prize–winning novelist Michael Chabon described how growing up in Columbia in the 1970s shaped his view of the world on both a personal and an artistic level.

But by the early 1980s, Columbia, like the rest of America, had started to grow a bit more conformist and conservative. On top of that, the Deadheads of the 1980s were starting to prove to be too wild for such an otherwise laid-back suburban town. When the Deadheads appeared, it seemed, tranquility disappeared.

Few people probably suspected the town was going to be turned into Hippie Central when the town's main local newspaper, the *Columbia Flier*, made casual mention of the Dead's first concert in town in the June 16, 1983, issue. "Only a few lawn tickets are left for the shows," read the pop music column. The column went on to explain that Dead concerts were a unique experience because the band "creates its own self-contained environment that is produced by the hypnotic length of the shows (three to six hours), the slow, mantric rhythms, the spacy solos and the unique rapport between the band and its devoted 'Deadheads.'"

Maybe that last word should have been a tip-off that something different was about to happen at the Dead's first Merriweather show, which occurred on June 20, 1983. What happened was rain, and lots of it. Thunderclaps and a brief power outage can even be heard on tapes made of the show that night.

The soaking rain caused Deadheads on the lawn to become covered with mud. A good number of Deadheads camped out overnight, because they planned on seeing the Dead's second Merriweather show the next night. Some camped under canopies at the local shopping area, the Mall in Columbia, located across the street from Merriweather. When the mall opened, dozens of campers trudged inside and proceeded to wash the dirt off themselves . . . in the mall's fountains.

The Deadheads' impromptu bathing ritual left a big impression—so much so that locals still recalled it some thirty years later when former Columbian Traci Balter Tyo put up a post about the Dead's Merriweather excursion in a Facebook group dedicated to growing up in Columbia. Annemarie Hunt Dauer was the most detailed in her recollections, remembering the scene as creating a mini-scandal: "Most of the 'bathing' I saw was very overheated people sitting on the edge of the fountain outside [Woodward & Lothrup's department store] soaking their feet [and] a few walking in the water and splashing each other. Someone poured a bottle of dish soap in the fountain and made bubbles."

Kathi Abernethy Dunsmore worked at the mall during that period and wrote that she remembered the mall's management sending notices to the stores, warning them about the arrival of Deadheads. "They would all have extra people working for fear the Deadheads would try to invade their stores," she recalled. "I always thought it was extremely unfair that the town of Columbia allowed the camping but they did not provide any water trucks or any other source of water. Then when the people camping used the creek and fountains as a water source, people had a fit. But if they [hadn't used the local water], the same people would have been having fits because [the campers] smelled bad."

Mike Duffy, who worked for the local government at the time, recalls that the county executive and his staff "fielded many phone calls from citizens. They objected on several fronts, and some claimed that the Deadheads were ruining [the county], trashing the landscape, endangering traffic."

Cathy Garland Meyers had memories of seeing Deadheads walking down the highway that divides the town, Route 29, and doing a double take. "I remember thinking we were being taken over by freaky zombies dressed as flower children with all of them walking down the shoulder," she recalled. Emily Vitullo Martin, who lived near Merriweather, remembers that her family "also took Deadheads to our house for showers." Sue Smith had memories of seeing girls with hula hoops dancing "and one girl walking her skunk. No lie, she had a skunk on a leash."

After the Dead finished their first two-night Merriweather run, the *Columbia Flier* did something atypical in its news section: it ran both an article and a feature photo devoted to a rock band.

"Deadheads Invade," read the main headline. The story describes how the town's downtown area "resembled the corner of Haight and Ashbury Streets when close to 28,000 'Deadheads' descended." The writer of the article, Susan

The crowds at the Grateful Dead's 1985 shows at Merriweather Post
Pavilion looked normal enough in the context of the concert hall,
but they unnerved locals when they wandered about the suburban
town of Columbia, Maryland. *Photo courtesy of Merriweather Post Pavilion*

Roberts, describes the throngs as if they were something out of an anthropologi-
cal study:

> Garbed like flower children, they could be seen all day Monday buying
> organic brownies . . . tossing Frisbees . . . and dancing down Little
> Patuxent [Parkway's] median strip, as if suddenly possessed by dervishes.
> Some of the women wore Indian-print skirts, silver bangle bracelets,
> and patchouli oil. Some of the men wore fringed vests, bandanas and
> T-shirts bearing the Grateful Dead [*sic*] cryptic insignia—a smiling skull
> in a pig-tail wig of roses.

At this point in American culture, the mainstreaming of tattoos, piercings, and weird facial hair was still a ways off, so the writer can be excused for seeming aghast at the out-of-style fashions Deadheads brought into town with them. Less excusable were the problems created by drug use. Roberts's article has Captain Ray Faith of the county's fire department noting that three concertgoers were taken to the hospital because of suspected overdoses. But beyond that, as far as Columbians were concerned, their experiences with the Dead were over. Until two years later, that is.

Like an Angry Stream

After the Dead played their standard two-night stand at Merriweather in the summer of 1985, a substantial number of Columbia's residents decided they'd experienced just about enough Deadhead culture for one lifetime, thank you. Why did it take until 1985 for residents to organize? Because the crowds were bigger. That year marked the Dead's twentieth anniversary as a band, and McNally had organized a promotional push around that theme. The group, which had experienced a mild lull in popularity when they stopped releasing studio albums in 1980, was starting to draw bigger crowds again.

Although the *Columbia Flier* did not run any articles related to the two Merriweather concerts the Dead played in the summer of 1984, it did run a full-page news story on July 3, 1985, following the June 30 and July 1 shows. Called "Invasion by the Deadheads," it functioned as something of a postmortem of the concerts. Writer Jeff Lowe described a carnival-like atmosphere, with "the scent of campfires and stranger things" burning in the air along with a young merchant hawking doses of acid "car-door to car-door."

That was the fun part. But the article also had a local official noting that scores of residents had called police, complaining about the unruly crowds that scattered trash, walked through traffic, and illegally camped overnight in Symphony Woods, the park that surrounds parts of Merriweather. In the article, Merriweather's manager, Michael Smith, praised Deadheads for "peacefulness and obedience."

By August 1, 1985, the paper's headline was blaring "Ban Grateful Dead, People Tell Police." The accompanying article describes how neighborhood association representatives had fielded complaints about Deadheads from residents and, in turn, passed those grievances along to authorities. One of the issues that arose was that some Deadheads had set off fireworks in the wee hours, waking up the residents of a neighborhood that bordered Merriweather called Sebring. "It's not because they dress differently or I don't like the music," explained Joan Lancos, the president of the neighborhood's association. "People dress in outlandish costumes at other Merriweather concerts, but they go home after four hours."

On August 22, nearly two months after the Dead had left town, the *Flier* ran an opinion column by writer Kay Wisnieswki questioning why authorities allegedly looked the other way when Deadheads broke countless laws and ordinances:

> If you can believe this newspaper, the four-day siege by the Dead and their camp followers, the Deadheads, included all of the following: drugs openly used and sold; adjacent neighborhoods overrun by bands of flower children gone to pot; fireworks at 3 a.m., well within earshot of the county general hospital. Yet only two arrests were made, both for disorderly conduct.

The column, titled "Breaking Law OK If 'Right' People Are Making Profit," goes on to claim that police and Pavilion management were afraid of Deadheads and their "potential to turn into an angry and destructive mob"—so much for that image of gentle flower children.

In that same issue, the *Flier* also ran a news story headlined "Efforts to Ban Grateful Dead Hit Police Snag." This time around, the article had the county police telling a room full of angry residents and neighborhood representatives that there was "no apparent legal basis for denying a permit for the concerts." Were there Deadheads in high places? No, just a county police chief, Paul Rappaport, who made it clear that the Dead did not meet any of the criteria for getting a permit to perform denied. According to the police chief, for a denial to be issued, a band or a promoter would need to have a history of violence, or the facility in question would have to have proven that it wasn't able to handle the expected crowds. Rappaport let the disappointed residents know that there were no real legal problems at the 1985 Dead concerts, save a few fence-jumpers. He recommended better fences. When questioned about the Deadheads' use of drugs in and around the concert area, Rappaport said that his police force tried to approach that problem in a levelheaded manner. He was quoted as saying:

> We don't look away. But I'm not going to jeopardize anybody's life or safety to make an arrest in the midst of 15,000 people for somebody smoking marijuana, whether it be at the Pavilion, at the lakefront or anywhere else . . . I think we enforce the law in a common sense way, not in a 'Rambo' way.

There was no word as to whether the police chief went home that night and cranked up the *Europe '72* album or a really crispy live soundboard tape of "Dark Star."

On August 29, 1985, two months after the Dead had left Columbia, the town's newspaper sported two full pages of letters relating to the Dead's appearance at Merriweather. There was also now a new problem about which the locals were complaining: noise from the Pavilion, as exemplified by the Dead's shows. Justin E. Morrill wrote a long diatribe, suggesting shutting the Pavilion down, enclosing it, or not allowing any electric amplification, among other ideas. Jay Vogel and Tim Krafft came down on the side of the Dead and in a joint letter wrote that banning the band would be a "gross over-reaction" because there were solutions to most of the problems posed by roving packs of Deadheads. One suggestion was to bring in "a spot-a-pot or two" to relieve the pressing problem of public urination. Once again, Merriweather's manager, Michael Smith, was tapped for a response and chimed in with a letter headlined "We Did Everything We Could." The contents of Smith's letter were pretty much an expansion on that thought. But Smith went on to defend the Dead's presence by noting that he had "a problem with censoring or limiting the public's access to all types of entertainment . . . That scares me a little bit."

All the controversy was a moot point, however. The Dead would never play Merriweather again. According to local lore, it was because they got banned. According to McNally, it was because after the band's twentieth anniversary in 1985, their popularity began to grow and by then "it was impossible to conceive of any venue that wasn't fully NBA arena size or larger."

But even if the Dead had moved on to larger venues, were they still banned from Merriweather? A Columbia-based Deadhead, John Sybert, looked into this issue almost ten years later when he wrote a letter to Merriweather's powers-that-be in 1994. The answer he received said the same thing McNally had explained. "When I wrote them, they just said the fan base had outgrown the venue," related Sybert, who saved the letter.

Sybert received a reply from Julie M. Kershner, Merriweather's customer relations manager, who wrote, in part, "Merriweather has never banned any acts from performing at its venue and, to my knowledge, neither has the community. Currently, the Grateful Dead has attracted crowds at sizes well beyond Merriweather's capacity."

I Know This Song It Ain't Never Gonna End

Once again, that should have been the end of things. And once again it wasn't. In 1989, Merriweather Post Pavilion booked Jerry Garcia's side group, the Jerry Garcia Band, to perform two shows in early September. Citizens didn't exactly revolt, but the controversy erupted on the town newspaper's editorial page, which ran a somewhat alarmist opinion piece two weeks ahead of the event. "Hang onto your hats, citizens," began the latest column by Wisniewski, who years earlier had shown no love for the Dead and their fans. "It's been four years since the last appearance of the Grateful Dead in Columbia. Now the Nederlander Company (which booked Merriweather) has decided it's safe to test the waters by booking the key elements of the band into Merriweather under an assumed name." Notwithstanding that no one at the paper had bothered to research the fact that the Jerry Garcia Band was not the Dead under an assumed name, the column would have made an important point had the Dead actually been playing.

By 1989, the band had attracted a younger, rowdier crowd in the wake of their 1987 Top 10 hit, "Touch of Grey," which also had an accompanying hit

As the 1980s progressed, some members of the Dead cut their hair and projected a more conventional image, making any furor surrounding their concerts seem ironic. Within a few years, the mainstream would fully embrace the band, making them one of the top-grossing touring acts around.   *Author's collection*

video that MTV played incessantly at one point. As Wisniewski noted in her column, when the Dead had played RFK Stadium earlier in the summer, neighborhood residents were so alarmed that they lobbied DC's city council to ban the group. It didn't, but instead provided outdoor toilet facilities and shower facilities, which Wisniewski noted kept the crowd from venturing out of the parking lot. But the Jerry Garcia Band had never attracted the type of audience fervor that accompanied the Dead, so the group's arrival never really was that much of a threat to the town's equilibrium.

Perhaps someone at the newspaper realized this, because the next week, on August 31, the paper changed its tune and ran an opinion piece that waxed positive about all things Dead-related. Written by Phyllis Kepner and jokingly titled "Piece 'n' Love from the Haightful Dead," it ran down all the benefits of having the Deadheads in town. This included the respect they showed to police after being told to move along and the massive business they brought to the mall.

But both columns were much ado about nothing. The Garcia Band came and went without making the paper's news section even once.

And so ended the Dead's dalliances with Merriweather, save post-Dead bands like Phil Lesh and Friends and Furthur. The Dead's shows at Merriweather Post Pavilion have never been released on CD or as downloads, but they can be heard online at Archive.org. The June 21, 1983, and June 27, 1984, shows were also surreptitiously filmed by fans and can be seen on YouTube. The recordings of the Jerry Garcia Band's 1989 Merriweather shows came out in 2005 as *Pure Jerry: Merriweather Post Pavilion, September 1 & 2, 1989*. The box set release was the fifth in a series by the Jerry Made label as part of the *Pure Jerry* series and is a four-CD set that comprises both full shows.

If you take Columbia's experience and multiply it by the number of towns the Dead played, it's easy to see how Deadheads earned a reputation for creating a circus atmosphere wherever they traveled. A few years down the road, things would get worse when the group's fan base expanded, resulting in gate crashings, open air drug dealing, and a much less friendly police presence. A gate crashing incident on July 2, 1995, at the Deer Creek Music Center in Indiana caused the next night's show to be canceled, depriving thousands of fans of seeing the band one last time before Garcia died.

As for Columbia, Maryland, the Dead did at least partially leave their mark there. They helped cause the fighting over the noise created by concerts at Merriweather to become an even bigger issue. The debate rages on to this day in the local newspaper's letters to the editor section.

33

I Was There

Toni Brown on Documenting the Dead

Toni Brown was editor of Relix *from 1979 to 1981 and publisher from 1981 to 2001. During that time, the Dead went from being cult figures to cultural icons, and the magazine grew from a fanzine to a renowned national publication. Now the co-author of* Relix: The Book *as well as a working musician, Brown talks here about documenting the Dead.*

R *elix* was founded as *Dead Relix* by early tapers Les Kippel and Jim McGurn as a way for them to connect and reach a broader audience to trade tapes with, just in case they missed a show from another state. It was a way to bring everybody together. When I first came into *Relix*, I was working with Jeff Tamarkin, who was the editor. He was trying to move *Relix* in a direction away from the Grateful Dead, and I knew that was wrong. Jeff decided I was going to be able to handle it just fine, so he stepped out and I stepped in.

At that time Les, whom I later married, went off to start Relix Records, which gave me the freedom with the magazine to feel out what our readers really wanted—and that was more Grateful Dead. It became somewhat of a voice for the Deadhead community, linking the Dead with their fans, because the Grateful Dead and the Deadheads really had no communication except for what went on during those musical moments. So *Relix* became that uniting force. Fans could learn what the band was up to, and the Dead could see in the magazine what their fans were saying in the letters to the editor. I could also pass on a lot of information, like whether their fans were being busted or if they want to hear Phil sing more or whatever.

I always tried to incorporate as many new writers and Deadhead writers as possible to make it a magazine by Deadheads for Deadheads. So, I always tried to stay very true to what I perceived as the spirit of the Grateful Dead, which was a community thing, not just a musical thing. In doing that, I actually kept myself out of the backstage loop and stayed away from the band, because whenever I was around them I felt as though I were seeing too much behind the scenes, and I didn't think we as fans belonged back there. Now I wonder if I maybe didn't gloss over some of the problems in the world behind the scenes. But then again, like I say, it was the Dead's private world. *Relix* was a very positive fan magazine.

I was really lucky. I was very young when I went to my first Grateful Dead concert, and eventually it became my job to publish *Relix* magazine.

No other band had a magazine so early in its inception that devoted so much energy to it. And I truly believe that without the tapers, the Grateful Dead would not have achieved the audience that they did. People were able to get a souvenir of the concerts they went to in the form of a tape. Then they'd turn other people on to it. I heard these kinds of stories all the time at *Relix*: "My buddy made me sit down and listen to this show, but my God, it was amazing."

In 2009, Toni Brown compiled a book about the history of *Relix* magazine called *Relix: The Book*. Since stepping down as editor in 2001, she has toured regularly with the Toni Brown Band.   *Photo by Ed Munson*

Wave That Flag

It was very difficult to document the Grateful Dead experience with a magazine coming out every other month. News was old by the time it came out, so I always had to think of creative ways to present old news, and also the same musicians would appear in the magazine constantly. It was very difficult to keep the story fresh.

So I just went with what I thought fit. What I tried to do was always include concert reviews, because that was really a major part of the Grateful Dead. So we put a lot of live reviews, but it wasn't easy to print every review of every show. We had to be selective. We'd miss things and people would freak out. Once, when Phil broke out "Unbroken Chain" in Philly and our reviewer just didn't happen to go to that show in the series of shows, I got such shit for it I couldn't believe it.

When I started printing set lists in the magazine, we didn't have the Internet. But the set lists were critical, and I just couldn't keep up with it. I didn't like giving all my space in the magazine to set lists, because by then you had Deadbase.com coming out, so I was very happy to let that go. By the time the Internet came out, I felt like it was a blessing, so I didn't have to worry about missing songs in a concert.

The difficult thing for me was always having to write all these stories about the same artists, so I tried to get other people to do the stories to get different slants. I had a lot of contributors outside of the magazine, so we just kept documenting everything about the Dead that we could basically keep up with. Eventually, our year-end "photo issues" turned into two special issues a year that were just crammed full of stuff, including advertising.

Doing an interview with Donna Jean was really a big deal for me because I knew how hard it was to be a female singer in a rock 'n' roll band, so that was pretty significant. I also loved finding the musicians who were around the Grateful Dead family and who worked with them. I'd have to say that some of the interviews that I did with the external people such as [Garcia collaborator] Sandy Rothman were wonderful. Merl Saunders was such a good person, too, of course. Then, of course, there was talking to Robert Hunter. He wrote our bible, you know? It was a religious experience.

Let It Grow

Once *In the Dark* came out, I have to say things really shifted. Advertising came in, sales of the magazine went through the roof, and you couldn't get tickets for shows. A lot of people were outraged at the band for selling out, but so many new fans came in. It was really a weird time. I mean, don't you want your band to be successful commercially and to make a lot of money so that they can keep on playing? It was really an interesting period to document. Fans were coming and going in opposite directions, and I thought my head was gonna split in half because of it.

I also did stories about issues that affected Deadheads. I did a cover story on the drug war, and I didn't want to put my name on it because I was straight-up against the Drug Enforcement Agency; I was on television a lot talking about it, so my assistant and I used a pseudonym. To me, that was one of the most important things I did: fight the mandatory minimum sentencing laws for first-time, non-violent drug offenses—and the targeting of Deadheads for arrests. I wouldn't be surprised to see this now, but at that time it was a very unusual situation to see our own culture being targeted.

When the Grateful Dead decided to champion protecting the rainforest, it was a pivotal time because very few people were stepping out for environmental causes then. There weren't a lot of celebrities coming out and endorsing things like saving the rainforest or the water. For the Dead to step out and do that, it was huge. Deadheads took it on and it was a big thing. But for me, it gave me the opportunity to take a segment of every issue and put in environmental issues pertinent to that time. I also included related things I felt our readers would be interested in, such as how to find healthy household products as opposed to the toxins that we still seem to buy.

So *Relix* became very environmentally involved because of the band. I donated profits from *Relix* to planting trees in the country. All of this also caused me to print the magazine with unbleached paper, as opposed to bleached paper, and to use soy-based inks in *Relix*. This was a huge expense, but I felt like if I was going to talk the talk, I was going to walk the walk. The music was great, but I felt I had this position to put important issues across, and how could I not take that responsibly?

34

Strange Deadfellows

Five Surprising Grateful Connections

ith thirty years together as a band, the Grateful Dead made a lot of history. As such, the band ended up developing some unexpected connections in strange places. Here are five of the strangest.

Bubblegum Music

There are dozens upon dozens of songs that mention the Grateful Dead, and most have been listed as part of the online Grateful Dead Family Discography, which has a page for such matters called "Songs with a Dead Connection." But the song that references the Dead everyone seems to have missed is likely the first one to do so: the Rock & Roll Dubble Bubble Trading Card Company of Philadelphia-19141's "Bubble Gum Music," which got to #74 in early 1969.

There are two good reasons this song has gone virtually unnoticed among Deadheads. First, it's not done by a jam band or a rock act or anyone even remotely related to the band. Second, it was only a minor hit and the lone record by a group that was a studio concoction. The oddly named Rock & Roll Dubble Bubble Trading Card Company of Philadelphia-19141 was an invention of the Kasenetz-Katz production team, the New York–based duo of Jerry Kasenetz and Jeff Katz, who were largely responsible for the explosion of the bubblegum genre in the late '60s. The team had produced such hits as the 1910 Fruitgum Company's "Simon Says," the Ohio Express's "Yummy Yummy Yummy," and the Music Explosion's "Little Bit O' Soul," among other songs.

"Bubble Gum Music," which stayed in the Top 100 for four weeks starting on January 18, 1969, was something of a statement of purpose for the genre. In the lyrics, the band declare all the reasons they love bubblegum music in the first verse, and in the second explain why they prefer bubblegum to other genres: "Well the Grateful Dead just leave me cold / and Herbie Alpert makes me feel too old." Since the Dead hadn't even clocked in with a Top 50 album at this point, this reference is a good indicator of how they were already being looked upon as culturally significant.

Another Kasenetz and Katz act, the Scoundrels, might also have tried to cop the Dead's cachet of cool when the Scoundrels renamed themselves Lt. Garcia's Magic Music Box. One of the reasons for the renaming might have been that there were a few Latin-flavored songs on the group's lone album from 1968,

'*Cross the Border*, but using the name "Garcia" was a bit suspect, especially because around this time the production team was producing wildly psychedelic albums such as Deviled Ham's *I Had Too Much to Dream Last Night*.

Conservative Commentators

The Grateful Dead may have shied away from getting overtly political in their early days, but they made a political statement by just being who they were, because they offered fans an alternative to the conservatives (or "straights") that made up the bulk of society. By the 1980s, the group had embraced environmentalism as a cause, and by the 1990s some members were invited to the Oval Office by Vice President Al Gore, who was a fan of the band, as was his former wife, Tipper Gore. So, it's not a stretch to say that the members of the Dead leaned toward the left side of the political spectrum, even if they weren't performing at rallies.

That makes it all the more incongruous that two of the country's best-known conservative voices, Tucker Carlson and Ann Coulter, would count themselves as Deadheads. Coulter especially waves the Deadhead flag whenever she can, the most notorious instance of which can be found in a 2006 interview with Jambands.com. In it, she spoke about keeping ticket stubs to Dead shows, flying out to attend the Jerry Garcia memorial ceremony in Golden Gate Park, and not having taken any drugs at concerts (not surprising, given her support of anti-drug laws).

Coulter's idea about why Deadheads and conservatives should "go hand-in-hand" seems to come from the perspective of viewing conservatives as small-government libertarians, which only represents one faction of conservative politics. "The Deadheads I just met casually and not through conservative politics were almost always right-thinking, whatever they called themselves," Coulter said. "Deadheads believe in freedom, not a government telling people how much water they can have in their toilets or where they can smoke or whether they should be allowed to own a gun."

A year before her JamBands.com interview, Coulter, like Carlson, had been the subject of a *New York Sun* article called "Jerry Garcia's Conservative Children," which reconciled their political beliefs and musical leanings by explaining how there is a "stark gap between the stereotype of the crew-cutted, humorless, Muzak-listening conservative of the past and the libertarian-leaning conservatives who came of age during the Reagan era." The article, which ran on the ten-year anniversary of Garcia's death, also included information about lesser-known conservative Deadhead Deroy Murdock, a columnist and contributing editor to the *National Review Online*.

It turns out that Carlson, who is best known as an MSNBC talk show host, is a veteran of more than fifty Dead shows. In the article, he says that he "always liked how apolitical the band was, at least in public" as well as the fact that Garcia wasn't didactic when it came to politics. "He was totally opposed to lectures—giving or receiving them," Carlson said. "He was the opposite of the self-righteous liberals who ran the schools I went to."

But merging a love of the Dead with conservative politics can only go so far. As the *Sun* article notes, it would be a stretch to think that Garcia would have appreciated Coulter's book that defended Joseph McCarthy, the Republican senator whose anti-communist witch hunts helped create the paranoid, repressive 1950s culture that the Dead represented a rebellion against.

Freaks and Geeks

According to the online Grateful Dead Family Discography, the Dead have been referenced in twenty television series, ranging from *Seinfeld* to *The Simpsons* to *The Big Bang Theory*. But the short-lived cult favorite *Freaks and Geeks* has the biggest Dead connection of all, because a storyline involving Deadheads shaped its final episode and would likely have continued to influence the show's plot had the series been given a second season (something for which lots of avid fans lobbied).

A bit of background: *Freaks and Geeks* was a coming-of-age dramedy that ran on NBC during 1999–2000 and centered on suburban teenagers during the 1980–81 school year. At the center of the stories was the character Lindsay (played by Linda Cardellini), a one-time good student who comes to identify more with the partying crowd (or "freaks") at her high school. The last episode, "Discos and Dragons," finds Lindsay stressed because she doesn't want to spend her summer attending an academic conference. She seeks advice from the school's hippie guidance counselor, Jeff Rosso (Dave "Gruber" Allen). "What do you want me to do?" he asks. It turns out he's quoting "Box of Rain" and is a Deadhead himself. He gives her a copy of *American Beauty* that he just happens to have sitting in his office.

When Lindsay walks through the cafeteria with the album tucked under her arm, she's spotted by a pair of high school Deadheads, Victor (Russel Harper) and Laurie (Samaire Armstrong), the latter of whom had been introduced two episodes back and inspired Seth Rogan's character, Ken Miller, to make the derogatory (but admittedly hilarious) crack "Grateful Dead. Music sucks. Chicks are hot!" Lindsay takes the album home, and the next thing you know she's twirl-ing to "Box of Rain" in her bedroom. While that sounds like a cringe-inducing made-for-TV cliché, the scene actually unfolds artfully and is surprisingly moving and convincing.

A while later, Laurie unwittingly entices Lindsay away from her academic conference by regaling her with tales of how she and Victor plan to go on tour with the Dead in the early part of the summer of 1981. "We're going down to Texas when school's out," she says. "We're gonna follow the tour out to Colorado—nine shows in a week and a half." A quick check of the band's where-abouts during that period on Setlists.net reveals that someone from the show actually took the trouble to make the information accurate. No one bothered to do this when the Rolling Stones' 1978 song "Miss You" was called "their latest single" in the same episode: the Stones had charted four American hits in the time between that song's release and the spring of 1981, when the episode is supposed to take place.

The show ends with Lindsay getting dropped off at a bus station by her family, but taking the bus to where her new Deadhead friends are waiting in front of their beat-up Volkswagen Bus (of course) replete with a *Steal Your Face* sticker pasted onto its side. "Ripple" plays as the scene unfolds. Even before this episode aired, *Freaks and Geeks* was in danger of getting canceled because of low ratings. Articles were written, websites started, and e-mail campaigns launched in the hopes of getting it renewed. It wasn't. Had fans of the show succeeded with their lobbying efforts, television would have had its first-ever show with a Deadhead theme running through it, as *Freaks and Geeks* would have had to address the ramifications of Lindsay ditching academic life to follow the band around.

NASCAR

If you happened to catch the Dodge/Save Mart 350 NASCAR race at California's old Infineon Raceway (now the Sonoma Raceway) on June 27, 2004, you would have heard Bob Weir sing the national anthem before the start of the event. Weir had previously sung the anthem with the Grateful Dead's Jerry Garcia and Vince Welnick on April 12, 1993, at the San Francisco Giants' home game opener, but he was on less familiar ground in NASCAR country. A press release had been sent out by the NASCAR folks a week earlier, explaining to the uninitiated who Weir is: "Weir is best known for forming one of Bay Area's most legendary musical groups, the Grateful Dead, which also featured the late Jerry Garcia," the release read. "The group, which was inducted into the Rock and Roll Hall of Fame in 1994, was formed in 1965 and still tours to this day."

Notwithstanding the inaccuracy of that last statement, what the release didn't mention was that the reason Weir was involved with anything NASCAR-related was that he has a sister-in-law who races. She's Leilani Münter, the younger sister of Weir's wife, Natascha Münter. According to her biography at Huffington Post, where she occasionally blogs, Leilani Münter was named one of the top ten female race car drivers in the world by *Sports Illustrated* and races in ARCA (the Automobile Race Car Association), a development league of NASCAR (National Association for Stock Car Auto Racing). In 2006, Münter set the record for the highest finish for a female driver in the Texas Motor Speedway's history with a fourth place race finish.

What Münter and Weir have in common is that they're both environmental activists. The Dead gave to environmental causes through their charitable Rex Foundation. Weir has publicly made his points of view known by speaking at events such as the September 1989 launch of Earth Train, an international organization that continues to help young people become leaders in the areas of environmental and cultural renewal. Münter holds a bachelor's degree in biology with a specialty in ecology, behavior, and evolution from the University of California, San Diego. Since 2007, she's been said to have adopted an acre of rainforest for every race she runs. She's also spoken with members of Congress to support clean energy legislation.

By the way, Münter didn't race on the day of Weir's big vocal performance at NASCAR. Forty-three other drivers competed, though, and Jeff Gordon placed first. Both Münter's racing and activism are documented on her website, carbonfreegirl.com.

Star Trek

The Grateful Dead and the science fiction television series *Star Trek* have two commonalities: both began in the mid-1960s and both spawned huge cult followings in the next decade. Where the Dead spawned the followers who came to be known as Deadheads and were often ridiculed for their devotion to the band, *Star Trek* begat a cult that was called "Trekkies," and they took just as much grief for their fanaticism. Deadheads swapped tapes and kept statistics about how many times songs were played; Trekkies held their own conventions where they shared their encyclopedic knowledge of every episode.

Both Deadheads and Trekkies were (usually) outsiders who bonded over commonalities that those not belonging to their subculture couldn't possibly understand. And both groups allowed individuals a way to flex their intellectual muscles outside of the confines of their everyday lives, by encouraging like-minded people to analyze the minutiae of the band or the TV show. Finally, both cults grew bigger by the fact that each enterprise (no pun intended) kept on keeping on. The Dead toured year after year, and the *Star Trek* franchise (after a period of inactivity in the late 1970s) churned out endless movies and TV series.

With this much common ground, it was probably inevitable that the worlds of both subcultures would collide one day. That collision came in the form of Gerrit Graham, an actor and songwriter. Graham is known in Dead circles for being friends with Bob Weir and having co-written the lyrics to Weir's "Victim or the Crime" from *Built to Last*. Graham also had a hand in writing "(I Want to Live in) America" from the second album by Weir's side project, Bobby and the Midnites (the album, *Where the Beat Meets the Street*, came out in 1984). He also co-authored four songs on the 2000 album *Evening Moods* by Weir's band RatDog.

But ask a Trekkie who Graham is and you'll learn that he played two roles on two different *Star Trek* series. In *Star Trek: Deep Space Nine*, Graham played a hunter of the Tosk species in the episode "Captive Pursuit." On *Star Trek: Voyager*, he was a member of the Q Continuum, Quinn, in the episode "Death Wish." He was also on *Babylon 5*, a series not officially affiliated with *Star Trek*, but beloved by some of the show's fans.

How did Graham and Weir come to collaborate? In 2004, Graham penned an essay about "Victim or the Crime" for the Annotated Grateful Dead

Gerrit Graham, who is best known as an actor, collaborated with Bob Weir on songs in the 1980s. The song "(I Want to Live in) America" was one of their collaborations for Weir's side project Bobby and the Midnites. Released as a single in 1984, the song did not chart or garner much radio play, but it could be heard easily on *Where the Beat Meets the Street*, the band's second and final album.   *Courtesy of Eric Schwartz*

Lyrics. In it, he tells of how he and Weir met in the mid-'70s through Andy Leonard, "an old and very dear friend who'd been brought into the scene by John Barlow and was working for Grateful Dead Records (he shot the cover pic for *Mars Hotel*)." A Los Angeles resident, he became friends with Weir and took to visiting him to "get the hell away from Hollywood for a minute." When Weir was writing songs for the second Bobby and the Midnites album in the early 1980s, Graham offered his services as a lyricist and an artistic partnership was born, even though Graham is quick to note that he's "an actor, not a musician or a poet."

35

Days Between

The Final Dead Album That Never Was

The Grateful Dead left us with only thirteen studio albums even though the band had a career that spanned three decades. On the plus side, you have to give the band credit for not going into the recording studio when they were uninspired and churning out low-quality "product" like so many other recording acts do. Because of that, the quality of the studio albums we did get is pretty high.

But on the other side of the coin, the Dead became almost phobic about recording in a studio setting during the second half of their career, most likely due to the drubbings they took from fans and critics who felt that the band's recorded output never measured up to the way they played live. Time has proven otherwise, and because of that it's raised the question of what could have been had the Dead buckled down one last time and delivered something of a goodbye album before Jerry Garcia's passing.

The Dead never did, though, and because of that, fans of Garcia never got their equivalent to Janis Joplin's *Pearl* or John Lennon and Yoko Ono's *Double Fantasy*—albums that gave us one final glimpse into an artist's mind before he or she passed on. But according to both Phil Lesh's *Searching for the Sound: My Life with the Grateful Dead* and Blair Jackson's biography, *Garcia: An American Life*, the band made an attempt to record what would likely have been their swan song.

In November 1994, they convened in a West Marin studio called the Site and laid down some basic tracks. Lesh notes that the studio's setting should have been conducive to creativity because it was located on a hill in rural Marin and offered panoramic views and even wildlife sightings outside its windows. But location couldn't spark inspiration. Both sources say that Garcia's lack of focus and interest in the project killed its momentum.

According to both Jackson's book and roadie Steve Parish's recollections in his memoir, *Home Before Daylight: My Life on the Road with the Grateful Dead*, Garcia was by this point using heroin again after having cleaned up following his health scare in 1986. Garcia would arrive late for some sessions, not show up for others, and sometimes show up and leave shortly afterwards. Heroin didn't have the same effect creatively on Garcia that LSD did in the early days, and no Garcia meant no creative focus. Lesh writes that out of the three weeks the band was booked at the Site, Garcia only played for a few minutes, and none of what he played was worth committing to tape.

But drugs can only explain away so much. Garcia's attitude was also a problem. It wasn't that he was totally against going into recording studios in the 1990s—it's more like he'd developed an aversion to it when the Dead was around. He sure liked recording with David Grisman, though. In 1991, Garcia sounded better than he had in years playing with Grisman on the acoustic *Garcia/Grisman* album. In 1993, the pair dropped the critically acclaimed *Not for Kids Only*. At this point, Garcia might have done well to discuss his relationship with his fellow band members and perhaps give them the classic "It's not you, it's me" line, as he'd essentially "broken up" with them, artistically speaking.

Another problem for the band was that they'd been away from the studio for so long that they were finding it difficult to perform in a non-live setting. Vince Welnick is quoted in Jackson's book as saying that he felt frustrated that the band "couldn't get a decent take." The band would start to perform a song, he continued, but "somebody would inevitably ruin it, which was kind of like how the way we played live came back to haunt us. You can get away with that onstage, but when it's supposed to be for keeps, that can be tough."

Welnick is also quoted in Jackson's book as saying that he felt that the Dead weren't capturing their sound properly in the studio, and that it was a "great studio, great view, great equipment and it just didn't sound good."

So Many Ironies

The biggest irony of the Dead's inability to record a new album in 1994 is that several of the songs were among the best the band had written in years. Back in 1991, Garcia had complained to *Rolling Stone* that the Dead had been "running on inertia" and needed to work up some new material. He got his wish. Lesh, Weir, and even Welnick came up with impressive material in the intervening years, and Garcia himself penned two of his most moving songs with Robert Hunter, "Days Between" and "So Many Roads."

One major impediment when it came to recording was that the Dead didn't operate like most major label groups of the era, who took a year (or two) off to record, then hit the road for a year to promote their newest record. The Dead gigged regularly, as if they were a journeyman rhythm and blues outfit that needed the cash. While it stands to reason that all of the band members at this point were fairly well off financially, the group did feel an obligation to its growing number of employees and as such stayed on the road. In the aforementioned *Rolling Stone* interview, Garcia told writer James Henke that the band had "a huge overhead" and "a lot of people that we're responsible for, who work for us and so forth, we're reluctant to do anything to disturb that. We don't want to take people's livelihoods away . . ."

The group played fifty-five shows in 1992, eighty-one in 1993, and eighty-five in 1994. All of that was not as backbreaking a workload as that of some working bands, but it was more than enough for a man who was around fifty and dealing with not only drug addiction but also health problems, including diabetes.

Had the Dead taken a break from touring after Brent Mydland's death in the summer of 1990, that might have resulted in Garcia getting medical treatment and cleaning himself up, which might have resulted in his full creative input on another album. But the Dead were a touring machine by this point. And if they (and Garcia himself) weren't going to call a time-out for Garcia's health issues, they certainly weren't going to do it for a recording project, especially not after the somewhat lukewarm critical reception of their 1989 studio effort, *Built to Last*, which even the usually sympathetic Robert Christgau had disliked, grading it a desultory C+.

The upside of this situation is that the Dead left behind enough live recordings that it's easy enough to piece together an idea of what could have been had their final trip back into a recording studio been productive. Six of these tunes were brought together in live versions and rehearsals on the fifth and final disc in the 1999 box set *So Many Roads (1965–1995)*. There are also six other original songs the Dead introduced at this late stage of their career that have not appeared on any release as of this writing.

The band could also have put out an album of previously unreleased new material recorded in a live setting at this point. That would have been a way to avoid dealing with recording studios and also would have functioned as a sort of a new edition of *Skull and Roses* or *Europe '72*. Besides giving a home to original Dead songs that have now become lost, it would have given Welnick the chance to have a composition or two on a Dead album.

What might the Dead's final album have sounded like? More bluesy and organic than their last two, judging from the tone of their new songs—and arguably artistically more substantial than anything the band had come out with since the 1970s, judging from the quality of that material. The following is a complete list of originals song, in alphabetical order, that the Dead introduced after Mydland's death and that could have made up a final studio album.

"Childhood's End"

This pensive Phil Lesh–composed song was performed a mere eleven times after its July 20, 1994, debut at the Deer Creek Music Center in Noblesville, Indiana. It's also the last original composition the band added into their set, so it's fitting that it's about growing up and finding your way in the world. The lyrics, which Lesh penned himself, juxtapose the commonplace ("hopping freights") with the otherworldly ("cosmic mystery"). They're anchored by a melancholy chorus that includes variations on the theme "River runs cold / River runs deep" and contains one of the most gorgeous pieces of melody that Lesh ever came up with. Phil Lesh and Friends performed a ragged-but-right unplugged rendition of this song on September 24, 1994, at the Berkeley Community Theatre with Weir, Welnick, and Garcia on acoustic lead.

Versions of this song can be found on Archive.org and YouTube, but it's become an obscurity of sorts, with its most popular video version only earning fifteen hundred or so views as of this writing.

"Corrina"

Not to be confused with "Corrina Corrina," an old blues that popster Ray Peterson had a #9 hit with in 1960 and which Bob Dylan tweaked on his second album in 1963. This "Corrina" is an original composition by Weir, Hart, and Hunter that made its debut on February 23, 1992, at the Oakland Coliseum Arena and was played seventy-seven times by the Dead (including at their last concert). It's a funky, rhythmic love lament with a stuttering beat similar to the Who's "Eminence Front." And it's become pretty familiar since it was put on the first RatDog album and has been performed over the ensuing years by the Other Ones, The Dead, and RatDog. Still, this started as a Grateful Dead song and would have been an upbeat inclusion on an album. (For anyone trying to track its performance history, it's spelled "Corinna" on Deadbase.com.)

This song can be found on the live set *Road Trips Volume 2, Number 4: Cal Expo 1993*, in a version recorded May 26, 1993. Other live versions are on Archive.org and YouTube, and a studio version found a home on RatDog's *Evening Moods*.

"Days Between"

If there is a raison d'être for arguing in favor of a final Dead album, this last great Garcia-Hunter collaboration is it. A sad, moving ballad that's as heartfelt as it is original in conception, it shows the pair moving toward a new maturity in their writing and makes you wonder what else they'd have come up with had Garcia lived longer. In the years that have gone by since its February 22, 1993, debut, "Days Between" has earned a reputation as such an impressive song that it's hard to believe that the band only played it forty-one times. The reason is probably that it's not a simple piece of music, being made up of wordy (in the best sense) Hunter lyrics that muse on mortality, scads of jazzy chords, and a melody line that rises and falls and couldn't have been easy for the aging Garcia to sing. But "Days Between" is almost as essential listening for Deadheads as any of the band's classics because it's a signpost of a future that never was.

"Days Between" is best heard in the live rehearsal from February 16, 1993, that's featured on the *So Many Roads* box set. That version is preceded by a seven-minute introductory jam from February 9 of the same year.

"Easy Answers"

The Bob Weir–sung "Easy Answers" didn't start out as a Dead song, yet the band played it forty-four times after its June 5, 1993, unveiling it at Giants Stadium in New Jersey. The song had its genesis as part of the 1994 album *Trios* by Rob Wasserman, a record on which the bassist gathered pairs of different musicians to collaborate with him on each track (hence its title). "Easy Answers" in its studio incarnation features Wassermen, Weir, and Neil Young. A rocking blues tune with a typically distorted guitar line by Young, "Easy Answers" has a Springsteen-like morality to its lyrics, which were co-written by Hunter and Weir. Welnick, Weir, Wasserman, and Dead keyboard tech Bob Bralove all get credit for the music, making it one of the band's more collaborative efforts—also one of the more rocking, as its drive takes it close to '90s grunge in its studio version.

Bob Weir and Rob Wasserman, shown here in a 1990 publicity photo, were frequent collaborators, and their composition "Easy Answers" (co-written with Bob Bralove, Robert Hunter, and Vince Welnick) made its debut on Wasserman's *Trios* album before the Dead ever played it live.   *Author's collection*

Besides being on Wasserman's album, the studio version of "Easy Answers" can be heard on *Weir Here: The Best of Bob Weir*.

"Eternity"

A lot of the time when rockers share co-writing credit with legendary bluesmen, the so-called collaboration comes about because the rocker in question stole part of an old song and has given credit to the blues player out of niceness or legality. The fact that "Eternity" does not fit this mold and is a real collaboration between Weir and blues legend Willie Dixon puts it in a special category of Dead songs. Beyond that, it's an interesting composition as well. The song is a jaunty, minor key shuffle penned by Weir, paired with deceptively simple love song lyrics by Dixon, about which Weir once said that they seemed simplistic on paper, but worked like a charm when sung. The Dead played this one forty-four times, first performing it on February 21, 1993, at the Oakland Coliseum Arena, a year after Dixon's death in early 1992. It often segued into another then-new Dead tune, "Liberty."

"Eternity" can be found on the *So Many Roads* box set in a rehearsal version from February 18, 1993.

"If the Shoe Fits"

One of the last originals introduced into the Dead's repertoire. This goodbye song by Lesh and friend Andrew Charles was first performed June 9, 1994, at the Cal Expo Amphitheatre in Sacramento, California, and was played only seventeen times. The song's negative lyrical thrust was atypical for the group, with its chorus of "Give it up 'cause you can't win" sounding more like something off an Elvis Costello record. The lyrics didn't come off as downbeat, though, because it was juxtaposed with Lesh's most pop-friendly melody since "Box of Rain" (and a chord scheme that bears a slight relation to Marty Balin's 1981 hit "Hearts"). When the band played it live, it sounded a bit like early R.E.M. and might have been a contender for a single had it been recorded in the studio.

"If the Shoe Fits" can be found by perusing the band's 1994 and 1995 concerts on Archive.org. Since 2009, YouTube has also featured a fan-shot performance from June 25, 1994, at the Sam Boyd Silver Bowl in Las Vegas, which has only a few thousand views, proving how obscure this song has become.

"Lazy River Road"

This slow Garcia-Hunter number (which can't quite be called a ballad) is one of those quintessentially American-sounding songs that seems like it dates from before the band's own genesis. It's also got one of Hunter's most romantically evocative lyrics.

After the song was unveiled on February 21, 1993, at the Oakland Coliseum Arena, it became a semi-regular part of the Dead's repertoire, showing up sixty-five times, including at the band's last-ever show. Since then, it's been kept alive by being played by Furthur, The Dead, RatDog, and Phil Lesh and Friends.

It can be heard in a rehearsal version recorded on February 18, 1993, on the *So Many Roads* box set.

"Liberty"

"Liberty" started life as a solo tune by Robert Hunter that was originally credited to just him and released on his 1987 album, *Liberty*. That version sounded a bit like the Dead's own "Touch of Grey," with its quick tempo and icy keyboard interjections. It also had very little to do with the version the Dead started performing beginning on February 21, 1993, at the Oakland Coliseum Arena. In the intervening years, Garcia had taken the lyrics and written a new melody to Hunter's ode to freedom that sounded a bit like "Brown-Eyed Women" in places. Which version has the edge? It's hard to say. The Dead's is more subtle, but Hunter's melody is more immediately catchy and puts more emphasis on some of his better lines, such as "Say what I mean and I don't give a damn / I do believe and I am who I am." The Dead liked theirs enough to play it fifty-six times through July 1995.

"Liberty" can be found on the *So Many Roads* box set in a version recorded March 30, 1994, at the Omni in Atlanta. An earlier rendition, from May 26, 1993, is on *Road Trips Volume 2, Number 4: Cal Expo 1993*.

"Samba in the Rain"

One of the original Vince Welnick songs performed by the band, both this one and Welnick's other contribution, "Way to Go Home," have lyrics by Robert Hunter. And it's one of Hunter's sexiest lyrics, replete with a classic opening couplet: "Ten and ten is thirty / If you tell me it is so / Let's get down and dirty, baby / Let's get sweet and low." Its Latin-tinged melody and chord progression take it far away from standard Dead

VINCE WELNICK

Had the Grateful Dead rallied and cut one final album before Jerry Garcia's death, it might have included songs the late Vince Welnick wrote while with the band, "Samba in the Rain" and "Way to Go Home." *Author's collection*

music, but the band seemed to enjoy chiming in on its big chorus. "Samba" made its debut on June 8, 1994, at the Cal Expo Amphitheatre in Sacramento, California. Welnick also performed this song with the Missing Man Formation in 1998, and Tom Constanten played it with Terrapin Flyer on the Vince Welnick Memorial Tour in 2006.

"Samba" can be found within concerts on Archive.org or on YouTube, with its best "video" rendition arguably being the October 14, 1994, performance at Madison Square Garden.

"So Many Roads"

Blair Jackson has written that this song sounds "as if it had been penned by (or for) some weird troubadour in the autumn of his life," and it's hard to argue with his assessment. With philosophical lyrics that drew imagery from old blues songs, this Hunter-Garcia ballad seemed to sum up something of what the Dead, specifically Garcia, was all about at that point. "Thought I heard a jug band playin' / If you don't—who else will?" goes one couplet. It's intended to be a "big" number in the style of Bob Dylan's "Knockin' on Heaven's Door," which it

The final Grateful Dead single, "Foolish Heart," was released with a picture sleeve and "When Push Comes to Shove" on the B-side. It did not make the pop charts.   *Courtesy of yesterdayandtodayrecords.com*

resembles during its long fade—so that makes it all the more surprising that the Dead only played it fifty-five times after its February 22, 1992, debut. Was it too emotionally draining for Garcia? Whatever the case, it's exactly the kind of song he should have been immortalizing in the studio then.

"So Many Roads" can be found on the *So Many Roads* box set in a performance from the Dead's final concert on July 9, 1995, at Soldier Field in Chicago, Illinois.

"Wave to the Wind"

It's ironic that Lesh, who didn't compose all that much for the Dead, caught inspiration during the final stage of the Dead's career and chimed in with three originals. As such, they ended up being his three most obscure numbers. This one, which the Dead unveiled on February 22, 1992, at the Oakland Coliseum Arena, went through at least one lyrical rewrite but never quite caught on with audiences. Part of its problem was Hunter's repetitive and somewhat confusing lyric, which was either an ode to personal pride, a goodbye song, or a tune for kids to sing along with (hence the repetition in the lyrics). It's much more interesting musically: its funky dance rhythms and slippery, unpredictable jazz chord progressions simultaneously look back to "Eyes of the World" and point forward to the acid funk that the British band Jamiroquai would popularize a few years later. The opening and closing riffs sound a little too much like the main riff of Peter Gabriel's "Solsbury Hill," but the song makes up for that with a chorus hook that's an earworm in the best sense of that word. With only twenty-one performances, this is one of the band's least-heard numbers.

"Wave to the Wind" can be found on Archive.org or on YouTube, with its strongest videotaped performance being from March 25, 1993, at the University of North Carolina's Dean Smith Center.

"Way to Go Home"

Welnick and Hunter's other collaboration was the first of the keyboardist's originals to be played by the band, having made its debut on February 21, 1992, at the Oakland Coliseum Arena. The song, which was played ninety-two times, is a mid-tempo rocker with lyrics that seems to be addressed to either critics or picky fans at concerts: "Who do you think you are? / What do you mean when you put us all down / Walking round in circles / Your nose to the ground."

"Way to Go Home" can be heard on the *So Many Roads* box set in a performance from July 31, 1994, at the Palace in Auburn Hills, Michigan.

Listening to these tracks back-to-back, it's not hard to think that, had the Dead been able to find inspiration in the studio in 1994, they might have come up with a genuine classic for their last outing. Beyond the originals, the Dead could have also drawn from some of the interesting cover versions they'd introduced in 1993 or afterward. Two examples include their versions of Robbie

Robertson's pensive "Broken Arrow" and Harry Belafonte's goofy-but-fun "Matilda Matilda," which Belafonte cut five years after recording "Man Smart (Woman Smarter)." It's a shame the Dead didn't leave us with a "goodbye" album, so to speak. But at least they left behind live versions of the songs they were writing at the time—because that makes it easy to at least hear a makeshift version of that last, great Dead album that never was.

36

Built to Last

Ten Places the Dead Left Their Mark on Popular Culture

T here are only a handful of recording artists whose influence extends beyond the sphere of popular music. The Grateful Dead are one of them. What differentiates the Dead from other influential artists such as the Beatles or Madonna, though, is that the Dead were far less commercially driven, which makes the ways their ideas and personae infiltrated society all the more intriguing. Here are ten ways the Dead left a mark on different facets of popular culture.

Academia

It's probably not a stretch to say that some Deadheads might have missed a few early morning college classes by staying up too late after weekend shows. But those same Deadheads might have been more enthusiastic about heading off to those early morning classes had those classes been about their favorite band. At least two professors have taught Dead-related courses over the years: Rebecca G. Adams of the University of North Carolina at Greensboro and Robert Weir of the University of Massachusetts (we're not kidding, that really is the guy's name).

Adams's most famous course was Applied Social Theory and Qualitative Research Methodology, which came to be known as "Deadhead 101" because it took students on tour with the group in 1989. But the sociology professor has also taught a course called Sociological Perspectives on the Deadhead Community and published articles in academic journals that centered on the Dead. Weir, a historian, taught a class called How Does the Song Go? The Grateful Dead as a Window into American Culture. According to an article in the *Boston Globe*, it came in for some criticism for "pandering to consumers," but attracted 110 students.

Archiving

For a long time, rock music was considered to be an ephemeral trend, a musical form that teenagers would outgrow when they entered the so-called real world. The Grateful Dead must have sensed that this wouldn't be the case and that rock music would take on historical importance as time went on, because almost from the beginning the band recorded their concerts and saved the tapes for future reference. Eventually, the Dead took to storing them in two temperature-controlled rooms in their Club Front office. These rooms came to be known as the Vault. In 1985, Dick Latvala became the band's official archivist, and one of his jobs was to organize the band's tapes for future reference. Some of the professionally recorded multi-track tapes started to trickle out with the *From the Vault* series, after which the band's two-track stereo mixing board tapes came out as part of the *Dick's Picks* series and then the *Dave's Picks* releases. The Dead's archive also yielded another live CD and downloads series, *Road Trips*, plus a myriad of live CDs that aren't part of any series. Clearly, the Dead were in the vanguard in rock music when it came to archiving their own tapes. The Dead's affinity for archiving also extended beyond the boundaries of music.

You know you've arrived when you get your own logo: a book, a rose, and two lightning bolts make up the insignia of the Grateful Dead Archive, the official resource for all Dead things. Grateful Dead Archive logo by Gary Houston.   *© Grateful Dead Archive*
Used with permission

In 2008, Bob Weir and Mickey Hart announced at a press conference that their archives were going to be stored at the library of the University of California, Santa Cruz, and two years later, counterculture historian Nicholas Meriwether was named Grateful Dead archivist. "What I'm doing is reconstituting the archive that never was," Meriwether told the *San Francisco Gate*. "They were a working band. They weren't sentimental about their history, and the idea of archiving it the way I am doing here was not something they were going to put their money behind or put their time into."

The Archive holds twenty-five thousand items and more than five thousand scans from the band's career. Some of the items have been displayed in exhibits at the Santa Cruz library, and some even made it across the country when the New York Historical Society opened an exhibit on the band on March 5, 2010. In 2012, digital facsimiles of much of the collection were made available for online viewing at www.gdao.org. Between the *Dick's Picks* CDs and the Santa Cruz collection, the Dead have become a leading light when it comes to archiving in the digital age.

The Business World

It's pretty ironic that a band that never had much of a plan for anything would be held up as a model for how to conduct business. Unlike Bon Jovi, who used marketing strategies in the 1980s to determine which singles to release and when, the Dead didn't call in consultants to make decisions. Still, their business acumen was savvy and they got by on instinct or by going with the flow in a lot of ways. Some of those ways are analyzed in two books that came out in successive years: David Meerman Scott and Brian Halligan's *Marketing Lessons from the Grateful Dead: What Every Business Can Learn from the Most Iconic Band in History*, from 2010, and Barry Barnes's *Everything I Know About Business I Learned from the Grateful Dead: The Ten Most Innovative Lessons from a Long, Strange Trip* from 2011.

Both books examine how the Dead helped "grow" their business model (to use marketing terminology) by doing things like selling tickets directly to fans, making each live show a unique experience, and creating a mailing list to communicate directly with Deadheads, something that could be considered an early form of social media. The idea of the Dead as entrepreneurial wizards dates back at least as far as 1997, when Glenn Rifkin wrote an article based around this idea, "How to 'Truck' the Brand: Lessons from the Grateful Dead," for *Strategy Business* magazine.

Two years later, Rifkin expanded on the ideas in his article when he included a chapter about the Dead in a book he co-wrote, *Radical Marketing: From Harvard to Harley, Lessons from Ten That Broke the Rules and Made It Big*. If you do some digging on the web, you can find even more of this sort of thing, such as a blog post by Deadhead-turned-management-guru Rob Kelly titled "7 Business Lessons I Learned from the Grateful Dead." Somewhere, Garcia is pickin' and chuckling. As for the Dead as businessmen? Well, they wore suits on one of their record covers . . .

Classical Music

Phil Lesh and Tom Constantan might have brought ideas from classical music to the Grateful Dead's music, but contemporary classical composer Lee Johnson did them one better: he took the Dead's melodies and fashioned them into a full orchestral piece. That led to the band's music becoming part of the classical music world when his work, titled *Dead Symphony No. 6*, made its premiere on what would have been Garcia's sixty-sixth birthday, Friday, August 1, 2008. The symphony (which had been released on CD a year before) was first played live by the Baltimore Symphony Orchestra at the Meyerhoff Symphony Hall.

This writer was present for the occasion, as was Garcia's ex-wife, Carolyn "Mountain Girl" Adams Garcia, and Weir's buddy and lyricist John Perry Barlow. Both were greeted with ecstatic cheers from the audience, which seemed to be made up of mostly Deadheads. Conductor Lucas Richman's *Skull and Roses* T-shirt was a nice touch, but probably a bit unexpected for the dressed-up denizens of the hall's exclusive box seats. The symphonic piece recast ten Grateful Dead tunes into a classical suite interpolating "St. Stephen," "Mountains of the Moon," "Sugar Magnolia," and "Blues for Allah," among other songs. One of the most moving sections centered on the gorgeous melody of "Stella Blue" and made you wonder what might have happened if Garcia had lived long enough to follow through with his plans to explore the classical music world with his daughter Heather Garcia, a classical violinist.

Drug Laws

When the Grateful Dead performed at the Acid Test parties held by author and LSD advocate Ken Kesey and his Merry Pranksters, the band helped popularize the use of the drug—and also helped make it illegal. The fact that the Acid Tests got so much attention put LSD in the crosshairs of elected officials, and the drug was made illegal on October 6, 1966, in California and on October 24, 1968, in the United States (as part of the Staggers-Dodd Bill). The Dead might not have caused LSD to become illegal per se, but the press they received for being "acid heads" definitely struck fear into the hearts of law-abiding Americans and hastened the passing of laws to ban it.

That's common knowledge, but what's less spoken about is the crackdown on drugs in the early 1990s by the Drug Enforcement Administration's LSD task force. This resulted in the arrests and/or imprisonment of thousands of the band's fans, some of which were documented in articles like the *San Francisco Examiner*'s February 2, 1993, piece titled "Jailhouse Rock: Deadhead Hedonism Meets New Age of Law Enforcement."

The Dead also had the dubious distinction of being named in various "drug prospectuses" put out by government agencies. Some of these can still be found on the web. In 1992, for example, the Maryland State Police issued an intelligence report called *Synthetic Drugs: Availability and Trafficking in Maryland*, which explains to police that although LSD use had subsided since the 1960s, "one remaining pocket of LSD loyalty remains with the followers of the popular rock music group, The Grateful Dead. These 'Deadheads' widely distribute and abuse LSD, as documented by police arrests and hospital emergency room admissions in areas where the Grateful Dead appear in concert."

Food

At this point, everyone reading this book should know about Ben & Jerry's Cherry Garcia ice cream, a chocolate-cherry flavor the brand introduced in the spring of 1987. What's not so well known is the fact that Cherry Garcia has long been the best-selling flavor and that it was the first flavor named for a rock legend. These facts come courtesy of Liz Stewart, a company spokesperson who also bills herself as a public relations "grasshopper," one of the quirky names the company gives its employees.

Having a boutique flavor named for Garcia was relevant in two ways. First, it signified that the Dead had become such a part of mainstream culture that a product bearing one of the members' names could not only be sold in grocery stores, but could become a best-selling item. And second, it opened the door for Ben & Jerry's and other food companies to give other products celebrity-related names. Ben & Jerry's followed up Cherry Garcia with both Phish Food and Wavy Gravy, but over the ensuing years, we've seen celebrity burgers and sandwiches as well.

The Hispanic Community

The Grateful Dead performed a lot of types of music, but one area they were never associated with was ethnic music, specifically Latin or Hispanic music—which is odd, considering Garcia's paternal heritage is Spanish. His name would connote ethnicity if it weren't so associated with rock music, hippies, the 1960s, and about a dozen other very American elements of popular culture, noted Ricardo Pimentel when he penned a eulogy after Garcia's death on August 25, 1995. Writing in the *Tucson Citizen*, Pimentel called Garcia "the ultimate mainstreamer" in the way he assimilated into mainstream culture:

> I don't know if Garcia possessed an ethnic identity. His father was a Spaniard. That makes him Hispanic. Heck, the *Newsweek* cover story didn't even say if Garcia was Hispanic. But he transcended ethnicity and his multitudes of faithful followers allowed him to. That says a lot about him and about us. And what it says, I think, is good. You just didn't run

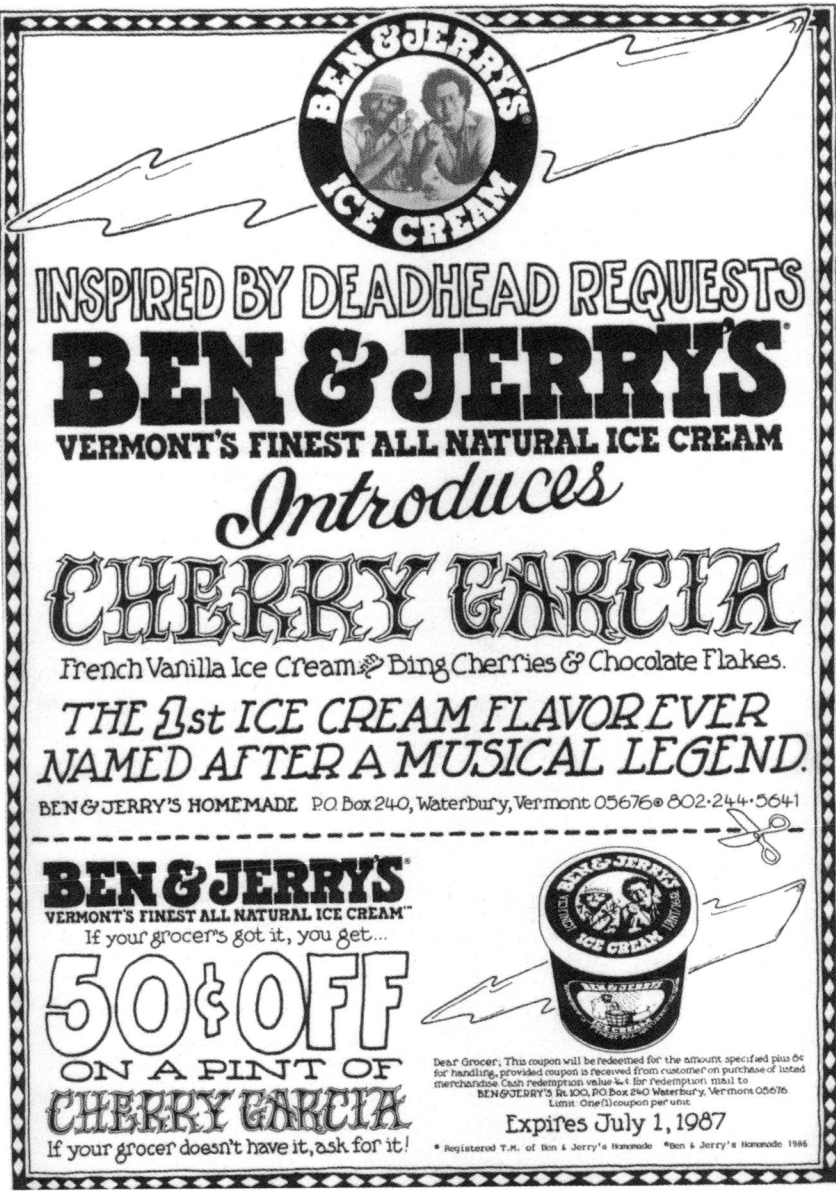

This vintage advertisement for Ben & Jerry's Cherry Garcia ice cream dates back to the summer of 1987, a few months after the flavor made its debut. According to company spokesperson Liz Stewart, the flavor has long been the company's best-selling product.

Courtesy of Ben & Jerry's Homemade, Inc.

into many Hispanic hippies. I marveled at how a guy named Garcia could fit in so seamlessly. He was, it seemed to me, mainstreaming since all the world appeared to be hippie back then.

According to Robert Hunter, Garcia had once thought about changing his name for reasons of its ethnicity. In an online journal entry from June 29, 2006, Hunter tells the story of how Garcia felt his surname "might be a hindrance to his acceptance" and considered using his mother's maiden name, Clifford, which had Anglo-Saxon roots. Garcia eventually decided to keep the name Garcia, thinking that Henry David Thoreau's adage that "any job that requires a change of dress style is probably the wrong job" should also apply to names. Around the same time, Paul Simon and Art Garfunkel made the decision to stop going by silly pseudonyms like Tom and Jerry and to use their obviously Jewish last names professionally (a bold move at the time). Garcia, along with that duo, and eventually others, brought a new ethnicity to mainstream culture by simply presenting himself honestly.

Philosophy

Were the parking lot vendors at Dead shows repudiating the capitalist economic system or representative of it? How do Robert Hunter's lyrics deal with such issues as freedom, fate, and gamblers' ethics? How do Buddhist concepts like discovering there is "no self" square with what the Dead represented? If you've ever found yourself having late-night conversations with friends on such topics, then you'll probably be interested in the 249-page tome *The Grateful Dead and Philosophy: Getting High Minded About Love and Haight*. The 2007 book gathered together twenty-one philosophers to muse on various aspects of the Dead and the Deadhead culture spawned by the band.

The task of bringing the Grateful Dead to the academic discipline of philosophy was devised by Steven Gimbel, the chair of the Department of Philosophy at Pennsylvania's Gettysburg College, who also occupies the Edwin T. and Cynthia S. Johnson Chair for Distinguished Teaching in the Humanities. Gimbel, who holds a PhD in philosophy from The Johns Hopkins University, has various writers in his book muse on subjects that range from art to collective consciousness, to conflict, to community, to cosmos. All of these are examined through Eastern and Western philosophical perspectives. The Deadhead community signified more than a group of fans who really liked the band, and *The Grateful Dead and Philosophy* explores some of the reasons for this.

Soundboard Recordings

If you go to a concert by one of today's jam bands or indie bands, after the show ends you might be able to buy a CD of the concert recorded from the mixing console (or "soundboard"). You might also be allowed to bring along a recording device and patch into one of the soundboard's auxiliary outputs and record the show yourself. Whatever the case, this method of recording was never commonplace until the Dead made it widespread, first by letting tapers patch into the mixing consoles during concerts, and second by releasing soundboard recordings via the *Dick's Picks* series.

How are soundboard recordings different from the concert recordings that are put on live albums or DVDs? Soundboards, as they're colloquially known, send the raw signal from the two stereo channels of the mixer directly to the recorder, capturing an artist's sound the way it comes through the board. Conversely, the sound on live albums and DVDs comes from a multi-track source where you can isolate each instrument and mix it to your liking. Soundboard recordings, in other words, deliver a "what you hear is what you get" sound. Only bands as confident about their live shows as the Dead were would let such unvarnished recordings out (and in the early days of *Dick's Picks*, even the Dead were self-conscious about what was released from such tapes).

But as the years passed and CD sales fell because of file sharing, soundboard recordings became more and more a way for bands to make money from performances and soon became commonplace for some acts. When YouTube arrived in 2005, non-professional videos of bands performing flooded that site and further expanded the number of un–touched up performances fans got to hear. But back when recording with a camera phone was the stuff of science fiction, the Dead were paving the way for non-professional recordings to go mainstream by taping concerts directly from their soundboard.

Not only did the Grateful Dead's organization create a mailing list to communicate with fans, but in 1983, they formed Grateful Dead Ticket Sales, which sold tickets directly to fans by mail, saving Deadheads the trouble of having to camp out overnight for tickets.

Courtesy of Stuart Dahne

The World Wide Web

It would be wrong for Deadheads to lay claim to inventing the Internet, like at least one politician did once upon a time. But the band's fans did play a part in the mainstreaming of cyberspace. In the late 1980s, back before most people even knew what 56K modems were, much less owned them, Deadheads were already sharing information via bulletin boards at www.well.com, also known as the WELL, or the Whole Earth 'Lectronic Link. The WELL bills itself as "the birthplace of the online community movement" and a "conversation-based community" where people from far and wide can get to know one another. While that doesn't seem very exciting in the age of Facebook, it was revolutionary back in the Reagan era, when fax machines were the quickest form of communication beyond telephones. Through the WELL, Deadheads discovered to their surprise that they could communicate with their brethren (or sistren) around the globe about everything from ticket sales to tape trading.

Back before websites and blogs were commonplace, Deadheads also shared information through an Internet bulletin board system called Usenet. It contained an area for discussions about the Dead, the group rec.music.gdead. The group still exists, but it has been hosted as part of Google Groups since 2001. Deadheads who couldn't log onto rec.music.gdead but could receive e-mails could become part of the electronic e-mail list called Dead-Flames, which distributed information about online discussions. Dead-Flames grew out of an online mailing list devised by Paul Martin of Stanford University's Artificial Intelligence Laboratory in the late 1970s, which shows just how deep the net roots of Deadheads run.

37

Garcia the Seer

How a Guitarist Became a Cultural Icon

In the late twentieth century, musicians graduated to the status of icon in one of two ways: by dying young or by selling a whole lot of records. Jerry Garcia did neither, which is what made his designation in the media as a cultural icon so unique.

Garcia didn't pass away as early as Jimi Hendrix, Janis Joplin, or Kurt Cobain, so he didn't become immortal by dying before his time. As for selling records, the Dead were never in the category of the Beatles or Bruce Springsteen. The Dead did end up filling stadiums toward the end of their career, but Garcia's icon status was long established by then, and not just among Deadheads, but in the mainstream media as well.

The Dead were sometimes referred to as a cult band, so it's tempting to characterize Garcia's iconic status as coming through his being a cult figure. But he wasn't quite that either. Garcia's name can't really be put alongside that of cult favorites such as Leonard Cohen, Morrissey, or Laura Nyro because those performers, impressive as they are, hold a much lesser place in the culture than Garcia did. What Garcia shares with them is a serious, devoted following. What he doesn't share with them is that his musical influence and name recognition extend far beyond the cult of Deadheads he helped spawn.

Garcia therefore holds a unique place in pop culture. He was neither a megastar who aimed to make music for the masses, nor an unsung hero who played for a small but devoted following. Garcia became popular and a commercial entity while playing the type of music that was almost designed to put off most listeners of popular, commercial music. By all accounts, he seemed to find this contradiction both humorous and unsettling.

Musical and Spiritual Adviser

Garcia's journey toward being a symbolic King of All Hippies started early on, almost before the Grateful Dead had an album out, in fact. On the back cover of Jefferson Airplane's *Surrealistic Pillow*, Garcia is credited as "musical and spiritual adviser." Although it's since been disputed whether Garcia actually played on the album, the fact that he's mentioned in such a manner turned out to be significant. A lot of people in the future would come to see Garcia as not just a musician but a spiritual guru as well.

Garcia thrived on interacting with other musicians, and his collaborations with Merl Saunders, pictured here, brought out the jazzy side of his chops. Their collaborative 1973 album, *Live at Keystone*, was reissued in 2012 as *Merl Saunders & Jerry Garcia: Keystone Companions—The Complete 1973 Fantasy Recordings*.   *Courtesy of Concord Music Group*

Then again, back in the 1960s, audiences saw a lot of musicians as spiritual gurus of sorts, because their music represented more than just music to a lot of people. It spoke to a way of life that seemed new, or at least new to listeners who had come of age in the more conformist era that preceded the mid-1960s.

And yet it's Garcia's name that people came to know, not Ian Bruce-Douglas, who led an even wilder psychedelic outfit in the Boston-based Ultimate Spinach (to cite one example). And it was Garcia who made the cover of non-musical magazines such as *People* and *Newsweek* when he died, not Bob Markley of the Los Angeles–based West Coast Pop Art Experimental Band (to cite another example). Out of all the musicians who emerged during the psychedelic era, it was Garcia who became an unelected spokesperson for hippie culture. To paraphrase an old advertising slogan, when he spoke, people listened.

The irony is that Garcia didn't take well to being called any sort of "leader." He was famously quoted as saying that he didn't like to be a leader because he was afraid he'd mislead people. He also once told *Magical Blend* magazine that he didn't like to think about the impact he had on people's minds because he felt that sort of influence "came close to fascism." Granted, he did allow his nickname, "Captain Trips," to be printed on the cover of the Dead's first album. But that was intended as a tongue-in-cheek touch in the same spirit as Phil Lesh's nickname, "Reddy Kilowatt," which was also printed on the album jacket. It certainly wasn't meant to designate Garcia as some sort of guru for a new age.

But it's the public that chooses leaders, not the other way around. And the public latched onto Garcia as being one of the leading lights of the hippie movement. Even if Garcia had set out to become a guru, it would have done no good unless the public had wanted that in some respect. In 1967, Garcia was a former bluegrass musician who had moved into playing rock, like many others of his generation. But as time ticked by, he not only acquired a reputation as a musician and songwriter par excellence, but he also became a symbol of a certain type of "new man"—someone who had freed himself from the shackles of society's stifling mores and conventions and was able to live as he chose.

As Blair Jackson said to this writer during an interview for a 2010 article on the fifteenth anniversary of Garcia's passing, "He's a guy that always sort of did what he wanted. He always played the music he wanted without any real consideration for commercial potential—and sort of got away with it."

All of this tied Garcia into a classic American archetype, the rebel. And like rebels ranging from Malcolm X to Igor Stravinsky, Garcia was barely tolerated at first, mostly because of fear, in his case due to long hair and an avowed love of drug taking (it's easy to forget how far out of the mainstream the Dead's early embrace of drugs was). But also like those rebels, Garcia was eventually embraced by mainstream society as an innovator and visionary—someone who became respected for being fiercely original, even by people who didn't particularly like what he did.

What makes Garcia's journey to the center of pop culture all the more impressive is that, unlike the rock stars of today, he had no team of publicists or "branding strategists" to help him craft an image that would "grow his brand" to a "targeted demographic." Garcia's infiltration into American life was not the stuff of marketing ploys or publicity stunts. This might be one reason he continues to interest new generations of fans who hunger for a more authentic musical experience than the music industry serves up these days. Even Garcia's insistence in keeping a scruffy beard long after beards went out of fashion gave him an air of singularity that other rockers didn't have.

The following are five of the reasons that Garcia went from being just another guitarist in a psychedelic band to a household name.

Built to Last

Garcia might have been a hippie, but he wasn't laid back, and his persistence over the years is the main reason he ensured his musical legacy would be "built to last," to quote a song of his and Hunter's. From the outset, Garcia played as much as he could and with a lot of different players. But most importantly, he never gave up. There were psychedelic bands that had more commercial success than the Dead early on (such as the Blues Magoos and the Peanut Butter Conspiracy), but then simply up and quit in the face of band friction or waning success. For Garcia, no matter what the crisis, he kept on playing on. During his time with the Dead, band members died, musical styles changed, money problems surfaced, and he suffered a major health catastrophe. But through it all, he kept on playing.

As such, the line "I will survive" from "Touch of Grey" was more than just a catchy chorus: it was actually something of a motto for Garcia. Perseverance is a quality that's admired in America, and as decades went by, Garcia's continued determination prompted even his naysayers to admire his strength and survival. Of course, most of the musicians who played in the Grateful Dead were "survivors" of one sort or another. But there were other things that marked Garcia as special.

If My Words Did Glow

One very important factor that made Garcia, well, Garcia was his keen intelligence, which came across in the interviews he did. Garcia might have looked like the quintessential hippie, and the general public might have expected him to speak in clichés out of the musical *Hair* (or some such thing), but he spoke like the well-read intellectual that he actually was. Garcia could be, at turns, articulate, educated, and sincere, the combination of which was not usually found in his peers. For example, as brilliant as Frank Zappa was, he usually sounded pompous or condescending when he addressed reporters. And as great a songwriter as John Lennon was, he came across in interviews as an inconsistent thinker because his opinions changed as quickly as his moods. John Fogerty's plainspoken earnestness is still eclipsed by his lingering anger over his lawsuits with Fantasy Records and the dissolution of his old band, Creedence Clearwater Revival. The tenor of Garcia's interviews, on the other hand, are remarkably consistent in tone over the years.

Garcia's talent for "improvising" his thoughts on the spot made him a fascinating interview subject. This was made clear when *Rolling Stone* put Garcia on the cover of its one hundredth issue in January 1972 and ran an interview so extensive that it was continued in the next issue. A book was even published that comprised the interview. It was titled *Garcia: A Signpost to New Space*, and it helped burnish Garcia's public image as a musician who was also something of a seer. Here was Garcia, expounding on meeting Ken Kesey and LSD changing his life, and coming off as articulate and perceptive. Only six years before, the Beatles were being forbidden from talking about the Vietnam War by their manager. Ten years before, rock stars weren't being asked about much more than their tastes in women. Times were changing, and Garcia, with his forthright honesty, was leading the charge. He was quoted as saying at one point in the *Rolling Stone* interview,

> There's been a lie about what freedom is, and the big lie is that freedom means absolutely and utterly free, and it really doesn't mean anything of the sort. The case in point is when you have your own scene like that. Somebody comes in and they're free to move in, but likewise you're free to tell them to get out. Freedom is a premise that's been put forth that's been abused.
>
> For any scene to work, along with that freedom there's implicit responsibility—you have to be doing something somewhere along the line—there is no free ride. And you have to know where you're going. It's helpful to have a scene that will indulge you long enough to let you find out.

These types of thought-provoking ideas weren't usually heard coming out of the mouths of rockers. It's little wonder that people came to see Garcia not only as a musician but also as a font of wisdom. Over the years, Garcia gave so many pithy quotes to so many interviewers that when the editors of *Rolling Stone* devoted a special edition to commemorating his death, they included a section composed solely of quotes, which they titled "'We Were Just Happy Freaks, Man': Garcia in His Own Words." One of the most interesting ones has him musing on the idea that you can't successfully put the idea of saving the world in your lyrics. However, he noted, you yourself can "be that idea."

You Get Confused, Listen to the Music Play

It seems self-evident to say that both Garcia's playing and his catalog of songs made him iconic. But a lot of performers play instruments well and write great tunes. Few of them hold Garcia's place in the cultural pantheon, though. While the songs Garcia wrote for the Dead proved to be especially durable, it was his playing that was truly special—not because he had the virtuosity of Jeff Beck or Eric Clapton, but because Garcia's improvisations were seemingly drawn from a bottomless pit of inspiration. There are thousands upon thousands of hours on tape of Garcia jamming away that people are still enjoying, if not analyzing. Where did the guy go creatively, to come up with ideas night after night?

As many have noted, Garcia didn't play the same parts exactly the same way in performance after performance. When you take into account how many concerts he played with both the Dead and with various solo groups, that's a hell of a lot of creativity. Garcia's ability to improvise on the spot was seemingly superhuman, and that's why his playing made him unique in a way that other

Garcia, shown here with Allman Brothers guitarist Dickey Betts, might not have invented Southern rock as we know it, but his improvisations on Donovan's "There Is a Mountain" (as heard on "Alligator" from *Anthem of the Sun*) inspired the Allmans to come up with one of the all-time Southern rock guitar classics, "Mountain Jam."   *Courtesy of BigHouse Archives*

musicians weren't. You'd have to look to jazz to find a musician who improvised as consistently during such a long period of time.

In Another Time's Forgotten Space

The public's perception of a musical performer is always borne out of the era from which that performer emerged. So no matter what Frank Sinatra did or said in the 1970s, he's still always going to be identified as an artist whose sensibilities were shaped by being part of the Greatest Generation. Similarly, no matter what Garcia did in the 1990s, he'll always be identified as a part of the hippie generation. Because that era was a time of profound social change, Garcia's emergence from it holds more weight than if he'd first appeared, say, a decade later, when times were less heady.

Garcia was first associated with West Coast hippies, but as time went on, he came to symbolize "the '60s" as we now know them. His words and actions were, by association, given an importance that those of other artists from other eras weren't. The fact that Garcia spoke so eloquently about issues relating to the 1960s made him a proverbial Spokesman of His Generation, whether he wanted that title or not.

Ripple in Still Water

Deadheads themselves helped Garcia achieve iconic status. Garcia himself would undoubtedly cringe at the following analogy, but he came to be seen as something of a high priest in popular music because of the devotion of his followers. The reason for this ties back into several other reasons that Garcia became so highly-regarded: Garcia's own perseverance and creativity.

When fans of most popular groups grow up, the music of their youth usually becomes little more than an adolescent memory. That wasn't the case with Deadheads. Most first- and second-generation Deadheads took the music of their youth with them right into adulthood, continuing to find inspiration in it. It also helped that the Dead continued on for decades and didn't retire and stage cheesy "comebacks" or morph into other configurations like Jefferson Airplane or Yes did. When Deadhead culture first started taking shape, it was viewed by some with disdain or bemusement. But after a while, the fact that any musical group could inspire the devotion of such a fanatical fan base became a point of interest. Because Garcia was the Dead's main writer and singer, he became, by default, a cultural phenomenon.

His reputation as a force in popular culture was bolstered when Deadheads started to be seen in high places, such as the White House (Second Lady Tipper Gore was a fan) and the management of Apple, Inc. (when Steve Jobs's Ping profile was shown during a keynote address, one of his favorite albums was revealed to be *American Beauty*). Because of the influence of many of his followers, Garcia's own influence spread wider, resounding like the crying wind he sang about in one of his and Hunter's most moving songs, "Stella Blue."

38

Unbroken Chain

A Dozen Artists Influenced by the Dead

How influential was the Grateful Dead, musically speaking? If someone were to look at most music that is commercially popular now, they might say "not very," as there's not much rock music in the Top 40 anymore. But in the world of music that's not hit-oriented, there's still quite a bit of Dead influence. Tune into any college radio station and you're bound to hear echoes of what the group did at some point in their career, especially the proto-Americana of their *American Beauty* period and the rhythmic grooves of their *Blues for Allah* era.

The Dead were never trendy, except inadvertently during a brief period when they first started out and the town of Haight-Ashbury was the hip place to hang out—so artists that have followed the Dead's lead have not, for the most part, been trend-oriented. The Dead were more about doing their own thing, and facets of that thing have resounded in other artists since the late 1960s and continue through today. The following is a roundup of artists and bands who either drew or continue to draw inspiration from the Dead in one way or another.

The Allman Brothers Band

These Southern rock pioneers were purportedly influenced by the Dead's two-drum, two-guitar set-up, but delivered a harder rocking, more commercially oriented style of music. While that style would eventually inform bands that had little to do with the Dead, such as Lynyrd Skynyrd and the Outlaws, the early Allman Brothers Band had a lot in common with the Dead in that they'd use their album tracks as jumping-off points for long, improvisatory jams. Band leader and lead guitarist Duane Allman's prowess on slide guitar really does live up to its reputation. He's best heard on the group's two early masterpieces, the double albums *At Fillmore East* and *Eat a Peach*, from 1971 and 1972, respectively.

The band's magnum opus, the thirty-three-plus-minute "Mountain Jam" (based on the Donovan hit "There Is a Mountain") even has its antecedent in Dead music. On "Alligator" from *Anthem of the Sun*, Garcia invents the guitar line that Duane Allman and Dickey Betts would later use in their reworking of the song. It can be heard at nine minutes in. The band's current guitarist Warren Haynes also praised the Dead in an entry he wrote for *Rolling Stone*'s "100

Greatest Artists" article (the Dead came in at #57). On the other hand, drummer Butch Trucks was less than complimentary about the Dead when interviewed for the website Classic Rock Revisited in 2006, so not everyone in the Allman Brothers was tuned into the Dead's wavelength. Duane Allman died in 1971, but the group still soldiers on live with the other Allman brother, Gregg, at the helm.

Elvis Costello

No, I didn't hear it either. I had a difficult time connecting Elvis Costello, the archetypal Angry Young Man of British punk rock, with anything related to the Grateful Dead, who put across anything but an angry vibe except on rare occasions. But the acclaimed singer-songwriter has gone on record as saying that the Dead were an influence on him as a young listener, and he performed on stage with Garcia in 1989. Costello has also spoken about how the Dead's music informed his own songwriting, and some of his praise of the band can be found in a joint interview he and Garcia did in a 1991 issue of *Musician* magazine that's well worth hunting down.

All of which raises the question: Where in Costello's music can we hear anything Dead-like? Well, there's the wordplay of his lyrics, which sometimes sound Robert Hunter–esque. There is the song "Shipbuilding," which definitely has its antecedent in "Ship of Fools" (which Costello covered), and there are the lazy shuffles on his first album, before he hooked up with the Attractions, who might be considered the anti-Dead because of their precise, hyped-up style. Costello's music is worth exploring even if you're not a Deadhead because his songwriting is so clever—but his best albums are generally considered to be the ones he did with the Attractions, so if you go exploring, don't expect "Row Jimmy."

The Disco Biscuits

It's easy enough to tell that this long-running electronica-infused jam band was influenced by the Dead. That's because they've come out and said so. Speaking to Billboard's Evie Nagy in August 2009, bassist Marc Brownstein said, "We were fans of the Grateful Dead." It doesn't get any more direct than that. There are more details about how the band was influenced by the Dead, however. The first, obviously, has to do with the music. The Biscuits make a droning, groovalicious, keyboard-infused sound that sometimes recalls the Dead during the period when their live sound incorporated the synthesizer sounds of Brent Mydland or Vince Welnick. You wonder if the Dead might have explored this area further had Garcia not passed away in 1995.

The other way this Philadelphia quartet is Deadicated is in their open approach to music. In much the way the Dead played on bills with Miles Davis and shared the stage with jazz saxophonist Branford Marsalis, the Disco Biscuits make a sound that edges toward hip-hop and host a festival called Camp Bisco, which has opened its stage to artists not part of the jam band scene. Such artists include rappers Snoop Dogg and Nas as well as the Grammy Award–winning reggae artist Damian Marley. In the above Billboard quote, Brownstein was likening his band to both the Dead and Phish because he felt the Disco Biscuits were getting by in the music industry by doing things their own way. It doesn't get more Dead-like than that.

Bruce Hornsby and the Range

This one is pretty obvious. Virginia keyboardist Bruce Hornsby liked the Dead so much that he joined in 1990 as an unofficial member. And he put his own career on hold to do it. Hornsby's musical career panned out differently than most. He started at the top with his first single, "The Way It Is," going to #1. At the time, his smooth, adult-oriented pop rock came off as tailor-made for the yuppies of that era, not its youth, and his playing on records by Don Henley made him seem only slightly cooler than Huey Lewis (who played harmonica on Hornsby's debut album). You half expected him to shill for the J. Crew catalog, which he and his band looked like they'd stepped out of.

Then the unthinkable happened. Hornsby outed himself as the polar opposite of a clean-living, law-abiding yuppie. He revealed to the world he was a Deadhead. Eek! OMG! He spoke of how seeing the band live made a huge impression on him, and how playing in a Dead cover band in college helped form his musical tastes, which he told me about when I once interviewed him. Well-coiffed Reagan-era yuppies probably spat out their Perrier when they'd heard he was regularly guesting with the Dead circa 1988. And they probably choked on their brie when he hooked up with the band as a regular member in the fall of 1990 after the death of Brent Mydland. Since then, Hornsby has considerably broadened his musical palette, playing with artists ranging from Pat Metheny to Branford Marsalis to Bonnie Raitt. His original audience will probably be relieved to know he played with Baby Boomer darling Phil Collins as well.

Phish

It's easy to see why Phish gets compared to the Grateful Dead so much. They both have Ben & Jerry's flavors named in honor of them (Cherry Garcia and Phish Food, if you're not an ice cream aficionado). Seriously, if you're a fan of the Dead, you probably know a little about Phish already, so there's no point in going on too much about the group, except to say that if any one band brought the jam band aesthetic to the masses and kept the Dead's tradition of jamming alive, it was Phish. The Vermont quartet, which started out playing a lot of Dead covers, exploded in popularity around the time the Dead was imploding. When Garcia passed away, it felt almost as if a torch had been passed from one band to another.

Phish was active from the early 1980s to 2004 and then reunited in 2008. Like the Dead, the group never had their music played much on radio, but they managed to create a huge fan base and sell a lot of albums anyway. Also like the Dead, Phish enjoyed surprising their audience by playing unexpected cover versions of songs in concert. But Phish took it a few steps further. Where the Dead would pull out the Beatles' "Revolution," Phish would play the entire *White Album* aka *The Beatles* (it happened on Halloween in 1994). Phish's songwriting isn't always up to par with their ambition, though. But whether or not every Dead fan liked Phish—and some clearly didn't—their presence on the scene reminded people of the Dead, which isn't such a bad thing.

Railroad Earth

In concert, Railroad Earth has been known to play versions of both the Grateful Dead's "Casey Jones" and "Peggy-O," a traditional ballad that was a favorite of Garcia's. That's just one way in which this Americana band from New Jersey carries on the Dead tradition. The other is in their sound, which can incorporate music ranging from bluegrass to Celtic to jazz to plain old rock 'n' roll. Railroad Earth roll all that together live, where they'll make like the Dead and extend songs when the mood strikes.

Railroad Earth are no Dead copy band, however, even if singer Todd Sheaffer's vocal inflections are sometimes similar to those of Garcia. Where they differ is in their instrumentation. Railroad Earth have a violinist in Tim Carbone, and a mandolin player in John Skehan. Along with Andy Goessling, who moves from guitar to banjo to dobro to flute and beyond, Railroad Earth craft a sound that's acoustic and jaunty, but with the mindset of a jam band that's plugged in. So far, Railroad Earth have released a half dozen albums, but fans have been known to say that (you guessed it) they're best experienced in concert.

Santana

Carlos Santana loved the guitar playing of Jerry Garcia so much that when *Rolling Stone* magazine put together one of its "100 Best Guitarist Lists" in 2011, the Mexico-born six-string virtuoso put down his guitar pick and wrote the entry, explaining what he thought made Garcia such a great player. His entry reads, in part:

> Most people who play the blues are very conservative. They stay a certain way. Jerry Garcia was painting outside the frame. He played blues but mixed it with bluegrass and Ravi Shankar. He had country and Spanish in there. There was a lot of Chet Atkins in him—going up and down the frets. But you could always hear a theme in his playing. It's like putting beads on a string, instead of throwing them around a room. Jerry had a tremendous sense of purpose.

That's no small praise coming from a guitarist who has received a lot of praise himself, alone and with his long-running band, Santana. Santana put his group together in San Francisco in the late 1960s, where they were part of the same scene as the Dead. Over the years, Santana has earned ten Grammy Awards, racked up a plethora of big-selling albums, and unexpectedly revived his career in 2002 when he teamed up with singer-songwriter Michelle Branch for the mega-hit "The Game of Love." Not bad for someone who was wowing 'em live way back in the Fillmore West days.

The String Cheese Incident

Back in 2008, this Colorado jam band dropped an archival release called *Trick or Treat*, which came out in two versions. The regular edition was a two-disc set that brought together some of the band's favorite performances from their Halloween gigs from 1998 to 2004. The other version was a nine-disc box set that contained music from all of those years plus bonus material from an October 29, 2005, show. Even if the band members of the String Cheese Incident professed to hate the Grateful Dead with a passion, the way they put out archival music is a testament to their carrying on a tradition that's almost sacred in Dead circles.

The SCI, as the band is casually known, formed around two decades ago and has kept its personnel intact, with all five original musicians still being members along with percussionist Jason Hann, who was added in 2006. The group's mix of rock, bluegrass, and electronic music is as danceable as it is listenable, the best example being popular cuts like "Joyful Sound" and "Rollover." The group has also become renowned for its stage show, which incorporates psychedelic lighting and "themed" events, the most popular one being their "Hulaween" Halloween shows, which has their fans grooving using hula hoops. The group has also collaborated with Dead disciple Keller Williams (see entry below).

Tea Leaf Green

Tea Leaf Green cut their musical teeth in the Dead's backyard. The band got started when two of the members met while attending San Francisco State University. The group released their first CD in 1999 and soon hit the road, which is where they've stayed for the most part. Like the Grateful Dead, Tea Leaf Green are first and foremost a road band, but unlike the Dead, they don't have a record company backing them since they've chosen to take a road way less traveled and put out their albums independently. The group made their name playing the festival circuit and built up a fan base from there.

The group found a fan in Phish front man Trey Anastasio, who joined them on stage in 2005. They also picked up a Jammy Award for Song of the Year for "Taught to Be Proud" from their 2005 CD of the same name. Tea Leaf Green also have a strong Dead connection in Justin Kreutzmann, the son of drummer Bill Kreutzmann. The younger Kreutzmann directed Tea Leaf Green's 2006

concert film *Rock 'n' Roll Band*, which showcased the band playing at the Fox
Theatre in Boulder, Colorado, that year.

Umphrey's McGee

Umphrey's McGee is a Chicago-bred jam band who make great records and wow
'em live but sometimes get nudged out of the spotlight by more popular acts
that play similar music. But Umphrey's McGee stand out because of the way the
group's members can stretch out while playing really strange chord progressions.
That's something Garcia liked to do in his more jazzy and funky moments, and
that's the main element that ties this sextet to the Dead. They are at their most
impressive on the live album *Live at the Murat*.

The group's follow-up to that album, *Mantis*, added more progressive
rock elements to its sound, yet ended up more accessible, with songs such as
"Cemetery Walk" and "Made to Measure" getting heavy rotation on college

Over the years, Widespread Panic has covered "Cream Puff War," "Morning Dew,"
and "Easy Wind." The long-running jam band also has been compared to the
Dead because they allow fans to tape their shows, and they never play shows with
identical song lineups.   *Photo by Jason Thrasher*

radio stations. They have been together more than ten years and have kept their lineup mostly intact, which is definitely one of the reasons they read each other so well on stage. And while Umphrey's might not get as much press as, say, Phish, the Disco Biscuits, or the String Cheese Incident, their CDs and live gigs hold their own against any of those groups. The crowd on *Live at the Murat* didn't get that excited over nothing.

Widespread Panic

Give this Athens, Georgia, ensemble credit where it's due: at the height of the post-punk era, when songs, not jams, were in fashion, Widespread Panic were fashioning a sound that did not avoid long-form jams and was based on equal parts Southern rock, jazz, and blues. As led by singer-guitarist John Bell, Widespread Panic make music that embraces the Dead aesthetic of stretching out without ever sounding like copy cats. The group occasionally make their Dead roots explicit, such as on their cover of Bonnie Dobson's folk standard "Morning Dew," which the Dead also covered. Bell also makes sure the group doesn't play an exact set twice, a very Dead-like move.

Widespread Panic have been putting out albums since its 1988 indie release, *Space Wrangler*, with their most popular efforts coming several years later. These include the albums *Ain't Life Grand* from 1994, which contained "Can't Get High," and the album *Bombs & Butterflies* from 1997, which had "Hope in a Hopeless World." Both were substantial hits on rock radio. They have also released a series of live albums that capture their versatility; one was done in tandem with the New Orleans Dirty Dozen Brass Band. How's that for variety?

Keller Williams

Keller Williams is an acoustic guitar virtuoso and singer-songwriter who built a reputation among the jam band set even though his approach to music couldn't be further from that of a band. He plays concerts virtually solo, aided only by his instruments, electronic gadgets, and vocals. Williams is also a longtime Dead enthusiast, and when he decided to gather together a group of "dream musicians" to assist him on his 2007 album *Dream*, one of the people on his wish list was Bob Weir. Luckily for Williams, Weir agreed to play with him, and so the former Dead guitarist's strumming graces one of the songs from that album, the funky country blues "Cadillac."

Williams has also cut an album with the String Cheese Incident (as the Keller Williams Incident), toured with Bob Weir's band RatDog in 2007, and played such festivals as the Bonnaroo Music and Arts Festival, the AllGood Music Festival, and the Rothbury Festival, so he's next to impossible to miss if you're a jam band fan. What Williams has in common with the Dead is that he usually builds his improvisations on a one-chord drone, similar to what the Dead did during parts of "Dark Star." These days, Williams has moved into playing music for kids, and although he's not exactly giving them "Son of Dark Star," it's amusing to think that the songwriter who once penned "Freeker by the Speaker" is crooning for impressionable youngsters.

Keller Williams is best known for playing stringed instruments, but he took to tickling the ivories for his digital release, *KEYS: A Collection of Grateful Dead Covers on Piano to Benefit the Rex Foundation*, released February 12, 2013. The one-man band tackled popular numbers such as "Touch of Grey" and obscurities such as "Can't Come Down" for the ten-song project, with 100 percent of the profits donated to the Dead's charitable non-profit organization. Photo by C. Taylor Crothers.   *Courtesy of Madison House Publicity*

39

With a Net

Online Resources for Deadheads

The Grateful Dead are among the most analyzed and researched groups in rock, so it makes sense that the web would be filled with great sites and blogs that center on all things Grateful Dead–related. Here are fifteen of the most interesting.

The Annotated Grateful Dead Lyrics

Author and researcher David Dodd's site is no longer being updated, but it remains a valuable resource because it provides footnotes for lyrics along with links that help explain obscure words and phrases. It also features essays and a bibliography of Dead-related books. http://artsites.ucsc.edu/GDead/agdl

The Compleat Grateful Dead Discography

Ihor Slabicky's website lacks design elements, but it makes up for it by being an exhaustive, ongoing chronicle of Dead releases. It encompasses everything from vinyl to downloads to songbooks and beyond. http://tcgdd.freeyellow.com

DeadBase

The online home of the small press that publishes the reference book *DeadBase: The Complete Guide to Grateful Dead Song Lists* and its succeeding volumes. The site also arguably has the most accurate search engine for show information on the web. http://www.deadbase.com

Deadlistening.com

Detailed reviews of old shows, with a mission to help "new and old-comers navigate through listening choices in the sea of Grateful Dead shows available on and offline." It also has sections about the best Dead shows and best audience tapes. http://www.deadlistening.com

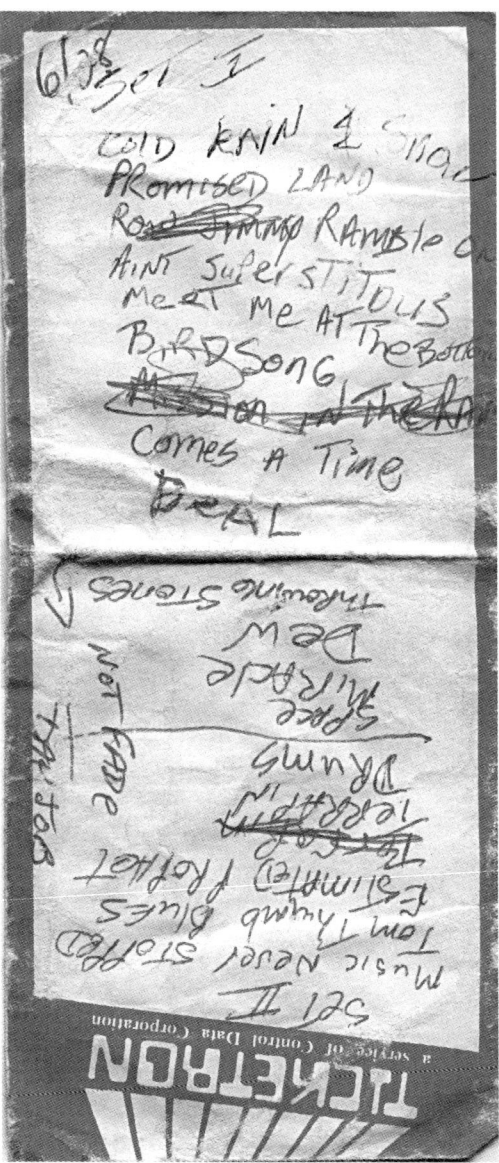

Before iPhones and the like let you store information electronically, the best way to remember what the band played was by writing up your own set list, which was often done on a scrap of paper, on a receipt, or in a notebook. This set list documents the Dead's June 28, 1985, show at Hershey Park Stadium.

Courtesy of Stuart Dahne

The DeadLists Project

A website that contains detailed information on shows, which are divided out by year and linked to streaming audio (when available) at Archive.org. There is also information on performances by Dead members in their pre-Dead days and a discussion forum. http://www.deadlists.com/default.asp

Dead.net

The band's official website, with current news; info on tours; a massive archive of photos, artwork, and news clippings; and links to buy CDs and DVDs. It also includes a weekly blog by Blair Jackson, interviews, and a forum and "community" section for readers. http://www.dead.net

GDRadio.net

This online station delivers nothing but full concerts by the Grateful Dead twenty-four hours a day, seven days a week. Dead-related groups such as the Jerry Garcia Band, and post-Dead bands such as RatDog, Furthur, and the Other Ones are also featured, as is David Gans's program *The Grateful Dead Hour*. http://www.gdradio.net

Grateful Dead Archive

The online home of the official Grateful Dead Archive at the University of California, Santa Cruz, which opened to the public in 2012. Curated by Nicholas

Meriwether, it contains forty-five thousand digitized items and digital content from Dead fans. http://www.gdao.org

The Grateful Dead Family Discography

A continually updated site of Grateful Dead–related recordings. Also includes discographies of musicians closely associated with the Dead and information about the band's DVD releases, movie appearances and references, streaming audio sites, and more. http://www.deaddisc.com

Grateful Dead Guide

Since 2009, this blog has featured a series of articles on songs and performances by the Dead in their early days. It explores subjects ranging from the band's use of train imagery to Pigpen's solo recordings to missing tapes of pre-1970 shows. Also of interest are the insightful comments from regular readers. http://deadessays.blogspot.com

Grateful Dead Reference Site

A discography of Dead albums with liner notes and (very convenient) links to lyrics, and a song finder with an index of nearly 350 songs. http://www.gdreferencesite.com

Grateful Dead Time Capsule

A history of the band with biographical data sequenced into "timeline" formats. Also includes discographies and book-related info through 2005, when the site stopped being updated. http://www.dead101.com

The Grateful Web

Launched in June 1995, the Grateful Web provides a platform for fans to post stories, reviews, pictures, and videos of the Dead and related acts. The website also has sections dedicated to tour dates and festivals. http://www.gratefulweb.com

Lone Star Dead Radio

The website for Eric Schwartz's long-running radio program, which runs Friday evenings, 9 p.m. Eastern Time, and can be streamed via KNON-FM. The site also includes scans of Schwartz's massive collection of vinyl records, ticket stubs, tour books, and other memorabilia. http://lonestardeadradio.com

Lost Live Dead

Allon Porter's blog details concerts by the Dead and the band's members that haven't been well documented. Subjects range from the Hartbeats shows to Kingfish's gigs with Bob Weir to the pre-Dead Jerry and Sara performances. http://lostlivedead.blogspot.com

Rukind.com

A musician-oriented fan site with guitar tabs, a forum discussion space, a news section, and auctions. There are also sections to find Dead cover bands, information on musical equipment, and instructional videos for guitarists. The name is, of course, a play on the phrase "Are you kind" from "Uncle John's Band." http://www.rukind.com

The Setlist Program

This site allows users to search through the Dead's set lists from 1965 to 1995 and comment on shows. There are also statistics about such topics as which cities and venues the band played the most. http://www.setlists.net

Selected Bibliography

Books

Constanten, Tom. *Between Rock and Hard Places: A Musical Autobiodyssey.* Eugene, OR: Hulogosi, 1992.

Cooper, Kim, and David Smay, eds. *Bubblegum Music Is the Naked Truth.* Port Townsend, WA: Feral House, 2001.

Dodd, David G., and Diana Spaulding, eds. *The Grateful Dead Reader.* New York: Oxford University Press, 2000.

Gillett, Charlie, and Stephen Nugent. *Rock Almanac.* New York: Anchor Books, 1978.

Greenfield, Robert, ed. *Dark Star: An Oral Biography of Jerry Garcia.* New York: Morrow, 1996.

Jackson, Blair. *Garcia: An American Life.* New York: Viking, 1999.

Lang, Michael, with Holly George-Warren. *The Road to Woodstock: From the Man Behind the Legendary Festival.* New York: Ecco, 2009.

Lesh, Phil. *Searching for the Sound: My Life with the Grateful Dead.* New York: Little, Brown, 2005.

Marcus, Greil. *Mystery Train: Images of America in Rock 'n' Roll Music.* New York: E. P. Dutton, 1975.

Marsh, Dave, and John Swenson, eds. *The Rolling Stone Record Guide.* New York: Random House, 1979.

———. *The New Rolling Stone Record Guide.* New York: Random House, 1983.

McNally, Dennis. *A Long Strange Trip: The Inside History of the Grateful Dead.* New York: Broadway, 2002.

Parish, Steve, with Joe Layden. *Home Before Daylight: My Life on the Road with the Grateful Dead.* New York: St. Martin's, 2003.

Scully, Rock, and David Dalton. *Living with the Dead: Twenty Years on the Bus with Garcia and the Grateful Dead.* Boston: Little, Brown, 1996.

Shenk, David, and Steve Silberman. *Skeleton Key: A Dictionary for Deadheads.* New York: Main Street/Doubleday, 1994.

Tamarkin, Jeff. *Got a Revolution! The Turbulent Flight of Jefferson Airplane.* New York: Atria, 2003.

Whitburn, Joel. *Top Pop Albums 1955–2001.* 6th ed. Menomonee Falls, WI: Record Research, 1991.

———. *Joel Whitburn's Top Pop Singles 1955–1990.* 5th ed. Menomonee Falls, WI: Record Research, 2002.

Zappa, Frank, and Peter Occhiogrosso. *The Real Frank Zappa Book.* New York: Poseidon, 1989.

Articles

Cavanaugh, David, Ken Hunt, Johnny Black, and Jaan Uhleszki. "Empire of the Sun." *MOJO* (June 1999).

Coleman, Mark, ed. "'We Were Just Happy Freaks, Man': Garcia in His Own Words." *Rolling Stone* (September 21, 1995).

Cullingham, James. "Love on the Tracks." *MOJO* (June 2000).

Fong-Torres, Ben. "A Grateful Man." *People* (September–October 1995).

Hull, Robert A. "The Sound and Vision of Psychedelia." *Creem* (January 1981).

Lowe, Jeff. "Invasion by the Deadheads." *Columbia Flier,* July 3, 1985.

Pimentel, Ricardo. "Jerry Garcia: He Was the Ultimate Mainstreamer." *Tucson Citizen,* August 25, 1995.

Roberts, Susan. "Deadheads Invade." *Columbia Flier,* July 23, 1983.

Sclafani, Tony. "Grateful Dead's Love and Haight." *Goldmine* (August 17, 2007).

Smith, Sam. "The Corporate Curse: How Business Culture Dragged America Down with It." *Progressive Review* (May 2008).

Index

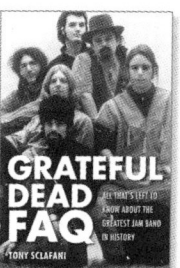